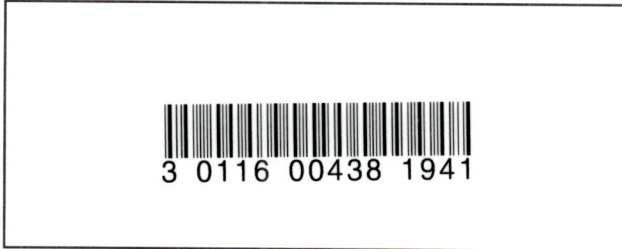

This book is due for return not later than the
last date stamped below, unless recalled sooner.

ITALY, EUROPE, THE LEFT

To Katryna-Maria Turner,
who profoundly understood
and appreciated *Scarface*

Italy, Europe, the Left

The transformation of Italian communism and the European imperative

VASSILIS FOUSKAS

Ashgate

Aldershot • Brookfield USA • Singapore • Sydney

Ashgate Publishing Limited
Gower House
Croft Road
Aldershot
Hants GU11 3HR
England

Ashgate Publishing Company
Old Post Road
Brookfield
Vermont 05036
USA

British Library Cataloguing in Publication Data
Fouskas, Vassilis
    Italy, Europe, the Left : the transformation of Italian
    communism and the European imperative
    1.Communism - Italy - History 2.Italy - Politics and
    government - 20th century
    I.Title
    320.9'45

Library of Congress Cataloging-in-Publication Data
Fouskas, Vassilis.
    Italy, Europe, the Left : the transformation of Italian communism
    and the European imperative / Vassilis Fouskas.
        p.   cm.
    Includes bibliographical references and index.
    ISBN 1-84014-450-5
    1. Partito comunista italiano--History. 2. Partito democratico
    della sinistra--History. 3. Communism--Italy--History. 4. Italy-
    -Politics and government--1945-1976. 5. Italy--Politics and
    government--1976-1994. I. Title.
    JN5657.C63F65 1998
    324.245 075--dc21   98-8636
                                                                           CIP

ISBN 1 84014 450 5

Printed in Great Britain by Antony Rowe Ltd, Chippenham, Wiltshire

Contents

**PART I: ROADS TO MODERNITY: THE POST-WAR
           STRATEGY OF THE PCI 1943-1980**

**PART II: POLITY CRISIS, THE EUROPEAN IMPERATIVE
          AND THE TRANSFORMATION OF ITALIAN
          COMMUNISM 1980-1992**

List of Tables

List of Abbreviations

ACLI	Associazione Cristiana dei Lavoratori Italiani (Association of Italian Christian Workers)
AN	Alleanza Nazionale
ARCI	Associazione Ricreativa Culturale Italiana
BOT	Buoni del Tesoro (Treasury Bonds)
CCD	Centro Cristiano Democratico (Christian Democratic Centre)
CESPE	Centre for the Study of Political Economy
CGIL	Confederazione Italiana dei Sindacati dei Lavoratori
CPSU	Communist Party of the Soviet Union
DC	Democrazia Cristiana (Christian Democratic Party)
EEC	European Economic Community
EFIM	Ente Partecipazioni e Finanziamento Industria Manufaturiera
ENEL	Ente Nazionale per l'Energia Electrica
ENI	Ente Nazionale Idrocarburi
FIOM	Federazione Italiana Metallurgici (Italian engineering union)
FUCI	Federal Democratic Movement
IRI	Istituto per la Ricostruzione Industriale
MSI	Movimento Sociale Italiano (Italian Social Movement)
NATO	North Atlantic Treaty Organization
OECD	Organization for Economic Cooperation and Development
OPEC	Organization of Petroleum Exporting Countries
PCE	Pardido Comunista de Espagna
PCF	Parti Communiste Francais
PCI	Partito Comunista Italiano
PDS	Partito Democratico della Sinistra (Democratic Party of the Left)
PDUP	Partito di Unità Proletaria (Party of Proletarian Unity)
PLI	Partito Liberale Italiano (Liberal Party)
PPI	Partito Popolare Italiano (Italian People's Party)
PRC	Partito di Rifondazione Comunista (Party of Communist Refoundation)
PRI	Partito Repubblicano Italiano
PSDI	Partito Social Democratico Italiano
PSI	Partito Socialista Italiano
PSIUP	Partito Socialista di Unità Proletaria
PSU	Partito Socialista Unificato (Unified Socialist Party)
RAI	Radiotelevizione Italiana
UDI	Unione Donne Italiane (Union of Italian Women)
UIL	Unione Italiana del Lavoro (Union of Italian Labour)

Preface

On 9 November 1989 the Berlin Wall collapsed. This unclenched a process which led to the demise of Communism throughout eastern and central Europe. In Italy, what was then the largest Communist party in western Europe, the PCI or *Partito comunista italiano*, transformed itself into the Democratic Party of the Left (*Partito Democratico della Sinistra* — PDS). The Italian Communists thus shared the fate of their 'comrades' in what was still called 'the Socialist camp'. Or so it would appear. Yet, just over a year after the transformation of the PCI, all the governing parties of what is now known as the First Italian Republic evaporated, punished by an indignant electorate, angry at the revelation of massive corruption unearthed by magistrates of great integrity. Fifty years of Italian Republican history were brought to a close. Thus, by the time the party of Antonio Gramsci and Palmiro Togliatti had jettisoned its name and symbols, a succession of events had led to the elimination or transformation of *all the parties* which had dominated Italian politics since 1945 and which had so rigidly kept the Italian Communists out of power. It is the great merit of the author of this book that he resists the temptation of proceeding as if one event (the collapse of Communism) led to another (the transformation of the PCI) which led to another (the end of the First Republic). Simplistic causal chains are best left to the billiard table.

The agony preceding the rebirth of the PCI as the Democratic Party of the Left was perhaps unduly prolonged. The decision of the Twentieth and last congress of the PCI (February 1991) when a new name and symbol were adopted, led to its acceptance in the ranks of Socialist International, a symbolic gesture signalling the reintegration of the party into the political family it had abandoned in 1921, when revolution was expected to spread throughout the world on the back of triumphant Bolshevism. Strictly speaking, this was not the first time the party had changed its name. Following the disbanding of the Communist International in 1943, what was then the *Communist Party of Italy* became the *Italian Communist Party*, to symbolise the fact that the party was no longer a section of an international organisation which has ceased to exist — at least in name.

Social anthropologists remind us, and rightly so, that names and symbols are important. The Communists themselves were aware of this. They came into existence when they accepted Lenin's 'Twenty-one Conditions' (July-August 1920) which included the obligation to call themselves Communists. If names were all that mattered, historians of the future would have their work cut out. The history of Italian communism could be encompassed within a measurable stretch of time: the seventy years from 1921 to 1991. Those who hold this position treat parties anthropomorphically, writing the history of a party as they would write a biography. Birth and death are relatively unproblematic historical facts.

It is the distinctive virtue of Vassilis Fouskas's inquiry to situate this metamorphosis in its proper historical context: the parallel disintegration of the Italian political system. This occurred essentially, though not exclusively, from endogenous causes: the corruption scandals, the long-term crisis of the DC, the rise of the Northern League. The PDS — to the extent that it was still the PCI under a new name — found itself as the sole survivor of the old party system. As recently as in 1994 it was still considered a Communist party by a sufficiently large number of Italians to enable the media tycoon Silvio Berlusconi to launch a new political party under the banner of stopping the red menace.

The author convincingly argues that, though the fall of the Berlin Wall and the collapse of Communism were the *immediate* causes of the metamorphosis of the Italian Communist Party, historians and political scientists require a far more complex analysis. He thus reconstructs the strategy of the PCI from its inception to 1989 and provides a coherent investigation of the interconnection between the PCI itself and all the other Italian parties. This set of relations is then systematically examined from the point of view of the social and economic evolution of Italy — evolution which is, in turn, mapped out in the wider European context. As he writes in the conclusion: 'the history of the PCI is inseparable from the history of the First Republic.' The context is a set of constraints which subjects all parties and limits their choices and freedom of action. Yet Fouskas eschews all forms of determinism: the recognition of constraints does not preclude that, at every historical conjuncture, real alternatives open up.

Twice before in its history the PCI considered giving up its name as part of a merger with the Italian Socialist Party. The first time was during the Resistance, when the leaders of the two parties, Palmiro Togliatti and Pietro Nenni, hinted that the close entente between their two organisations could lead to the creation of a single party. Togliatti was not enthusiastic, presumably because the only merger Moscow would have approved was one controlled by the Communists; this would have simply brought about a new anti-Communist Socialist party. For similar reasons Nenni gave up the attempt.

The second time occurred in 1964. After the death of Togliatti, Giorgio Amendola, in a somewhat prescient article, noted that both West European Communism and Social Democracy had not been able to establish a socialist society. He believed that the 'thaw' in East-West relations had made the division between Socialists and Communists irrelevant and that the two parties should merge. The proposal was firmly opposed by the majority of the PCI and met the indifference of the PSI, by then part of the ruling coalition. Had this unlikely merger occurred, it would probably have been on terms chosen by the Socialists, but this would not have prevented a sizable dissenting part of the PCI from forming their own Soviet-backed party. In either case, however, the merger would have meant the abandonment of the name and of its distinctive identity.

But the identity of a party is never entirely self-constructed. It requires the participation of the 'semiotic' universe within which the party operates, that is it requires the accord of other parties, other forces, other agencies who have the power and the ability to validate this identity. This struggle is at the heart of all politics. In the eyes of the party leadership it is necessary to establish the 'true' identity (that is, the identity which they wish to establish as the only true one) among all members of the party, its actual supporters, its potential supporters, its potential allies, its opponents and the entire network of communication whose task is to 'communicate' the image of the party. 'Being perceived' is as important a condition of existence of a political party as are its perception of itself and its actual being. But all 'communications' involve interpretations, filtering and, hence, redefinition. Thus the battle is never won once and for all. This is the reason why it is not possible to account for the metamorphosis of a party purely on the basis of the inner debates of that party, and this is why Fouskas's account is so timely and valuable.

Donald Sassoon

Acknowledgements

I would like first of all to express my profound gratitude to Donald Sassoon, friend and mentor, whose moral and intellectual contribution to the direction of my research was of inestimable value.

Percy Allum and Tobias Abse read and commented on every word I wrote. I am immeasurably indebted to them for their advice and enviable editing skills. I should also like to thank Beppe Vacca and Lucio Sponza, who have been constant discussants of mine on the post-1992 Italian crisis.

I am indebted to all the politicians, practitioners, trade unionists and researchers who, despite their busy schedules, kindly accorded me interviews. Their names are acknowledged at the end of the book, after the bibliographical section. I would like, however, to mention specifically Pietro Ingrao, whose personality and culture have uniquely impressed me. My particular thanks are also due to Piero Fassino, who kindly gave me permission to research his archives.

Though I cannot thank here all my Italian friends who so generously, in one way or another, assisted and encouraged my project, I would like to recall my friends Renato Giallombardo and Claudia Prestipino for the inestimable assistance they offered me throughout my research. I would also like to acknowledge my debt to Armando Giallombardo and his family for their exceptional hospitality and help during my stay in Rome. Thanks are also due to my friend Marco Bianchini for his constant support and many stimulating discussions.

I will always be grateful to my old friend Tolis Malakos for many illuminating conversations about the notion of modernity. Roberta Lo Sardo supplied useful material to me and Ilaria Favretto helped me with the background chapters of my research.

I owe a great deal to the personnel of *Botteghe Oscure* (the PDS headquarters in Rome), the Parliamentary library of Rome, the Centre for the Study of Political Economy (Cespe), the CGIL and the Gramsci Foundation of Rome. Special thanks are due to Camillo Danieli, archivist in *Botteghe Oscure*, and Elettra Palma, secretary in the Department of International Affairs of the PDS. In particular, I would like to recall Franco Romagnoli for his massive help with the use of microfilm and photocopy machines in the Parliamentary library, though once I heard him mumbling *fortuna che pazzi come lui si vedono qui ogni vent' anni*.

I thank the seminars organised by ASSEB (Association for the Study of Southern Europe and the Balkans) at the London School of Economics and FILEF (Federation of Italian Emigrants in London) for giving me the opportunity to present my views on Italian politics.

Thanks are due to the Hellenic Scholarships Foundation (IKY) for a 42-month full bursary which enabled me to complete my research. I am also indebted to the Department of History of QMW for financing my travels to Italy (research purposes) and Canada (where I participated in a conference).

I am immeasurably indebted to Donald Rayfield for his assistance in formatting the camera-ready copy for this book, and thank Sheila Blankfield for her prompt editing.

Last but not least, I would like to thank Vasso Agathidou for her immense support and encouragement during the difficult years of researching and writing the book (1993-97).

Introduction

In a famous passage in his prison essays concerning the theory of the political party, Antonio Gramsci argued:

> To write the history of a political party, it is necessary in reality to confront a whole series of problems of a much less simple kind than Robert Michels, for example, believes — though he is considered an expert on the subject. In what will the history of a party consist? Will it be a simple narrative of the internal life of a political organisation? How it comes into existence, the first groups which constitute it, the ideological controversies through which its programme and its conception of the world and of life are formed [...]. The study will therefore have to have a vaster and more comprehensive framework [...]. The history of any given party can only emerge from the complex portrayal of the totality of society and State (often with international ramifications too). Hence it may be said that to write the history of a party means nothing less than to write the general history of a country from a monographic viewpoint, in order to highlight a particular aspect of it. A party will have had greater or less significance and weight precisely to the extent to which its particular activity has been more or less decisive in determining a country's history.[1]

Gramsci's insight is unique not only because it offers a *methodological locus* for the study of political parties, but also because it incites the awareness of the researcher to look for the necessary *holistic mélange* of the processes to be reconstructed in the presentation of the arguments. Gramsci in fact says that the history of a political party is inextricably linked with national and international developments and that the more the party is important for a country, the more its specific history will be linked with that country's broader history. In the light of this, *the first major hypothesis under examination here is that the process of the crisis and dissolution of the PCI is inseparable from that of the crisis and collapse of the political class of the First Italian Republic.* This is a *methodological* point of view: we are dealing with the political history of the PCI and its transformation by way of 'mirroring' the whole variety of political events and intrinsic societal trends that each particular conjuncture encompasses.

The concepts of *polity* and *modernity* that figure in our analyses do not require an *a priori* strict definition to be 'implemented' *a posteriori* in the course of the investigation. Rather, the narrative presents them through the discourse of the PCI/PDS, that is, the ways in which Italian communists have conceived these concepts. Nevertheless, there is no reason, in the first place, to avoid speculation upon these exciting topics. In short, our theoretical definitions of *modernity* and *polity* draw on the works of Karl Marx and Max Weber, for a synthesis which can be found in Nicos Mouzelis' study *Post-Marxist Alternatives*.[2] By 'modernity' we mean capitalist processes of decomposition/recomposition — e.g. technological restructurings and innovations shaping and re-shaping society and the modes of production — which pertain to historically determined forms of *rationalisation* (the Weberian claim of the 'rationality of capitalist enterprise and bureaucracy') and *de-rationalisation* (from which the Marxian critique of liberal capitalism, market and forms of domination is drawn). As a cultural project, 'modernity' achieves its 'maturity' with the growth of the Enlightenment along the values of liberty, fraternity and equality. In this context, we can also define the notion of 'polity' as an autonomous terrain of hegemonic political strategies and social interests, which are periodically articulated by social and political subjects. At any event, it will become clear that the analyses of the PCI/PDS involve an almost identical speculative framework.

My plan is to present the history of the PCI/PDS and the First Republic through two major historical periods, hence the division of the study into two Parts. The first outlines the political strategies of Palmiro Togliatti and Enrico Berlinguer in the context of post-war reconstruction and the crisis that followed the prosperity of the 1950s and the upheavals of 1968-69. My major claim is that the period stretching roughly from 1943 to 1980 can be read along the lines of *political and social compromises* whose fundamental conceptions, shared mainly by the PCI and the DC, were that the state constitutes the privileged 'battlefield' and lever of socio-economic development. This was no accident: all over Europe and the world, the state could boost aggregate demand management and play a substantial role in the so-called 'golden age of capitalism' (1950-1970). However, that was no longer the case after the breakdown of the Bretton Woods system (1971), the oil-shock (1973), the strong inflationary trends and the first signs of the state's serious fiscal crisis.

The second Part of the study corresponds to the abandonment of the strategies of *compromesso* on the part of Berlinguer with the formation of a new Centre-Left government, with the PSI of Bettino Craxi becoming an organic part of the DC-based system of power. Meanwhile, on the international front, we had already experienced the second oil-shock and Margaret Thatcher's and Ronald Reagan's neo-liberal economics in Britain and the USA respectively. It is in this particular conjuncture that the PCI of Berlinguer introduced the line of *alternativa democratica* and began to contest the ability of the nation-state to determine social and economic developments: hence, the whole party strategy had to be revised. In this context, the thesis I suggest here is that the underlying process of European integration along neo-liberal lines underpinned the shaping of a *new revisionist identity*[3] for the PCI, well before the crisis of the USSR and, even, before the coming of Mikhail Gorbachev to power. By its 18th Congress in March 1989, the PCI was already a fully-fledged neo-revisionist party of the European Left. I deal extensively with these issues in the chapter 'The crisis of Keynesianism and its impact on the PCI's strategy, 1980-1987'.

Subsequently I examine the very process of transformation of the PCI which is seen, as I have mentioned above, in parallel with the transition process to the Second Italian Republic. The crisis and, in the end, the dissolution of PCI involved three major interlinked, but relatively distinct, parameters:

a The internationalisation of capital and the crisis of nation-state and mass parties.
b The decay of the DC-PSI political axis of power.
c The collapse of 'actually-existing socialism' and the end of the Cold War.

The focus of my final essays is entirely an attempt to theorise the contradiction between *new revisionism* and *communist refoundation*, a contradiction which pertains to Italy's Centre-Left political spectrum, lending it a unique dimension. Further details describing the content of each particular section of the study are given in the introductory comments of each such section.

The arguments advanced here are only hypotheses put forward for discussion and eventual rectification. There is nothing definitive about them, whatever originality the book claims for itself. This also explains the critical and sometimes even polemical character with which my arguments are formulated. Instead of suppressing differences, I have preferred to dwell on them, insofar as criticism alone can advance our knowledge of modern Italian politics. Having said this, the critique that I have on certain points levelled against some authors in no way detracts, in my view, from their analyses on other points which have been of great help to me personally.

Notes

1   A. Gramsci, *Selections from the Prison Notebooks* [ed. Q. Hoare and G.N. Smith] (London: Lawrence and Wishart, 1973), pp. 150-51.
2   N. Mouzelis, *Post-Marxist Alternatives; the Construction of Social Orders* (London: Macmillan, 1990).
3   For the concept of *new revisionism*, see D. Sassoon, *One Hundred Years of Socialism* (London: I.B. Tauris, 1996), pp. 730-54. Although 'neo-revisionism is not a finite doctrinal corpus', Sassoon explains, its main tenets are that 'markets should be regulated by legislation and not through state ownership [...]; that regulation of the market will increasingly be a goal achieved by supra-national means; that national — and hence parliamentary — sovereignty is a limited concept; that the concepts of national roads to socialism should be abandoned [...]. Neo-revisionism entails accepting important aspects of the conservative critique of socialism — including the association between collective provision and bureaucratic inertia' (pp. 734-35). Neo-revisionism, Sassoon's argument goes, has many variants, because it is compelled to build on specific national contexts and political environments. However, 'a national road to social democracy — or even modernisation — was no longer possible: *here lies the authentic neo-revisionism of the 1990s*' (my emphasis), ibid., p.739.

PART I
ROADS TO MODERNITY:
THE POST-WAR
STRATEGY OF THE PCI
1943-1980

Experience of the working class movement in Turin was to lead Gramsci to abandon his attachment to nationalism as such, but he never lost the concern, imparted to him in these early years, with peasant problems and the complex dialectic of class and regional factors. A unique surviving essay from his schooldays at Cagliari shows him, too, already progressing from a Sardinian to an internationalist and anti-colonialist viewpoint, as vehement in his opposition to European imperialism in China as in his repetition of what (he recalled in 1924) was the favourite slogan of his schooldays: 'Throw the mainlanders into the sea!'

Quintin Hoare and Geoffrey Nowell Smith, 'Introduction', in Hoare-Smith (ed.), *Antonio Gramsci: Selections from the Prison Notebooks* (London: Lawrence and Wishart, 1971), p. xix.

1 Modernisation or Populist Insurrection? Consensus Pattern of Reconstruction, 1943-1950

Trasformismo, fascism, modernity

Well before the foundation of the Italian State (1861), Camillo Benso di Cavour inaugurated a political practice which was known in the Piedmontese establishment as *connubio* (wedding). As political parties were deprived of any sound organisational structure, ideological principles and parliamentary majorities were formed on a day-to-day bargaining basis among political elites. Progressively, this sort of 'parliamentary centrality' came to depend on the consensus of civil society: the more the relationship between the public and social spheres was developed, the more their politicisation assumed a central role. The question of *clientelism*, that is, the exchange of favours between political class and ordinary people for the historical reproduction of dominance — the establishment of voting rights in 1919 for all male citizens underpinned this process — thus linked up with what Agostino Depretis and Giovanni Giolitti, in the late 19th and early 20th Centuries, named *trasformismo*.[1] These overlapping of functions between 'clientelism' and 'trasformismo' — Luigi Graziano defines clearly *trasformismo* as 'the parliamentary counterpart of clientelism'[2] — assumed a specific form in relation to the South. In point of fact, given the unfeasibility of the labour force being reproduced in the underdeveloped conditions of the South, state apparatuses and state parties took over this role on their behalf.

Having said this, *trasformismo* is a specific mode of political management of power and bears clientelistic networking and corrupt political practices. Accordingly, the very problem of modernity is how to get rid of these parasitic forms of governance which constitute real barriers for further advance. In other words, the requirement of modernity in this case is identified with the wiping out of clientelism in order to achieve growth.[3] However, had this been accepted in full, it would have been almost impossible to explain the social and economic progress of Italy from 1861 to 1920.[4] In addition, the thesis implies that there can exist a 'perfect' and 'moral' capitalism, purified from any sort of irrationality and mismanagement.

Drawing on the analyses of Leonardo Paggi and Massimo D'Angelillo, we consider *trasformismo* as a historically concrete form of hegemony which, in turn, does not pertain exclusively to Italy.[5] Inasmuch as *trasformismo* was able to guide the first capitalist accumulation in Italy by way of excluding the labour movement from the leading role in this process (political power *plus* organisation of production), it was only a specific political form of historical development. Consequently, 'the fundamental problem of *trasformismo* was not how to govern by circumventing modernity, but how to modernise against the labour movement'.[6] In this context, any sort of liberal criticism against *trasformismo* assumes the form of criticism against the elements of welfarism, the form which *trasformismo* takes under the pressure of the class struggle.[7]

We can now give substance to our historical analyses. I will survey the strategy of the PCI and the role of the Third International before and during the fascist regime. In this context, I will pay attention to Gramsci's thesis with regard to the specific form of modernity guided by fascism.

Italy's social economy experienced a deep crisis after World War I, despite its tumultuous and exuberant development during the wartime period.[8] Decline, stagnation, daily bankruptcies and a huge wave of unemployment followed the golden era of imperialism in Europe:

> There was a great falling off in the production of iron and steel which had boomed during the war and was suffering from the cancellation of war orders. In fact, the production of pig iron fell from 471,188 tons in 1917 to 61,381 in 1921 and that of steel from 1,331,631 to 700,433 tons in the same period. Imports, which were 26,8 million lire in 1920 as against exports of 11,6 million lire, fell to 16,9 million in 1921 as compared with exports of 8 million. The number of bankruptcies almost trebled from 1919 to 1921, gross national product went down from 114,8 million lire (value of 1938) in 1917 to 106,7 in 1921, and, along with rapidly rising prices, there were food riots (July 1919), because of shortages in supply.[9]

At the time, the electoral balance of forces was in favour of the Socialist Party, the Catholic *Partito Popolare* and Liberals.[10] The fascists, even during the first half of 1920, were a limited phenomenon of little importance. However, no political party or politician had a clear view on how that critical economic situation could be confronted and solved.

When Benito Mussolini and the fascists had achieved their march on Rome — with the consent of King Victor Emmanuel III — the Communist Party of Italy had already been founded during an extraordinary Congress of the Socialist Party held at Leghorn in January 1921. The leadership of Amadeo Bordiga and Antonio Gramsci (the former being secretary) accepted the Third International's twenty-one conditions. It had the name

Communist Party of Italy; Section of the Communist International (PCd'I), and it kept this name until 15 March 1943 when the International dissolved. Then, Palmiro Togliatti gave it a 'new' name: PCI.

Despite the adoption of Leninism and the conditions imposed by the International, the party lacked both a concrete political strategy and a sound ideology for dealing with fascism. Serious theoretical and political disagreements existed between Gramsci's group of *Ordine Nuovo* settled in Turin, and that of Bordiga, whose group had been publishing the review *il Soviet* in Naples.[11] The inner-party conflict became sharper when Grigori Zinoviev, then President of the Comintern, intervened in order to convince the PCd'I and Bordiga to advance a policy of alliance with Socialists vis-à-vis the rise of fascism. Gramsci, for his part, supported Zinoviev's proposal and, reluctantly enough, this strategy was accepted 'within the spirit of international discipline'.[12]

As a result of this profound contradiction, the party took several sectarian positions at home, such as its attitude towards the spontaneous anti-fascist movement of the *Arditi del Popolo*. This is Togliatti's judgement on Bordiga's strategy: 'The decision not to participate in the *Arditi del Popolo* movement, which was taken in the first months of 1921 when the movement had only just appeared on the political scene, was a serious mistake of sectarian rigidity.'[13] In short, the political attitudes which were adopted by the entire spectrum of the Italian Left and liberal-democratic forces during the crucial years 1921-1922, helped the fascist conquest of power. Neither the Left nor the Centre-right and liberal forces had a coherent political strategy to pursue. Thus, fascism was a combined result of the economic and political crises, accompanied by the failure of both the *trasformismo* and the Left to elaborate a viable democratic political solution. From then onwards, 1922 has symbolised for the PCd'I/PCI the 'terrible mistake' of democratic Italy, since all the democratic political parties had proved unable to present a united front to prevent the advent of fascism. Let us focus now on the PCd'I itself and the positions taken by Gramsci on the question of fascism.

The provisional arrangement between Gramsci, the Third International and Bordiga was resolved during the 3rd party Congress held in Lyons in France (January 1926).[14] Gramsci's and Togliatti's theses were approved by 90 per cent of the votes. Bordiga and his followers, having no alternative, abandoned the *gruppo dirigente* (ruling group). Meanwhile, with the fascists gaining absolute power, the PCd'I had to deal with its own problems and, first of all, the imprisonment of Gramsci, secretary of the party after the split. Thus, in essence, Togliatti led the party from 1926 onwards.[15] When the tenth Plenum of the Third International (1929) imposed the sectarian political strategy 'class against class' on all national Communist parties, believing the proletarian revolution to be imminent and Social Democracy to be the 'left-wing' of fascism, Togliatti was forced to obey.[16]

According to the Comintern, fascism represented a mere decline of capitalist society which, having no more possibility of developing its productive forces, was bound to collapse. In the characteristic spirit of 'economic catastrophism', the Comintern considered imperialism itself to be a stage of 'the general crisis of capitalism'. This thesis turned out to be utterly unfounded and misleading. In fact, fascism represented a development of social productive forces, advanced industrial development, technological innovation, and increased the productivity of labour.[17] When *trasformismo* ceased to be a historical necessity for Italy's modernisation — so when it no longer represented that specific 'political form of historical development' (Gramsci), while the existing political forces as a whole failed to cover the void — fascism arose as the only political option. In essence, fascism was the successive political form of Italy's modernity, a fact which was recognised by Gramsci.

The leader of the PCd'I had no hesitation in formulating the idea that *fascism was a progressive phenomenon* because it had the capacity of developing the productive forces of the country and, therefore, carried out the unification of the most advanced factions of the financial and industrial oligarchy.[18] This homogeneous and nationalist character of fascism was the very element which gave cohesion to the post-war fragmented political and socio-economic structures. The means of mobilisation for the re-vitalisation of all those social strata which had been neutralised by the political inertia of Giolitti's liberal era of *trasformismo*, gave fascism the characteristics of a real movement.

The fascist modernity, however progressive it might have been in its economic aspects, remained for Gramsci a *passive revolution*, because it was being realised by a reactionary and authoritarian polity: *the fascist polity*. Fascism's modernity meant repression of political and civil liberties, reinforcement of class exploitation and domination, circumvention of the principles of equality, fraternity and justice. In this context, *economic modernisation was against modernity and Gramsci became a Marxist intellectual who attempted the formulation of a different road to modernity for the West.*

Under the threat of fascist expansion throughout Europe, the Comintern changed its political priorities. The strategy of the *Popular Front* announced by Georgy Dimitrov and approved by the Comintern in its 7th Congress (Summer 1935) proposed co-operation amongst all democratic forces, thus overcoming its previous sectarianism.[19] Adopting this conception, the PCd'I started to become a mass party during the anti-fascist and the national resistance struggle. A leading force in the latter, it later claimed that it was one of the founders of the First Italian Republic.

'Liberal' reconstruction

The allied army landed in Sicily in July 1943 and pushed on to the mainland. Marshal Pietro Badoglio formed a new government that was recognised by the USSR.[20] The fascist organisations were all liquidated, but Benito Mussolini, rescued by German parachutists, escaped to the North, on September 23, 1943, where he was permitted to create, under German protection, the Social Italian Republic, with its capital at *Salò* in Lake Garda.

La Repubblica di Salò, with its structures being established in the North, was much better organised than the South which was under the management of the allies. The example of control over prices, i.e. that of inflation, is the most typical. As a student of Italian economic history wrote:

> For the most part, prices were kept down better under the Republic of Salò than under Allied Military Government. In the North, fascist price control machinery remained operative and prices could be dictated to large producers in both agriculture and industry. In the South, with its most primitive economy, the Allied Military Government (AMGOT) did not have the advantage of an effective pre-existing organization for enforcing price controls, nor concentrated production upon which it could centre its authority.[21]

However, the outcome of the war was sealed. The allied army moved northward and the Germans were on the run everywhere. In April 1945, Mussolini was captured by partisans and shot. In point of fact, fascism's very system of power, which was based on a war-oriented model of capitalist development and corporatist mass participation, disintegrated during the *hot war*. The allied troops remained in Italy until 1 January 1947 and guaranteed the peaceful return to democracy and the insertion of Italy into the western capitalist sphere.

By the beginning of the post-war period the question of the country's reconstruction was posed. Inflation, unemployment, poverty and severe deprivation, all caused by the war, remained to be solved. In particular, what had to be done was the implementation of a concrete economic strategy of reconstruction, which had also to include a concrete programme for agrarian reform, a very pressing problem particularly in the South. Accordingly, the whole institutional and political framework had to be re-designed so as to provide stable democratic cabinets in a new Constitutional framework which required drafting. In other words, a new *historic bloc* (Gramsci) to lead Italy's new phase of modernity had to be formed in order to express the given social relationship of forces. In this context, both the dominant and the dominated classes had to decide if, and whether, a joint politico-economic formula to cope with the acute crisis was possible.

Vis-à-vis the post-war social and economic problems, the Italian bourgeoisie was divided. The dispute concerned disagreements upon economic arrangements. Policy-makers were divided between those supporting *laissez-faire* conceptions and those arguing for an *indicative planning* rather similar to the French model.[22] The former prevailed for three main reasons. The first factor was *economic*. Exponents of *laissez-faire* argued that the establishment of trade liberalisation could solve Italy's perennial problem, which was the absence of raw materials (oil, coal, iron), so that the basis of industrial development could be reinforced.[23] By developing this process, inflation could be curbed and the development of the South plus the agrarian reform would become feasible. The liberal front had argued for the targets of low-priced imports of raw materials, export-driven growth and full integration of the Italian economy into the international and European markets.[24]

Ideological and *political* factors also played a role. Admittedly, the 'common sense' after the war was against any pattern of autarky and Keynesianism that strongly resembled the fascist corporatist/interventionist model in the collective imagery. There had been a clear identification of *liberalism* with *anti-fascism*. Thus, the American dream of freedom triumphed, and the first signs of an internationalisation of Italian capital appeared.[25] At the institutional/political level, liberal democracy gained momentum with the abolition of Monarchy through a referendum (1946), whereas a constituent assembly drafted a Constitution that was very progressive with respect to civil and social rights. In order to avoid any future authoritarian rule, a weak executive was shaped, a parliament composed of two houses with the same powers was created, and a pure proportional electoral system was introduced. The Liberal Luigi Einaudi, first governor of the Bank of Italy, then vice-President of the Council and minister of the budget in the government of De Gasperi in 1947, became President of the Republic from 1948 to 1955 and guaranteed these liberal directions.[26]

However, the Italian economy did not recover only on the basis of *laissez-faire*. Alongside the element of *discontinuity* with respect to fascist policies (the establishment of a liberal democracy), serious consideration should be given to that of *continuity*.

First of all, during the period 1945-50 as well as later, the Italian State intervened 'to the extent of favouring a particular kind of economic growth based on low wages and sustained exports'.[27] The effort had some success from the beginning, since 'wartime destruction had failed to seriously damage Italian industry's productive capacity'.[28] The case of IRI — *Istituto per la Ricostruzione Industriale* created on January 23, 1933, with capital provided by the State or by the sale of its own bonds — is the most striking. IRI contributed decisively to Italy's 'economic miracle' and turned out to become one of the largest industrial conglomerates in Europe.

Secondly, political and economic institutions as well as various corporatist practices inherited from fascism, were neither destroyed nor abandoned. On the contrary, they were invigorated, expanded and metamorphosed under the new liberal-democratic regime. This was not the simple transforming continuity that characterises any transition from one type of a political regime to another: *what distinguished this continuity was the fact that it took place with the consent of the PCI.* Thus, students of modern Italy will point out the 'unfulfilled aspirations of the Resistance' and castigate Togliatti who, being minister of justice from June 1945 to October 1946, 'made no serious effort whatsoever to reform the judiciary or purge it of its fascist elements'.[29]

To recapitulate: after the war, the neo-liberal anti-fascist bloc loomed large in economic and political matters; this, in turn, did not imply a total break with the corporatist and interventionist policies of fascism. On the contrary, these were crystallised and re-shaped whithin the institutional framework of the newly formed Republic. Therefore, the PCI of Togliatti, by compromising with the DC, could either be praised for being a prominent co-founder of the First Italian Republic *and/or* be accused of succumbing to the post-war capitalist institutional arrangements.

The *compromesso* of Palmiro Togliatti and the *questione salariale*

The PCI supported, participated in, or gave its consent to, all the post-war coalition governments from 1943 to 1947. The political conceptions of *national unity* and *democrazia progressista* (progressive democracy) were proclaimed by Togliatti to enable the country overcome its profound crisis and postopone the awkward question of *structural reform*, the main concept in the party's economic policy agenda.[30] In addition, the strategies elaborated by Togliatti 'were a direct continuation of the political strategy which triumphed at the Seventh Congress of the Comintern in 1935', that is, the *Popular Front* strategy.[31] This policy abandoned the sectarianism of the 'class against class' conception formulated at the tenth Plenum of the Comintern (1929) and gave national Communist parties the opportunity of advancing a line of cooperation with other democratic forces. Nevertheless, nothing could prevent the PCI's expulsion from government in 1947, which was dictated by the new international balance of forces: it was the beginning of the Cold War and the insertion of Italy into the western sphere of influence.

The political theses which the PCI presented to cope with the bourgeois bloc had a clear theoretical reference. This was Togliatti's interpretation and implementation of Gramsci's political thought.[32] According to Togliatti, who at the time and up to 1945-6 had exclusive possession of Gramsci's *Quaderni del Carcere* (Prison Notebooks), Gramsci had elaborated a specific theory of the hegemony of the proletariat in the developed West which was implicitly different from that of V.I. Lenin, whose analyses pertained to the underdeveloped socio-economic and political contours of the East.[33] Western civil societies enjoy robust political and economic institutions, thereby every revolutionary crisis could be solved and absorbed by them. This deprives the proletariat of employing any sort of 'frontal attack' strategy (the leninist paradigm), since western states are not entrenched citadels (the Russian case), but rather an open battlefield with many dykes and bridgeheads: hence the complicated relational nexus between state and civil society in the West. Indeed, what is needed is a prolonged *war of position* instead of the Leninist *war of manouevre*. To this end, both politics and strategy of the vanguard party, of the *Modern Prince*, need to be focused on the *mechanisms of consensus* (the role of the intellectuals, the question of national culture, folklore and tradition, including the Catholic tradition in particular). This, from a political point of view, implied in turn a more intensive concentration on the *real political and social processes of the formation of consensus*. In other words, the *Modern Prince* should reconsider the question of gaining the majority vote in a fully-advanced mass democracy of formal civil liberties and rights. Overall, and taking account of the negative experience of the Greek guerrilla movement, Togliatti argued that the post-war critical situation required a *constructive* and *positive*, instead of an *intransigent* and *negative* (revolutionary) dialectic to deal with the 'class enemy'.[34] To put it more succinctly, the Togliattian conception implied an *evolutionary* rather than a *revolutionary* notion of Socialism and Communism. From this perspective, the ripening of the social productive forces and the education of the masses were becoming the *conditio sine qua non* for the transition to Socialism. Once this interpretation of Gramsci was made, a new road to Socialism, strictly democratic and, if possible, totally peaceful, should, in practice, be envisaged.

In the post-war conjuncture, in accordance with his political philosophy, Togliatti formulated analogous theses on economic policy issues. In August 1945, at a special economic Conference of the party, the PCI leader opposed subsidies and state economic planning. In the present situation, Togliatti argued, both are *utopian.*[35] Consequently, Soviet-type control over the economy would be a catastrophe. Quite the opposite, what was needed was an increase in the productivity of labour, British-type wartime controls and an anti-inflationary policy to protect small savers. In this context, Togliatti asked the trade unions to be less concerned with wages and more with increasing production. Thus, Togliatti was in line with the dominant *laissez-faire* positions over economic policy arrangements so, in essence, with the Einaudi-De Gasperi project of class appeasement and reconciliation. The party's strategy of *compromesso* at the political level assumed the form of a *compromesso salariale* at the socio-economic one. The indifference the PCI showed when the trade union federation, the CGIL, put forward a 'Labour Plan' in 1949 which was essentially Keynesian, is attributable to the compromising stances adopted.[36]

We can now turn our attention to the crucial question of the *type of party*: How was the *Modern Prince*, inherited from Gramsci, to be transformed in order to play its hegemonic role as organiser of the national culture and political democracy? We know that Togliatti gave a single answer to this question: *the PCI must be transformed into a mass party.*

Mass democracy and the mass party

Well before the eruption of war, Togliatti had diagnosed the absence of a mass party in Italy. The origins of this phenomenon, Togliatti said, is traceable back well before the advent of fascism. In his famous *Lectures on Fascism* (1935) he wrote:

> The bourgeoisie had never possessed a strong, unified political organisation; it never had an organisation in party form. This was one

of the characteristics of the Italian situation before the war [he means World War I]. Before the war, you could not find a bourgeois political organisation having the name, the character, of a political party; I mean a centralised organisation linked with the masses and having a definite programme and line of action equal throughout the country. Make an effort to find one such organisation; no use, you will not find it.[37]

According to Togliatti, since Fascism represented a further revolutionary advance in the development of social productive forces, it created conditions in which broad social strata, directly or indirectly, got increasingly involved in political and economic affairs. The post-war democracy should therefore become the 'political lever' of mass participation in the democratic mechanisms of the state and political parties are the most suitable mediators to do it. It follows that the PCI could not remain a 'cadre party', such a party being suited to underdeveloped political and civil societies (e.g. the party acting under a ban). Hence, the whole question was the creation of a mass democratic party which should aim at the expansion of political democracy, civil liberties and human rights in directions which tended to go beyond capitalism. Thus, Togliatti's conception of *progressive democracy* is linked with that of a *partito nuovo* (mass party) and *Socialism*: these are the real contents of the *svolta di Salerno* (Salerno 'turning point'), or what later came to be known as *La via Italiana al Socialismo*, the Italian road to Socialism. However, in practice, the whole operation encountered several difficulties.

Once Togliatti arrived in Italy following a long exile in Moscow and after having said his famous *deponete gli armi*! (lay down your arms) to the partisans once the war was over, he had to deal with two conspicuous and urgent problems.[38] Firstly, the existing gap in the movement itself between North and South Italy was *de facto* a political drawback since it deprived the party from evenly balancing its strategy throughout the country. Secondly, Togliatti had to cope with the hard-line opposition of Pietro Secchia within the party. Despite the fact that the contrast between them was manifested after 1947,[39] it was implicit during the entire operation of the *svolta di Salerno*. In fact, Secchia had a solid orientation toward a rigid organisation based on working class militancy and gave significance to the role of the party-cadre at the expense of the mass character of the party.[40] This fact, which was seen by Pietro Ingrao as Secchia's 'lack of Gramscian culture',[41] added another set of problems for Togliatti. Broadly speaking, the arguments the leader of PCI put forth to deal with the situation as a whole can be summarised as follows:

The post-war balance of forces in the country did not feature a typical *dual power* situation consistent with the Soviet pattern of 1917. The main social contradictions in Italy were the North/South axis, and not the Centre/Periphery one, as in Russia or Greece. A civil war would probably have split the country in two. It is unlikely that the South, with its large mass of peasants, inexperienced in partisan warfare and untouched by socialist ideology, would have supported a communist insurrection. Quite the opposite, Southern areas would, almost certainly, have provided a strategic counter-revolutionary 'rampart' inasmuch as fascist and monarchic forces enjoyed exceptionally strong influence there.[42] The way that the Nazis' retreat took place, as well as the dynamic presence of the allied army, which often became quite hostile to the PCI and partisan forces, meant that the Italian Resistance could not *de facto* have the concentration of forces that the Greek and Yugoslav Resistance had. Thus, the unsuccessful, though glorious, experiment of the second *hellinikou antartikou* (the Greek guerrilla fight, 1946-49), became Togliatti's *Realpolitik* verification.

Having said this, Togliatti had no intention whatsoever of jeopardising the opportunity for bringing the PCI to a fully-fledged democracy and exposing it to that political experience. He precisely argued for the mass *partito nuovo*, presenting it as a *national force* of the new Italian Republic. For this reason, *class hegemony* was achievable through the articulation of a *national political discourse*:

> In basing our immediate political programme on the convocation of a national Constituent Assembly after the war, we find ourselves in the company of the best men of our Risorgimento, in the company of Carlo Cataneo, of Giuseppe Mazzini and Giuseppe Garibaldi, and we are happy to be found in this company.[43]

Yet, the *partito nuovo* should not be a 'discussion club'. The PCI kept its rigid skeleton, and the principle of *democratic centralism* was never rejected by Togliatti.[44] Skillfully combining 'democracy' and 'centralism', the PCI became a mass party with more than two million members.[45]

Notes

1   Before the outbreak of World War I, Antonio Gramsci distinguished two main periods through which the phenomenon of *trasformismo* had unfolded: the first one from 1860 to 1900 had to do with a 'molecular' *trasformismo*, as Gramsci maintained, where political personalities of the opposition passed to the conservative 'political class'; the second one took place from 1900 onward, and here left-wing groups embraced the conservative politics (Gramsci refers to the formation of the nationalist party by ex-trade-union and anarchist groups). Gramsci also described a mid-period between 1890-

1900 which was marked by the shifting of bulk of intellectuals to the parties of the democratic Left, see A. Gramsci, *Quaderni del Carcere* (Torino: Einaudi, 1977), vol. II, pp. 962-63.

2   See his 'Patron-client relationships in Southern Italy', *European Journal of Political Research*, vol. 1, n.4, 1973, pp. 3-34, the citation on p.13.

3   This is, among others, the thesis of Giulio Sapelli, *Southern Europe since 1945: Tradition and Modernity in Portugal, Spain, Italy, Greece and Turkey* (London: Longman, 1995), L. Graziano, 'Partito di regime e clientelismo di massa', *Rinascita*, 33, 8-8-1975, p.14-15; for further discussion on this point and bibliography, see the perceptive study of L. Paggi, M. D'Angelillo, *I Comunisti Italiani e il Riformismo; Un Confronto con le Socialdemocrazie Europee* (Torino: Einaudi, 1986), pp. 60-70, passim.

4   On the rates of growth in Italy between 1861 and 1920, S. B. Clough, *The Economic History of Italy* (New York: Columbia Univ. Press, 1964), pp. 370-73, 375-76, V. Zamagni, *The Economic History of Italy; Recovery after Decline, 1860-1990* (Oxford: Clarendon Press, 1993), pp. 75 ff.

5   In the absence of mass parties and organised civil interests, loose political elites underpinned by clientelistic practices were the case almost everywhere in Europe and other parts of the world, see my review of Sapelli's book, *Southern Europe since 1945* (op. cit.), in *Modern Italy*, vol. 1, n.2, Autumn 1996, pp. 127-28.

6   L. Paggi, M. D'Angelillo, *I Comunisti Italiani...*, op. cit., p.67.

7   Ibid., p.72.

8   V. Zamagni, *The Economic...*, op. cit., pp. 209-42.

9   S. B. Clough, *The Economic...*, op. cit., pp. 202-03.

10   Catholicism's popular ideology invaded social and political life in the beginning of the 20th Century after the abolition of the Pope's *non expedit*. The first Catholic Party was founded in 1919 by Luigi Sturzo under the name *Partito Popolare* (Popular Party). As Italian people have said ever since: *le anime alla chiesa, i corpi alla politica* (souls to the church, bodies to politics).

11   Gramsci, as he was influenced by the historicism of Antonio Labriola and the idealism of Benedetto Croce, argued that Communist institutions are already present in capitalist society assuming the form of *consigli di fabbrica* (factory councils). For this, he was severely criticised by Bordiga; see Q. Hoare (ed.), *A. Gramsci: Selections from Political Writings (1910-1920)* (London: Lawrence and Wishart, 1977), where a summary of Bordiga's polemic with Gramsci can be found in pp. 199-237, also P. Togliatti, 'Our ideology', in D. Sassoon (ed.), *Palmiro Togliatti; On Gramsci and other Writings* (London: Lawrence and Wishart, 1979), p.20 ff., G. Galli, *Storia del Partito Comunista Italiano* (Milano: il Formichiere, 1976), pp. 50-53.

12   See G. Galli, ibid., p.80, P. Togliatti, 'The formation of the leading group of the Italian Communist Party in 1923-24', in D. Sassoon (ed.), ibid., p.271.

13   P. Togliatti, ibid., p.270. For this movement, see also the unsigned essay 'Gli Arditi del Popolo' (originally published in *Ordine Nuovo*, 15-7-1921), in Q. Hoare (ed.), *A. Gramsci: Selections from Political Writings (1921-1926)* (London: Lawrence and Wishart, 1978), pp. 56-58, where on page 57 we can read: 'Are the communists opposed to the *Arditi del Popolo* movement? On the contrary: they want the arming of the proletariat, the creation of an armed proletariat force which is capable of defeating the bourgeoisie and taking charge of the organisation and development of the new productive forces generated by capitalism'.

14   For the Lyons Congress and the joint platform of Gramsci-Togliatti, see Q. Hoare (ed.), *A. Gramsci: Selections from Political Writings*, op. cit., pp. 311-76.
15   On this topic, P. Spriano, *Gramsci in Carcere e il Partito* (Roma: Riuniti, 1977).
16   See D. Sassoon's comments in his 'Introduction' in the volume *P. Togliatti...*, op. cit., pp. 7-20.
17   N. Poulantzas, *Fascism and Dictatorship; the Third International and the Problem of Fascism* (London: NLB, 1979), p.98. The thesis that fascism advanced capitalist modernisation, is unquestionable; however, what must be stressed here is, on the one hand, that 'fascism failed to narrow the gap between Italy and other industrialised countries' (V. Zamagni, *The Economic...*, p.274) and, on the other, to modernise Southern Italy.
18   See A. Gramsci, *Sul Fascismo* (Roma: Riuniti, 1974), pp. 382 ff., 394-95, passim.
19   Basically, from then onwards, left-wing criticism of the PCI's political strategy, from Togliatti to Berlinguer, would be based on the concept that the PCI followed, *mutatis-mutandis*, the strategy of the Popular Front. See for example the *Manifesto* group's attitude (Aldo Natoli, Luigi Pintor, Lucio Magri, Rossana Rossanda, Luciana Castellina) as argued by Sergio Dalamasso in his *Il Caso 'Manifesto' e il PCI degli Anni '60* (Torino: Cric Editore, 1989), and also, G. Amyot, *The Italian Communist Party; The Crisis of the Popular Front Strategy* (London: Croom Helm, 1981). All these points will be clarified below.
20   It occurred on March 13, 1944, thirteen days before Togliatti's arrival in Rome.
21   S. B. Clough, *The Economic History...*, op. cit., p.284 and P. Ginsborg, *A History of Contemporary Italy; Society and Politics 1943-1988* (London: Penguin Books, 1990), pp. 17-38.
22   See D. Sassoon, *Contemporary Italy; Politics, Economy and Society since 1945* (London: Longman, 1986) pp. 15-28.
23   Among others, P. Ginsborg, *A History...*, op. cit., pp. 73ff., 93-98, V. Zamagni, *The Economic...*, op. cit., pp. 322 ff., passim.
24   See in particular the 'Introduction' by Augusto Graziani (1972) in his *L'Economia Italiana: 1945-1970* (Bologna: il Mulino, 1972) pp. 13-96 and esp. pp. 15-31.
25   Private capital, for the first time since the *Risorgimento* (the Italian movement for national unification), was a participant in political power. As Sassoon has pointed out: 'This was one of the rare moments of Italian history since the Risorgimento when the entrepreneurial class could feel that it shared in political power, perhaps even that it was at the centre of it. Guido Carli who was for many years the Governor of the Bank of Italy and then led the Confindustria (Employers' Federation) has stated that since 1876 the Italian State has always been the State of the petty bourgeoisie and never that of the "productive" classes', in *Contemporary...*, op. cit., p.135.
26   On the deflationary liberal policies of L. Einaudi-A. de Gasperi, see L. Paggi-M. D'Angelillo, *I Comunisti Italiani...*, op. cit., pp. 70-80, 122.
27   D. Sassoon, *Contemporary...*, op. cit., p.22.
28   V. Zamagni, *The Economic...*, p.321.
29   P. Ginsborg, *A History...*, op. cit., pp. 71, 107; on this topic, see also the interesting discussion between E. Hobsbawm and G. Napolitano, *The Italian Road to Socialism* (London: Journeyman, 1977) pp. 14-18.
30   We deal with these issues below.
31   D. Sassoon, *The Strategy of the Italian Communist Party; From the Resistance to the Historic Compromise* (London: Frances Pinter, 1981) p.8 ff. See also, P. Togliatti,

'The Communist Policy of National Unity' (1944), in D. Sassoon (ed.), *P. Togliatti...*, op. cit., pp. 29-65.

32   We do not wish to be involved here in a theoretical debate, i.e. whether a continuity between Gramsci and Togliatti really exists. These are questions which also have to do with the Social Democratic and revolutionary aspects of Gramsci's work, especially that produced in prison, as well as which one of these aspects is predominant (let us put aside here the question of interpretation of Gramsci since he codified many of his manuscripts written under prison censorship). What concerns us is the historical connection that existed and developed between the PCI's political strategy and Italy's immediate post-war capitalist development. Thus, I will deal with the above questions through Togliatti's *concrete* political action, not in theory. In this context, it is worth mentioning that Togliatti himself did not try to legitimatise new political concepts (i.e. 'progressive democracy', 'structural reform') with references to Marx, Lenin, or even Stalin, see D. Sassoon, *The Strategy...*, op. cit., pp.24-25, 39.

33   Along the same lines, G. Vacca, *Gramsci e Togliatti* (Roma: Riuniti, 1991) and 'Alle origini dell'eurocommunismo: gli apporti del PCI' (written April-May 1979) in G. Vacca, *Gorbachev e la Sinistra Europea* (Roma: Riuniti, 1989) pp. 83-116. The Togliattian interpretation of Gramsci and, thereby, its practical political function, had already appeared in Togliatti's essays on the Spanish civil war. Pietro Ingrao has commented on the positions taken by Togliatti as follows: 'Togliatti, for years, was indicating a way out and a democratic road for Italy, both of which were the extreme opposite of an armed insurrection. There is a clear sign of it already in his reflections on the Spanish war. Let us say it with a certain plainness: *Togliatti, over this perspective, had risked his entire prestige and role as leader of the PCI*' (our emphasis), P. Ingrao, *Le Cose Impossibili* (Roma: Riuniti, 1990), p.47.

34   In September 1990, a magnetic tape appeared on which Nikita Khrushchev's voice was recorded, saying that Stalin, during the period of the German retreat, had stopped Togliatti at the moment he was ready for an armed insurrection. However, in June 1944, Togliatti was talking about an insurrection against the German Nazi fascists, since they were still strong and could thus delay the march of the allies towards the North. So rather, twenty years after (Khrushchev's speech is dated Oct. 1964), Khrushchev's memory had played tricks on him; see on these questions the documented analysis made by N. Tranfaglia, 'Ma la storia dice il contrario', *La Repubblica*, 23/24-9-1990, p.14.

35   P. Togliatti, 'Ricostruire', in PCI, *La Politica Economica Italiana, 1945-1974; Orientamenti e Proposte dei Comunisti* (n.d.), Roma, pp. 7-17.

36   See among others, D. Sassoon, *Contemporary...*, op. cit., p.135. One can read Togliatti's remarks on the question of European federalism formulated as early as 1948 — an issue linked with the views expressed by Altiero Spinelli — in the context of these 'liberal' views expressed by the PCI leader. In a leading article in *Rinascita* under the title *Federalismo Europeo?* Togliatti argued that 'a "European federation", if it wanted to be something serious, should become, more or less, a new State, unique and multinational'. Despite the fact that Togliatti opposed federalism along capitalist lines, this particular reading of history, a reading that wanted to foresee and reaffirm a *minimalist* assessment of the nation-state, goes *pari passu* with the liberal tradition of state theory, see P. Togliatti, 'Federalismo Europeo?', *Rinascita*, 11, Nov. 1948, p.378.

37   P. Togliatti, *Lectures on Fascism* (New York: International Publishers, 1976), p.29.

38   See M. Valenzi, 'La difficile victoria di Togliatti', *Rinascita*, 13, 29-3-1974, pp. 29-30. At the first National Council of the PCI which was held in Naples there were party cadres still under the influence of Bordiga (e.g. L. Manucci).
39   On this question, see in particular the very interesting article by G. Amendola, 'I contrasti fra Secchia e Togliatti (1944-1954)', *Rinascita*, 17, 4-5-1979, pp. 23-26.
40   See P. Secchia, 'Introduzione' (1954) in his *I Comunisti Italiani e l'Insurrezione, 1943-1945* (Roma: Edizioni di Cultura Sociale, 1954), pp. VII-XXXIII.
41   P. Ingrao, *Le Cose...*, op. cit., p.77.
42   See G. Pajetta, 'Alle Origini del Partito Nuovo', *Rinascita*, 35, 7-9-1973, pp. 13-17.
43   P. Togliatti, 'The Communist Policy of National Unity' (1944), in D. Sassoon (ed.), *P. Togliatti: On Gramsci...*, op. cit., p.49.
44   See P. Togliatti, 'Un Partito di Governo e di Massa' (25-9-1946, speech at the party's Federation in Reggio Emilia), in *Rinascita*, 32, 24-8-1973, pp. 11-13. Togliatti's platform is fundamental. He related the problem of the PCI mass organisation and its development to the question of an altering of the relationship of forces *within* the State. We need not mention here the Kautskian core of such an approach — which, otherwise, is well formulated by Nicos Poulantzas in his last theoretical statement, *State, Power, Socialism* (London: NLB, 1978).
45   *Inter alia*, D. Sassoon, *The Strategy...*, op. cit., pp. 24, 31.

2   Roads to Modernity, 1950-1980: Rapid Development, Social Mobility, Crisis and Compromise

The expansion of capitalism: the 'miracle'

In retrospect, the overall results of the liberal economic strategy which was adopted after the war were positive. There is no doubt that liberalism laid the basis upon which the 'economic miracle' of Italy was developed. What remains debatable, however, is the thesis defended by Augusto Graziani that the entire period of the 'miracle' — in his view, from 1950 to 1963 — was due chiefly to liberal strategies and that Italy's rapid development was only export-led (primacy given to foreign demand). Graziani explicitly maintains that the 1950-1963 period was characterised by private economic initiative, while that of 1963-1975 (crisis and slowdown rhythms of development) was marked by the expansion of state ownership and public investment.[1]

The Graziani thesis has been criticised to by several authors.[2] Their chief argument is that the economic cycle from 1951 to 1958 was characterised 'by a development which was largely internal in origin'.[3] Michele Salvati also clearly maintained that from 1949-50 a shift to Keynesian economic policies began.[4] However, the only certainty for all authors without exception and including Graziani, is that the peak years of the period (1958-63) were undoubtedly stamped by export-driven growth: in this, the integration of Italy in the European Community area has played a very important role.[5] Thus, the 'economic miracle' of Italy was based on a twofold precondition, each of which was predominant during the period in question: both Liberalism (1944-50) and Keynesianism (1950-58) helped Italy's economic recovery and laid the basis for it to become a major European and world economic force. Let us examine more concretely the reasons which permitted the rapid growth of the years 1958-63.

As we have seen, the dominant line of trade liberalisation after the war, which was supported by the PCI, was in practice unquestionable during the 1940s. A more decisive role for the state began at the turn of the decade with the creation of a development fund for the rebirth of the South called *Cassa per il Mezzogiorno*. During the same year, and before the creation of the *Cassa*, the agrarian reform was promulgated. The De

Gasperi government decided to distribute 40,000 hectares of land in Calabria.[6] This initiative did not take place only under the PCI's pressure. Certainly, it was politically determined — the DC, for instance, was also afraid of the fascist and monarchist parties in the South — however, the main reason which lay behind it was the battle of the DC's left faction of Amintore Fanfani and Giuseppe Dossetti. This group, always in favour of state intervention, rightly thought that the DC could lose the support of the peasant masses to the PCI.[7] Thus, the governmental party, the DC, must introduce the reform defended by the opposition.[8]

In 1953, the National Agency for Hydrocarbons (ENI) was established and in December 1954 the famous *piano Vanoni* (Vanoni plan) was launched;[9] The ENI, responsible for energy and petrochemicals, exploited the methane gas deposits in the Po Valley in straight opposition to private enterprise. Headed by Enrico Mattei, who was in close collaboration with the left-wing of the DC, the ENI 'broke the hold exercised by Montecantini over the price of many basic chemicals, and, especially in late 1950, the economy as a whole benefited from a substantial reduction in the price of chemicals and fertilisers'.[10] Both the ENI and the fascist-created conglomerate IRI played a substantial role in the creation of the 'miracle'. In this context, both liberalism of the 1940s and state intervention of the 1950s not only laid the basis of the 'economic miracle', but also promoted a deep cleavage between the dominant social classes of Italy: that between 'state' bourgeoisie and 'private' bourgeoisie.[11] How could the long-term interests of both these groups be simultaneously expressed via the DC's lasting dominant role, given that it had already begun the so-called 'occupation of the state' (clientelism, corruption, connection with the Mafia and the Masonic Lodge P2)?[12] To put it another way, how could the logic of national state and, especially, of *this nation-state*, easily dominate the internationalisation of social economies and also dominate the new social order that the crisis of the Bretton Woods system and the 1973 oil-shock opened up?

The questions posed above constitute the guide-lines of this study. As we shall see below, the PCI was operating within this context and the evolution of its strategy was determined by it. Here, it is sufficient to further specify the basic features that the rapid development of the 1958-63 period was based on:

a The *Cassa* and the agrarian reform increased agricultural productivity, which rose rapidly.[13] Indeed, the 1950s were years of a remarkable agricultural growth[14] which 'provided a sustained demand for industrial output, following the increase in the use of fertilizers, the spread of mechanisation, and the extension of land reclamation; and it maintained a surplus in the trade balance of foodstuffs'.[15]

b The South offered *cheap labour* to the Northern industries: *low wages* were one of the most prominent factors of the 'miracle'.[16] This huge reserve of cheap labour that the South provided helps explain the competitiveness of Italian exports. The North had provided the historically advanced *structures*; the South supplied the *subjects*.

c The very rapid growth of fixed investment which was promoted by both the public and private sector. The IRI and ENI, for their parts, 'succeeded in establishing those industrial infrastructures (cheap steel, cheap petrochemicals, a motorway system, cheap energy) which allowed rapid Italian economic growth'.[17]

Table 1   Growth of GNP and selected demand components, 1951-1963
(average annual percentage changes)

	1951-63	1951-58	1958-63
GDP	5.8	5.3	6.6
Private Consumption	5.5	4.5	7.0
of which: durables	8.9	5.0	14.5
Gross Fixed Investment	9.9	9.8	10.1
of which: resid. construction	12.8	15.5	9.0
Machinery/equipment	9.3	6.0	14.0
of which: agriculture	8.3	10.0	5.8
industry	9.1	7.1	12.1
Exports of Goods and Services	13.2	12.9	13.7
of which: goods	11.9	8.8	16.3
Imports of Goods and Services	13.6	9.4	19.8
of which: goods	12.9	7.2	21.3

Source: G. M. Rey, 'Italy', op.cit., p.507, table 17.3

d No serious strike, on a national level, took place between 1950 and 1960, while price stabilisation was remarkable.[18] In this climate of social peace, the CGIL-PCI's momentous defeat at FIAT in 1955 occupied a distinct position.[19]

e There was a rational utilisation of Marshall Aid, which was incorporated into the fixed investment achieved by the public sector. It has been estimated that Marshall Aid represented some 2 per cent of the Italian gross national product between 1948 and 1952.[20]

f Tourist earnings and migrants' remittances are two further relevant factors. Once stabilisation had been secured, Italy became a delightful place for tourists from all over the world, while the migrants' remittances must be seen as a result of the fact that Italy exported both *capital* and *labour.*[21]

All in all, the years of rapid development in Italy must not be seen separately from the European prosperity cycle of the 1950s and 1960s:[22] mass production for mass consumption (the *Fordist* model), scientific organisation of labour (Taylorism) particularly implemented in the big Northern industries, competitiveness, high profits, investment strategies and once again accumulation: 'the original propulsive mechanism of the Golden Age of capitalism in a limited group of privileged nations[…]. In the Italian case, it is well known, the division cut off the half of the country with perverse effects.'[23]

The problems for Italy had only just begun. Neither the *Cassa* nor the 'economic miracle' as a whole developed the South. Vanoni's plan failed to coordinate a rational policy of public works and capitalist urbanisation assumed distorted features.[24] Direct investment from northern industrialists, in addition, was orientated to the external front, not to the South.[25] Given the whole fluid social and cultural framework, the mass migrant conurbations in the northern cities as well as the lasting unemployment in the South, one can talk about a 'miracle' only with regard to the North. And this is a conditional thesis.

The rapid development further aggravated the distortions of Italian capitalism, and as it has started to 'falter' by October 1963, it brought simultaneously another anomaly of Italy, a political one: the Centre-Left government, based on the PSI-DC axis, developed by the experts of politics and power as a long-term strategy for overcoming organic crises of the regime, in fact, coincided with the end of 'miracle'. Certainly, negotiations between the DC and PSI dated from before it.[26] We shall take this thread up again, as well as that of economic and political crisis, in order to shape a logical explanation for the 'Hot Autumn' and of Berlinguer's 'historic compromise'. What we now have to deal with are the different interpretations that Italian Communists gave to this type of development which, using Ingrao's terminology, was called *neo-capitalism.*[27]

Communist interpretations of capitalist modernity; the PCI in the 1960s and the question of 'duplicity'

From the Popular Front to 'structural reforms'

As we saw earlier, Togliatti, by the adoption of the Popular Front strategy after the war, was able to compromise with the bourgeoisie and have no particular problems with the Soviet Communist Party. Problems began with the inception of the Cold War, when the era of the anti-fascist coalition was over. The Cominform, set up in September 1947 at a meeting held in the small Polish town of Szklarska Poreba and aimed at imposing a uniform strategy for all western Communist parties, accused the PCI, as well as the French Communist party, of having been too subordinate to their respective bourgeoisies. Stalin and the Cominform proclaimed the era of intransigent opposition which had to be adopted by the western Communists. This strategy was *also* in continuity with the spirit of the Popular Front. Let us throw some light on this point.

The basis of the Popular Front ideologies included two strategic phases which, in the first instance, were not contradictory. Dimitrov presented the Popular Front as a *tactic* which did not imply 'a reconciliation with Social Democratic ideology and practice'.[28] So the first phase of broad anti-fascist alliances in which some fractions of the bourgeoisie could also participate was a *tactical* not a *strategic* moment in the development of the revolutionary movement. The second phase (the strategic moment) was more decisive and, as it was prepared by the first, it had to deal with the real construction of socialism, that is, the dictatorship of the proletariat, once fascism had really been defeated. As the resolution of the Comintern stated:

> In the circumstances of a political crisis, when the ruling classes are no longer in a position to cope with the powerful sweep of the mass movement, the Communists must advance fundamental revolutionary slogans (such as, for instance, control of production and the banks, disbandment of the police force and its replacement by an armed workers' militia, etc.), which are directed toward still further shaking the economic and political power of the bourgeoisie and increasing the strength of the working class, toward isolating the parties of compromise, and which lead the working masses right up to the point of the revolutionary seizure of power.[29]

These two phases were to have been developed together in order to present a uniform anti-fascist political strategy as long as fascism was a real threat and/or a party leadership could not use, *in practice*, the first component at the expense of the second. As we have seen, Togliatti, through his *svolta di Salerno*, embodied in the PCI's policy the concept of *progressive democracy* which enabled him to postpone the question of revolution, as well as that of 'structural reforms'.[30] This allowed Togliatti to lay the basis for the *Italian Road to Socialism*, to incorporate in the party's strategic views the question of a lasting alliance with the DC and Catholic masses,[31] to initiate the process of autonomy vis-à-vis the despotic role of CPSU and, among other things, to press Italian capitalism for the development of the South.[32] In this context, 'progressive democracy' implied a completion of Italian capitalism first, and then socialist solutions could be initiated. This perspective was quite the opposite of the Stalinist.

Grant Amyot has argued that a revolutionary potential could be recognised in the concept of 'structural reforms', a kind of qualitative leap, once it was going toward the point of a decisive rupture with the bourgeoisie, that is to say, it implied an *alternative model of economic development*. It was impossible to implement these in the immediate post-war period; they could only be postponed.[33] Thus, 'structural reforms', having been interpreted in this way — the linking-up with the mass movement is always postulated — were nothing but reforms which could be achieved *before* an exhaustive development of Italian capitalism took place. The 'structural reforms' were not *sectorial reforms* — this is the reformist concept — but they had to question the entirety of the capitalist productive system. However, Togliatti himself left the concept with 'reformist' rather than 'revolutionary' connotations.

After the end of the anti-fascist coalitions and the inception of the Cold War, Togliatti tended to define 'structural reforms' as *transitional objectives* of the movement, objectives, however, which *could be achieved*. In his Report to the party's VIII Congress in December 1956, Togliatti stated:

> Our struggle for structural reforms is one of the main points of our search for the road of development towards socialism in the present conditions. *It is a mistake to confuse the demand for these reforms with what used to be called transitional demands* [...]. Structural reforms are a *positive objective* which we want to achieve and which *can be achieved* in the present conditions of political struggle. We do really want a general agrarian reform according to the principles endorsed by the Constitution (our emphasis).[34]

Some pages below, the PCI leader systematised the view that 'structural reforms' were established by the Constitution, so they were written in the unstable balance of compromises achieved by the PCI, DC and the PSI in the critical post-war conjuncture and it was up to the mass movement to get them implemented.[35] In this context, the two concepts 'progressive democracy' and 'structural reforms' can be seen as a uniform strategic project, with no contradiction, and where the former constitutes the 'superstructure' while the latter is the 'base'. 'Progressive democracy', as Giuseppe Vacca has written, is the institutional form of 'structural reforms'.[36] It follows, therefore, that the problem Togliatti had to cope with was *how* he could present to the International Communist movement and, above all, to the Soviet Communist Party, the 'Italian Road to Socialism' as a political project which included *in se* only the contents of the first phase of the Popular Front strategy. This was a very difficult task especially after 1947. Consequently, and taking into account Pietro Secchia's opposition within the party as it was developed, not accidentally, after 1947 (Secchia was very close to the Soviet leadership), the famous *walking on two legs* of Togliatti, as Michele Salvati called it, is located just here and can be politically dated to this period.[37] Indeed, Togliatti had to present his own distinct concept of the construction of socialism in Italy, while, at the same time, being consistent with the rigid orthodox strategy of the Soviet party. This is the so-called *doppiezza* (duplicity) of the PCI.

Togliatti never rejected socialism as a *different* model of economic development. He rather attempted to present his conceptions of the Italian road and 'polycentrism' by way of insisting not only on the idea that different roads to socialism do exist, but also implying that *different models of socialism* can also exist.[38] In his last political statement, written shortly before his death (Yalta, August 1964), Togliatti, in developing the relations between 'structural reforms', economic planning and internationalisation of national economies, wrote:

> It is obvious that the working class and democratic movement cannot be uninterested in this question; we must fight on this terrain too. This requires a development and coordination of immediate structural reform (nationalisation, agrarian reform etc.), in a general plan for economic development to be counterposed to that of capitalist planning. *Certainly, this will still not be a Socialist plan, because the conditions for this are lacking, but it is a new form and a new means of struggle for the advance towards Socialism.* The possibility of a peaceful road for this advance is today closely bound up with how this problem is presented and solved (our emphasis).[39]

However, the above statement on 'structural reforms' constitutes in itself a problem, rather than a solution. Indeed, the real question lies in how 'structural reforms' could be presented as a long-term policy which should simultaneously be *realistic* and not organically absorbed by the capitalist political and economic system.[40] As Donald Sassoon put it:

> The problem was the *practical application* [...]. As long as the party tended not to press coherent short-term demands to counterpose the government's short-term plans, structural demands could not but be seen as a propagandist exercise removed from a situation which urgently requested immediate decisions. In the dialectic between Centre-Left government and Communist opposition there was a clear asymmetry. On the one hand the government was unable to formulate organic long-term proposals for the solution of fundamental structural disequilibria, or when it actually did so they were unrelated to its day-to-day policies. On the other hand the opposition seemed to be able to counter-pose little except long-term proposals [*our emphasis*].[41]

In fact, Togliatti did not oppose the economic platform of the DC-PSI axis because he had no precise alternative economic proposal. His thesis of *constructive opposition* was firmly against any leftist conception, including the left-wing socialist faction of Riccardo Lombardi. Thus, a cross-party agreement was created on the issue, rather than two firmly opposing blocs.[42] The PCI leader left some important essays on the Centre-Left that support our thesis: 'We are considering this shifting of the government towards the Centre-Left as positive. Of course, we understand this position in a critical sense, that is, we support an effective shifting of economic, political and even ideological policies of the government.'[43]

Thus, it raises the problem as to what extent, *de facto*, the 'structural reforms' represented an advance towards socialism or simply pointed to an advance towards a more democratic management of capitalist development. There is no room to address such a broad question in this study; however, further clarification on the question of 'duplicity' is necessary.

The importance of being Communist and maintaining a radical anti-capitalist discourse while rejecting any sort of utopianism in dealing with concrete questions regarding a country's modernisation is decisive. Togliatti never rejected socialism as a *different* mode of production. However, he was always able to postpone it by appealing to *realpolitik*. To put the question more succinctly, there was a theoretical amalgamation of subversive Marxist ideas in the party's discourse and a practical application of reformist notions which contest neither the structure of the state apparatuses nor the intrinsic mechanisms of capitalist production, both being the nub of any revolutionary strategy. *Our thesis is that this fact constitutes a duplicity in itself, thereby either aspect could be used by the future ruling party generations to forward radical or reformist strategies alternatively.* Accordingly, Togliatti's political behaviour of 'walking on two legs' is strictly linked to the question of the PCI's internal debate, that is, to its political strategy proper. The following discussion aims, amongst other things, to present the two distinct factions in the PCI, showing that Togliatti's bi-lateral attitude is not unconnected with their formation.

Giorgio Amendola vs *Pietro Ingrao: is capitalism still progressive?*

The Popular Front ideology did not represent a definite break with the rhetorics of 'class against class' and that of 'capitalism's stagnation', views which had prevailed during the so-called 'third period' (1928-1934). As we have seen, the first phase was presented as a tactical manoeuvre rather than a strategic perspective which should have been adopted forever. Once fascism was defeated, Western Communist parties had to radicalise their respective political strategies at the national level. It was here that the legitimation of Stalinist discourse against the PCI lay.[44]

Thinking within this context, throughout the 1950s and well into 1960-62, when the 'miracle' was at its peak, many Italian Communists still had the fatal belief that Italian capitalism lacked propulsive mechanisms and that it could not further develop the social productive forces.

In May 1962, at the Conference on the tendencies of Italian capitalism held in Rome, the PCI, through its principal speaker Amendola, recognised not only this profoundly political mistake, but admitted the possibilities conceded by the EEC for the modernisation of the country:

> Our position, a politically responsible one, in criticising the EEC, was accompanied, however, by an extreme overestimation of the economic difficulties which would have followed the application of the Community regulations and by an underestimation of the new possibilities for the expansion of the Italian economy which arose out of the initial formation of a European market. In reality, the working class has an interest in favouring an economic development which permits the Italian economy to acquire a competitive position in the international market. Modernisation and technical progress of the Italian economy are requirements which must be supported by a policy of democratic development and not of conservation of the backward positions of lesser

groups of the Italian bourgeoisie. Inevitably the EEC accelerates the processes of centralisation and capitalist concentration and sweeps away positions which are working on excessively high unit costs. But all this requires a working class which develops a 'European' struggle, in full agreement with the labour forces of the other EEC countries against the monopolistic concentration which controls the executive organs of the EEC.[45]

Amendola, who was in charge of Southern and then of European affairs for the PCI, saw the rapid capitalist development as a result of the 'democratic thrust operated by the anti-fascist victory and the Resistance'.[46] The country was transformed from 'agrarian-industrial' into 'industrial-agrarian' (I use Amendola's terminology). Therefore, in the last analysis, the 'miracle' represented a positive outcome for Italy and for the workers, since it had been able to develop the productive social forces.[47] This kind of growth, however, had a number of negative aspects and distortions (failure of state policies to develop the South, mass migration, nonchalant welfare institutions etc.). The Centre-Left government, which was based on the DC-PSI axis, failed to implement a substantial programme of social reforms so as to eliminate these distortions. Basically, it was due to the PSI's failure which, once in government, has been patronaged by the DC's conservatism. To shift this alliance axis to the left and lay the basis for the PCI to lead a rational development, Amendola proposed provocatively the re-unification of the PCI with the PSI.[48] In any case, and following Togliatti's analyses on the Centre-Left, Amendola was aware of not totally rejecting the policies of the DC-PSI axis.[49]

Above all, this conservative political bloc was strictly linked with the economic processes of modernisation, so the developmental possibilities of the bourgeois revolution in Italy were not yet exhausted. Amendola, in his interview with Renato Nicolai, cited a long extract from Togliatti's speech at the Congress of May 1954 in Naples:

Can we be confined [...] to preaching socialism, and that is it? Or in the minds of the working class, we must work concretely to find a solution — favouring the interests of workers and of the people — on all the questions arising from the fact that in our country *the bourgeois democratic revolution has not yet been carried through to the end*? Lenin and Stalin gave a clear answer to this question, when they said that the working class, through its struggle towards the socialist revolution, simultaneously fights in carrying the bourgeois democratic revolution through to the end.[50]

Ingrao's analyses were quite different. According to him, and even though asymmetries between the North and South still existed,[51] Italian capitalism was not suffering from the absence of further industrialist development. Since capitalism always reproduced itself unevenly, the problem of the South was seen as a *result* of capitalist development, rather than as a problem which could find a final solution via reformist programmes of capitalist industrialisation and rationalisation. In addition, 'neo-capitalism' in Italy promoted the entire model of production and labour relations which had been fully developed in America during the 1930s and thoughtfully analysed by Gramsci. Indeed, the Fordist/Taylorist model implied an increase in the rate of exploitation and an increase in the alienation of labour-power; subjectivities further lost any sense of creativity with the means and objects of their labour since the entire production process was subsumed to profit and machine structures. Moreover, this constant technical modification and progress in the factory increased the physical and psychological strain on the workers. All in all, capitalism in Italy was mature and what was needed was a concrete political project putting forward reforms of a *socialist* character: thus, a different model of development was on the agenda.[52] 'Neo-capitalism', as the Centre-Left experiment showed, was trying to incorporate the working class into its mechanisms of accumulation, thus lending a Social Democratic character to reforms. In this context, Ingrao was not seeking, as Amendola was, the shifting of the political centre to the left via a common initiative based on the PCI-PSI axis.[53] Ingrao was arguing for a new 'historic bloc' which firstly had to be constructed from the bottom up: to this end, a *socialisation of politics* was the only real path through which a concrete content could be given to democracy.[54] Thus, he emphasised the creation of local power centres and saw left-wing local administrations as the hotbeds of direct democracy.[55] Accordingly, a grass roots alliance with the Catholic left-orientated movement and the PSIUP was much more substantial than one with a social-democratising PSI at the top.[56]

Another sharp discrepancy with Amendola, as well as with the PCI's ruling group, was on the question of intra-party democracy. Even though Amendola was first to raise the question, his attitude was marked by a conjunctural simulacrum rather than a real long-term intention.[57] Had the PCI wanted to be a prefiguration of a future communist society, a harbinger of a new, not authoritarian, social order, then it would prove to be so only in the course of the struggle against capitalism. In this context, the question of internal democracy, that is, an opening up of the party's dialogue to the rank-and-file, was becoming increasingly decisive for the battle towards socialism.[58]

Ingrao suffered an acrimonious defeat on all the questions he raised; even on that of inner-party democracy. The peak of his defeat took place at the eleventh Congress of the PCI (Jan. 1966). Ingrao's speech was rather moderate and inspired by a sense of party unity. He made no explicit critique of the PCI's strategy, but he stated many of the characteristic elements of his position. From his concluding remarks addressed to Luigi Longo, then secretary of the PCI, a phrase on the question of intra-party democracy has remained famous: 'Comrade Longo has expressed his criticism and his preoccupations on the question of the publicising of debate. I should not be sincere if I said to you that I have been persuaded.'[59]

Ultimately, but not least importantly, Ingrao was the PCI leader who integrated in the PCI's political discourse the problematic of *new social subjects* (youth, pacifism, women, ecology) engendered, in Europe and Italy, by the movements of 1968. Moreover, on his theoretical and political ideas the *Manifesto* group was developed.[60] It was expelled from the PCI (1969), then it took the shape of a party (1972),[61] while its main body, after the death of Berlinguer (1984), returned to the fold.[62] Furthermore, as if this trajectory never comes to an end, a strong theoretical and political link between Ingrao and *Rifondazione Comunista* (the newly created Communist party after the foundation of the PDS) can easily be detected. We shall deal with these themes in later chapters; however, and as far as Ingrao is concerned, he never broke with the PCI: *dobbiamo costruire nel gorgo* (we must build within the maelstrom), where the masses are getting involved, was the phrase he constantly liked to repeat after the second major defeat of his political career at the hands of the new PCI/PDS ruling group (Achille Occhetto, Massimo D'Alema, Walter Veltroni, Piero Fassino, Fabio Mussi) as well as of its rightist ally, the *miglioristi* of Giorgio Napolitano and Emmanuele Macaluso. History's irony in this case is that Occhetto, the leader who sealed the PCI's transformation into the PDS, used to be an 'Ingraiano' when he was general secretary of the FCGI (the youth Communist organisation).[63] Ingrao, without provoking any split, resigned from the PDS on May 15, 1993.[64]

Concluding the debate: the two dimensions of Marxist modernity

We can now attempt to list the crucial differences between these two distinct factions in the PCI and assess the importance of some significant common links between them. The ruling centre of the party (Togliatti, Longo, Berlinguer) had always tried to 'straddle the two extremes', by having them 'equally' represented in the party's strategy, ideology and organisation. As long as this centre was competent enough in managing and re-composing the divergencies and outside constraints, this kind of 'duplicity' could even be functional for the party's development in terms of aggregating various political and social groups along its strategic conceptions.[65] In other words, the requirement was for the 'reasonable' and fruitful management of 'duplicity', not its transcendence.

We can epitomise the two tendencies as follows:

Table 2   The PCI's discourse of Marxist modernity

P. Ingrao	The leading centre (Togliatti-Longo-Berlinguer)	G . Amendola
Italian capitalism is mature; socialist demands should be put forward; the 'miracle' aggravated the problem of the South;		The bourgeois revolution in Italy is incomplete (the South); Italian capitalism still has modernising capacities (the 'miracle');
Mass struggle from bottom up; emphasis on the working class and factory; direct democracy and regional autonomy;		Parliamentary strategy; opening up to European Community, fighting in its representative institutions;
Grass roots alliance with the radical Catholic masses and left-wing socialists;		Privileged interlocutor: the PSI;
Internal party democracy; publicity of dissent;		Centralised action; unfavourable to an 'insatiable' intra-party democracy;
Critical positions on Soviet socialism;		Hesitancy;
The role of new social movements;		Against radicalism of the youth;
Socialism is a different model of economic/social development;		Is Socialism a different model of economic/social development?;
The mass physiognomy of the PCI.		The mass physiognomy of the PCI.

The duplicity of PCI was thus a duplicity over the interpretation of capitalist modernisation. This interpretation encompasses, as two distinct moments of one and the same process, both dimensions of the Marxist discourse of modernity.

Ingrao attempted primarily a radicalisation of the societal process which, via its various radical subjectivities arising from within capitalism, would undermine the system's irrationalities (e.g. production for profit's sake) and the organisation of class power (towards a socialisation of politics). Amendola, on the contrary, saw capitalist development as a rationalisation process in itself, something which is also assisted by the extension of the public sphere being, especially in that period of time, in the ascendant.[66] Therefore, the two leaders neither shared a common conception of Socialism nor an agreement on the ways to pursue it. Nevertheless, there are two decisive points on which both Amendola and Ingrao never disagreed.

The first fundamental element shared by both leaders was that a *socialist* mode of production could exist in the future. On this point, what allied Amendola and Togliatti against Ingrao was the fact that socialism was not an immediate goal: its attainment still lay in the future, since the PCI's battle which collaborates in the completion of bourgeois revolution in Italy is gradually leading to this end. As Amendola put it: 'Our conception of the path to socialism is very pragmatic: it is founded on a historicist understanding of social revolution as a process which has come a long way and is going a long way.'[67]

There is no doubt that Amendola had a *linear* conception of capitalist history, a conception, indeed, which characterises *Social Democracy*, not *Communism*, the latter conceiving history via qualitative leaps and breaks/discontinuities. Ingrao was seeking an alternative model of economic development; Amendola sought a way of reforming capitalism. Grant Amyot has attributed Ingrao's defeat at the XI Congress also to this point, among other reasons:

> The 'alternative model of development' which was the central feature of [Ingrao] his programme remained too vague, and was not sufficiently linked to concrete problems. It therefore failed to gain acceptance among the mass membership, who could not really understand it; it appeared to many an abstract, intellectualistic exercise with little relationship to the practical, day-to-day struggle.[68]

Both discourses constituted the pillars of Marxist modernity; they shared the common ground of an enlightened idea for the future, another society more rational and just, organised and run in a different way. It is necessary to bring out the chief implication of this proposition, the principal *means* through which Socialism and/or Communism can be reached.

Indeed, the second fundamental conception shared by Ingrao and Amendola was the notion they had about the *Modern Prince*, the mass party. They disagreed on how the party should complete its functions, but none of them rejected its mass character as a cardinal pre-condition for democracy both in the party and in Italy. The party is the dialectical articulation of social partialities, the collective intellectual which deciphers social contradictions in order to go beyond them and unify humanity alongside the universal values of equality, justice and solidarity.

All the points made above entail that both Amendola and Ingrao based their own analyses on the common grounds of Marxist modernity, developing specific aspects and tensions existing within this theoretical tradition. The 'political language' advanced by both leaders, although conflictual, could articulate a viable and fruitful co-existence within the party. The cultures of the Second and Third Internationals, the tradition of austro-Marxism (Ingrao) and the elaborations of Mao Tse Tung (the *Manifesto* group) constituted the main points of ideological reference both for the PCI elite and the wider Italian Left. This was one of the reasons, if not the most crucial one, which permitted the broad electoral aggregation around the PCI — by far the strongest pole of the Left — in the 1970s.

After the death of Togliatti, Luigi Longo became general secretary of the PCI. He held this position up to 1972. He did not succeed in solving the PCI's *doppiezza*, which was passed on to his successor Enrico Berlinguer. However, Longo, by taking two decisive initiatives, and overcoming his traditional rigidity, very much helped the work of Berlinguer and the shaping of the culture of *Eurocommunism*.[69] Firstly, he took a quite positive stance vis-a-vis the student movement and blamed the party which had become too bureaucratic.[70] At the same time, Amendola was arguing for the necessity of a battle against government *and* students.[71] Secondly, the PCI of Longo energetically condemned the 1968 Soviet invasion of Czechoslovakia.

Meanwhile, and during the critical years 1962-1972, the party had clearly become pro-European. The EEC was no longer a capitalist foe, but a *conditio sine qua non* for the progress of social productive forces in Italy.[72] The Eurocommunist strategy attempted to envisage a perspective and a political project which would have the possibility of going *beyond* 'existing socialism' and the model of Western European Social Democracies. Accordingly, the overall foreign policy of the PCI was a 'phasing out of the blocs'. In this context, the inner-party tendencies presented above can be considered as the main components of Eurocommunist ideology and political strategy based on two different interpretations of post-war capitalist modernisation: that of the left Eurocommunism (Ingrao-Manifesto) and that of right Eurocommunism (Amendola-Napolitano); the latter has had an outright vocation for Social Democratic reformism. Communism, certainly, is the political matrix of the former. Both the principal aspects of Marxist modernity were found in a single Western European Communist Party.

Political economy and political strategy: the dynamics of a crisis and the *compromesso storico* of E. Berlinguer

A polymorphous crisis

The year 1963 was a distinct dividing-line for the Italian post-war socio-economic picture. A price inflation and the emergence of a balance of payments deficit appeared, a situation which was further aggravated by a concomitant increase in illegal capital exports.[73] From then onwards, and right up to 1969, the economy witnessed a consolidation of the growth achieved in the previous years accompanied by the stagnation of investment: *lo sciopero del capitale* (the strike of capital), as Salvati called it, was in fact a preparatory period for *lo sciopero del lavoro* (the labour strike, 1969-1973), when the revolutionary eruption of labour-power changed and gave shape to the entire system of industrial relations.[74] Social peace ceased to be the dominant feature and the increase in the class struggle brought Italian capitalism face to face with a new economic reality: *high wages* were the chief problem the Italian bourgeoisie had to solve, especially after the first oil-shock (1973) and the deep recession of 1975.[75]

The above general framework — which will be examined in more detail below — constituted the basis for a decisive intervention of state economic and political forces. The political axis which characterised the first crisis period, that of Centre-Left, tried to follow the classic path: improvement of macro-economic imbalances, enlargement of public sector, that is, increase of the state's role in the *management-reproduction* of labour-power, and to introduce counter-tendencies to the tendency of the falling rate of profit.[76] Apart from the traditional and, in essence, *anti-institutional* function of the Italian state,[77] that of the reproduction of labour-power via clientelistic networks for political-electoral purposes, we know that all the above state activities compose the core of a Keynesian type reform policy: introduction of welfare institutions — although a bit slender in the Italian case — nationalisations, social contracts between labour and capital under the aegis of the state, in other words, energetic intervention into aggregate demand.

The second crisis cycle was politically marked by the crisis of the Centre-Left and Berlinguer's proposal of a 'historic compromise'. The PSI began its self-criticism and grew reluctant to form a governing majority with the DC, while the PCI was excluded from the ruling coalition (the *conventio ad excludendum*). As a consequence, 'stable majorities could not be formed during the middle 1970s' and thus, 'unlike the de Gaulle and Pompidou governments after May 1968, the Italian governments of the IV Legislature (1968-1972) lacked the political strength to pursue an anti-union strategy'.[78] Hence, one real wound opened within Italian capitalism by the social and labour movement of 1960s and 1970s, that of *high wages*, was difficult to ease. The PCI's moderation, as it was going towards compromising attitudes with the DC in order, among other reasons, to get full legitimation *status*, proved to be the only viable solution, and the finest brains in the DC, like Aldo Moro, recognised this fact. With its inclusion in the government, the trade unions would be more conciliatory. Berlinguer's famous speech, *Discorso sull'Austerità*, at the Eliseo theatre of Rome (January 1977), when the PCI aimed clearly to be a party *of* government, shows not only the PCI's accommodation within capitalist structures, but something more: following Togliatti's general ruling strategy, the PCI had to present itself as a responsible national force ready to govern the country by *positively* resolving the economic and social crisis; so not as a striking-force which is seeking to exploit the crisis and the contradictions of capitalism in order to gain political power and to impose a dictatorship (the Leninist paradigm), but a positive force which was working and elaborating solutions *within* the boundaries of capitalist accumulation.

I shall attempt to present the entire period 1962-1980 within the general framework already outlined.

Towards the 'Hot Autumn' and beyond

In Italy, the increase in political mobility and in class struggle were bound together with the crisis of the social economy. The growth rate dropped from 6.3 per cent in 1962 to 2.9 per cent in 1964 and the first signs of unemployment appeared. Meanwhile, labour militancy and inflation were increasing. Real wages were virtually stable, while the partial recovery of 1966-68 could not put a halt to the deep-rooted problems. The lack of investment which, basically, entailed an absence of *fixed* capital investment, created a type of industrial relations which was based upon the use of *existing* capital equipment. Thus, the working class witnessed an intensification of the labour process inasmuch as enterprises wanted to increase labour productivity and profits. Accordingly, 'both the worsening of working conditions on the factory floor and the shift in income distribution away from labour must have contributed to the autumn 1969 industrial relations crisis'.[79]

The above explanatory scheme, if set within a broader sociological framework, can be further developed. A reasonable starting point is the migration question. As long as capitalism is able to create revolutionary changes in the social/technical division of labour, social mobility becomes one of its dominant features. The masses move towards places where there is job availability. This process, which is 'supervised' by big capital and/or the state, does not entail a rational utilisation of its *variable* component, that is, *labour-power*. Marx, in *Capital*, wrote that capitalist production, as it collects the population together in great centres, 'destroys at the same time the physical health of the urban worker, and the intellectual life of the rural worker[...]. The more a country proceeds from large-scale industry as the background of its development [...], the more rapid is this process of destruction. Capitalist production, therefore, only develops the techniques and the degree of combination of the social process of production by simultaneously undermining the original sources of all wealth — the soil and the worker.'[80] Under these conditions, and as long as the mass dissatisfaction is translated into militancy and participation, then social mobilisation is transformed into *political* mobilisation.[81]

In the Italian case the analysis developed above is widely applicable. The human costs for migrants who settled in Northern Italy were enormous. They had to deal not only with the hostility of the local population, but also the considerable inadequacy of housing, social services and education which contributed decisively to the 1969 eruption. The former problem which the Italian economy had already had during the years of the 'miracle', that of *distortion of consumer goods*, was aggravated afterwards.[82]

Table 3   Urbanisation in Italy, 1955–1968

Average rates of the population increase in urban centres with
more than 100,000 inhabitants (per year average percentage composed)

Towns between 100,000 and 500,000 inhab. (a)	Towns with more than 500,000 (b)	Total Population (c)	(a)/(c)	(b)/(c)
North 3.5%	1.9%	0.9%	3.9%	2.1%
Centre 4.9%	3.2%	0.9%	5.5.%	3.6%
South 3.4%	1.3%	0.3%	11.3%	4.3%

Source: A. Graziani, 'Introduzione', op.cit., p.50

The Centre-Left proved unable to integrate the mass movement and to institutionalise its demands through a concrete programme of social reforms. The 'Hot Autumn' of 1969, which altered the entire system of industrial relations in Italy, must be seen from this analytical angle.[83]

The immediate impact of the strike wave was the strengthening of labour in comparison with capital: large wage increases, reductions in hours worked and, in particular, in overtime work. This shift in the balance of power in favour of labour was crystalised in a new legal schema, broadly known as the *Statuto dei Lavoratori* (Workers' Charter).[84] Among other radical things, this labour law provided a reduction of productivity and of differentials between skill levels, while it managed to drastically limit the scope of employers in dismissing workers.[85]

Under these conditions which were favourable for labour-power, it is not difficult to understand the acceleration in inflation. This strategy, which was put forward in order to maintain the profit equilibrium, was followed by the devaluation of the lira, thus trying to limit negative repercussions on foreign trade.[86] For many reasons this twofold economic design failed and, in addition, in 1975, the year of the deepest recession, trade union bargaining power managed to reform the mechanism of the *scala mobile* (index-linked wage increases) and thus to offset the rate of inflation.[87]

This, therefore, resulted in the Italian social economy as a whole being under great pressure in the mid-1970s. The picture we have just given becomes worse if the gradual increase of the public sector deficit is added. However, the international crisis was the most important factor.

In August 1971, the American President Nixon declared, in essence, the end of the Bretton Woods system: gold convertibility of the dollar was suspended and an extra import tax of 10 per cent was introduced; thus, the International Monetary Fund, set up at a mountain resort in Bretton Woods, New Hampshire, in 1944, was requested to make new proposals regarding a new international monetary system. The dollar was devalued and the entire framework of American proposals, in spite of France's objections, was ratified by the group of the richest countries in the world in their *Smithsonian Agreement*, reached in Washington on 18 December 1971.[88] The resulting international financial uncertainty was coupled with the 1973 oil-shock, when the Organisation of Petroleum Exporting Countries (OPEC) decided on a 70 per cent increase in the price of crude oil.

There are no difficulties in recognising the degree of importance that such international developments had on the Italian economy as a whole. An export-led economy, deeply rooted in the post-war international division of labour, and increasingly affected by shortages of raw materials, meant that any negative fluctuation in the global economic indicators would inevitably also produce negative results on it. The average annual rate of growth of total output in Italy fell from 5.7 per cent in 1960-1969 to 3.2 per cent in 1970–1979.[89] Industrial production dropped from 9.07 per cent in 1959-1963 to 6.20 per cent in 1964-1970 and to 3.38 per cent in 1970-1974. Since 1974, double digit inflation has been a constant problem and the public sector deficit has been expanding. In addition, the lack of modernisation in agriculture and in the South decreased the ratio of exports compared to imports.[90]

The multiple combination of factors which had contributed to the Italian crisis, all led, in the last analysis, to the fall in *capitalist profitability*. It was within this critical socio-economic conjuncture that a new business-tendency appeared. As an economist put it:

The decline in profitability had accelerated, as firms were under pressure from the labour costs side on the one hand, and the rise in import penetration on the other. Rather than increase productivity by raising the capital-labour ratio, entrepreneurs, particularly in medium-sized and small firms, often preferred to decentralise their productive activities towards smaller-scale establishments or even self-employed operators working at home in order to depress their wage bills and circumvent trade-union restrictions.[91]

These small firms were located in the North-East of the country as well as in the central regions of Emilia Romagna, Tuscany and Umbria. The era of flexibility and of *small is beautiful*[92] had begun, and this phenomenon led to the crystallisation of the so-called 'third Italy': the North-Centre and North-East could now clearly be distinguished as 'third Italy' compared to the 'first' (North-West) and 'second' (South) one.[93] The PCI was always aware of the fact that this threefold division of Italy profoundly affected political/electoral tendencies.[94]

So far, we have presented the most salient features of the polymorphous Italian crisis as well as the contribution of the critical international conjuncture to it. An important final point, however, is worth mentioning: it concerns the divisions *within* the bourgeoisie.

The existing clash between *public* and *private* interests in Italy has already been noticed. How this clash came to characterise the various political processes as they were expressed by the DC alliance system, is not the object of this study. However, we shall mention only two points, otherwise strictly linked.

Firstly, the contradiction between private and public interests must not be seen separately from the question of the orientation of enterprises towards the markets. Augusto Graziani has distinguished two types of economy: a. that of advanced technology orientated toward foreign markets (e.g. cars, chemicals); b. that of low technology innovations orientated toward the domestic market (e.g. food).

Secondly, the entire question cannot also be differentiated from that of *political power* and the management of public enterprises. To give only one example, the big private interests, through their chief exponent, Giovanni Agnelli, attacked the DC system of power and the Centre-Left.[95] According to FIAT and its main ally, the Pirelli group, the Centre-Left experiment had been a failure. It did not modernise the country and the chief reason for this was the 'parasitic' clientele system of the DC which had raised a cement-wall in front of the productive classes (private entrepreneurs plus workers), that is, the *real modernising units* of society. In the early 1970s, the clash between FIAT and the 'statist-populist' faction of the DC led by Amintore Fanfani, 'took the form of a struggle within the Confindustria between the chemical giant Montedison and the FIAT-Pirelli group'.[96]

At the same time, Giorgio Amendola put forward similar *reasonings*. In essence, he identified the parasitic groups among subservient classes as the enemies of modernisation and development of the economy, and proposed an alliance between the working class and advanced capital to eliminate them.[97]

The historic compromise: another compromesso salariale?

In a widely studied article written after the PCI's withdrawal from the governmental majority, Berlinguer argued that the fundamental difference which distinguishes Togliatti's compromise from his own, regards the highly qualified leading role the working class should play in the present phase of capitalist accumulation. In Togliatti's years the compromise was the way to re-build the country and advance modernisation. Today's compromise has to do with 'what' should be produced and for 'which purposes'.[98]

Further to this thesis, one could add another, equally important, difference which concerns Berlinguer's revisionism vis-à-vis the party's foreign policy: no doubt, Eurocommunism enlarged the distance from 'existing socialism', a distance which Togliatti never had.[99]

These important and real differences between Togliatti's and Berlinguer's compromising strategies would nevertheless depict a misleading picture if a cardinal *common* element is not added: we are referring to the question of the 'price' of labour-power, that is, the way in which the strategy of *compromesso* was the necessary, if not the only, means to ease the trade unions' demands for high wages. The requirement, therefore, is to present Berlinguer's compromising attempt by way of emphasising this particular aspect of the party's strategy.

The proposal of Berlinguer to build a governmental policy together with the PCI's major rival, the DC, was explicitly formulated in Autumn 1973 in three series of articles in *Rinascita*.[100] Berlinguer seized the opportunity offered by the Chilean experience where the government of the *Unidad Popular*, headed by the socialist Salvador Allende and backed by the Communists, had been overthrown in a *coup d'état*. The parties of the *Unidad Popular* had no majority either in the Senate or in the Chamber of Deputies. In fact, Allende's coalition was unable to scrape together much more than 41 per cent of the popular vote.

The leader of the PCI, interpreting the Chilean facts, did not come to a sectarian conclusion according to which rigidity and emergency measures should be taken on behalf of the *Unidad Popular* (such as the dictatorship of the proletariat), but on the contrary, he concluded that even a left government which enjoys a 51 per cent of the vote cannot guarantee its permanent location in power. In Italy, a very broad governmental alignment which, in addition, can pledge democracy and civil liberties, can only be constituted by the joint action of the three main components of the Italian Republic: the Communists, the Socialists, and the Catholics. In that way, Berlinguer somehow created a predicament both for Ingrao's left and the reformist faction of Amendola-Napolitano.

Ingrao, who advocated an alternative left strategy,[101] including Catholic activists, could hardly convince his followers not to support Berlinguer, inasmuch as the proposed *compromesso* created possibilities for a larger aggregation on the grounds of a radical platform.[102] As far as Amendola and Napolitano were concerned, the possibility of establishing a more lasting alliance with the PSI could not be excluded beforehand, since the PSI would be part of the future coalition, a fact, moreover, which should be exploited in order to marginalise the DC. Therefore, Berlinguer's strategy of 'a new great 'historic compromise'[103] created an intra-party equilibrium which, as marked by steps and turns, facilitated rather than blocked his effort to build a solid hegemonic majority in the party.

The dramatic events in Chile were only the motivation in the formulation of Berlinguer's proposal. The reasons which counted most for the leader of the PCI were rather of *internal* origin, as was the question of the legitimation of the PCI vis-à-vis the Atlantic Pact.

First of all, Berlinguer aimed at guaranteeing the *continuity* of the Republican institutions in Italy; he wanted to avoid a right-wing shift of the masses at a moment in which both the MSI and terrorism were at their peak: the famous *strategy of tension*.[104] In this situation, where an unsuccessful *coup d'état* had also been attempted,[105] the official political thesis of the DC was that of identifying of the PCI with the MSI, by placing both in the field of terrorism: this was the so-called conception of *gli opposti estremismi*. In this context, the PCI drew parallels with the symbolic year 1922, when the democratic forces failed to prevent the empowerment of fascism. Indeed, the party's ruling group tenaciously argued that any sectarian decision at these critical moments of the Republic could very well lead to a reactionary take-over. Thus, once again, anti-fascist political logic prevailed, and the principal opponent was not the capitalist establishment but the dangerous reactionaries seeking to subvert the institutions of parliamentary democracy.

Secondly, Berlinguer's strategy aimed to transform the DC and shift policy to the left. The DC had always included a revolutionary democratic potential, that is, the left-wing populist and religious anti-capitalist values, a potential whose release was a *conditio sine qua non* for the democratic socialist transformation in Italy. The general secretary of the PCI openly argued that the strategy of *compromesso* deepened the crisis of the DC: 'Trying to confront our policy, the DC can be exercised in various tacticisms [...], but the crux of the matter is that our strategy put its back to the wall and accelerated its crisis.'[106]

The third and equally significant reason was the fact that the PCI seemed to be the only real force which had succeeded in electorally expressing the social radicalism and diffuse popular discontent of the 1960s and mid-1970s.[107] It had had the great advantage of being the sole rising political body. The PCI, despite its ambiguities,[108] beat the DC of Fanfani in the divorce referendum in May 1974 and had spectacular gains in the regional election of 1975. The results of the election of 20 June 1976 gave the party its biggest post-war percentage: it polled 34.4 per cent of the votes, as against the 38.7 per cent of the DC, while the PSI gained less than 10 per cent. The MSI dropped to 6.1 per cent. The Social Democrats (PSDI) and the Republicans (PRI) got little more than 3 per cent each. Thus, the line of the *compromesso* appeared to be a triumphant one.

Meanwhile, *Eurocommunism* was also at its peak and thus increased German and American fears, particularly those of Helmut Schmidt and Henry Kissinger.[109] On July 12, 1975, the joint declaration by the Italian and the Spanish parties was signed. On November 15, of the same year, there was the joint declaration of the French and Italian Communist parties. The PCI, PCF and the PCE were to draw up another joint document on March 3, 1977, as a result of a meeting held in Madrid.[110]

However, and apart from these justifications, the important matter for this study remains the *economic* component of the PCI's strategy. Which was the appropriate policy that, on the one hand, could capture the hegemony from the DC and, on the other, open the way to socialism through an ascending process of gaining social support? Was the implementation of the project of 'structural reform' in the 1970s possible? And, indeed, was this project still appropriate for coping with the present crisis and the post-1973 era?

Berlinguer and the PCI proclaimed the need for a *new type* of economic development, claiming it to be a necessity for the country and its economic renewal.[111] The overall programme can be described as a rational design aimed at putting forward anti-inflationary measures while, simultaneously, claiming to keep wages stable and to guarantee employment. While direct productive investments were the lasting solution for the industrialisation of the South, as far as the state was concerned, the whole platform was arguing for a rational utilisation of resources available, and against the DC's clientelism, corporatism and *malgoverno* (mismanagement). At the end of September 1975, Napolitano launched the idea of a medium-term programme, *programma a medio termine*, which tended to justify the governmental deflationary policies, and asked for the understanding of the workers, since any economic recovery would be linked with the *long-term* goal of an advance towards democratic socialism.[112]

However, this project, including that of Napolitano, still remained quite vague and rather blurred. For instance, Napolitano had claimed an increase in productivity without intensifying exploitation of labour-power.[113] Despite the fact that the medium-term plan of Napolitano was very close to the conceptions of his great teacher, Amendola, founder and then President of *Cespe*, only the latter would have had the courage to call things by their names: that is, within such a critical socio-economic (national and international) conjuncture, inflation can be curbed only by hitting the *social status of wages*, i.e., the real living standard of the workers. As Amendola himself put it:

> A consistent struggle against inflation calls for an increase in the productivity of labour and, at the same time, a reduction in the deficits, deficits in all the balances [...]. This calls for serious measures, far more serious than those that have been taken and those that have been announced by the government, measures that we should criticise not only because they are contradictory and unfair, but before all else because they are *insufficient* if we do not wish to continue to slither down a slope that will lead to the unleashing of uncontrollable inflation (emphasis by Amendola).[114]

Not only Ingrao but also Berlinguer and the majority of the PCI's ruling group, were against the Amendolian concept. However, as Berlinguer approached power, he not only started to feel 'safer within the Atlantic Pact',[115] but, being additionally forced to deal with the real tendencies and economic constraints, he had the opportunity to deliver his two famous speeches on the question of *austerity*: both, symbolically, took place in January 1977, the first in front of intellectuals (Rome, 15-1-1977, *Teatro Eliseo*) and the second at a workers' assembly (Milan, 30-1-1977, *Teatro Lirico*).[116]

The Berlinguerian discourse of *austerità*, although highly sophisticated, was, in essence, an appeal to the Italian people who had now to 'tighten their belts' in favour of capitalist economic recovery: 'Austerity means rigour, efficiency, seriousness, and it means justice'; it brings *in sè* a 'new morality' and thus tends to seriously challenge the existing order, which is, corruption, scandals, irrationality and the *parastato*.[117] In brief: the Berlinguerian design aimed at a 'purification' of capitalism, at a rationalisation of its own structures rather than an undermining of its social and political powers (the latter remained the Ingraian line). Within this context, and *also* from this point of view, one can easily recognise Berlinguer as the major PCI leader who kept up the Togliattian tradition of *compromising* with the DC while Italian economy and society were experiencing deep crises. Thus, we have witnessed not only a simple deal at the political level, but, and this is the key-issue, also a compromise along *strategic lines* concerning the equilibria between labour and capital where the DC and capitalist forces have always had the upper hand. The PCI has adapted its policies to the needs of capitalist economy and not vice versa. Paggi and D'Angelillo in their perceptive study on the PCI's economic policy, would even say that the main difficulty the PCI had in justifying its exit from the government of Giulio Andreotti stemmed precisely from its incapacity to develop an alternative economic policy.[118] The PCI itself, in a rather rare extract found in the official document of the party's XV Congress (Rome, March 1979), would suggest:

> Any programmatic projection implies an income distribution policy [...]. It is therefore correct that the trade unions give their battle for the programmatic projection which guarantees the real expansion of the South's productive basis and the employment, while considering it detrimental and harmful to base themselves on a further increase of wages without taking into account the compatibilities and priorities of political economy in general.[119]

Having said all this, our thesis is that *the policies of compromise could not be anything other than policies of subordination to the DC.*

Berlinguer, like Togliatti, proved able and flexible in proposing *positive* and *constructive* solutions, within a capitalist framework, in order to cope with the crisis while, however, at the same time he could argue for a *new model of development*, and it is that, as we have seen, which constitutes a fundamental aspect of *duplicity*.[120] Thus, any of the two major factions within the PCI could, to some extent, recognise itself via the official party discourse: consequently, even though that *anomaly* of the party has remained, party unity was never seriously at stake, *ingraiani* and *amendoliani* could co-exist under the same umbrella.

There are, certainly, further points for discussion. One can see, for instance, that all these efforts made by the PCI throughout the post-war period in order to get full legitimation, to take over national responsibilities, to build a stable democratic bloc and so forth, also had negative aspects. Undoubtedly, as we have already pointed out, the most serious one was that the PCI, however much it wanted to hit authoritarian tendencies and corruption, did not succeed in presenting itself as a *Modern Prince* which had nothing to do with the omnivorous and corrupting state machine of the DC and, later, of the DC-PSI inherited from fascism. And this fact, as we shall see below, lessened its prestige at the moment of its transformation into the PDS.

The strategies of *compromesso* also encompass an ideological contradiction. Togliatti and Berlinguer — but this notion is traceable back to Gramsci — claimed that no democratisation of Italian society is possible without the significant contribution of the Catholics. However, the point at issue is that the Catholics, and particularly their left-wing radical group at which the PCI aimed, had an anti-secular ideology which contradicted the very notion of modernity. Thus, in the single-issue divorce referendum, an unbridgeable cultural gap between the DC and PCI appeared. An American student of Italian politics commented on this point as follows: 'The PCI cannot expect to construct a secular alliance for modernisation and social justice with a party that contains a strong traditional religious and cultural base and maintains links with some of the most conservative elements in Italian society.'[121]

By the end of 1978, the balance of power, both in the party and the country, was no longer in favour of the *compromesso*: it had already become a *linea perdente* (a failed strategy).[122] Berlinguer himself, extremely conscious of this fact, would have been less aware if two additional events, which assisted the strategy's failure, had not happened.

In fact, the kidnapping (16-3-1978) and killing (9-5-1978) of the distinguished DC leader Aldo Moro by the Red Brigades as well as the intransigent stance of the PSI, initiated the collapse of the governments of National Unity. Craxi, who was elected as PSI secretary-general in July 1976, led his party successfully to adopt a position favouring compromise with the Red Brigades over the Moro affair, while the PCI and, finally, the DC, were opposed to this. From a political point of view, and understandably enough, Craxi argued for a withdrawal of the PSI from the governmental coalition, since 'it is not so clear that a Socialist Party of 10 per cent would be necessary to participate in a Communist/Christian Democrat coalition which already sums up more than 72 per cent of votes'.[123]

The leader of the PCI abandoned the *compromesso* and returned again to the *alternativa democratica*, taking advantage of a government crisis triggered by the earthquake in Irpinia in November 1980. To him, the *alternativa democratica* had never had anything to do with the *alternativa di sinistra* (Ingrao's claim): 'The difference between democratic alternative as proposed by Communists, and left alternative is very clear. The democratic alternative is a governmental perspective including those who do not belong to the left but who, however, are faithful to the Republican Constitution.'[124]

It is said that Berlinguer's post-1980 strategy had had a left-wing political hue.[125] However true this position is, we shall commit ourselves to show, among other things, that the whole issue is much more complicated and, therefore, much more fascinating.

Notes

1 A. Graziani, 'Introduzione', in his *L'Economia...*, op. cit., p.14.
2 See, *inter alia*, Michele Salvati, *Economia e Politica in Italia dal Dopoguerra a Oggi* (Milano: Garzanti, 1984), D. Sassoon, *Contemporary...*, op. cit., G. M. Rey, 'Italy', in Andrea Boltho (ed.), *The European Economy. Growth and Crisis* (Oxford: O.U.P., 1991), pp. 502-28.
3 G. M. Rey, ibid., p.504.
4 M. Salvati, *Economia...*, op. cit., pp. 52-3, 58.
5 Italy was one of the founding members of the European Economic Community (EEC), an original signatory of the treaty of Rome (March 1957).
6 D. Sassoon, *Contemporary...*, op. cit., p.35. In the PCI's programme of 'structural reforms' the target of the agrarian reform and of land distribution was a basic component, see in particular, PCI, *La Politica Economica Italiana: 1945-1974* (n.d.), Rome, pp. 19 ff.
7 We remind the reader here that the expansion of the *via Italiana al socialismo*, led by Giorgio Amendola and Mario Alicata in the South and backed by Togliatti himself (both were against Secchia, then in charge of the labour movement in the North), was successfully promoted on the basis of a broad alliance between middle classes and poor peasants, see on these points in particular, Grant Amyot, *The Italian Communist Party...*, op. cit., pp. 89-95.
8 See M. Salvati, *Economia...*, op. cit., pp. 46, 52-4.
9 The *piano Vanoni*, from the name of the Christian Democrat Minister of Finance Ezio Vanoni, among others, aimed at the creation of 3,200,000 jobs, but this goal has never been realised; see on this point in particular the comments of L. Paggi, M. D'Angelillo, *I Comunisti Italiani...*, op. cit., pp. 121-25.
10 D. Hine, *Governing Italy; the Politics of Bargained Pluralism* (Oxford: Clarendon Press, 1993), p.38.
11 P. Ginsborg, in his study on Italy (*A History...*, op. cit., passim) pays particular attention to the question of divisions within the bourgeoisie. In spite of its contradictions, he concludes, the bourgeoisie remained united.
12 On these points, see the excellent essay by C. Donolo, 'Social Change and Transformation of the State in Italy', in Richard Scase (ed.), *The State in Western Europe* (London: Croom Helm, 1980), pp. 164-97.
13 See G. M. Rey, 'Italy', op. cit., pp. 506-08.
14 M. Salvati, *Economia...*, op. cit., p.54.
15 G. M. Rey, 'Italy', op. cit., p.507.

16   Massive migration took place between 1955 and 1963. With a brief break in the mid-1960s, it resumed strongly in the period 1967-71. In all, between 1955 and 1971, some 9,140,000 Italians were involved in inter-regional migration (see, among others, P. Ginsborg, *A History...*, op. cit., p.219). Particular attention will be paid below to migrational phenomena which were the basis of the 'Hot Autumn' (1969) and of the lasting crisis.

17   D. Sassoon, *Contemporary...*, op. cit., p.41.

18   Among others, A. Graziani, 'Introduzione', op. cit., pp. 40, 43.

19   The CGIL at FIAT tried to control the activities of the Agnelli family by the elected assemblies. The immediate object was to put an end to political discrimination and repression and to the worst forms of 'super-exploitation' (G. Amyot, *The Italian...*, op. cit., pp. 118-23). The entire effort collapsed when 'at the FIAT plants where the CGIL, which had previously relied on the support of 65 per cent of the workers for the elections of their representatives to the shop-floor organizations (the workers' commissions), fell to 36 per cent (March 1955)' (D. Sassoon, *The Strategy...*, op. cit., p.92), see also, Vittorio Foa, *Sindacati e Lotte Operaie, 1943-1973* (Torino: Loescher, 1975), pp. 101-13.

20   P. Ginsborg, *A History...*, op. cit., p.159. See also the following formulation by V. Zamagni (*The Economic...*, op. cit., p.332): '90 per cent of counterpart funds were used for investment purposes, which in turn enabled Italian industry to renew a massive amount of plants with the aid of mainly American technology.'

21   On this point in particular, M. Salvati, *Economia...*, op. cit., p.94.

22   We cannot examine here the reasons why the Italian 'miracle' was halted in 1963, while in the rest of Europe it went on well up to 1970-72.

23   M. Salvati, *Economia...*, op. cit., pp. 23-24.

24   A. Graziani, 'Introduzione', op. cit., p.57.

25   Giovanni Agnelli, at a conference held in Naples in June 1980 pointed out that, compared to the past and after the 'miracle', the South closed its gap with the North which, in turn, gained ground in Europe, and he added: 'If Southern Italy were to regard mere financial subsidies from the EEC as a solution to its problems, it would be deceiving itself. The real solution — I repeat — consists in the extension and reinforcement of local industry' (G. Agnelli, 'European Industry and Southern Italy', *Questions for Debate*, 27-28, 6-6-1980, Naples, pp. 15-24, the extract on p.23). Two points are worth stressing here: **a.** Italy's uneven internal development on a lasting economic/territorial basis has continued, since the South's gap with the rest of Europe remains; **b.** the statement of Agnelli argues for 'extension and reinforcement of local industry' in the South, but he gives a blurred description over *who* can transfer resources and develop the South bringing it up to a European level; Agnelli's argument implies an absence of private capital investment towards the South, rather than an active participation to its development.

26   The dates of *rapprochement* are given in detail by Giuseppe Tamburrano, *Storia e Cronaca del Centro-Sinistra* (Milano: Feltrinelli, 1971), pp. 335-43.

27   The term *neo-capitalism* was common amongst the Ingraian Left, left-wing Socialists (e.g. Raniero Panzieri), and various leftist groups in the 1960s and 1970s (e.g. 'Lotta Continua', 'Potere Operaio' etc.), see, *inter alia*, S. Dalmasso, *Il Caso...*, op. cit., passim. The remark made above, of course, does not include the use of the term by various scientists, journalists and scholars. For instance, Gino Germani used the term *neo-capitalism* in describing the third stage of capitalism, that extended from the end of the Second World War up to 1973 (oil crisis) — the previous two stages were

labelled *paleo-capitalism* (the epoch of Marx), and *transitional capitalism* which ended in 1945. The post-1973 stage is marked, according to Germani, by the *crisis of neocapitalism*, see G. Germani, 'Lo Sviluppo dei Ceti Medi', in Gerardo Ragone (ed.), *Mutamento e Classi Sociali in Italia* (Napoli: Liguori Editori, 1981), pp. 13-21.
28   See, J. Degras (ed.), *The Communist International; Documents (1929-1943)*, v.3 (Oxford: O.U.P., 1965), p.356.
29   'Resolution of the Seventh Comintern Congress on Fascism (20-8-1935)', ibid., pp. 364-65.
30   The Togliattian concept of 'structural reforms' is examined in depth by Donald Sassoon in his *The Strategy...*, op. cit., pp. 140-67. The concept, as it was presented in the PCI's documents, indicates nationalisation of large monopolies (including electrical energy), credit institutions, steel and mechanical firms, complete implementation of the Constitution, agrarian reform, see *La Politica Economica Italiana*, op. cit., pp. 20, 25, 37-38, passim.
31   See in particular the following formulation of the communist leader: 'Our search for an Italian road to socialism must necessarily comprise a political alliance with these Catholic forces [...]', P. Togliatti, 'Rapporto all'VIII Congresso', in L. Gruppi (ed.), *Teoria e Politica della Via Italiana al Socialismo* (Roma: Riuniti, 1979), p.116.
32   Togliatti, in his famous interview with the review *Nuovi Argomenti* (May-June 1956) after the twentieth Congress of the Soviet Communist Party (14-16 Feb. 1956) where the distortions of Soviet socialism were attributed to the 'cult of personality' of Stalin, stated: 'At the time of the Seventh Congress (1935) the parties which had gained strength were united and well directed, already felt that an international centre should do no more than lay down general strategies on the situation and on the duties of our movement, but that decisions of practical policy and their implementation should be the work of the individual parties, entrusted fully to their initiative and responsibility', in P. Togliatti, *On Gramsci...*, op. cit., p.139.
33   G. Amyot, *The Italian...*, op. cit., pp. 41-54, passim.
34   P. Togliatti, 'Rapporto all'VIII Congresso', op. cit., pp. 97-98 and also G. Vacca, *Saggio su Togliatti e la Tradizione Comunista* (Bari: De Donato, 1974), pp. 393-99.
35   P. Togliatti, ibid., p.102, passim.
36   G. Vacca, *Saggio su Togliatti...*, op. cit., p.395.
37   See the following formulation of M. Salvati ('The Travail of Italian Communism' *New Left Review*, 202, Nov.-Dec. 1993, p.121): 'Togliatti's strategy of "walking on two legs" — ideological fidelity to the principles of Communism and to the Soviet Union, on the one hand, defence of the concrete interests of the working classes and of local communities, on the other — was paying handsome electoral dividends. Activists, militants, young people, intellectuals were attracted by the first; unions, cooperatives, local interests by the second, and the weight on either leg was shifted according to political opportunity.'
38   See, P. Togliatti, 'Rapporto all'VIII Congresso', op. cit., pp. 91-93, passim.
39   P. Togliatti, 'Yalta Memorandum', in P. Togliatti, *On Gramsci...*, op. cit., p.231.
40   In this context, the most striking example was the nationalisation of electricity by the Centre-Left, a lasting target of the PCI's structural reform policy. The same analogies on the question of the agrarian reform, which was gradually realised by the DC, can be found.
41   D. Sassoon, *The Strategy...*, op. cit., p.153.
42   See L. Paggi, 'Comunismo e riformismo', *Rinascita*, 32, 24-8-1979, pp. 3-7 and L. Paggi-M. D'Angelillo, *I Communisti Italiani...*, op. cit., p.135.

43   P. Togliatti, '"Operazione di Centro-sinistra" o crisi del monopolio politico della Democrazia Christiana?', in Instituto Gramsci (Sezione di Firenze), *Togliatti e il Centro-Sinistra, 1958-1964*, v.Ib (Firenze: Cooperativa Editrice Universitaria, 1975), p.604.

44   However, it was not only the Soviet party which blamed the PCI for being too tolerant vis-à-vis the Italian bourgeoisie. Roger Garaudy, the respectable Communist philosopher of the French party, after the eighth Congress of the PCI (1956), made a harsh attack on the Italian Road to Socialism. Togliatti responded to Garaudy by defending the PCI's strategy of 'polycentrism' and inveighed against any 'politics of principles' because it leads to 'not having any policy at all', see P. Togliatti, 'Postilla a Garaudy', in *Il PCI e la Svolta di Salerno* (attached leaflet of *Rinascita*, 14, 12-4-1986, pp. 101-10).

45   G. Amendola, 'Lotta di classe e sviluppo economico dopo la liberazione', in Instituto Gramsci (ed.), *Tendenze del Capitalismo Italiano* (Roma: Riuniti, 1962), p.202. See also Napolitano's formulation in his discussion with Eric Hobsbawm (op. cit., pp. 24-25). There Napolitano maintained that the PCI was unprepared to face the 'economic miracle' since 'the idea circulated, and in some measure influenced us' was that of 'stagnation in the development of productive forces and of production in the present historical phase'. Giuseppe Di Vittorio, leader of the CGIL, was among the first to understand the positive role that the EEC could play. In October 1957, at the fourth Congress of the World Federation of Trade Unions (WFTU) in Leipzig, Di Vittorio defended the above position and he was severely criticised for that especially by Benoit Frachon, secretary of the French General Confederation of Workers (CGT), see, A. M. Gentili-A. Panebianco, 'The PCI and international relations, 1945-1975: the politics of accommodation', in S. Serfaty-L. Gray (ed.), *The Italian Communist Party; Yesterday, Today and Tomorrow* (London: Aldwych Press, 1980), pp. 118-19.

46   G. Amendola, 'L'avvento della Repubblica' (originally published in *Critica Marxista*, 1966), in G. Amendola, *Gli Anni...*, op. cit., p.58.

47   In particular, G. Amendola, 'La classe operaia nel decennio 1961-1971' (originally published in *Critica Marxista*, 1973), ibid., pp. 243-62.

48   G. Amendola, 'Ipotesi sulla riunificazione', *Rinascita*, 47, 7-11-1964, pp. 3-4. A long debate followed and even Secchia intervened, and insisted on 'class unity'. In general, Amendola was severely criticised.

49   For a reformist, although very substantial, account of Togliattian views on the Centre-Left experience see, among others, G. Chiaromonte, 'La sua analisi del Centro-Sinistra', *Rinascita*, 35, 6-9-1974, pp. 17-20; on the reform programme of the Centre-Left — which, mainly, is focusing on the 1960-1964 period — see G. Tamburrano, *Storia e Cronaca...*, op. cit., pp. 139 ff.

50   P. Togliatti as is quoted by G. Amendola, *Il Rinnovamento del PCI* (interview to R. Nicolai) (Roma: Riuniti, 1978), p.53.

51   See Ingrao's testimony to N. Tranfaglia, in *Le Cose...*, op. cit., p.129. The following analysis is based on the two fundamental books of P. Ingrao: *Masse e Potere*, Roma: Riuniti, first edition in May 1977, and *Crisi e Terza Via* (Interview with Romano Ledda and with Pietro Barcellona's contribution), Roma: Riuniti (Nov. 1978). Both books appeared when Ingrao was President of the Chamber of Deputies (1976-1979) with the PCI at the threshold of government (the peak years of the 'historic compromise' experiment).

52   In particular, P. Ingrao, *Crisi...*, op. cit., pp. 141ff. Along the same lines and very interesting, P. Ingrao, 'Sistema di potere e tipo di sviluppo economico-sociale',

Rinascita, 21, 25-5-1973, pp. 18-19, P. Ingrao, 'Il sistema di potere del capitalismo di Stato', *Rinascita*, 47, 30-11-1973, pp. 15-16.
53   Ingrao: 'To explain myself: I did not believe in the possibility of a change in the Centre-Left, I mean from inside. I always maintained that the substance was the defeat of the Centre-Left,' in *Le Cose...*, op. cit., p.131.
54   P. Ingrao, *Masse...*, op. cit., p.40.
55   See P. Ingrao, 'Novita dalle regioni', *Rinascita*, 19, 11-5-1973, pp. 1-2.
56   The PSIUP (Italian Socialist Party of Proletarian Unity) set up in January 1964, as the PSI's left-wing faction led by Lelio Basso had refused to support the Centre-Left government of Aldo Moro–Pietro Nenni. Initially, it constituted a body of 25 deputies.
57   Amendola proposed the deepening of inner-party democracy in the convention of the party's Central Committee in November 1961 (see *L'Unità*, 12-11-1961, p.10). However, his proposal was determined by the democratic decisions taken by the XXII CPSU Congress which further developed the openings made by the XXI and XX Congresses. As a matter of fact, Amendola never insisted on this question after the defeat of Nikita Khrushchev in the USSR; Pietro Ingrao, personal interview (Rome, 14-7-1995).
58   See, P. Ingrao, *Masse...*, op. cit., pp. 179-211.
59   P. Ingrao, 'Intervento all'XI Congresso del PCI', in *XI Congresso del PCI. Atti e Risoluzioni* (Roma: Riuniti, 1966), p.265; see also, S. Dalmasso, *Il Caso 'Manifesto'...*, op. cit., pp. 32-34.
60   On the differences between Ingrao and the *Manifesto*, see, *inter alia*, P. Ingrao, *Le Cose...*, op. cit., pp. 165-67. Here Ingrao points out his different assessment of Maoism, as well as on how the struggle *within* the party should be conceived. He concluded: 'The comrades of the Manifesto — I think this is the point — perhaps have already seen as mature new political subjectivities on the left, completely different from the PCI, and have maintained that potentialities for a real and proper revolutionary rupture existed within the international situation', ibid., p.167.
61   The *Partito di Unita Proletaria* (PdUP) in the 1979 general election gained 1.4 per cent of votes and 6 seats in the Chamber of Deputies. It is worth noting here that the PdUP was not freed from the catastrophic ideology of the Third International, or that of the Fourth (the Trotskyist International). See, for instance, the following thesis of Lucio Magri: 'The European workers' movement has arrived at a new critical point in its history. Once again it faces great possibilities and great dangers. *Capitalist society is again in crisis. Regarding the stagnation of the productive forces, this crisis is as grave as any in the past*' (our emphasis), L. Magri, 'Real Socialism and Possible Socialism: The Problems of the East European Societies and the European Left', in *Power and Opposition in Post-Revolutionary Societies* (London: Links, 1979), p.181.
62   See L. Magri, 'Non è solo un ritorno, siamo cambiati tutti', in *L'Unità*, 20-10-1984, p.4.
63   In addition, Occhetto was backed by Ingrao to become the party's leader, a fact now faced resentfully by Ingrao (personal interview, cit.).
64   See in particular the brilliant account by Roberto Roscani, 'Il Comunista Eretico', *L'Unita*, 16-5-1993, p.6.
65   As we shall see below, for instance, none of these two conditions helped in the period of Alessandro Natta's secretaryship (1984-1988): on the one hand, we had a weak party leadership whereas, on the other, inextricable contradictions and insuperable international and national constraints (e.g. the internationalisation of national

economies and the crisis of Keynesianism). Thus, the PCI's 'duplicity' in the 1980s was bound to fade away.

66   An extreme example is an interview of Amendola in the *New Left Review* (106, Nov.-Dec. 1977, pp. 39-51). He responded to the question whether Swedish social democracy too had undertaken structural reforms, in the following way: 'No. It [Swedish social democracy] wanted to start doing so some months before its defeat; but for half a century it confined itself to intervening at the level of redistribution of income, and left ownership of the means of production intact. Whereas in Italy a large proportion of the means of production are already in the hands of the state' (ibid., p.44).

67   Ibid., p.44.

68   G. Amyot, *The Italian...*, op. cit., p.167, passim.

69   The term 'Eurocommunism' was first used by Frane Barbieri, the Madrid correspondent of *Giornale Nuovo* in an article published on June 26, 1975.

70   L. Longo, 'Il movimento studentesco nella lotta anti-capitalistica', *Rinascita* (special insert: *Il Contemporaneo*), 18, 3-5-1968, pp. 13-16.

71   G. Amendola, 'I communisti e il movimento studentesco; necessità della lotta su due fronti', *Rinascita*, 23, 7-6-1968, pp. 3-4.

72   See in particular, D. Sassoon, 'The Italian Communist Party's European strategy', *The Political Quarterly*, v.47, n.3, 1976, pp. 253-75.

73   G. M. Rey, 'Italy', op. cit., pp. 512 ff.

74   M. Salvati, *Economia...*, op. cit., passim.

75   The year 1962 can be considered as the symbolic starting point of the new phase of social tension. The riots of the *Piazza Statuto* in Turin as provoked by the FIAT (semi-skilled) workers and without the support of the trade unions, of the PCI and PSI, signalled three main tendencies in the movement: **a**. The young Southern immigrants were in the forefront of struggles; **b**. Political and ideological aversion towards the left national parties; **c**. A new left-wing connection between Marxian and Catholic culture appeared; both were deeply against consumerism, social injustice and individualism, all produced by 'neo-capitalism'. The journals *Quaderni Rossi* and *Quaderni Piacentini* were clear indications towards this direction. Moreover, what exactly gave rise to the post-1968 terrorism was a leftist mix of Communist and Catholic culture; see, among others, P. Ginsborg, *A History...*, op. cit., pp. 361 ff., passim.

76   On this point, reference should be made to the original analyses of Karl Marx, *Capital*, v.3 (London: Lawrence and Wishart, 1959), pp. 211-67.

77   See the following formulation of C. Donolo ('Social Change...', op. cit., p.169): 'The Christian Democratic party acts as a mediator between the state and those large sections of the subordinate classes who are outside the organisation of the working class movement. Chief among these are the agricultural workers. In this case the relationship between the masses and the Christian Democrats is a more intrinsic one based on a *vaguely social ideology, broadly populist and moderate* (but in some matters decidedly reactionary). The relationship of these masses with the state, particularly in the early stages of development of the political system, say up until about 1960, *is not based therefore on legitimate procedures designed to confirm constitutional democracy but on confidence in the protection offered by the dominant party*. This relationship is maintained by the distribution of favours (jobs) and subsidies, especially in the country areas of the South. In this way, private relations are developed with the state (and primarily the dominant party) which subsequently develop into more or less organised, more or less political forms of clientelism, culminating in the more complex present day phenomena of corporatist group clientelism. Faith in the Christian Democrats is

confidence placed in the party which remains dominant, 'central', immovable, indispensable. *Legitimacy is given to the institutions only indirectly'* [*our emphasis*].
78   M. Salvati, 'Muddling through: economics and politics in Italy 1969-1979', in P. Lange, S. Tarrow (ed.), *Italy in Transition; Conflict and Consensus* (London: Frank Cass, 1980), p.35.
79   G. M. Rey, 'Italy', op. cit., p.515. For such an explanation see, among others, D. Hine, *Governing...*, op. cit., pp. 44-45.
80   K. Marx, *Capital*, v.1 (London: Penguin Books, 1976), pp. 637-38.
81   Gino Germani, the Italian sociologist working in Argentina, used this analytical scheme in order to interpret Latin America populism as well as Italian fascism, see in particular, G. Germani, *Autoritarismo, Fascismo e Classi Sociali* (Bologna: il Mulino, 1975).
82   Graziani has remarked ('Introduzione', op. cit., p.44, passim) that while some goods were rapidly developed (e.g. cars, televisions), some others, such as health, housing etc. were not, or scarcely, developed.
83   See, Serafino Negrelli-Ettore Santi, 'Industrial Relations in Italy' in Guido Baglioni-Colin Crouch (ed.), *European Industrial Relations; The Challenge of Flexibility* (London: Sage Publications, 1992), pp. 154-99.
84   See, V. Foa, *Sindacati...*, op. cit., pp. 193-197.
85   See also D. Hine, *Governing...*, op. cit., pp. 46 ff., G. M. Rey, 'Italy', op. cit., p.518.
86   D. Sassoon, *Contemporary...*, op. cit., pp. 69 ff.
87   The *scala mobile* was introduced in the national contracts of 1945 and 1946. It was an automatic mechanism which aimed to protect workers' real wages against the effects of inflation. A referendum in 9 June 1985 (45.7 per cent for and 54.3 per cent against) resulted in the reduction of the *scala mobile*.
88   On these issues in particular, our basic reference is H. Van Der Wee, *Prosperity and Upheaval; The World Economy, 1945-1980* (London: Viking, 1986), pp. 347-48, 472-94.
89   Ibid., pp. 50-51.
90   Also, D. Sassoon, *Contemporary...*, op. cit., pp. 70-76. However, this pessimistic picture does not touch the Italian economy only. Throughout the 1970s, the most developed western economies witnessed a deep crisis. The underlying trend was that of *stagflation*, stagnation accompanied by inflation. Unemployment was a common problem, while world trade was in decline. Moreover, 'further oil price rises in 1979 and 1980 brought the problem of balance of payments and the problem of the international monetary system once again to the fore and triggered a new economic recession at the beginning of the 1980s', see S. V. Der Vee, *Prosperity...*, op. cit., p.87, passim.
91   G. M. Rey, 'Italy', op. cit., pp. 519-20.
92   It is around this period when the texts of E. F. Schumacher, under the title *Small is Beautiful* appeared (first published in Great Britain by Abacus Edition, London 1973).
93   The pioneering study in this field is that of Arnaldo Bagnasco, *Tre Italie; La Problematica Territoriale nello Sviluppo Italiano* (Bologna: il Mulino, 1977).
94   See for instance, A. Accornero, 'Nella 'terza Italia' maggiore coesione', *Rinascita*, 25, 23-6-1978, pp. 15-17.
95   We are presenting the point as outlined by D. Sassoon, *Contemporary...*, op. cit., pp. 137-40.
96   Ibid., p.138. The Montedison group was formed in 1966 as a result of the merger between the Montecantini group (Chemicals) and Edison (Electricity). The DC managed

to control the Montedison through Eugenio Cefis who became, in 1970, its President, see ibid.

97   See, the criticism made by L. Magri 'Spazio e ruolo del riformismo' and A. Lettieri, 'Le illusioni del riformismo', in V. Parlato (ed.), *Spazio e Ruolo del Riformismo* (Bologna: il Mulino, 1974), pp. 15-42 and 143-56. Despite their different points of view, both authors argued in common that the proposal of Amendola would have made sense if Italy was under fascism's threat. In fact, the reformist PCI leader, by taking such a position, did question the entire classic anti-monopolistic strategy of the PCI. By summing up the *progressive modernising* forces of Italy, he rather argued for a *cross-cutting* of the political system. The same, *mutatis-mutandis*, can be said as far as Ingrao's case was concerned; the only difference is that Ingrao, as a communist, was trying to sum up the *anti-capitalist forces* as they were cutting across the entire political and civil society.

98   E. Berlinguer, 'Il compromesso nella fase attuale', originally published in *Rinascita*, 24-8-1979, now in A. Tortorella (ed.), *Berlinguer aveva Ragione* (Rome: Critica Marxista, 1994), p.84.

99   Paggi and Angelillo suggested that this sort of revisionism on Berlinguer's behalf was made only for the party to be inserted in the government coalition and assure the USA of the PCI's acceptance of NATO, L. Paggi-M.D'Angelillo, *I Communisti Italiani...*, op. cit., pp. 115-16, passim.

100   E. Berlinguer, 'Imperialismo e coesistenza alla luce dei fatti cileni', *Rinascita*, 38, 28-9-1973, pp. 3-4, 'Riflessione sull'Italia dopo i fatti del Cile', *Rinascita*, 39, 5-10-1973, pp. 3-4, 'Riflessioni sull'Italia dopo i fatti del Cile; alleanze sociali e schieramenti politici', *Rinascita*, 40, 12-10-1973, pp. 3-5 (the last one was the most important). Berlinguer, maintained openly that the 'historic compromise' was not a *tactical manoeuvre*, but a *strategy*, see, for instance, E. Berlinguer, 'Compromesso storico, crisi della DC, rapporto dei sindacati con i partiti e con il governo' (originally published in *La Tribuna dei Lavoratori*, 9-2-1975), in E. Berlinguer, *La Questione Comunista* (Roma: Riuniti, 1975), v.II, pp. 967-76. In addition, it is worth stressing here, that Berlinguer was seeking a privileged alliance with the DC even before 1973, see, E. Berlinguer, 'La DC ha paura?' (originally published in *Rinascita*, 29-5-1970), in *La questione...*, op. cit., v.I, pp. 195-200.

101   See, *inter alia*, the very interesting discussion between P. Ingrao, N. Badaloni, G. Napolitano, G. Fanti and L. Lama, 'La politica del PCI per una nuova direzione del paese' in *Rinascita*, 4, 24-1-1975, pp. 7-12. In this discussion the common 'left-wing' views which both Ingrao and Badaloni shared, as against the moderate stances of Lama and Napolitano, become clear. Characteristically, Ingrao maintained: 'But the response — just what I would like to stress — cannot be the stabilisation of a confused coexistence with conservatism which, in turn, is going to finish up by detracting force and cohesion from our choices, thus bringing impotence to democracy', ibid., p.9. In his *Le Cose...* (op. cit., p.169), Ingrao had clearly stated: 'The formulæ of the 'historic compromise' [...]. I have never sympathized with it, and I have continuously insisted upon a strategy which would tend to split the DC at the moment in which it was at the risk of not finding a political veil, because of the crisis which has shaken the Socialist party.'

102   P. Ingrao had made a strict distinction between the 'centrist DC', a traditionally reactionary current in Italian politics, and social Catholicism, a firm advocate of peace, social justice and solidarity. Ingrao had in particular developed very good relationships with ACLI (Association of Italian Christian Workers), see personal interview, cit.

103 E. Berlinguer, 'Riflessioni...' (12-10-1973), op. cit., p.5.

104 In the national vote of May 1972 the MSI enjoyed 8.7 per cent and 56 seats in the Chamber of Deputies; it was very strong in the South and, particularly, in Naples and Catania (Sicily) where it gained more than 20 per cent of the vote.

105 We are referring to the attempt made by the Prince Junio Valerio Borghese during the night of 7-8 December 1970. This coup was much less serious than that attempted by the General Giovanni De Lorenzo in the Summer of 1964, see P. Ginsborg, *A History...*, op. cit., pp. 276-79, 334.

106 E. Berlinguer, 'Compromesso storico, crisi della DC...', op. cit., p.969.

107 It occured not without the decisive contribution of the Berlinguerian political practice. The leader of the PCI had always tried to link, along Togliattian strategies, mass mobility and political reforms, thus further deepening democracy and civil liberties. On this point, Berlinguer's statement is clear: 'It is only this interaction between struggle of the masses and united political initiative, between social and political spheres that can push forward our perspective which is to change the present situation and the unification between the left and democratic forces in order to construct a new majority', E. Berlinguer, 'Costruire una nuova unità internazionalista e compiere un passo avanti verso in socialismo' (Conclusion in the XII Party Congress, Bologna, February 1969), in *La Questione...*, op. cit., v.I, p.35. Along the same lines, and equally interesting, is his text 'A un anno dall'«Autunno Caldo»' (originally published in *Rinascita*, 16-10-1970), in ibid., pp. 225-38. The schema that social struggles can be institutionalised and take the shape of political reforms, can be applied, according to Berlinguer, even *within* the core of state power: the bureaucracy, army, police, see in particular, E. Berlinguer, 'La nostra lotta per l'affermazione di una alternativa democratica,' in ibid., pp. 393-94.

108 It is well known the phrase of Berlinguer 'contro il referendum della discordia' (against the referendum of discord), meaning the separatist nature of such a referendum vis-à-vis the compromising line toward the DC; see in particular, T. Abse, 'Judging the PCI', *New Left Review*, 153, Sept.-Oct. 1985, pp. 5-45.

109 At a conference held in Washington in June 1977, Kissinger publicly declared: 'We must frankly recognise the problem that we will face if the Communists come to power in W. Europe and we must understand the practical decisions this will impose on us as a nation [...]. We must have a programme for encouraging the forces of moderation and progress in this critical period and for rallying them should a Communist party nonetheless prevail', H. Kissinger, 'Communist parties in W. Europe: challenge to the West', in A. Ranney-G. Sartori (ed.), *Eurocommunism: the Italian Case* (Washington: American Enterprise Institute for Public Policy Research, 1978), p.194, also pp. 184-86.

110 All three documents can be found in Peter Lange, Maurizio Vannicelli (eds), *The Communist Parties of Italy, France and Spain; Postwar Change and Continuity* (London: George Allen, 1981), pp. 357-62.

111 See *La Politica Economica...*(n.d.), op. cit., pp. 277-99.

112 See G. Napolitano, 'Proposte per un confronto su un programma a medio termine', *Rinascita*, 38, 26-9-1975, pp. 3-5.

113 Ibid., p.4. Two years later, his economic proposal appeared as a collective party document for further discussion (PCI, *Proposta di un Progetto a Medio Termine*, Roma, 1977). The Commission's work was coordinated by A. Occhetto; among the participants were M. D'Alema, E. Macaluso, A. Reichlin, A. Seroni and A. Tortorella.

114 G. Amendola, 'Inflation is the main danger' (speech to the Central Committee, Oct. 19, 1976), in D. Sassoon, *The Italian Communists...*, op. cit., p.129.
115 We are referring to Berlinguer's interview in *Corriere della Sera* (June 15, 1976), also in P. Lange-M. Vannicelli, *The Communist Parties...*, op. cit., p.301.
116 See E. Berlinguer, *Austerità, Occasione per Trasformare l'Italia* (Roma: Riuniti, 1977).
117 Ibid., pp. 13, 19, passim.
118 L. Paggi, M. D'Angelillo, *I Comunisti Italiani...*, op. cit., p.21, passim.
119 PCI, *La Politica e l'Organizzazione dei Comunisti Italiani; Le Tesi e lo Statuto Approvati dal XV Congresso del PCI* (Roma: Riuniti, 1979), p.83, and also p.119.
120 See especially, E. Berlinguer, 'Una sola via per uscire dalla crisi: cambiare il meccanismo di sviluppo' (Dec. 1973), in *La Questione...*, op. cit., v.II, p.672, passim.
121 S. Tarrow, 'Historic compromise or bourgeois majority?; Eurocommunism in Italy 1976-9', in H. Machin (ed.), *National Communism in Western Europe; A Third Way for Socialism?* (London and New York: Methuen, 1983), p.148.
122 See on this point the very interesting extracts from the diaries of A. Natta, first published in 1994, which describe the discussion which took place in the party's Central Committee in January 1979, in A. Tortorella (ed.), *Berlinguer...*, op. cit., pp. 53-63.
123 B. Craxi, quoted by N. Bobbio, 'Compromesso a alternanza nel sistema politico Italiano', in *Quale Riforma dello Stato?* (Roma: Mondo Operaio-Ed. Avanti!, 1978), p.34. Bobbio gave a positive assessment of Craxian position. Craxi became the first Socialist Prime Minister of Italy, and still holds the record for the longest lasting cabinet (1,060 days, August 1983-June 1986).
124 E. Berlinguer, 'Governo diverso e alternativa democratica' (from a press conference in Salerno, 28-11-1980 after the Irpinia earthquake, and from an interview in *L'Unità*, 7-12-1980), in E. Berlinguer, *Attualità e Futuro* (Roma: L'Unità, 1989), p.45.
125 Berlinguer, for instance, supported the struggle of the FIAT workers and vigorously defended the *scala mobile*. As Ingrao put it: 'Is it true that Berlinguer, during the 1970s, was looking for a compromising ground also with a section of the big entrepreneurs and, in the 1980s, on the contrary, arrived at the perspective of a support in the case of the Turinese workers when they had occupied the FIAT? You can discuss whether these things were good or bad. But to maintain that there is a continuity between the two strategies, seems to me to be a paradox', in *Le Cose...*, op. cit., p.191. From this point of view one can read the Berlinguerian speech of 24 August 1979, just after the kidnapping and killing of Aldo Moro which initiated the collapse of the governments of National Unity (1976-1979), in a sense that he had started to propose not only a new model of development based mainly on the purification and rationalisation of capitalism, but something more: 'Our discourse did propose and does propose to the Italian society and to its various components a new economic policy [...], a new intervention of the working class not only on the distibution of income [...] but also on the form and the qualities of consumer goods, therefore, on the process of accumulation *per se*', E. Berlinguer, 'Il compromesso nella fase attuale', in *Attualità...*, op. cit., p.38.

PART II
POLITY CRISIS, THE EUROPEAN IMPERATIVE AND THE TRANSFORMATION OF ITALIAN COMMUNISM 1980-1992

Qualche tempo fa Roberto Benigni ad Enzo Biagi – che gli chiedeva perchè avesse voluto bene a Berlinguer, lui che di regola prende in giro i politici — ha risposto: 'Berlinguer non era un politico, era un poeta'. Certo questo paradosso illumina solo una parte della verità; ma una parte importante.

Massimo D'Alema, 'Il comunismo di Enrico Berlinguer', in E. Berlinguer, *Attualità e Futuro* (Roma: L'Unità, 1989), p.8.

3　The Crisis of Keynesianism and its Impact on PCI Strategy, 1980-1987

The setting of the problem

The two main arguments advanced in this section of the study, concern the evolution of the PCI's national (democratic alternative) and international (Eurocommunism/New Internationalism) strategies in the 1980s. In particular, I shall examine the evolution of Eurocommunism and the reasons which gave rise to the new culture of the *Euroleft*.[1]

I proceed to present the transition from the strategy of *democratic alternative*, to that of *nuovo corso* put forward by the PCI's new ruling group and Occhetto. The latter line heralded the end of the PCI and precipitated the process of the *constituent phase* which aimed at the reconstruction of the Italian Left and the dissolution of the PCI in it.

The aim of the presentation is to distinguish, but not isolate, the effects the following historical processes had upon the strategic performance and identity of the PCI: I am referring to the crisis and, finally, the collapse of the Stalinist regimes in the Central and Eastern Europe, as well as to the crisis of the Keynesian interventionist State in the West, triggered by the process of the internationalisation of capital along neo-liberal lines. This latter process, it should be added, already questioned the identity of the PCI in the early 1980s, thus preceding the repercussions that Gorbachev's experiment excercised upon the party during the second half of the decade.

Simplifying in advance the thesis I shall defend here, I would say that the crucial reasons for the PCI's transformation into the PDS lie in the above interrelated processes. Therefore, its transformation seemed to be inevitable.

From Eurocommunism to the Euroleft

The international balance of forces

The 1980s began with extreme tensions in Poland. The mass character that Lech Walesa's independent trade union *Solidarność* enjoyed forced the pro-Soviet general Jaruzelski to proclaim a state of emergency in Poland, during the night of 12/13 December 1981. Two days later, Berlinguer, interviewed by RAI 1, declared 'the propulsive force that began with the October revolution has come to an end' and reaffirmed that the PCI's *terza via* aimed at going beyond both the traditional pro-capitalist Social Democratic road and the Eastern European models.[2] For the time being, the famous *strappo* (break) of the PCI from the Soviet motherland of Socialism still remained within a Communist horizon.

Meanwhile, the Soviet Union began a more dynamic promotion of its new foreign policy. It invaded Afghanistan in December 1979 — an event which was strongly condemned by the PCI with the sole exception of the pro-Soviet faction of Armando Cossutta — and deployed in Europe a new generation of missiles, the SS 20. The Americans responded with the creation of Pershing and Cruise missiles. In the light of this, the PCI's international policy could hardly go beyond a dry 'neither SS 20 nor Pershing and Cruise' while appealing for disarmament.[3] 'Instead of competing in the arms race', Berlinguer argued in his Report at the party's XVI Congress (Milan, March 1983), 'we should start competing for disarmament'.[4] And again: 'The Communists declare the gradual overcoming of Europe's division in two opposing military blocs, on the basis of precise warranties of security.'[5] Eurocommunism, in the last instance, was the logic of blocks reversed: both would have to exist for the PCI to develop its 'third way out' policy.[6]

International tensions continued and reached a very critical point when, on September 1, 1983, a Soviet pursuit plane attacked a Korean Boeing 747 which had violated the USSR's air space. This time, the USA responded in a different manner. On 25 October of the same year, some thousands of the USA marines landed on Grenada, where governmental power was controlled by a pro-Cuba movement. This extremely tough and dangerous competition for international security between the two super-powers, ended with the defeat of the USSR. The crucial point was the militarisation of space.

The USA President Ronald Reagan announced the new project of a *spatial shield* which could protect the United States from any sort of international ballistic missiles. It was the beginning of the *star wars scenario* and on this terrain the USSR was utterly defeated. Indeed, having serious domestic economic problems, the USSR could not drive the policy of military competition any further. Western capitalist economies and new free market policies have proved much more durable than the quasi state-centred economies of the East. After the defeat, the new reformist leader of the USSR, Mikhael Gorbachev, having no alternatives began to shift Soviet foreign policy from the military terrain to the political one.[7]

The political strategy followed by Gorbachev both at national and international level was multi-dimensional and seemed to be a justification, rather than a frustration, of the PCI's former critical stances vis-à-vis the Soviet Union. Gorbachev claimed that Europe should become the Common House of its own people and began strengthening political ties with the PCI, Beijing and even Social Democracy. On the domestic front, he started a courageous programme of political and economic reforms. By using first the political conception of *glasnost* (transparency) and later that of *perestroijka* (re-structuration), Gorbachev attempted to advance institutional democratisation and economic modernisation. Once his power was established — a difficult course if one takes into account not only the immobility of the *ancièn regime* but even more imponderable factors, such as the nuclear accident at Chernobyl on 28 April 1986 — Gorbachev rehabilitated the historical figures of the October revolution who had been condemned to death during the great Stalinist purges in the 1930s (Bukharin, Zinoviev, Kamenev et al.). In addition, the reformist Soviet leader revised the hitherto prevailing conception of Communist orthodoxy about the leading role of the CPSU, and developed Togliatti's conception of *polycentrism* by virtue of a 'dialectical unity of diversity'.[8] The CPSU no longer claimed the leading role among the other sister parties and instead wanted to share with them the principle of being 'equal among equals'. This idea, deeply rooted in the PCI of Togliatti and Berlinguer, was praised by Gorbachev himself on more than one occasion.[9]

In the light of all these evolutions, the strategy of Eurocommunism automatically ceased to be a *terza via*, since it had no substantial divergences from the new policy employed by Gorbachev. As a matter of fact, after the Natta-Gorbachev meeting in March 1988, Italian newspapers, understandably enough, alleged that the PCI 're-patches up the *strappo*' and that 'Gorbachev conquers the PCI'.[10] This common sense view no longer made the PCI's Eurocommunism a distinct reference point and the roads seemed rather to be two: Gorbachev's reformism or capitalism. But was that the case? In addition, did Eurocommunism overcome itself due only to the bi-polar developments?

At this stage, I would like to advance two points. My first claim is that the very strategy of Eurocommunism implied a much broader notion than that of 'phasing out' of the blocs on the grounds of transcending the capitalist mode of production. Even though Berlinguer had *never* rejected that conception, as we shall see, he left the reformist horizon open enough, thus leaving room for the next ruling party generation to capitalise on it. In the last analysis, Berlinguer himself was an expression of the party's post-war duplicity and was constrained by it. My second claim is that what extensively influenced Eurocommunism's metamorphosis *well before* the mortal crisis of the Eastern bloc became apparent, were the processes of internationalisation and European integration along neo-liberal lines. Both interwoven advances, which aimed at the restructuring of the whole socio-economic and political system, implied that nation-state as well as political parties were no longer able to organise cultural, political and economic hegemony at the national level. Therefore, the PCI had to re-adjust itself vis-à-vis this new reality in order to capitalise politically on the crisis of Italy's ruling power bloc.

Eurocommunism, New Internationalism, the Euroleft

To start with, Eurocommunism was not a mere Eurocentric strategy. Europe was simply the privileged terrain for action and it was so for obvious geo-political reasons. A number of issues such as the state of détente and world security, the potentialities Europe opened for a strong united labour movement, questions of the Southern peripheries of the world as well as the increasing environmental destruction, new social movements, were all included as part and parcel of Eurocommunism. As Berlinguer put it:

> We intend to contribute in bringing the labour movement of western Europe to a point where it would be able to become the new ruling force of Europe [...]. We propose this, because Europe [...] can promote and implement the broadest and most fruitful international cooperation [...]; for peace, for progress and for the advancement of western working class and for the peoples of the Third World. This is our view of Eurocommunism, this is the gist of what we intend by the 'third road'.[11]

Yet, according to Berlinguer, *Eurocommunism* and *New Internationalism* were seen as identical concepts. Both notions could guarantee cooperation and autonomy for all the political and social forces sharing the general strategic principles and concepts:

> Universal models are no longer possible, cathedrals of ideological orthodoxy or exclusive centres of political leadership. The necessary process which points to *rapprochement* and collaboration, should take place by virtue of recognising the respect for autonomy and independence in every state, party and movement [...]. Precondition of the *New Internationalism* is, above all, the achievement of rules of equality [*our italics*].[12]

And again:

> A new phase for the struggle towards socialism has opened worldwide: a phase in which the question of socialist transformation [...] can and must be strictly linked with the mass movement of liberalisation, social justice, human and civil progress as well as all the poor and oppressed masses in the underdeveloped areas [...]. This is what we want to say when we are talking about a new internationalism. The research of Italian communists around the themes of 'terza via' and Eurocommunism is located in this perspective.[13]

The concepts, however, could be used in different ways. Instead of having Eurocommunism's ambivalent practical and theoretical utility which contained a revolutionary notion in itself as the second passage shows, the concept of *New Internationalism* could address a friendly discourse to European Social Democracy and argue for a new political project which goes beyond the Left's historical division (the question of the Second and Third Internationals). In addition, this interpretation had the advantage of being politically operational and useful inasmuch as the PCI had lacked the support of strong Communist Parties in Europe since the early 1980s. Slowly but constantly, and under the inner-party pressures of Napolitano's reformist faction, the German SPD, the French Socialists of Mitterrand and the British Labour Party were becoming privileged interlocutors.[14] This move was made on the grounds of transcending the traditional division between Socialism and Communism in the labour movement and the times were ripe for that. Napolitano left us in no doubt: 'The objective location of the PCI's strategy has not only overcome national frontiers, but it has also gone beyond an old postulate: that of considering Social Democracy as the major opponent.'[15]

Certainly, this position did not imply any notion of subsumption of one ally to another: as we have seen, the PCI of Berlinguer argued that there are no leader-states or leader-parties any more and each political or social force should enjoy its own political, ideological and organisational autonomy. Nevertheless, 'autonomy does not mean isolation' and Berlinguer himself went on to argue: 'It is no longer adequate to speak strictly of an International Communist movement; not because we underestimate the role of Communist Parties and Socialist states, but because we maintain that *Communist Parties should become part of a broader and more varied alignment that moves towards the transformation and unification of the world*' [*our italics*].[16]

The fact that this statement was made during the governments of *national solidarity* (the peak years of the 'historic compromise' experiment) does not lessen its significance. In essence, independently from the political situation, Berlinguer never clarified the relationship between his Eurocommunist party and European Social Democracy and was rather contradictory on the issue. Therefore, as we shall try to show in more detail below, a distinction between the Berlinguer of *compromesso* (more rightist) and that of *alternativa* (more leftist), although justifiable up to a certain point, is completely misleading if it assumes a strict sense.[17] Let us give two characteristic examples.

In an interview with Eugenio Scalfari in *La Repubblica* (28-7-1981) when the *compromesso* strategy had already been abandoned, Berlinguer argued that the only substantial difference between the PCI's Eurocommunism and mainstream European Social Democracy (SPD, Labour Party), was the emphasis which was given by the PCI to the new social movements (ecology, youth, women, marginal people etc.). Social Democracy, Berlinguer maintained, had lagged in recognising these new realities.[18] Nonetheless, in another interview in the party's daily *L'Unità* (21-2-1982), Berlinguer was quite clear where the PCI's 'peculiarity' lay: 'Vis-à-vis Social Democracy, our peculiarity above all lay in the fact that we have a vision fixed towards socialism, that is, the transcendence of capitalism...'[19]

Other issues that have left opportunities for the reform of Eurocommunism were the questions of peace, and the recognition by the PCI that democracy has a *universal value*[20] and that it is not only *a means* but an *end in itself*: 'We are proving that the PCI considers democracy neither as a favourable and indispensible terrain for the development of class struggle, nor as a method and *means* of our political action, but rather as an *end in itself* as directed by its own transforming strategy...' (emphasis by E.B.)[21].

This statement, made by Berlinguer in September 1983, came to reinforce Togliatti's conception in foreign affairs according to which the *class* character of democracy should be considered as a sub-ensemble of its *universal* dimension, inasmuch as the problems of guaranteeing peace, security and cooperation in the atomic era assume a dominant position. This ideology played a crucial role to the formation of the new ruling group and had a specific influence over the next party secretaryship. For instance, during the second half of the 1980s, the new party secretary Alessandro Natta balanced the party strategy over the question of Euromissiles and the Gulf crisis — after the government had decided to send some warships to the Persian Gulf — in line with that reformist aspect of the party's tradition:

> In the atomic era, peace and coexistence are a supreme requirement and mankind's fate and future are linked to them [...]. With Togliatti, we were among the first to realise and say that the nature of war has profoundly changed, that no ideology, progress or prospects for liberalisation can be achieved without safeguarding the conditions for peace. But it is not just a problem of getting together. The very facts of an increasingly interdependent world, a world which is a single whole, points to a new conception of international relations and the need for deeper and wider cooperation.[22]

I would argue, therefore, that the conception of the *Euroleft* which was adopted by the PCI at its 17th Congress (February 1986), was already embodied *in nuce* into the notion of *Eurocommunism*. What Giuseppe Vacca, in his penetrating analysis of the 15th Congress of PCI, had called *insertion of Eurocommunism in the search for a New Internationalism*,[23] had now become a *dominant* issue: Eurocommunism had wholeheartedly acquired the *form* of 'new internationalism' with the latter needing only a revisionist ruling group to detach it from the class and Marxist contents of Eurocommunism.

In the light of all this, Gorbachev's reformist policy in the second half of the 1980s should not be seen as an *original* contribution to the Communist and Social Democratic movement in Europe, even if the international weight of the USSR and the overall prestige of its leader gave added importance to Gorbachev's strategy. The Euroleft ideology, which was first clearly formulated in the book of the leading German Social Democrat Peter Glotz in 1985, *Manifesto for a New European Left* (the result of a long discussion in the SPD for the revision of its Bad Godesberg programme of 1959), had very little to do with Gorbachev and the crisis of 'really-existing socialism' in the 1980s. The themes of the book were the crisis of the Keynesian nation-state and welfarism, the recognition of the universal value of democracy — Glotz calls it 'societal democracy' — the end of the old Social Democratic reformism and the responses, if any, which a united European Left could marshal vis-à-vis neo-liberalism, the technological revolution, as well as the two/thirds society the new development stage promotes. This sort of problematic, was particularly familiar to neo-Marxist theorists in the 1970s,[24] and had strongly affected some prominent PCI intellectuals and politicians in the early 1980s.[25] However, they were either not influential in political terms and/or the solutions proposed had a leftist rather than a neo-revisionist orientation.[26] On the contrary, as far as the new rising ruling group was concerned, its attempt to interpret and understand the crisis of the nation-state began to fortify the Social Democratic/neo-Socialist, and not the radical Marxist elements of the Eurocommunist policy.[27] As regards the PCI as a whole, the debate took on a clear, open form only after the death of Berlinguer and the appearance of Glotz's book. So in effect, from 1985 onwards, the PCI gradually began the reform of Eurocommunism by first drawing advantages from Eurocommunism itself.[28] On this basis, the 17th Congress was able to establish the conception of *New Internationalism* as follows:

> The party's New Internationalism expresses [...] the necessity of stabilising new relationships between Communist, Socialist, Social Democrat and Labour parties; [between] national liberation movements and progressists; lay democratic forces of Christian and/or Catholic inspirations; trade unions, pacifist and environmental movements. With that vision employed in full autonomy and without establishing any privileged relationship with someone, the PCI will intensify its initiative at the international level [...]. The PCI is an integral part of the European Left.[29]

And again: 'The PCI is and always wants to be, in the best of ways, a decisive component of the European Left. The PCI draws its own unitary inspiration from socialist ideals aiming, above all, at the Left's unification and its reforming will.'[30]

The term 'Eurocommunism' had disappeared from the document of the XVII Congress. 'Natta', wrote Antonio Rubbi, 'could no longer go to Moscow as a Eurocommunist [...], but as someone who represents either the Euroleft and/or another political alignment'.[31] We can turn now to the examination of our second claim.

The crisis of the State-Civil Society Nexus and the analyses of PCI

The XVI Congress of the party held in Milan in March 1983 — the last Congress under the leadership of Berlinguer — had widely discussed the crisis of the welfare state as a process triggered by the internationalisation of national economies alongside the neo-liberal policies of Ronald Reagan in America and Margaret Thatcher in Britain. Accordingly, it diagnosed the crisis of European Social Democracy whose main policy focus was based on the efficiency of Keynesianism at the national level: the famous *corporatist* model as centred on a national social contract between government, trade unions and entrepreneurs. In addition, the PCI was conscious of the difficulties and even of the the failure of Mitterrand's Keynesian experiment in France (1981-83)[32] and recognised that political parties, nation-states and societies in the West are in a deep crisis: 'There is a crisis of parties in the West as they are involved in the general complex crisis of state and society. This phenomenon has also manifested itself in Italy.'[33]

Nevertheless, the diagnosis did not lead to any re-evaluation/revision of the PCI's physiognomy as a *mass party* and a *collective intellectual*. Instead, the PCI insisted on the general role of political parties as organisers of democracy and mass participation in it, alongside the democratic centrality of the 1948 Republican Constitution: 'We need to act in order to reaffirm the democratic character and function that political parties should have within our democratic system ratified by the Constitution.'[34]

In this context, the PCI of the late Berlinguer gave the general impression of a *left-wing turn* vis-à-vis the neo-liberal economics introduced in the USA, Britain and the rest of Europe, rather than an adaptability to them. In point of fact, the PCI believed that the crisis of European Social Democracy would be solved by way of acquiring a less modest political image and thus shifting its policies to the left, alongside the *terza via* of Eurocommunism. In the words of Berlinguer in his Report to the XVI Congress: 'In essence, Europe is discussing and searching for something new; in particular, Europe is shifting towards what we have called the Third Road.'[35]

Having said this, our thesis is that *the PCI as a whole* began to revise its Eurocommunist positions only after the death of Berlinguer. Such positions, in turn, as promoted by the new generation of party cadres, particularly reinforced their validity after Gorbachev's coming to power in the USSR. A new way of thinking started to prevail in the PCI: more pragmatic and technocratic, less utopian and populist; the image should be moderate, decisive and competent; politics must be based on a clearly defined and feasible programme: that is, the principles which had characterised the post-war reformist wing of the party.

The PCI began to take into account the new politico-economic developments in the European Community under Jacques Delors' leadership and proposals. The French Socialist became Commission President in January 1985 and he is generally credited with the Community's metamorphosis. Apart from the enlargement regarding the Southern European countries (Spain and Portugal) which, broadly speaking, coincided with his years of influence,[36] Delors promoted a single market economic programme on a monetarist basis, along with a strengthening of Europe's political cohesion and decision-making in terms of a common foreign and defence policy. A number of intergovernmental European initiatives culminated in the Single European Act (1986) which, in turn, adumbrated the Maastricht Treaty and the deadline of 1992. The PCI tried to keep pace with the changing European reality:

> The democratic unity of Europe, a unity which considers as actors the forces of the Left, is a necessity stemming from objective needs: the increasing internationalisation of the economy and the difficulties any individual country has to cope with, if coordinated efforts vis-à-vis the challenges due to technological innovation are lacking.[37]

Despite the fact that PCI's 17th Congress outlined an economic programme which was mainly Keynesian insisting on a strong state intervention — a state which, of course, should be totally reformed — [38] the above *technologically determined* position goes *pari passu* with Glotz's Euroleft conception: nation-states lost their power, that is, their own bureaucracies are no longer capable of operating viable solutions vis-à-vis multinational trusts, international financial institutions, new information systems and transnational markets.[39] These processes of internationalisation and technological innovation are now guided by the Right which, meanwhile, has been renewed, whereas the Left runs the risk of becoming a *nationalist* force by virtue of still insisting on the strong interventionist role of the state.[40] In the words of Glotz: 'It is the Left that finds itself in a dangerous identity crisis. Its own strongholds become now imperceptibly eroded by technological progress.'[41]

In essence, neo-liberal economics contested the welfare state itself — what Italians call *stato assistenziale*. With regard to the PCI's strategic performance, it came to have some important consequences.

In the Euroleft's conception, that is, according to the efforts of the leading European Social Democratic parties to renew themselves, the internationalisation of capital and the crisis of the nation-state must be taken as *given* and *irreversible* facts. In this context, tasks of the European Left include a new and just European order, the developing of a *concrete* common programme for employment and progress, fighting against the two/thirds society of neo-liberalism, putting forward the environmental question and women's emancipation, in other words, the entire discourse of the Enlightenment. Last but not least, fighting for a *societal* and *economic democracy*,[42] with the latter term becoming one of the main focuses of attention in the PCI's internal debates thereafter. Thus, the Euroleft's conception integrated the strong ideological and rational background of modernity, now being employed at the European level, and aimed at the construction of a new transnational social contract alongside the universal values of justice, equality, liberty and fraternity. Under those circumstances, the PCI saw the German SPD as an ideal model and as the really strong Social Democratic party which could legitimate its entry into the Euroleft, that is, in concrete terms, the Socialist International.[43]

These issues, which had been entirely adopted by the PCI new ruling group as it was prepared by Natta himself,[44] undermined the anti-capitalist aspect of Eurocommunism. As we have seen, Eurocommunism argued that democratic extension of the state and political democracy go *pari passu* with the gradual transformation of the *capitalist* relations of production at a national, European and/or world level. The Euroleft, nevertheless, operates only *pro*-capitalist alternatives *ab imo pectore*, that is, within the very boundaries of capitalist development and without challenging the power relations between capital and labour. Therefore, my thesis is that what distances Eurocommunism from the Euroleft is the inherent Communist radicalism of the former, its persistence that democracy and civil liberties go hand in glove with the overcoming of the capitalist mode of production. I also suggest that, in terms of international policy criteria, this was the point of the *total rupture with the past* the new PCI ruling group carried out with respect to Berlinguer's and Togliatti's tradition. That was the end of the PCI's famous *duplicity*.

After the death of Berlinguer in June 1984, the PCI found itself divided on these issues. The new party secretary, Natta, contributed to the promotion of the new ruling party generation of *quarantenni*, but he did so on a pure technical/organisational basis without advancing any sound theoretical analysis and political assessment of national and international developments. Ingrao's judgement speaks for itself:

> There is no doubt that the real decline of the PCI started with Natta's secretaryship. Italian capitalism has initiated its restructuring process since 1980 and achieved spectacular gains compared with the conquests of the labour movement. The peculiar crisis of public industries had started. There was an entire social process which changed the relationship of forces at the expense of the trade union and the party. In my view, the criticism I still feel the need to address to Natta, is that, under his secretaryship, all these phenomena had not been studied, comprehended, analysed. There was a total lack of social analysis.[45]

The lack of analysis and political initiative had created a weak party centre with Natta swinging between the party's left and right wings. Thus, at the same time as he pushed on the generational renewal of the PCI and promoted the revisionist ideas of the new ruling group around Occhetto, he could also have formulated clear-cut pro-Keynesian theses.[46]

Nevertheless, leading economists and politicians of the PCI clearly emphasised the novelties brought about by the new phase of development and did not hesitate to openly attack the defects of the existing Italian welfarism. Alfredo Reichlin, a former supporter of Ingrao's faction, together with the ruling group, recognised the validity of Glotz's analyses and went on to claim that, 'the public sphere all over the world, either in the West and elsewhere, has become synonymous with inefficiency, privileges, wastage etc [...]. The fact that these themes come from the Right, must not prevent us from recognising their objective validity'.[47] Reichlin, who was President of *Cespe*, adopted the Euroleft platform and presented similar positions in the debates taking place during the transformation of the party.[48]

More concretely, according to the new ruling group, the Keynesian state in Italy could not play its interventionist role any longer. Above all, the state's functioning in the economy was seriously questioned especially after the breakdown of the Bretton Woods system (1971) and the first oil-shock (1973). The more the internationalisation of capital deepened, the more the role of the nation-state in the economy diminished. Thus, Occhetto, three days before the party's famous Central Committe gathering on 27 November 1987, which came to characterise the real turning-point in the party's transformation, argued in *Rinascita* that 'the true question today is that of a European Left capable of guiding the processes of transformation in our modern society, beyond the pillars of Hercules of the old Keynesian compromise'.[49]

Moreover, the new modernisation process was reversing the relationship between the private and the public sphere, leading to a more globalised world and, in addition, revolutionised social and labour relations. Reichlin also maintained that the partial transition to post-fordism, that is, flexible specialisation, increasing number of part-timers, the proposed de-bureaucratising models of enterprises as well as the moulding of productive output according to the market demand, should all be taken into account by the PCI and, finally, lead to a serious revision of its Eurocommunist strategy.[50] These phenomena which, in the last analysis, affect the mass and interventionist role of the trade unions (the question of *fragmentation/segmentation of the labour force*) as well as female labour-power, especially as far as part-time jobs are concerned, were seen by the PCI cadres in the early 1980s but were not properly scrutinised.[51] Yet, vis-à-vis Gorbachev's reformist revolution, which was not moving towards a *socialist* democracy but towards capitalism, Eurocommunism proved to be unrealistic and lacked initiative.[52]

Concluding remarks

We can now attempt to draw a few conclusions. What has been said so far, enables us to begin with the most important point: the transition from Eurocommunism to the Euroleft seemed to be for the PCI an *actus essendi*, an act of being. So it was, as we shall see, the transition from Berlinguer's *alternativa democratica* — a strategy which contained a strong revolutionary potential — to Ochetto's *new course* that led to the PCI's dissolution alongside the claim for a *constituent phase*, implying a re-constitution of the Italian Republic *via* the re-constitution of the Italian Left. More specifically, the adoption of the renewed Euro-Social Democrat project by the PCI after the death of Berlinguer had been underpinned by the following historical and political factors:

1 Gorbachev's reformism which overshadowed Eurocommunism and gave the impression that the PCI's inventive political capacity no longer existed. This reformist process had *de facto* deprived Eurocommunism of its dynamism, that of being the 'transcendental' anti-capitalist logic of the two opposing blocs. In particular, after the collapse of 'really-existing socialism', no-one could argue for a *terza via* any longer. Even the *Ostpolitik* of Willy Brandt no longer made sense. In the light of these developments, the adoption of the Euro-Social Democrat identity constituted the *chief point of discontinuity* with Eurocommunism's radicalism and mass conception of democracy.
2 Eurocommunism itself, which comprised a classless and pacifist conception of international relations as well as an inclination towards favouring the Western bloc, backed revisionist/reformist conceptions in the party. As we have seen, here lies the *major point of continuity* between Eurocommunism and the Euroleft.
3 Last but not least, the new phase of development, which opened in the late 1970s and early 1980s under the aegis of the internationalisation and further European integration, weakened the nation-state and its capacity to promote growth. Considering this process as irreversible, the PCI had to readjust its international as well as its domestic strategy by way of enlarging its potential allies and making its political image more competent and pragmatic. To this end, it was necessary to put forward a concrete and realistic programme which took into account the new international

constraints. As regards international allies, these were mainly the German SPD, the British Labour Party and the French Socialists. We are not far from the PCI's request to become a member of the Socialist International in the late 1980s, a claim which was in concert with Gorbachev's opening to the SPD.[53]

From the 'Democratic Alternative' to the 'New Course'

The political relationship of forces

The First Republic and the post-fascist mass democracy in Italy, reinforced as they were by a strictly proportional electoral system, had mainly experienced three political forms of government. The governments of *National Solidarity* with the full participation of the PCI (1945-47) or only with its political and parliamentary backing ('historic compromise', 1976-79); various types of coalition centred around the DC's indisputable control of the executive, such as those formed by the inception of the Cold War under De Gasperi's Premiership; the Centre-Left (DC with PSI) management of political power that was first practised in full at the end of 1963. The latter political form has governed Italy, with some interruptions, from 1964 to 1993-94 and gave the death blow to the First Republic. None of these coalitions, it should be noted, ever succeeded in removing the DC from the centre of the political system. (See **Table 4** p. 72.)

In the 1980s, the Centre-Left assumed the name of *pentapartito* (five-party coalition). It comprised Craxi's PSI, the DC under the influential figures of Andreotti, De Mita and Forlani, the Socialdemocrats (PSDI) of Pietro Longo, Franco Nicolazzi and Antonio Cariglia, the Liberals (PLI) of Alfredo Biondi and Renato Altissimo and the Republicans headed by the historian Giovanni Spadolini. In effect, Spadolini was the first non-Christian Democrat Prime Minister since Parri, who guided the first *pentapartito* government in July 1981.[54] If compared with past experience, this ruling bloc in the 1980s contained some specific features. Basically, I am referring to the PSI's upgraded function within the coalition; to the influential figure of its leader, Craxi, as well as to the serious party and intra-party rivalries that cut across the ruling bloc itself.[55]

Craxi's chief aims, in particular, were to take the political initiative away from the PCI and lead the opposition against specific factions of the DC by taking advantages of the managerial and bargaining positions the PSI enjoyed within the state apparatuses and the world of business.[56] The basis of this strategy, fully employed in the 1980s, was laid down at the PSI's 42nd Congress in April 1981 in Palermo. The key words were now 'governability' and 'decisionism' in the sense that — as Occhetto put it commenting on Claudio Martelli's speech at the socialist Congress — 'we [the PSI] need to make the Left stronger but staying with the DC' and 'inasmuch as the DC does not accept the PCI in office, we [the PCI] should reinforce the PSI'.[57]

Pursuing these strategic objects, leading the party according to the *Führerprinzip* — as Ricardo Lombardi, the old leftist figure of PSI, once put it — and employing a populist rhetoric, Craxi believed that his party would overcome the PCI's political and electoral strength: that was the famous conception of *sorpasso* (overtaking).

As regards the DC, and worth mentioning here are, on the one hand, the declared reformism of Ciriaco De Mita that dates back to the DC's XV Congress (Rome, May 1982), where he became party secretary; and, on the other, the importance of the progressively developed Andreotti-Forlani alliance which, after the political defeat of De Mita during the second half of the 1980s, ended up with the formation of the so-called Craxi-Andreotti-Forlani (CAF) governmental axis.

According to De Mita,[58] the government had to accomplish two imperatives: firstly, it needed to promote institutional modernisation (e.g. reform of bi-cameralism, stable Cabinets, overcoming clientelism etc.); secondly, it had to take some neo-liberal economic measures for the 'relaxation' of bureaucratised economic institutions (e.g. privatisations). In fact, De Mita was the first leading Italian politician who, at least on paper, formulated the idea of a *constituent phase* along with a *centre-left/centre-right* conception of the Italian political game, an idea which was categorically rejected by Berlinguer himself: 'We are clearly arguing against political bi-polarism. On the contrary, we have always been thinking of a collaboration with the other parties on the basis of mutual respect and autonomy in order that each party may make its own specific contribution to the country's recovery.'[59]

Although intentions for the implementation of reformist policies were scarce — De Mita himself was a *maestro* of clientelistic practices in Avellino[60] — the leader of DC represented the thin end of the wedge: *the question of the constitution of the Second Italian Republic was posed.*[61]

Table 4   The Italian Governments from 1945 to 1998

Prime Ministers	Government Coalitions	Duration
1 Parri	DC-PCI-PSI-PLI-DL-Pd'A	21-6-45/24-11-45
2 De Gasperi I	DC-PCI-PSI-PLI-DL-Pd'A	10-12-45/1-7-46
3 De Gasperi II	DC-PCI-PSI-PRI	13-7-46/20-7-47
4 De Gasperi III	DC-PCI-PSI	2-2-47/13-5-47
5 De Gasperi IV	DC-PLI-PSDI-PRI	31-5-47/12-5-48
6 De Gasperi V	DC-PLI-PSDI-PRI	23-5-48/12-1-50
7 De Gasperi VI	DC-PSDI-PRI	27-1-50/16-7-51
8 De Gasperi VII	DC-PRI	26-7-52/29-6-53
9 De Gasperi VIII	DC	16-7-53/28-7-53
10 Pella	DC	17-8-53/5-1-54
11 Fanfani I	DC	18-1-54/30-1-54
12 Scelba	DC-PSDI-PLI	10-2-54/22-6-55
13 Segni I	DC-PSDI-PLI	6-7-55/6-5-57
14 Zoli	DC	19-5-57/19-6-58
15 Fanfani II	DC-PSDI	1-7-58/26-1-59
16 Segni II	DC	15-2-59/24-2-60
17 Tambroni	DC	25-3-60/19-7-60
18 Fanfani III	DC	26-7-60/2-2-62
19 Fanfani IV	DC-PSDI-PRI	21-2-62/16-5-63
20 Leone I	DC	21-6-63/5-11-63
21 Moro I	DC-PSI-PSDI-PRI	4-12-63/26-6-64
22 Moro II	DC-PSI-PSDI-PRI	22-7-64/21-1-66
23 Moro III	DC-PSI-PSDI-PRI	23-2-66/5-6-68
24 Leone II	DC	24-6-68/19-11-68
25 Rumor I	DC-PSU-PRI	12-12-68/5-7-69
26 Rumor II	DC	5-8-69/7-2-70
27 Rumor III	DC-PSI-PSDI-PRI	27-3-70/6-7-70
28 Colombo	DC-PSI-PSDI-PRI	6-8-70/15-1-72
29 Andreotti I	DC	17-2-72/26-2-72
30 Andreotti II	DC-PSDI-PLI	26-6-72/12-6-73
31 Rumor IV	DC-PSI-PSDI-PRI	7-7-73/2-3-74
32 Rumor V	DC-PSI-PSDI	14-3-74/3-10-74
33 Moro IV	DC-PRI	23-1-74/7-1-76
34 Moro V	DC	12-2-76/30-4-76
35 Andreotti III	DC	29-7-76/16-1-78
36 Andreotti IV	DC	11-3-78/31-1-79
37 Andreotti V	DC-PRI-PSDI	20-3-79/31-3-79
38 Cossiga I	DC-PSDI-PLI	4-8-79/19-3-80
39 Cossiga II	DC-PSI-PRI	4-4-80/27-9-80
40 Forlani	DC-PSI-PSDI-PRI	18-10-80/26-5-81
41 Spadolini I	DC-PSI-PSDI-PRI-PLI	28-6-81/7-8-82
42 Spadolini II	DC-PSI-PSDI-PRI-PLI	23-8-82/13-11-82
43 Fanfani V	DC-PSI-PSDI-PLI	1-12-82/29-4-83
44 Craxi I	DC-PSI-PSDI-PRI-PLI	4-8-83/27-6-86
45 Craxi II	DC-PSI-PSDI-PRI-PLI	1-8-86/3-3-87
46 Fanfani VI	DC	17-4-87/28-4-87
47 Goria	DC-PSI-PSDI-PRI-PLI	28-7-87/11-3-88
48 De Mita	DC-PSI-PSDI-PRI-PLI	13-4-88/19-5-89
49 Andreotti VI	DC-PSI-PSDI-PRI-PLI	23-7-89/29-3-91
50 Andreotti VII	DC-PSI-PSDI-PLI	13-4-91/24-4-92
51 Amato	DC-PSI-PSDI-PLI	29-6-92/28-4-93
52 Ciampi	DC-PSI-PSDI-PLI	28-4-93/17-1-94
53 Berlusconi	Forza Italia-Lega Nord-An-CCD-UCD	11-5-94/22-12-94
54 Dini	PDS-PS-Lega Nord	13-1-1995/11-1-96
55 Prodi	PDS-PRC-PPI-Dini	9-5-1996+

DL: *Democrazia del lavoro*; Pd'A: *Partito d'Azione*; AN: *Alleanza Nazionale*; CCD: *Centro Cristiano Democratico*; UDC: *Unione di Centro*; PS: *Patto Segni*; PRC: *Partito Rofondazione Comunista*; PPI: *Partito Popolare Italiano*.

Italian democracy was a *democrazia zoppa* ('lame democracy'):[62] no political alternative in the central government was possible, that is, no different policies could be implemented and judged by the electorate. The principle of PCI's quasi exclusion from power, the *conventio ad excludendum*, was still in force. *The First Italian Republic was an anti-PCI Republic*. Moreover, a whole series of prodigiously anomalous phenomena had been reinforced further: I am referring to the trend for the occupation of the state by the ruling parties which engendered serious phenomena of corruption and institutional distortions, to the hidden structures of the *parastato* and the relationship with the Mafia, the list is endless. The corrupt management of power and the institutional decay were two of the reasons, perhaps the most decisive ones, which caused Italy's chief 'malady' in the 1980s: *the fiscal crisis of the state alongside the question of institutional reform*.[63]

In conclusion, the 'new regime' was not 'new' at all and Occhetto, soon after the formation of Spadolini's Cabinet, rightly argued much in advance that 'as far as the structure and composition of the government are concerned, the continuity with the post-1948 regime remains unchallenged'.[64] It was within this context that Berlinguer raised the *moral question*:

> Political parties today are machines of power and clientelism; these have a mystified and scarce knowledge of social problems, of people, of ideals; their political programmes are very vague and of low quality; without having civil passion and sentiments, political parties today are just zero [...]. [The parties] occupied the state, its institutions and, above all, the government [...]. According to the Communists, the moral question in Italy today is one and the same thing with the occupation of the state by the governmental parties and their own internal factions, it is one and the same thing fighting against spoils as well as against their understanding of politics and management methods. That is why I say the moral question is the crux of the Italian problem.[65]

Strictly speaking, the 'moral question' posed forcefully by Berlinguer was embodied in the strategy of 'democratic alternative' occupying a straightforward relationship to the renewal of the Republic. The complex evolution of this strategy in the 1980s, the intra-party debates and the rise of the new ruling group will be presented along with the two constructive hypotheses which shaped our arguments when examining the metamorphosis of Eurocommunism. More concretely, I will first attempt to show that the strategy of the *alternativa* implied a revolutionary *plus* a reformist notion, the latter being developed by the *quarantenni*. Secondly,

I shall examine the overall impact of European integration on the shaping of a revisionist evolution of the *alternativa*, which effectively culminated in Occhetto's 'new course' and his proposal for the party's dissolution. Then I will pass on to outline a critical aspect of the institutional system, namely, the fiscal crisis of the state alongside the theses of the PCI.

Democratic alternative, programmatic alternative, 'New Course'

Despite the failure of the *compromesso storico* to produce an alternative to the DC's system of management, the PCI, in its 15th Congress held immediately afterwards, still insisted on the political correctness of the strategy.[66] Under the new political conditions, however, this political project proved not to be successful. Thus, as we have already seen, Berlinguer introduced the *alternativa democratica*, taking advantage of a government crisis triggered by the earthquake in Irpinia in November 1980. This strategy, which replaced that of *compromesso* and constituted the 'domestic' aspect of Eurocommunism and New Internationalism, was equally affected by the same sort of duplicity: it included, on the one hand, a revolutionary potential as well as an 'insatiable' expansion of political democracy and civil liberties whereas, on the other, it could be interpreted as a mere exchange of political personnel and rationalisation of public apparatuses without seriously challenging the dominant power bloc, that is, its hegemonic position in politics, economy and society. To be more precise, the *alternativa democratica* was based on the following key features:

a. It was a democratic strategy aimed at the construction of a new ruling bloc, beyond the *pentapartito's* capitalist and corrupt horizon of administering the crisis. Social mobilisation for the gradual transformation of the capitalist mode of production had to be widely used. In continuity with the revolutionary aspects of Gramsci's and Togliatti's legacy, the PCI of Berlinguer had not distanced the political from the economic, political reforms from economic ones. From this standpoint, and *only* from this, the *alternativa democratica* re-formulated the alliance system and priorities of the *compromesso storico* whilst still articulating the ideological structure of Eurocommunist discourse in its 'domestic' strategic framework. Indeed, Berlinguer was fully aware of the ruthless neo-liberal trends and warned of the negative aspects such a process would have upon Italy's social cohesion. He pointed out the increase of individualism, mass unemployment and marginalisation that the implementation of neo-liberal policies could entail, as well as the hazards the technological revolution brings *in se* in proportion to the crisis of mass politics and mass participation in democratic procedures.[67] Accordingly, the welfare state and mass political parties were in profound crisis and neo-liberal economics drives society towards *barbarism*, rather than to a *new civilisation*. Therefore…

> to avoid all these tendencies, reformism and welfarism are no longer enough: what is needed is a profound renewal of the order of the system as well as its leadership. This strategy stems from objective tendencies and this is our policy, our commitment. In addition, Swedish Social Democrats are moving towards this strategy; almost half of the German Social Democracy does the same […]; Mitterrand won with a similar programme.[68]

Here, I do not intend to comment on either the historical validity or the possible voluntarism of Berlinguer's statement, since they do not fit the scope of my arguments. I would like to stress, however, that a fundamental aspect of the 'democratic alternative' strategy was designed to be pursued by means of a long-term opposition battle against the *pentapartito*, always within the spirit of a gradualist anti-capitalist political perspective.[69] This was the result of Berlinguer's faith that, after the crisis of Keynesianism, European Social Democracy, devoid of alternatives, would adopt the PCI's *terza via* of Eurocommunism.[70] Ingrao's faction drew advantages from, and participated in the debate over the transformation of the party, as it agreed with this aspect of the party's policy.

b. The strategy of the *alternativa* ceased to regard the DC as a privileged interlocutor: 'The democratic alternative is an alternative to the DC and its system of power.'[71] This strategy, Berlinguer argued, addresses its message equally to all those who are faithful to the Republican Constitution. With regard to the political and institutional crisis, the *alternativa's* strategic horizon should embrace the notion of the renewal of the rest of the party system, including the DC. So this operation can be considered as an *open political and social procedure towards the remodelling of the blocked political system as a whole*. Here, various social and political forces, such as the new social movements and left-wing social forces (e.g. the PDUP of Lucio Magri), but even enterpreneurs and elderly people, could join.[72] In the final instance, the big advantage the *alternativa* enjoyed is that it contained a democratic government and an institutional solution by virtue of a *concrete realistic political programme*: populist rhetoric and political vagueness *a là* Craxi did not belong to the *alternativa's* baggage. The *alternativa* did not imply an *organisational* alliance with other political forces, but a *political* agreement between them on a *programmatic* basis. The target, we repeat, was the renewal of the Republic. Thus, the democratic alternative becomes transformed into a *programmatic alternative*, into a concrete and pragmatic governmental proposal. However, the boundaries determined by this rather linear democratic dialectic under-represent the *class character* both of the political procedure and of the state. To put it bluntly, the political could be seen separately from the economic, political reforms could be isolated from their capitalist economic structures. In this context, the notion of the *alternativa*, being itself subject to the PCI's historical duplicity, included also a revisionist potential placed *within* the capitalist horizon of progress and evolution. Consequently, it could be used in such a way that any perspective of transcending the *capitalist* relations of production could be rejected. The conception of *riformismo forte* (strong reformism) which was to have been established at the 18th party Congress (Rome, March 1989), was being conceived within that theoretical and political horizon. It was this precise interpretation of the *alternativa* which was to have been fully employed by the PCI's new ruling group. Berlinguer himself left enough space for such a *classless* political use of the term:

> As a need, the democratic alternative — which in the present conditions could also put the DC in opposition — [...] lies in the degeneration of the government system, in the degradation of political power being always the result of DC-based government coalitions. Thereby, we posed the objective of the democratic alternative as an indispensable operation of efficient and radical exchange of political personnel, of its directions, of its behaviour.[73]

I would argue, therefore, as I have in the previous chapters analysing the concept of Eurocomunism and the transition to the Euroleft, that a reformist interpretation of the 'democratic alternative' was possible and could prepare the ground for Occhetto's group to advance the conceptions of *programmatic alternative* and *nuovo corso*. These in turn led to the proposal of the *fase costituente*, during which the PCI should be dissolved, acquiring the characteristics of a neo-revisionist and reformist political force.

In this context, I would like to point out my disagreement with some interpretations of Berlinguer's strategy which distinguish between *compromesso* (a pre-1980 strategy) and *alternativa* (1980-84), attributing a reformist character to the former and a revolutionary to the latter.[74] This chronologically determined conceptualisation corresponds to historical reality only if invested in an 'ideal-typical' theorisation. In *concrete* historical and political terms, Berlinguer never abandoned both hues of the party strategy, either when it refers to the pre-1980 *compromesso* or the post-1980 *alternativa*. He simply gave priority to one or the other. In the final analysis, had Berlinguer's post-1980 *alternativa* achieved a clear-cut break with reformism and Social Democratic conceptions, the formation of the new ruling group of *quarantenni* and the promotion of neo-revisionist ideas during the second half of the 1980s would have been far more difficult and perhaps even impossible. Thus, as we shall see below, Occhetto's majority capitalised greatly on Berlinguer's duplicity by way of picking up its reformist and pro-capitalist discourses regardless of any chronological determination.

From 1984 (the year of Berlinguer's death) to 1986 (the year of the 17th Congress in Florence), the PCI abandoned Eurocommunism and achieved its transition to the Euroleft. However, it was a very 'bizarre' transition: between 1984 and 1987 neither the entire platform of the Euroleft was adopted (e.g. a 'third way out' policy beyond the two blocs was still strongly present in the party documents and speeches), nor were the full consequences of the European integration process on economic policy arrangements drawn. Analyses advanced by both Ingrao's faction and the rising group of *quarantenni* were either badly edited and/or entirely omitted from the endorsed official documents. Ultimately, the whole debate in which a large part of the broad Italian Left had been involved in the period extended well up until 1988 was a debate over the question of *identity*, not over the party's *name* and *symbols*.[75]

At this stage, some fundamental points, developments and even inextricable condradictions concerning the analyses crystalised in the party's document of the XVII Congress, should be mentioned.

Firstly, alongside the Euroleft's conception and SPD's leading role, the party began to realise the demand for further institutionalisation of the new social movements, paying particular attention to gender and environmental issues. Secondly, the questions of institutional and political reforms (e.g. mono-cameralism), were based on the grounds of a 'government alternative, i.e. a programmatic alternative',[76] in the wake of constitutional (strengthening the executive) and even electoral reforms. In this context, the PCI proposed to all political forces a *programmatic convention*, a proposal which constituted a great advantage for Occhetto's majority, since it included *in nuce* the reformist notion of the *constituent phase*. Thirdly, Eurocommunism was abandoned and the passage to the Euroleft endorsed, but principal conceptions of the former, such as the overcoming of the blocs and the neo-Marxist notion of 'uneven development', were maintained. In addition, once concrete analyses of the party's economic policy start, the document becomes disguised as a Keynesian paper. Thus, whilst, on the one hand, corporatism, clientelism, Mafia and *parastato* as well as the blocked character of democracy were assessed as being major obstacles to the advance of the new phase of capitalist development, a thesis which was correct, on the other hand, it rather saw the *pentapartito* as a political bloc which applies, or is prone to apply, fully-fledged neo-liberal measures, a thesis which has proved incorrect.[77] I will focus on this point while examining the manner in which the party conceived the institutional crisis, because it constitutes the core hypothesis along which the PCI realised the full implications of the institutional crisis and, in relation to this, claimed both its own transformation *and* that of the First Republic: *the PCI transforms itself in order to change Italy*. This 'slogan', which accompanied the neo-revisionist political campaign of the *quarrantenni*, can be found, slightly metamorphosed, in the theses of the 17th Congress.[78] Fourthly, the crisis of the PCI as a mass party was admitted, but apart from old recipes, no real solutions to the problem were suggested;[79] the principle of 'democratic centralism', although inactive in practical terms, was enshrined in the party statute. Fifthly, following an inherent difficulty in the conception of the *alternativa*, the PCI did not succeed in specifying who its privileged political ally should be: the DC or the PSI? Finally, the document argued, on the one hand, for the reinforcement of the executive and, on the other, proposed a democratic expansion of parliamentary powers, but it did not specify how this could be done.[80]

This is an appropriate point to examine the evolution of the *alternativa democratica* since the death of Berlinguer. I will also look at the analyses made by each party faction, trying to pinpoint the most important intra-party ideological cleavages and tensions. In this context, we shall meet once again the issue of internationalisation and the crisis of the nation-state. Indeed, the European integration process tended to restructure the entire axis of the state/civil society relationship, thus putting into reconsideration and challenging the most important functions of the polity: the *economic* (intervention in aggregate demand and the main counter-tendency of the falling rate of profit); the *politico-institutional* (parliamentary sovereignty as expressed through mass organised national parties); the *ideological* (organiser of cultural activities of the nation and principal disseminator of the dominant ideology).

In a conference organised by the Centre of Marxist Studies (CMAS) in Athens in April 1983, Ingrao addressed a speech that caused a great sensation among Greek Eurocommunist politicians and intellectuals.[81] Any form of action organised by individual states was at stake, Ingrao said, chiefly because of advances in technological and information systems.[82] The state apparatuses were in a serious crisis and political practice was changing. The Left should capitalise on these processes by promoting a new public power encouraging devolution and self-managerial economic activities. Ingrao had placed this project within the party's conception of *New Internationalism*: 'The new public power we are fighting for must also advance international integration.'[83] Elsewhere he argued in favour of 'de-nuclearised zones' and pointed out that 'new internationalism' meant socialisation of state and military apparatus.[84]

The core of Ingrao's analyses concerned the potentialities the PCI had in capitalising on 'splits' created inside the *pentapartito's* power bloc, 'splits' that were caused by the process of capitalist restructuring. The new contradictions produced were reflected within the ruling political class and accentuated its crisis. Therefore, a libertarian move of the societal was possible inasmuch as it was being freed from the state's encumbrance. It was high time for Communists, the Left and various social forces to undertake serious anti-capitalist initiatives and get rid of the DC-PSI corrupt power axis once and for all.[85] Consequently, the line of the *alternativa* did make sense if it was invested inside a radicalising social bloc which was prone to exploit the contradictions inside the ruling political class of the *pentapartito* and created the necessary preconditions for the *socialisation of politics*: Ingrao has never really abandoned this proposal which had informed his *Masse e Potere (The Masses and Power)*. At this stage the project of institutional and electoral reforms needed to be forwarded. In the words of Ingrao:

> Even when I have argued for the so-called 'parliamentary centrality', I have also always asserted the need for a strong and agile executive; and I maintained that without it even Parliament is weak [...]. First of all, a reform is necessary which abolishes the absurdity of bi-cameralism which does the same legislative work and has exactly the same powers [...]. I do not wish to make electoral reform the object of one party alone [...]. I simply maintain that if you want to confront alternative positions, on the agenda of institutional reforms you should also include the electoral system.[86]

It is clear, therefore, that Ingrao did not reduce the PCI's strategy to a mere social radicalisation, but he also tried to link new forms of social dynamics with political reforms in order to intensify the crisis of the dominant political class and take away its political initiative. Admittedly, the *alternativa* strategy was neither seen in continuity with the line of *compromesso* nor as a mere *alternanza* (alternation) implying an institutional exchange in power between opposing party formations. The 'historic compromise' failed because it was much subjected to 'solidarity policies', thereby very often leaving on one side the declared commitment to the renewal of the other political forces.[87] After all, a change of political personnel in the ruling positions of the state and power will not solve the question of socialist trasformation. As Magri put it:

> In fact, what we have been asked for, is not whether or not we are a reformist force having the commitment to partial modifications of the social axis: the point at issue is that if we are continuing to think that the reforms for which we are fighting, still contain in themselves [...] a radical transformation of the capitalist system.[88]

In one way or another, these views were shared by a number of PCI intellectuals and political cadres whose stances will be considered in detail while dealing with the party's transformation. The point I wish to make here is that the above analyses as well as a number of amendments in the party's Congressional theses stemming mainly from the left factions of Ingrao (e.g. Luciana Castellina, Mario Santostasi) and Cossutta (e.g. Guido Cappelloni), were rejected. Characteristically, the statement of Cossutta that 'Communists are working for the transcendence of capitalism', was categorically repudiated.[89]

However, if extreme anti-capitalism was rejected, so were the analyses of Occhetto and the group of *quarantenni*. They insisted on four principal points: the concrete programmatic character the *alternativa* must assume; the cross-cutting of the political system vis-à-vis the modernisation process underway as well as the centrality of institutional reform; the need for further institutionalisation of the new social movements; the reform of the party. All these points were badly presented and/or omitted in the theses approved by the 17th Congress.

'Recalling the democratic alternative in such an abstract way', Occhetto wrote as early as February 1985 in his attempt to inculcate concrete contents to the strategy, 'is not something which should be done. The strategy of democratic alternative should measure itself with the capacity of "being politics", that is, to "produce politics" which, in turn, implies the indication of a non ideological road'.[90]

The rejection of utopian theses by the rising ruling group already constituted a clear demarcation line. According to the *quarantenni*, any analysis of current political and socio-economic developments must lead to a *pragmatic agenda*, not to abstract radical formulations. More concretely, if capitalist modernisation reshapes social reality and class groupings then it does not refract its effects instrumentally at the political and institutional level, but it rather creates cross-cutting alignments alongside the conservatism-progress cleavage. This reality goes beyond the class conception of politics according to which progress was identified with a quasi (motionless) progressive working class and also a quasi (motionless) reactionary bourgeoisie. The latter includes progressive elements *ad hoc* — as long as they are able to advance development and modernisation — whereas the working class might comprise conservative fractions — as long as they resist the advances provoked by technological innovations.[91] The new social movements constitute the most conspicuous case that was not reducible to class analysis and contradictions. In this context, the conservatism-progress cleft cut across the social, political and party system and pointed to the formation of a *new ruling political class for the country*. To do so, the PCI's political credibility needed to be re-created and re-thought. Allies should be formed inside and outside the existing political and social forces on the basis of a concrete programmatic platform. Thus, Occhetto's majority emphasised the *programmatic* character of the *alternativa* and the concrete functioning it should assume for the re-organisation of the Italian polity. As early as November 1985, interviewed about the Achille Lauro affair, Occhetto pointed out that '*a programmatic government*' should be seen as a '*Copernican revolution which opens a transitional phase between the construction of the alternative and the present situation*' (our emphasis).[92]

The above analyses might have signalled a fundamental political difference with Ingrao, had he himself realised that the so-called 'progressive bourgeoisie' could participate in a communist-led 'historic bloc'.[93] He would never have accepted a position based on an alliance with the 'progressive bourgeoisie' which was the main point of his divergence from the Amendola-Napolitano strategy. Thus, for instance, in the above mentioned essay on the question of *New Internationalism* written in 1985, Ingrao noted:

> The contradiction that arises within the labour process is not slackening; but it is becoming interlinked with new contradictions, produced or revitalised or exacerbated by the type of development dominant today, which involves the expressive side of life and our capacity to give a creative meaning to the activity of groups and individuals. This is the level at which the conflict is taking place. Therefore I do not believe in any strategy based on an alliance between the so-called 'productive sectors'.[94]

Some further claims by Occhetto concerning the crucial link between the *reform of the party* and the *constituent reform of the Republic* did not prevail in the debate. The following statement, for example, received little attention from the centrist majority of the party: 'The party's theses claim that to open a new political phase, the PCI has, first and foremost, to renew itself. These are not pretentious words [...]. Change ourselves already means contributing to changing the country.'[95]

Since then, however, the aforementioned thesis has constituted the most crucial notion of the *quarantenni*. As a matter of fact, it was the main slogan in support of their campaign over the question of party's transformation. The transformation of the political system and the renewal of the PCI were seen as a single transforming process. The key problem was the institutional decay of the state because, after all, the economy as such was doing rather well. Thus, as early as 1986, Occhetto went so far as to say that, 'even the suggestion for a shadow cabinet is, in my view, a question which the party should think about [...]'.[96]

The PCI formed its shadow cabinet three years later. Apart from the difficulties the idea encountered in Italy, which shall be discussed below, what needs to be stressed here is the conspicuous transformation of the radical contents of the *alternativa*: these have now assumed a clear revisionist character as they were bound to within the framework of new constraints imposed by capitalist restructuring.

The fiscal crisis of the state and the theses of the PCI

Whether overtly or not, the most fashionable view shared by a number of economists, political scientists and columnists, is that the exhaustion of the First Italian Republic under way in the 1980s was due to the inability of its polity to shape new policy dimensions functional to capitalist restructuring. The account is informed by a cogent rationale and always comes down to the following proposition: the *pentapartito* and, more in general, the DC system of power showed an extreme profligacy in using resources and public finance; it was more in tune with the Mafia, the *parastato* and the underground economy, than the real developmental needs of the country; its political reproduction was a matter of subsidising its own *clientele*, rather than applying concrete modernising policies in keeping with European requirements; this fact, the account goes on, dovetails with the perennial problem of 'corporatism' and the political inefficacy caused by that gloss of democracy which David Hine labelled 'bargained pluralism' and Arend Lijphart 'consociationalism'. Some writers have gone so far as to see the collapse of the First Republic as a mere reflection of the monstrosity of 'consociationalism', which was no longer able to advance growth along neo-liberal lines.[97] Others located the fiscal crisis in the welfare reforms of the 1970s. In the words of Filippo Giavazzi and Luigi Spaventa:

> The 1970s were a period of big social reforms: extension of years of compulsory schooling, reform of the health-care system, the decision to link pension benefits to earnings, rather than to contributions, etc. The gap that those social bills opened in public finances has never since been closed [...]. Italy now faces the effects of the fiscal imbalance created in the early 1970s. Revenues will have to increase: this, however, is the delayed price to be paid for the social reforms of the early 1970s.[98]

Similarly Schioppa Costoris argued: 'Our studies emphasise that the unwieldiness of the Italian welfare state and its consequent development [...] are attributable to the superimposition of the conflictual model on the particularistic-corporatist model, and to the effects of the political cycle.'[99]

These views embrace in fact considerations formulated by OECD assessors on the fiscal crisis of the Italian state, seen in a completely neo-liberal framework. The *OECD Survey of Italy of 1984-5*, which thoroughly examined the question of the fiscal crisis and public debt, pointed out that both general government borrowing requirement and high interest rates policy should be reduced because they aggravated the fiscal problem and suggested that Italy become more competitive. 'It is thus important', the OECD analysts continued, 'that the authorities pursue and increase their efforts *towards achieving these targets by implementing measures which currently encounter political obstacles*' (our emphasis).[100] Certainly, the set of measures proposed were the implementation of the neo-liberal agenda in full, that is, privatisation of state holdings, deregulation of the financial system, flexible adjustment of the labour market, drastic reductions in welfare contributions (health, pensions, various benefits etc.) and a squeezing of labour costs. Sabino Cassese and Michael Braun also saw that the three main public corporations, IRI, ENI and EFIM[101] were under the management and bargaining power of the *pentapartito*, refracting the latter's internal contradictions.[102] Yet, Paolo Bianchi stated clearly that, while Professor Romano Prodi — the then manager of IRI — was calling for privatisation in an attempt to re-launch the autonomy of the corporation from the political parties and their rivalries, Craxi favoured public share-holdings in a permanent government holding, to be politically controlled in order to ease social problems and to consolidate the autonomy of the political class.[103]

The neo-liberal critique of 'the life and times' of the First Republic enjoys its own merits. As Riccardo Azzolini has argued, no one can really deny the fact that, for example, the increase of public spending in the 1980s, as reinforced by the deficit of the *Cassa Integrazione Guadagni* (Wage Supplementation Fund) — a fund aimed at financing unemployment — as well as the anticipated generous pension schemes, contributed to the worsening of the fiscal problem. On the revenue side, the real blow to the state authorities derived from mass tax evasion, which was the result of inefficient tax collecting mechanisms.[104] In short, the neo-liberal critique saw the fiscal crisis of the state as the most critical institutional aspect of the Italian polity in the 1980s. Yet, it diagnosed that the *pentapartito* was part and parcel of the problem, rather than the real solution to it. However, the *way of approaching* the question as well as the solutions proposed, were far from those in fact needed for the construction of a new social and political pact. Yet, there are some *historical* inaccuracies in this argument.

The misleading thesis within the neo-liberal notion stems from the fact that it considers the *pentapartito* as a body wholly alienated from neo-liberal policies throughout the 1980s. None the less, as we saw earlier while examining the PCI's strategy between 1980-87, we asserted that Italy underwent some very important structural changes during that period. They concerned the degree of internationalisation of the Italian economy, the decline of public industry, the introduction of flexible labour schemes and the gradual liberalisation of financial markets. The national currency could hardly be controlled at the national level (e.g. Italian authorities alone were unable to decide on the devaluation of lira in order to improve competitiveness as they did in 1976). The partial recovery from the 1970s recession was achieved through a marked growth of private fixed investment and private consumption, having been triggered by exports and the positive contribution of stockbuilding. Meanwhile, the first set of privatisation policies appeared. Under these circumstances, state authorities succeeded, as we have seen, in curbing inflation while defeating the labour movement over the referendum for the *scala mobile*. In order to ease social tensions caused by the restructuring process, the ruling political forces increased public employment in general government jobs, whereas the slight decrease in state-controlled companies as seen in the table below, should be attributed to the realisation of the first privatisation plans.

Table 5   Public employment in Italy, 1980–1987

Year	Empl. in general govern. ('000s)	Empl. in state-controlled companies ('000s)
1980	2,954.0	715.5
1981	3,013.0	714.9
1982	3,041.0	702.5
1983	3,080.0	706.8
1984	3,108.0	679.2
1985	3,120.0	653.1
1986	3,263.0	588.7
1987	3,309.0	564.7

Source: F.P.S. Costoris, *Italy: the Sheltered Economy*, op.cit., p.136

The average annual percentage of real GDP growth in 1985 constant prices was around 3.0, as against 1.5 in Denmark, 2.7 in Netherlands, 3.1 in W. Germany and 2.9 in France. In 1986, the Milan stock exchange grew faster than any other stock market in the world. FIAT led this modernisation process by assuring itself the leading place amongst European car manufacturers, and when the 1985 referendum resulted in the reduction of the *scala mobile* and the PCI's acrimonious defeat, investment projects increased. In point of fact, due to the massively accumulated public debt — by the end of the decade it succeeded in going over 100 per cent of GDP and the cash requirement of the public sector which was (absolute value in billion of constant **lira 1988**) 159.755 in 1975 and 289.627 in 1980, soared to 528.384 in 1988 — [105] the *pentapartito* was forced to privatise some important public holdings.

Table 6   The Italian deficit in billions of current Lira, 1980–1988

Year	Total Revenue	Total Expenditure	Deficit
1980	162.681	129.667	-33.014
1981	213.941	160.929	-53.012
1983	315.346	248.155	-67.191
1985	414.977	313.315	-101.662
1987	494.361	391.429	-102.932
1988	551.651	437.438	-114.213

Source: F.P.S. Costoris, *Italy: the Sheltered Economy*, op.cit., pp.20-1, also pp.24-27

The sale of Alfa Romeo to Fiat in 1986 was the most striking. Finally, between 1983 and 1989 the IRI sold seventeen large enterprises.[106] In this context, the 1983-1988 period had rightly been characterised as the 'mini-boom' of the 1980s because it involved 'rolling back' the bargaining power of the trade unions and keeping pace with neo-liberal trends. Yet, fragmentation and segmentation of unionism apart, the modernisation process under way was but a *jobless growth*. Unemployment rates went up from 7.6 per cent in 1980 to 11.1 per cent in 1986 and 12 per cent in 1988 with the South always having a double-digit, and gradually increased, percentage. In short, the achievements of Italian private capitalism did take place with the assistance of the *pentapartito*, and not independently from it. Therefore, the ruling bloc was not so 'dysfunctional' for the new phase of growth as was claimed by some neo-liberal commentators.

Inevitably, all this reminds us, *mutatis-mutandis*, of the old critique addressed by liberals to the notion of *trasformismo* which, as we saw earlier, was described by Paggi and D'Angelillo as a criticism against the elements of welfarism that the *trasformismo* undertakes under the pressure of the class struggle.[107] *Consequently, the fundamental problem for the 'consociationalism', or 'corporatism'' or 'bargained pluralism' of the pentapartito was not so much how to govern by circumventing modernity, but how to modernise against the labour movement.* Indeed, the *pentapartito*, via its 'consociationalism', played a major role in 'modernisation against the labour movement' throughout the 1980s. Therefore, the view according to which the ruling power bloc was wholly 'dysfunctional' to the intrinsic needs of the neo-liberal developmental cycle, was groundless.

The *methodological assumption* lying behind the neo-liberal argument is also debatable. Whatever their intentions ought to have been, neo-liberals conceived the nexus state/civil society in a mere technocratic/quantitative version, purified of any form of articulation between autonomous instances, social subjects and human needs. They in fact think of a 'pure' capitalist development in which the economy reproduces itself without any state intervention at all. The polity thus comes to be seen as an entity quasi determined by the economy, the only 'ontological' structure capable of achieving growth and prosperity. *However, this is the most extreme form of reductionism, also as regards certain interpretations of Marxism along which the 'superstructure' is quasi determined by the ontological principle of the 'economic base'.*[108]

How did the PCI deal with it? This is a very difficult question to answer, mainly because the PCI itself was in a transition period, its theses being as yet uncrystallised. My attempt, therefore, will be a rather speculative one. I will focus on the few documents the party produced during the second half of the 1980s on the topic, documents which, as we shall confirm, are deeply contradictory.

As we saw earlier, a first-class illusion of the party in 1984-87 was the belief that the *pentapartito* was implementing neo-liberal policies *in full*.[109] Accordingly, and despite the fact that the *XVII Congress* — a *transitional* Congress — left room for revisionist manœuvring,[110] the PCI could argue for institutional reform *and* a strong economic presence of the state. No clarification on how this could be done was given. The problems did not stop here. In struggling to avoid any sort of exaggeration with regard to the predominance of international factors over the national ones, the PCI theses went on to argue:

> Even internationalisation is a necessity and a condition for development. It is the only way through which many economic sectors can advance their output. At the same time, however, the loss of national control over fundamental centres of productive apparatus due to the internationalisation, must be prevented.[111]

In point of fact, as we have stressed above, the Congressional theses were highly reluctant to advance any consistent set of policies which would have enabled the party to go beyond both neo-liberal economics and old-fashioned Keynesianism. The real problem for the economic institutions were their structural adjustment vis-à-vis the European imperative and the Maastricht deadline, the convergence criteria being postulated for inflation, interest rates, the budget deficit and the public debt.[112]

At the time the *Theses* were drafted, the Research Institute contributing to the formation of the party's economic policy attempted to tackle the fiscal question. On October 28, 1985, *Cespe* organised a joint seminar with the PCI and the parliamentary group of the Independent Left on the fiscal crisis of the state and the prospects for modernisation. The discussion took place vis-à-vis the Budget approved by the *pentapartito's* parliamentary majority. The main contributions were collected in a volume edited by the party's weekly *Rinascita* and prefaced by Alfredo Reichlin who stated:

> The negative effects of governmental policies — in terms of unemployment, halting the development [...] — have been purposely ignored or underestimated [by the Budget] [...]. [the government] instead of facing the challenge of innovation and the process of

transformation by going beyond the crisis of the welfare state, has been reduced to Reagan's recipes.[113]

We are confronted here with a twofold 'paradox': Reichlin, on the one hand, accused the *pentapartito* of applying neo-liberal economics in full, whereas the neo-liberals, on the other, castigated it because of its unwillingness to back capitalist restructuring along neo-liberal lines. It is clear that both conceptions fail to pinpoint the crux of the matter: that neo-liberal capitalist development was advancing with the partial backing of the *pentapartito*, whilst its institutional framework remained unreformed. Piero Fassino, one of the key figures in Occhetto's rising team, was quite categorical on this point:

> We began to realise in full that the economy was doing well, whereas institutions were going through a very serious crisis; therefore, we concluded that it is not the economic crisis which inevitably leads to a political one, inasmuch as in Italy we were experiencing a political and institutional disaster while a conspicuous economic modernisation was taking place. That is why we decided to break with reductionism and confer on the political and institutional spheres the autonomy they deserve.[114]

The essay of Silvano Andriani,[115] then President of Cespe, argued for a reduction of interest rates via a qualified public intervention accompanied by specific strategies of investment. Andriani said that interest rates should stop being financed by the state budget through the perverse mechanism of the BOT, introduced by the Bank of Italy in 1981. This mechanism, in effect, instead of positively financing the debt, tended to damage public finance and increase the debt.[116] Andriani pinpointed the problem but did not indicate any concrete solution. The account of Massimo Paci went so far as to see the Italian welfare state as a 'residual' one, which tended to be classed alongside the US model, state intervention covering only the relationship family/market, as long as the latter cannot provide 'prosperity' for the former.[117]

We are witnessing, therefore, the same sort of ambiguities in both PCI intellectuals and policy makers: either a pro-Keynesian qualified state intervention is proposed in order to stave off crisis (Andriani) without, however, specifying concrete ways of achieving it; or the illusion that an 'americanisation' of the *stato assistenziale* was underway (Paci). In the latter case, the Italian state, pressumably, applied neo-liberal policies *à la* Reagan. Having said this, I would not hesitate to argue that the PCI, under the centrist leadership of Natta, oscillated between two avenues without following either. The *first* was along neo-revisionist lines, recognising some policy constraints imposed by the process of European integration and the capitalist restructuring of the 1980s. This implied the achievement of institutional reform, including electoral reform, and application, in part, of supply-side economic policies in order to mitigate the fiscal crisis of the state. The *second* was steady resistance to capitalist restructuring and the deepening of political democracy and welfarism. This solution seems close to left-wing Eurocommunism, although this was not always the case: as we have seen, Ingrao was the first PCI leader who firmly argued in favour of institutional and electoral reform. In point of fact, there were a number of other PCI senior cadres who, having a strong pro-Keynesian culture, took the declarations of De Mita and Craxi for real while being impressed by some privatisations that took place. Thus, it was believed that the *pentapartito* was keen to follow a neo-liberal doctrine in full. By opting strongly for the first avenue in 1987, the new ruling group around Occhetto resolved any policy ambivalence on the subject.

In conclusion, and given the fluid inner-party political and ideological environment, the Florence Congress was not a 'triumph of new internationalism' as Joan B. Urban has argued.[118] It was rather an apotheosis of centrism, i.e., an unstable balance of compromises between Eurocommunism and the rising Euroleft. In fact, the party achieved a real breakthrough in the understanding of the crisis, including its own, only after 1987: it was the serious defeat at the June 1987 general election which brought Occhetto's group to the party's leadership.

Concluding remarks

We have examined the evolution of the 'democratic alternative' strategy since Berlinguer and have affirmed its *dual* and *ambivalent* strategic character. On the one hand, it was conceived as an anti-capitalist strategy contesting the 'historical bloc' of bourgeois power (*alternative*); on the other, it was potentially understood as a realistic programmatic project aimed at achieving a functional political democracy of *alternation* on the British model. *The neo-revisionist strategy of Occhetto's group which was to be launched, was in accord with the latter, reformist aspect of the party tradition.*

By examining the theses of the party with regard to the institutional question, we have noted certain contradictions in it, concerning the articulation between the political and the economic instances. Namely, the PCI's policy makers became confused by the reluctant neo-liberal policies of the *pentapartito*, its declared reformism as well as the process of capitalist restructuring. Thus, they were unable to cope with the public sphere *per se* and proposed concrete institutional reform which would have meant, first and foremost, solving the fiscal crisis of the state and dealing with electoral reform. For more than three years (1984-87) the party was oscillated between Eurocommunism and the Euroleft (neo-revisionism). This fact had some further implications.

In contrast to its prompt revisionism on the international front, the PCI was rather sluggish in 'domestic policies'. To put it another way, the joining of the Euroleft, apart from the fact that the initiative as such did not represent a PCI initiative — as was the case with Eurocommunism — was not accompanied by a dynamic 'endogenous' strategy — as was the case with the *compromesso* which constituted a dynamic Communist notion. In point of fact, *the pair Euroleft/alternative seemed much more 'feeble' and nonchalant than that of Eurocommunism/compromise*. What are the main reasons lying behind this sluggishness?

The general inherent weakness of the *alternativa* in producing coherent strategies constituted a first set of difficulties. Here lies the above-mentioned problem of interpretation and the ambiguities inherited from Berlinguer himself (vagueness of the alliance policy). Moreover, as a *Communist* party, the PCI had not only to face national and international constaints to shape its policy, but also to decipher the contradictions of the present phase of capitalist development so as to sketch out a visible outcome *beyond* this development. True, this problem had to do, as we have seen, with the question of *duplicity*. Seen in this context, however, any *realistic* amalgamation of the *alternativa* through which the PCI could improve its political and electoral performance, proved impossible.

Another difficulty for the PCI as a whole — that is, militants, cadres, leadership and broader electorate — was the PSI. The proclaimed discourse of the Euroleft for the reconciliation of the Communist and Socialist traditions — the demand of going beyond the Second and the Third Internationals — in Italy would have meant that the PCI should open up to the PSI, a party which had been collaborating with the DC for more than 25 years and which was integrated into its corrupt system of power.[119] Indeed, the main problem the reformist wing of Napolitano had to face while attempting to advance the Euroleft's conception in the party was the inner-party resistance to any collaboration with the PSI of Craxi. This attitude of abhorrence towards the PSI not only had the backing of the party's left-wing faction; broader sections of the non-PCI Independent Left paid lip service to this political perspective, from the Communist journal *il Manifesto* of Luigi Pintor to the Liberal-Socialist Left of the review *Micromega* around Paolo Flores d'Arcais, the list is endless. In practice, however, the whole problem meant that the *alternativa democratica* could hardly be incorporated and implemented as the functional domestic aspect of the Euroleft's project, thus functionally replacing the strategic axis of the *compromesso*.

A third difficulty was the triple crisis — political, organisational, ideological — of the PCI itself. Here a whole series of factors were involved and I do not intend to go into this problem as a whole here, as I shall return to it in the following chapters. I shall merely mention the deeply transitional character of the 1986 Congress, *the first Congress of the non-Eurocommunist PCI* which, in the words of Fassino, was also 'the last Congress of the old ruling group'.[120] Indeed, in 1987, Giuseppe Chiarante, Giorgio Napolitano, Alfredo Reichlin, Aldo Tortorella and Gavino Angius left the politbureau of the party. Natta alone would simply give the party over to Achille Occhetto, Massimo D'Alema, Claudio Petruccioli, Piero Fassino, Livia Turco and Fabio Mussi. As Piero Ignazi did not fail to mention, the only element of continuity between the 1983 politbureau and that of 1989 was Occhetto.[121] The Italian Road to Socialism was about to come to a close.

Notes

1   The landmark of this conception was the book of the German Social Democrat Peter Glotz, *Manifesto for a New European Left*, which appeared in Italy in 1986, only a year after the original German edition, and prefaced by Occhetto.
2   E. Berlinguer, 'Si è esaurita la spinta propulsiva' (15-12-1981), in *Attualità...*, op. cit., pp. 86, 88, and PCI, 'Riflessione sui dramatici fatti di Polonia: aprire una nuova fase della lotta per il socialismo' (Resolution of the CC, 29-12-1981), in *Rinascita*, 1, 8-1-1982, pp. 26-30; see also the contributions of G. Napolitano, 'Polonia, una vicenda cruciale' *Rinascita*, 50, 18-12-1981, pp. 1, 31 and P. Ingrao, 'In Polonia e altrove c'era altro da fare', ibid., pp. 3-4.
3   As best testimony — although the author clarifies that the line of *terza via* concerns not only the 'military blocs' but the social and economic ones — A. Minucci, 'La logica dei blocchi', *Rinascita*, 51, 25-12-1981, pp. 1, 43.
4   E. Berlinguer, *Relazione al XVI Congresso Nazionale del PCI* (Milano: Bozze di Stampa, 2-3-1983), p.6 and PCI, 'Documenti approvati al XVI Congresso Nazionale del PCI', in *XVI Congresso del Partito Comunista Italiano; Atti, Risoluzioni, Documenti* (Roma: Riuniti, 1983), pp. 664 ff., thereafter: *XVI Congress.*
5   E. Berlinguer, 'Inderdipendenza dei problemi dell'umanità' (Report to 15th party Congress in 30 March 1979, Rome), in *Attualità...*, op. cit. p.31. Exactly the same formulation can be found in the document of the Congress, see, *XV Congress*, p.39.
6   Much later, towards the end of the 1980s, the PCI officially recognised the validity of this point: 'Even those who had been neither located in, nor recognised themselves through, the logic of blocs, however, were constrained to examine the problems of the

world in the light of its division in two', *XVIII Congresso del PCI* (supplement in the party's daily *L'Unità*, 272, 4-12-1988), p.5, thereafter: *XVIII Congress*.

7   See in particular, A. Pravda, 'Introduction: linkages between Soviet domestic and foreign policy under Gorbachev', in T. Hasegawa-A. Pravda (ed.), *Perestroika: Soviet Domestic and Foreign Policies* (London: Sage, 1990), pp. 1-25 and J. Cooper, 'Soviet resource options: civil and military priorities', ibid., pp. 141-55. This reality was grasped by the PCI. Antonio Rubbi, the leading PCI cadre in charge of the party's international relations, argued: 'The great novelty which the new Soviet ruling group brought to foreign policy affairs, consists in shifting world competition from the military field to the political one. It consists in emphasising a new conception of the problems of security and the need for growing cooperation', A. Rubbi, 'Let us discuss the USSR, socialism and our choices' (originally published in *Rinascita*, 13-2-1988), in *The Italian Communists*, Foreign Bulletin of the PCI, 1, Jan.-March 1988, p.53, also, A. Rubbi, *Incontri con Gorbachev* (Roma: Riuniti, 1990), pp. 65-68, 87, 194.

8   On this subject, see S. Gundle, 'The Italian Communist Party: Gorbachev and the end of "really existing socialism"', in D. S. Bell (ed.), *Western European Communists and the Collapse of Communism* (Oxford: Berg, 1993), J. B. Urban, 'The PCI's 17th Congress: a triumph of the "new internationalism"', in P. Corbetta-R. Leonardi-R. Nanetti (ed.), v.2, *Italian Politics: A Review* (London: Pinter,1987), pp. 48-9.

9   See for example, M. Gorbachev, *Le Idee di Berlinguer ci Servono Ancora* (Roma: Sisifo, 1994), pp. 11-22.

10   For the reconstruction of the events, A. Rubbi, *Incontri...*, op. cit., pp. 197-200.

11   E. Berlinguer, 'Per salvare e cambiare il mondo' (Conclusion in the party Conference, Rome, 3-4-1977), in *Attualità...*, op. cit., p.24, also, *XV Congress*, pp. 25-48, passim. It is worth stressing, moreover, that Eurocommunism foresaw and fought against the expansion of nationalism, which prevents the integration and construction of Europe on a pro-popular basis, see, *XV Congress*, pp. 49-50.

12   XV Congress, pp. 6, 53. Berlinguer, in his Concluding speech in the Congress (Rome, 3-4-1977), argued: 'On the basis of our conception of the *New Internationalism* [...] the rigid principle of autonomy and independence of each party, movement or state remains. This is something irreversibly accepted by our party', E. Berlinguer, 'Per salvare...', in *Attualità...*, op. cit., p.23. Two years ago, in his Report at the 14th party Congress, Berlinguer had already put forward the hypothesis of a *world administration* as a realistic historical aim, see E. Berlinguer, 'Cooperazione internazionale' (18-3-1975), in *Attualità...*, op. cit., p.11.

13   *XVI Congress*, p.672.

14   See for instance the following articles by Napolitano, 'Le condizioni del dialogo tra Eurocomunismo e Socialismo Europeo', *Rinascita*, 19, 8-5-1981, pp. 3-4, 'Le nuove dimensioni della via Italiana', *Rinascita*, 25, 23-6-1984, pp. 6-7, 'Un polo europeo per le forze di progresso', *Rinascita*, 42, 27-10-1984, pp. 22-23 and G. Chiaromonte, 'La via Italiana che noi proponiamo' *Rinascita*, 23, 22-6-1985.

15   G. Napolitano, 'Le nuove...', ibid., p.7.

16   E. Berlinguer, 'Per Salvare e cambiare il mondo' (3-4-1977), in *Attualità...*, op. cit. p.23. The official *Theses* of the XV Congress were extremely careful in judging Social Democracy (see, *XV Congress*, pp. 7 ff., 49-56). The party document stated that 'the PCI encourages and proposes to contribute to the stabilisation of solidarity assuming an international commitment which goes beyond the communist parties' (ibid., pp. 5-6, passim). However, it reiterated its faith in Eurocommunism, polycentrism and *terza via* (ibid., pp. 9-10, passim).

17   Recent contributions on this question construct their arguments along this mendacious line, see M. Battini (ed.), *Dialogo su Berlinguer* (Firenze: Giunti, 1994), A. Tortorella, *Berlinguer Aveva Ragione; Note sull'Alternativa e la Riforma della Politica* (Roma: Critica Marxista, 1994), G. Chiarante, *Da Togliatti a D'Alema* (Bari: Laterza, 1996), M. Mafai, *Dimenticare Berlinguer; La Sinistra Italiana e la Tradizione Comunista* (Roma: Donzelli, 1996).

18   E. Berlinguer, 'La crisi Italiana', in *Attualità...*, op. cit. p.71.

19   E. Berlinguer, 'Ragioniamo su pace e terza via' (*L'Unità*, 21-2-1982), now in M. Gorbaciov, *Le Idee di Berlinguer...*, op. cit., p.72.

20   Berlinguer did not hesitate to develop the party theses in Moscow, à propos of his speech on the 60th anniversary of October revolution (3-11-1977): 'Democracy today is not only the ground where the class enemy is forced to retreat: it is also the historically *universal value* upon which an original socialist society should be founded' (my italics), E. Berlinguer, 'Democrazia, valore universale', in *Attualità...*, op. cit., p.29.

21   E. Berlinguer, 'Consenso e Cambiamento' (originally published in *La Repubblica*, 11-9-1983), now in *Attualità...*, op. cit., p.116.

22   A. Natta, 'Disarmament, Europe, the Left' (originally published in *Rinascita*, 10-10-1987) in *The Italian Communists*, Foreign Bulletin of the PCI, 4, Oct.-Dec. 1987, pp. 5-6.

23   See G. Vacca, '"Nuovo internazionalismo" e "terza via": riflessioni sul XV Congresso del PCI', in his *Gorbachev...*, op. cit., p.146.

24   The works of P. Sweezy, M. Nicolaus, N. Poulantzas, E. Mandel, R. Murray, C. Palloix, S. De Brunhof show the sensibility of neo-Marxists on the issue. However, there was no common agreement. It is possible, at least schematically, to locate two major tendencies in the positions taken on this question. The first tendency maintained that the nation-state does not lose its powers vis-à-vis internationalisation. In the words of N. Poulantzas: 'The current internationalisation of capital and the emergence of "multinational giants" alongside the state cannot be discussed in terms of two entities "possessing" power and distributing it. In particular, to argue that the more "economic power" increases and is concentrated, the more it takes away power from the state, is not only to fail to understand that the state does not possess any power of its own, but also the fact that it intervenes decisively in this very concentration' [N. Poulantzas, *Classes in Contemporary Capitalism* (London: Verso, 1978) pp. 80-1, first French ed. in 1974]. The second tendency saw a decline of nation-states inasmuch as the economy is becoming more and more integrated, see, *inter alia*, R. Murray, 'The internationalisation of capital and the nation-state', *New Left Review*, 67, May-June 1971, pp. 84-109.

25   Thus, G. Vacca talked about a *legitimation* and *fiscal* crisis of the state (G. Vacca, 'Per non dire crisi si discute di governabilità', *Rinascita*, 6, 6-2-1981, pp. 23-25) and P. Barcellona would write on the 'decline of planning' formulating a new social compromise based exclusively on the societal etc. [P. Barcellona, 'Oltre la crisi del Welfare, più autonomia sociale', *Rinascita*, 12, 20-3-1981, pp. 11-12 and his book *Oltre lo Stato Sociale* (Bari: Laterza, 1980)]. Ingrao, through his various initiatives as President of the Institute for the Reform of the State, was also equally aware, see his 'Le forme della politica e il rapporto tra masse e democrazia', *Rinascita*, 23-1-1981, pp. 18-22. We should also not fail to mention the pioneering article of E. Somaini in *Critica Marxista* in 1979, which provoked much discussion on these issues, see E. Somaini, 'Crisi della sinistra e ripresa neo-conservatrice in Europa; dinamiche distributive e mediazioni politiche', *Critica Marxista*, 5, Sept.-Oct. 1979, pp. 17-47.

26   Personal interview with C. Mancina (Rome: Botteghe Oscure, 16-4-1995).

27   For a leftist interpretation of the term 'new internationalism', see P. Ingrao, 'The European Left and the problems of a new internationalism', *Socialism in the World*, 53, 1986, pp. 54-73 [also published in *Socialism in the Threshold of the Twenty-first Century* (London: Verso, 1985), pp. 101-19].
28   See, A. Bolaffi, 'Il teorema Glotz incrocia il dilemma PCI' *Politica ed Economia*, 12, Dec. 1985, pp. 4-5, H. Mattfeldt, 'Eurokeynesimo: una base per un programma economico alternativo', *Politica ed Economia*, 5, May 1985, pp. 8-9.
29   PCI, *Tesi, Programma, Statuto: I Documenti Approvati dal XVII Congresso del PCI* (attached leaflet of *Rinascita*, n.4, 31-1-1987) (Roma: L'Unità, 1987), pp. 27, 32. Thereafter: *XVII Congress*.
30   *XVII Congress*, p.8.
31   A. Rubbi, *Incontri...*, op. cit., p.75.
32   See, among others, G. Napolitano, 'Governare da sinistra un arduo periodo di transizione', *Critica Marxista*, 1, Jan.-Feb. 1983, pp. 61-73, where the PCI's most influential reformist discusses the contributions of E. Hobsbawm and S. Holland; in the same issue: M. Boffa, 'La difficile prova di Mitterrand', *Rinascita*, 13, 1-4-1983, p.33.
33   *XVI Congress*, p.678.
34   Ibid.
35   E. Berlinguer, *Relazione al XVI Congresso...*, op. cit., p.11.
36   We should remind the reader at this stage that the PCI, as a strongly pro-European party, was not against the enlargement of Europe and, in particular, encouraged the entry of Greece, Spain and Portugal, see *XV Congress*, p.44.
37   *XVII Congress*, p.27.
38   For the PCI's proposal of state planning see ibid., pp. 96-99, 103 ff. We examine these points in detail below while dealing with the fiscal crisis of the state and the strategy of *alternativa democratica*. The PCI wholeheartedly adopted and integrated the Euroleft's platform only in the document of the 18th Congress (March 1989, Rome). There it drew up a balance sheet of the 1980s and its self-criticism.
39   P. Glotz, *Manifesto...*, op. cit., p.39.
40   Ibid., p.50.
41   Ibid., p.51.
42   Ibid., pp. 81-106 and *17th Congress*, pp. 99-101, passim. It is true that in the PCI's document *Materiali e Proposte per un Programma di Politica Economico-Sociale e di Governo di Economia* (*Rinascita*, 50, 18-12-1981), the term was used, but in a different context. In it 'economic democracy' was defined as a feasible project which guarantees the participation of workers in the production process thus 'enabling them to enjoy the rewards of their labour'; from this perspective, the document argued that, 'economic democracy is essential for policy planning', ibid., p.21. Thus, the real meaning of the term was identified with the Communist conception of 'industrial democracy, self-management and cooperative institutions' rather than with the Euroleft's notion (economic democracy as achieved by less regulated measures and rationalities emanated by the public sphere). In the XVI party Congress a left-wing explanation of the term can also be found, see *XVI Congress*, pp. 634 ff.
43   As a typical example of this, see the articles of H. Ehmke, 'SPD — PCI, le ragioni di un confronto' and G. Napolitano, 'Senza timidezze per nuove prospettive di progresso e di unità'; both appeared side by side in *Rinascita*, 5, 9-2-1985, pp. 40-42.
44   See Natta's resignation letter to the CC of the PCI in *The Italian Communists*, Foreign Bulletin of the PCI, 2, April-June 1988, pp. 30-31 (originally published in

L'Unità, 14-6-1988), where he clearly points out that his basic commitment was to prepare the formation of a new ruling group.

45   P. Ingrao, personal interview (Rome, 14-7-1995).

46   See, among others, the following formulation of the PCI secretary: 'The objectives of the expansion of democracy and the complete assertion of its rules, inasmuch as they constitute the diametrically opposed visions to conservatism and moderatism, have characterised and characterise Italian Communists [...]. And we have once again taken up the question of economic democracy. It can no longer be considered as an imaginary threat, at the moment when an extraordinary expansion of capitalism is taking place [...]. This is not the birth of a 'popular capitalism', as is said, but the concentration of power and choice in the hands of few', A. Natta, 'Il programma e la lotta del PCI per aprire una nuova fase politica', *L'Unità*, 29-7-1987, p. 13-15.

47   A. Reichlin, 'Note per un programma', *Politica ed Economia*, Nov. 1987, 11, p.35. Certainly, Reichlin was very cautious. In his article, he declared in advance that these were 'personal notes' and had nothing to do with the party's official policy. However, a year earlier and in the same magazine, Reichlin was much more hesitant about matching the Euroleft's positions, even under the pretext of 'personal notes', see A. Reichlin, 'L'economia si fa progetto', *Politica ed Economia*, Nov. 1986, 11, pp. 3-5. But he gave no signs of the Euroleft's positions in his 'Se l'Italia discende di un gradino', *Rinascita*, 3, 25-1-1986, pp. 40-43.

48   See for example, A. Reichlin, 'La sinistra del post-Reaganismo', *L'Unità*, 12-9-1990, p.6.

49   A. Occhetto, 'Un nuovo modo di pensare e fare politica', *Rinascita*, 41, 24-10-1987, p.4.

50   Apart from the internal party pressures of the *miglioristi* of Napolitano and of the *ultra-miglioristi* of Emanuele Macaluso, it should also be noted that the Ochetto-D'Alema aggregation was exposed to pressures exercised by the *sinistra indipendente*, independent Left, which was elected in the PCI lists (G. Pasquino, S. Rododà, L. Pintor et al.), as well as by the *sinistra dei Club* (Paolo Flores D'Arcais, Massimo Cacciari, Gianni Vattimo, et al.), as gathered around the prestigious theoretical review *MicroMega* (founded in 1986). In both groups, the *reformist* and *liberal* elements were dominant. Basically, they favoured the PCI's opening towards a Socialist-Liberal Left alongside the positions of Norberto Bobbio; see in particular G. Francesco Serra (ed.), *Una Magnifica Avventura: Dalla Sinistra Sommersa alla Sinistra dei Club* (Roma: Associate, 1990); the book is prefaced by Bobbio. We deal with these issues below.

51   See, *inter alia*, Maria Luisa Boccia, 'Part-time tra passato e futuro', *Rinascita*, 15, 16-4-1982, pp. 16-17, Licia Perelli, 'Part-time, perchè non diventi un ghetto', *Rinascita*, 19, 21-5-1982, p.15.

52   See, P. Hanson, 'Gorbachev's economic policies after four years', in T. Hasegawa-A. Pravda (ed.), *Perestroika...*, op. cit., pp. 109-123. Even towards the end of the decade, PCI Leftist intellectuals and cadres tended to believe that the crisis of the East did not lead to a capitalist restoration but, on the contrary, to a Communist liberalisation process. The daily *il Manifesto* was very fond of this interpretation; see, *inter alia*, the article of Cesare Luporini, 'L'Utopia della liberazione ha un futuro?' (originally published in *il Manifesto*, 19-11-1989) now in G. Moltedo, N. Rangeri (ed.), *PCI: La Grande Svolta; il Nome, il Simbolo, il Nuovo Partito* (Roma: Associate, 1989), pp. 143-46.

53   See A. Rubbi, *Incontri...*, op. cit., pp. 282-83, 295.

54   The previous four-party coalition government of Forlani was forced to resign after the enormous repercussions that the revelation of the existence of the Masonic Lodge P2 had upon the coalition. The PCI had substantially contributed to the debate: see, *inter alia*, E. Macaluso, 'Le domande sulla P2 alle quali Forlani poteva rispondere', *Rinascita*, 21, 22-5-1981, pp. 4-5, U. Pecchioli, 'Armi, petrolio e P2', *Rinascita*, 23, 5-6-1981, pp. 1, 31, E. Berlinguer, 'Il partito di cambiamento', *Rinascita*, 25, 19-6-1981, pp. 1, 31.

55   The *pentapartito* was far from being a monolithic bloc without internal contradictions. Soon after Craxi became the first socialist PM of the Republic (4-8-1983), a series of inner-government disagreements surfaced. The election of Francesco Cossiga in the Presidency of the Republic (26-6-1985), accentuated existing contrasts between De Mita, who was then DC secretary, and Craxi. The 'Achille Lauro affair', from the name of an Italian ship captured by a group of Arab terrorists in 7 October 1985, pitted Craxi and Andreotti against Spadolini, who was then Minister of Defence. The *pentapartito* was also divided about economic policy arrangements, for each party faction claimed to set its own control over particular public holdings: see, *inter alia*, M. Braun, *L'Italia da Andreotti a Berlusconi* (Milano: Feltrinelli, 1995), pp. 37-115.

56   In particular, during the second half of the 1980s, Craxi established a privileged relationship with the businessman and, later, media magnate and PM Silvio Berlusconi, a member of the Masonic Lodge P2. In essence, Craxi provided the legislative framework which enabled Berlusconi to establish his three private channels; on the famous *legge Mammì* (Mammì law), from the name of the Republican Minister Oscar Mammì, which enabled Berlusconi to develop his media empire, see, among others, M. Braun, ibid., pp. 101, 184, passim.

57   A. Occhetto, 'La sinistra dopo Palermo', *Rinascita*, 18, 1-5-1981, p.31. In practice, however, this conception of politics was dominant since 1979, after the failure of *compromesso* (see in particular, E. Berlinguer, *Relazione al XVI Congresso...*, op. cit.). Needless to point out, the PCI had refused to play that subordinate role.

58   I am basically referring to C. De Mita, *Politica e Istituzioni nell'Italia Repubblicana* (Mialano: Bompiani, 1988).

59   E. Berlinguer, *Relazione al XVI Congresso*, op. cit., p.20.

60   Thus, one can see, for example, that the criticism of PCI of the neo-liberal theses of De Mita, was chiefly based on the fact that these proposals neither clarified nor offered any solution to the question of clientelism in the South, see G. Chiarante, 'Le ricette di De Mita, le alternative di Ruffolo', *Rinascita*, 4, 27-1-1984, pp. 3-4.

61   The PCI and — surprisingly enough — Ingrao, through his *Centre for the Reform of the State*, was the first leader who argued for institutional and electoral reform since 1985. His proposal, which encountered particular resistance from Nilde Iotti, was not accepted by the party; we deal with the issue below.

62   The phrase belongs to Giuseppe Chiarante, 'Compromesso, solidarietà, alternativa', *Rinascita*, 25, 23-6-1984, pp. 7-8.

63   During the IX legislature (1983-87), the parliamentary Commission set up in order to examine and formulate proposals for institutional reform, reached similar, if not identical, conclusions. The Commission — the famous *commissione Bozzi* — reported that 'the relationship between parties and institutions has been a relationship of occupation' and pointed out the *blocked nature* of political democracy; see, U. Indrio, *Dieci Anni: la Lotta Politica in Italia dal 1978 al 1988* (Roma: Edizione Lavoro, 1989), pp. 112-13 (among the participants in the Commission were A. Natta, S. Rodotà, M.

Segni, G. Pasquino, R. Formica, S. Cassese, L. Balbo, N. Iotti, M. Pannella); see also M. Braun's analyses, *L'Italia...*, op. cit.

64   A. Occhetto, 'Una contrastata partenza', *Rinascita*, 27, 3-7-1981, p.1.

65   E. Berlinguer, 'La crisi Italiana' (28-7-1981), in *Attualità...*, op. cit., pp. 65-66, 73, also *XV Congress*, pp. 58, 87-91, passim.

66   See *XV Congress*, pp. 23, 102-109, passim. The aim of the PCI was to become part of the government in full, otherwise it would return to opposition.

67   See in particular Berlinguer's Report at 16th party Congress (*Relazione al XVI Congress*, op. cit., pp. 26-27, passim), also his discussion with F. Adornato (originally published in *L'Unità*, 18-12-1983, à propos of the fortieth anniversary of the appearance of G. Orwell's book *1984*, 'Il duemila, l'avvenire', in *Attualità...*, op. cit., pp. 121-31. It is worth noting here that Stefano Rodotà has expressed similar — if not identical — concerns; see for example his article 'Potere e democrazia nel futuro elettronico' (*Rinascita*, 15, 16-4-1982, pp. 23-4); the jurist and, much later, President of the PDS for a short period, argued that new technologies tend to reinvigorate vertical communication among people, thus increasing the isolation of individuals; fears of transforming every house into an electoral cabin, thereby dissociating the masses from direct participation in politics, were also expressed by Rodotà.

68   E. Berlinguer 'La crisi Italiana' (interview with E. Scalfari, *La Repubblica*, 28-7-1981), now in *Attualità...*, op. cit., p.71.

69   As Napolitano maintained: 'Yes, Berlinguer has always held the view of permanently renewing the party strategy, but this renewal should be done within a Communist, however flexible, horizon', personal interview, cit.

70   See E. Berlinguer, *Relazione al XVI Congress*, op. cit., p.8, passim.

71   E. Berlinguer, ibid., p.20; the same formulation can be found in the document of the Congress, see *XVI Congress*, op. cit., p.616, 625-26, passim. On this point I would disagree with the thesis expressed by Occhetto, who emphasised the element of continuity between *alternativa* and *compromesso*, providing a one-sided view of this complex question, see A. Occhetto, 'Compromesso storico e alternativa democratica', *Critica Marxista*, 2-3, May-June 1985, pp. 149-57.

72   See *XVI Congress*, pp. 619-24 where the party's alliance policy is discussed.

73   E. Berlinguer, 'Consenso e cambiamento' (originally published in *La Repubblica*, 11-9-1983), now in *Attualità...*, op. cit., p.116.

74   In the words of A. Tortorella (*Berlinguer aveva Ragione...*, op. cit., p.7): 'During Berlinguer's secretaryship there is a clear-cut distinction between a first and a second phase. This distinction applies — it is understood — to politics: from national solidarity to the democratic alternative.'

75   This point was strongly stressed by Napolitano in our conversation, personal interview, op. cit.

76   *XVII Congress*, pp. 64 ff.

77   Thus, one can read in the *Theses*: 'The policies applied by the *pentapartito* cabinets in these years are strongly determined by the neo-liberal notion according to which cuts in social spending [...] and general deregulation in the relationship between the market and the state would create conditions for an economic recovery. It has been an unsuccessful attempt', ibid., pp. 43-44. However, the economy was doing well and the *pentapartito* had very little, if any, intention of applying neo-liberal economics and promoting institutional reform. The mistake was openly and officially admitted at the 18th Congress (Rome, March 1989).

78   See, *XVII Congress*, p.73.

79   Ibid., pp. 73-87.

80   Ibid., pp. 125-35.

81   The Centre for Marxist Studies (CMAS) should be clearly distinguished from the Centre of Marxist Research (CMR). The former was the research Institute of the Greek Eurocommunist party (KKEes) whereas the latter was the equivalent for the orthodox Greek Communist party (KKE). The KKE (11.5 per cent of the vote in the 1981 election) had a clear predominance over the KKEes (2.5 per cent).

82   P. Ingrao, 'La sinistra oltre i limiti dello stato-nazione', *Rinascita*, 17, 29-4-1983, pp. 6-9.

83   Ibid., p.9. Certainly, Ingrao also mentioned the classic points of Eurocommunism, i.e., beyond the two blocs, the question of the Southern world peripheries, etc.

84   P. Ingrao, 'La grande politica dell'epoca atomica', *Rinascita*, 39, 19-10-1985, pp. 40-42.

85   Along the same lines the theses of Magri who, meanwhile, brought large part of his PDUP party in the PCI, see for instance his 'La spesa sociale è un falso imputato', *Rinascita*, 35, 21-9-1985, pp. 6-7.

86   P. Ingrao (interviewed by A. Gambino), 'Alternativa di stato', *L'Espresso*, 7, 23-2-1986, pp. 13-14.

87   See, G. Chiarante, 'Compromesso, solidarietà...', op. cit., pp. 7-8.

88   L. Magri, 'Alternanza o alternativa: omologazione o nuova identità comunista?', *Critica Marxista*, 1, Jan.-Feb. 1986, p.126.

89   Cossutta protested openly about it, see for example his 'Per il superamento del capitalismo', *Critica Marxista*, 1, Jan.-Feb. 1986, pp. 51-65. All the proposed amendments — which were published — can be found in *Documenti per il Congresso; Progetto di Tesi, Programma, Emendamenti; Statuto, Criteri e Proposte*, attached leaflet of *Rinascita*, 5, 8-2-1986, pp. 129-149. So far we have purposely used the document *approved* by the 17th Congress which includes all the amendments and additional comments — especially chapters regarding gender issues — thus avoiding confusion.

90   A. Occhetto, 'Non un cartello di potere ma un programma riformatore', *Rinascita*, 4, 2-2-1985, p.5.

91   See, P. Fassino, 'La sinistra e la questione delle modernità', *Critica Marxista*, 1, Jan.-Feb. 1986, pp. 65-81. In essence, this thesis is in continuity with Amendola's notion in the 1970s (alliance with the 'progressive bourgeoisie'). It can be found in the document of the 17th Congress: 'A positive relationship and a convergence are possible with those bourgeois classes which are interested in fighting against disequilibria and backwardness [...]', *XVII Congress*, p.50.

92   A. Occhetto, 'PCI: sulla Lauro occorre un'indagine parlamentare', *L'Unità*, 2-11-1985, p.2.

93   P. Ingrao: 'I did support Occhetto to become the party's vice and then general secretary. I thought he had drawn up some reasonable theses on the question of capitalist development in the 1980s. But I was wrong and I recognise this very serious political mistake', personal interview, cit.

94   P. Ingrao, 'The European Left...', op. cit., p.70.

95   A. Occhetto, 'Il partito di programma', *Rinascita*, 8, 1-3-1986, p.17; as we have already remarked, the citation Occhetto refers to can also be found in *XVII Congress*, op. cit., pp. 33-34.

96   A. Occhetto, 'Il Partito... ', op. cit., p.17.

97   This is the case, among others, of G. Pasquino, 'Introduction: a case of a regime crisis', in G. Pasquino-P. McCarthy (ed.), *The End of Post-war Politics in Italy; the*

Landmark 1992 Elections (Oxford: Westview Press, 1993), pp. 1-12, S. Fabbrini, 'The end of consensual politics in Italy', paper presented in the Conference *Contesting the Boundaries of Italian Politics* (Ottawa: Carleton University, 22-23 March 1996).
98 F. Giavazzi, L. Spaventa, 'Italy: the real effects of inflation and disinflation', in M. Baldassari (ed.), *The Italian Economy: Heaven or Hell?* (London: St. Martin's Press and SIPI, 1994), pp. 49, 52. Along the same lines, A. C. Masi, 'Economic performance, government policies, and public opinion in Italy', in A. Gottlieb, E. Yuchtman Yaar-B. Strumpel (ed.), *Socio-economic Change and Individual Adaptation: Comparing East and West* (Connecticut: JAI Press, 1994), pp. 193-213.
99 F.P.S. Costoris, *Italy: The Sheltered Economy; Structural Problems in the Italian Economy* (Oxford: Clarendon Press, 1993), p. 173.
100 *OECD Economic Surveys, Italy 1984-5* (Paris: OECD, June 1985) p.51. In this context, the famous question of the *Bot, Buono Ordinario del Tesoro*, Ordinary Treasury Bond, introduced by the Bank of Italy in 1981, created a vicious cycle where the state, instead of positively financing its debt, would continuously find itself paying more than it had been receiving; see, *inter alia*, R. Azzolini, personal interview (Rome: Cespe premises, 25-7-1995), F.P.S.Costoris, ibid., pp. 153 ff., passim.
101 The EFIM was created in 1962 to receive the shares held by the fund for Financing Mechanical Engineering Industry, which was an autonomous administration formed in the post-war period to support firms producing weapons. In the 1960s EFIM started to diversify from the original sector of weaponry and operate in railway rolling-stock, engines, aluminium and food-processing.
102 S. Cassese, 'Italy: privatisations announced, semi-privatisations and pseudo-privatisations', in V. Wright (ed.), *Privatisation in Western Europe: Pressures, Problems and Paradoxes* (London: Pinter Publishers, 1994), pp. 122-38, M. Braun, *L'Italia...*, op. cit.
103 P. Bianchi, 'The IRI in Italy: strategic role and political constraints', *West European Politics*, v.10, n.2, April 1987, p.285.
104 F.P.S. Kostoris, *Italy...*, op. cit., pp. 153 ff., passim, R. Azzolini, personal interview, op. cit.
105 CENSIS, *Italy Today: Social Pictures and Trends* (Rome: F. Angeli, 1990), p.244.
106 See P. Bianchi-S. Cassese-V. Della Salla, 'Privatisation in Italy: aims and constraints', *West European Politics*, v.11, n.4, Oct. 1988, pp. 87-100.
107 L. Paggi-M. D'Angelillo, *I Comunisti Italiani...*, op. cit., pp. 67-73, passim.
108 For a speculative critique of reductionism, N. Mouzelis, *Post-Marxist Alternatives*, op. cit., pp. 45-92.
109 *XVII Congress*, pp. 43-44, 68.
110 For instance, it will argue against crude neo-liberalism, but it will not *a priori* exclude privatisation policies, see ibid., pp. 96-99, passim.
111 Ibid., p.99.
112 In particular, *OECD Economic Surveys, Italy 1992-93* (Paris: OECD, 1992), p.51.
113 A. Reichlin, 'Prefazione', in A. Reichlin (ed.), *La Riforma del Welfare; Materiali per un Programma di Politica Economica*, special insert attached to *Rinascita*, 47, 14-12-1985, p.5 (thereafter: *La Riforma*).
114 P. Fassino, personal interview, op. cit. The same thesis by A. Reichlin (M. Villari, 'La grande...', op. cit.): 'We should step out of an economicist analysis that would have helped us very little in understanding the present situation [...]'.
115 S. Andriani, 'Il governo dello sviluppo', in *La Riforma...*, op. cit., pp. 17-27.

116 For general account on this specific subject, see in particular A. Lopes, 'Scelte di portafoglio, tassi di interesse e debito publico in Italia. Una verifica empirica per gli anni '80', in A. Giannola, U. Marani (ed.), *Tassi di Interesse a Debito Publico* (Napoli: Edizioni Scientifiche Italiane, 1990), pp. 219-34.

117 M. Paci, 'Stato sociale e redistribuzione del reddito', in *La Riforma...*, op. cit., pp. 37-54. See also by the same author, 'Quali principi per il welfare', *Politica ed Economia*, 4, April 1985, pp. 7-10, 'Il mercato e la sfida della cittadinanza sociale', *Politica ed Economia*, 11, Nov. 1986, pp. 9-13.

118 J. B. Urban, 'The PCI's XVII Congress...', op. cit.

119 A. Rubbi remarks: 'When the PCI declared its joining the Euroleft, efforts for an extension of contacts with all principal European Socialist and Social Democrat forces was intensified [...]. Only with the PSI tensions continued to exist and/or were reinforced, especially after the visit of Natta to Hungary in September 1986', in *Incontri...*, op. cit., p.116.

120 P. Fassino, personal interview (Rome: Botteghe Oscure, 31-7-1995).

121 P. Ignazi, *Dal PCI al PDS* (Bologna: il Mulino, 1992), p.116.

4   New Revisionism and Alternative Discourses of Transformation

The setting of the problem

I will deal here with the actual process of the transformation of the PCI. We shall try to see this process not as an introverted story concerning the PCI itself, but as an amalgamation of many international and national determinants: in particular, I shall propose that the transformation of the PCI was, in certain ways, inseparable from the crisis and the transformation of the First Italian Republic, the latter being triggered by the processes of European integration and the irreversible crisis of 'actually-existing socialism'. For three main, strictly interlinked, reasons it seems to me that this setting of the problem is the most adequate.

Above all, as we have seen, as early as 1979-80, the PCI started to discuss the crisis of Keynesianism caused by the process of European integration along neo-liberal lines. Berlinguer himself was aware of it, although, mistakenly, he foresaw a left-wing outcome and a move of European Social Democracy towards the PCI's Eurocommunist positions. In point of fact, this was not a simple issue: *it had to do with the identity of the party itself.* This question was debated under the centrist leadership of Natta and in 1986 the PCI declared that it was an 'integral part of the European Left'. From November 1987, when Occhetto's neo-revisionists took over the party leadership, the Communist identity of PCI floundered. This narrative of events demolishes, *in toto*, any argument that the transformation of the PCI was *primarily* triggered by the collapse of Eastern communism. The events in the East facilitated the transformation, but they did not by any means start it. If they had any impact at all, these events mostly affected the *name change*, not the *identity* of the party.

Secondly, it is true that Gorbachev's coming to power in the USSR created problems for the PCI, in terms of difficulties it had in presenting itself in the usual distinctive manner, vis-à-vis both Social Democracy and Eastern Communism. Besides, the PCI was losing ground on the international front, being overshadowed by Gorbachev's activism. It seemed that the crisis these regimes went through at the end of the decade would have caused immense damage for the PCI alone. This was a false conception. The entire political power of the First Republic was affected by the events in the East, events which put a definite end to the *conventio ad excludendum* principle in Italian politics. In short, with the end of the

Cold War, the DC-PSI government axis could no longer base itself on America's backing in order to keep the PCI out of office. For good or bad, the ruling political class failed to understand this reality promptly.

Thirdly, and equally importantly, we have seen that the party was searching throughout the decade for a *concrete programmatic platform*, and that Berlinguer's 'democratic alternative' seemed quite inadequate. Between 1984 and 1987, the PCI refers to a certain 'programmatic alternative', that is, a more competent and pragmatic, less ideological, projection. The 'new course' of Occhetto which was about to be launched, would break with any rhetoric and contain concrete proposals for the most crucial aspect of Italian polity: the *institutional reform*. Also from this perspective, the PCI was in a state of continuous transformation throughout the 1980s. The March 1989 Congress which confirmed the hegemony of those ideas, did not come 'out of the blue'. *Considering the changes in the East and the European unification process, the PCI tended to adopt a new revisionist discourse linked to a new analytical framework concerning the relationship between the public and the private spheres, between the national and international instances.*

These are the three principal reasons why the transformation of the party should be viewed in very close association with the transformation of the First Italian Republic, European integration and the collapse of 'really-existing socialism'. My narrative will be largely chronological, except when specific topics demand it. I will first speculate about the crisis of the party in the 1980s. After that, I will present the overall proposal of the neo-revisionist ruling group. Thus, readers will have the necessary yardstick to compare the analyses of the 18th Congess (March 1989), 19th (March 1990) and 20th (February 1991) that will follow. The study will deal with a wide range of questions posed and the narrative will be accompanied by theoretical speculation drawn from the debates presented. Finally, an account of the conflicting relationship between *new revisionism* and *communist refoundation* notions in Italian politics will be given.

The crisis of the PCI in the 1980s

Despite the massive accumulated public debt, the institutional crisis in which the *pentapartito* was increasingly involved, despite pressures from the European authorities to modernise the state apparatuses, the ruling class and Premier Craxi in particular could, at least, claim the credit for economic growth and for halting inflation. The PCI, however, could claim for itself no success at all. Let us discuss aspects of the party crisis.

a For thirty years (1946-1976) the PCI's electoral force had expanded (table 7). Since the 1979 national election — but some clear signs of decline were already present in the regional and local elections before this — when the policies of *compromesso* had met the mass disapproval of the electorate, the PCI was in a constant electoral decline (table 8).

Table 7   Electoral results of the three main Italian political forces, 1946-1976

		Chamber of Deputies		
	DC	PCI		PSI
1946	35.2	19.0		20.7
1948	48.5		31.0	
1953	40.1	22.6		12.7
1958	42.2	22.7		14.3
1963	38.3	25.3		13.9
1968	39.1	27.0		14.5
1972	38.8	27.2		9.6
1976	38.8	34.4		9.7

Note: In 1948 PCI and PSI candidates were on a joint list; in 1968 PSI and PSDI presented a joint list. Source: PCI archives (collated data supplied by Camillo Danieli)

Table 8   The national elections of 1979, 1983 and 1987

	Chamber of Deputies		
	3 June 1979	26 June 1983	14 June 1987
DC	38.3	32.9	34.3
PCI	30.4	29.9	26.6
PSI	9.8	11.4	14.3
MSI	5.3	6.8	5.9
PRI	3.0	5.1	3.7
PLI	1.9	2.9	3.7
Radicals	3.5	2.2	2.6
PSDI	3.8	4.1	2.9
PdUP	1.4	—	—
DP	—	1.5	1.7
Greens	—	—	2.5
Lega Lombarda	—	—	0.5

Source: PCI archives (data collection supplied by Camillo Danieli)

The only exception was that of the June 1984 European election, when the party succeeded in achieving the famous *sorpasso* (overtaking) of the DC (table 9). The new PCI secretary, Alessandro Natta, saw the electoral result as a 'triumph' of the democratic alternative strategy and asked the government to resign.[1] The successor of Berlinguer committed a serious political mistake, simply because the electoral result was substantially affected by the people's emotional feelings caused by the loss of the popular leader. As a matter of fact, the PCI suffered such a serious defeat in the extensive local election on 12-13 May 1985 that many tart comments against Natta followed immediately afterwards.[2]

Table 9   Results of the European elections, 1979, 1984 and 1989

	1979	1984	1989
DC	36.4	33.0	32.9
PCI	29.6	33.3	27.6
PSI	11.0	11.2	14.8
MSI	5.4	6.5	5.5
PSDI	4.3	3.5	2.7
PLI-PRI	6.2	6.1	4.4
Radicals	3.7	3.4	—
Fed. Greens	—	—	3.9
Rainbow Green	—	—	2.4

The PLI and PRI presented a joint list in 1984 and 1989 but not in 1979, where they gained 3.6 per cent and 2.6 respectively. Source: PCI-International Relations department/P. Fassino archives (data collection supplied by Elletra Palma); *Rinascita*, 41, 23-6-1984, p.2

One can also notice a certain recovery in the 1989 Euro-election vis-à-vis the serious electoral defeat of 1987, but this is a rather misleading comparison. It represents neither a triumph of the Euroleft's line nor a definite recovery at the national level. Italians had always given particular credit to the PCI in the Euro-election, their concern being basically for domestic matters.[3] Hence, if a comparison is to be made, it should be between the 1984 and the 1989 Euro-elections, where the PCI presents a substantial retreat at the latter. On the whole, many not only believed in the irreversible decline of the party, but also predicted a leak of the Communist vote towards the Socialists and assumed that Craxi's dream of overtaking the PCI's lasting electoral advantage on the Left was possible.[4] In this context, the thesis of Walter Veltroni which, immediately after the European election of 1989, defined the PCI's 'victory' as an affirmation of the party's 'new course' and Euroleft identity, proved to be totally mendacious.[5]

b. The consequences of capitalist restructuring was yet another indicator of crisis affecting both the PCI and the trade unions. Leading the new era of capitalist modernisation and flexible production in Italy, the car industry of Giovanni Agnelli and Cesare Romiti (managing director), at the turn of the 1980s, announced redundancies for about 23.000 workers. They had to resort to the *Cassa Integrazione* for three months. On 25 September 1980, Berlinguer came to the gates of FIAT-Mirafiori. The leader of the PCI defended the workers' interests and tried to prevent the lay-offs. However, the entire effort of both the PCI and the trade union failed. At the institutional level, the defeat was far more serious. By promoting a law for the reduction of the *scala mobile*, Prime Minister Craxi succeeded in dividing the trade union movement, isolating the CGIL and pushing the PCI into an unsuccessful referendum in defence of the *scala*.[6] On 9 June 1985, 54.3% of Italians opted against the PCI proposed referendum. Thus, the restructuring of the most advanced sectors of the Italian business classes was in line with the tendencies of international capitalism and began to show their dynamism to the PCI and the working class. The defeat of 1985 was in fact the defeat of the model of industrial relations established by the bargaining power of trade unions in the 1970s after the victory of the *Autunno caldo* and the sharp class conflict of the period. The new era of post-Fordism, flexibility and market-oriented policies had started, and the basis of their operation in Italy was about to stabilise. To complete this picture, the appearance of the autonomous associations *Cobas, Comitati di base* (grass roots unions) in the second half of the 1980s, came to contest the bureaucratic nature of the three big trade unions and thus to accentuate further the crisis of the CGIL and established trade-unionism.[7]

c. A third indicator of crisis is the decline of party membership and militancy, as well as the PCI's ageing membership.[8] This fact is undoubtedly linked to the general crisis of *mass politics* in the 1980s throughout Europe.

Table 10   PCI membership, 1980-1990

Year	Membership	Rates of recruitment
1980	1.751.323	5.20
1981	1.714.052	4.80
1982	1.673.751	4.05
1983	1.635.262	3.89
1984	1.619.940	4.02
1985	1.595.668	3.88
1986	1.551.576	3.31
1987	1.508.140	3.28
1988	1.462.281	2.91
1989	1.421.230	3.35
1990	1.264.790	3.42

Source: P. Fassino archives-official data of the PCI's organisation

This should be seen as a consequence of the crisis of the nation-state, its incapacity to control and promote economic development at the national, regional and local levels, resulting in the incapacity of mass parties to manage and satisfy their own *clientele* through patronage networks in the state controlled enterprises: the economic failure of the state is thus becoming a political failure, because the management crisis of mass parties is no longer able to sychronise policies of consensus with the international development cycle and budgetary constraints. The PCI, although it had never been in office, was increasingly involved in local government and administration duties and controlled a large number of cooperatives and various party enterprises. Therefore, it was impossible to remain unaffected in the face of the process of socio-political restructuring.

The organisational crisis of PCI in the 1980s reflects the crisis of Fordism, the fragmentation of the trade union movement and the fall in workers' militancy in general. These critical processes are manifested through a socio-economic *continuum*, whereby the crisis of mass production is associated with the crisis of mass politics and vice versa. This *continuum* must not be seen in a 'cause-effect' ('the chicken or the egg') relationship, but rather as a dual process acting simultaneously. Thus, both the defeat at FIAT and the referendum over the *scala* should be seen as parts of a dual process of crisis concerning both aspects of opposition: the political (PCI) and the socio-economic (trade union-CGIL). It should be added, however, that that was the mainstream explanation which had been progressively adopted by the PCI itself. Indeed, as early as January 1981, Ingrao remarked that capitalist restructuring affects crucial organisational links between the party and the masses, 'disbands' traditional types of recruitment and disarticulates the social structures.[9] Society becomes more complex and new contradictions emerge. The *mass media* become more and more influential, Ingrao argued, whereas party propaganda and politics was still based on the *comizio* (party political rally) and the grass roots *sezione* (party branch). All this required a further democratic opening up on the party's behalf and de-bureaucratisation of its rigid apparatuses. As far as information technology and the mechanisms of disseminating ideology were concerned, these, Ingrao said, should be gradually transformed by the Left 'from within'.[10] Four years later, Michelangelo Notariani, epitomising the results of a party Conference on organisational issues held in Cascina (4-5-6 June 1984), reached similar conclusions: the crisis of the party is strictly linked with the new process of capitalist modernisation and technological innovation.[11]

d. Since the early 1980s, the party had been experiencing a profound identity crisis, that is, a crisis along political and strategic lines. The crisis was chiefly reflected in the conception of the *alternativa democratica*, the incapacity to provide a concrete alternative project as well as the allies the party should choose in order to govern. To these, the 'centrist' leadership of Natta should rather be added as an additional source of inefficiency. We have earlier attempted to throw some light on this conception by examining the evolutionary/historical side of it. The political/structural aspect as such, however, is equally important.

For an entire decade, the PCI was divided over who its principal ally should be. The whole problem constitutes a real jungle, and any attempt at recording all the views expressed to reach a sound typology, if not impossible, might prove misleading and totally false: there was such a fluidity and a mutability of views in the system of inner-party groupings and alliances throughout the 1980s, that typologies have no validity whatsoever. At this stage, we can refer to some interesting examples and tendencies to show the size of the problem.

Commenting on the 1983 election in an article published in *Rinascita*, Napolitano makes the *alternativa democratica* his central theme and conceives of it as a 'strategic pact' with the PSI. The reformist leader went so far as to say that this was a very favourable conjuncture for the alliance between the two parties of the Left, because the PSI now only had a 18 per cent difference with the PCI, whereas in 1976 the electoral difference was as high as 25 per cent.[12]

In addition, Massimo D'Alema, one of the key figures of the *svolta*, maintained that the battle for the achievement of the *alternativa* would make sense only if it created such conditions that would favour an alternation in power between government and opposition. The future leader of the transformed PCI, the PDS, vehemently defended the Communist identity of the party and excluded any possibility of working together with the reformist PSI.[13]

Ingrao and Magri shared the conceptions already examined and Natta's leadership was uninspiring. All these tensions were reinforced rather than appeased by the interference of the Independent Left elected in Parliament in the PCI lists. Some attempted to theorise the problem, but the typology proposed was rather unsuccessful:[14] the PCI might ally with the DC (first type); the PCI might ally with the PSI (second type); the PCI might claim a *programmatic alternative* and, in this case, whoever signs the 'programmatic declaration of intent' automatically became an ally; in the latter case, however, it is obvious that the declaration might be signed by both, the DC and PSI, or by some factions of them (the case of a *cross-cutting political and government pact*). The other option, certainly, is that no one signs the declaration. This is what indeed happened in the 1980s.

e. The political crisis coupled with the *ideological* crisis of the party. As we have seen, Gorbachev's initiatives deprived the PCI of the monopoly of democratic-Communist ideas among Western Communist Parties. Moreover, the crisis of the Soviet-type Communism was leading to the crisis of Communist ideals in general. The 'Italian Road to Socialism', the enlightened views of the founder of Italian Communism, Antonio Gramsci, had already been elaborated in the 1960s and 1970s and started to lose their attractiveness. In Italy and Europe theoretical production and attention around these issues became rather parochial during the 1980s. And on the top of all this, as we shall assert further on, 'sacred' party figures, such as Palmiro Togliatti, came under fierce criticism not only from the Socialists and other political rivals, but also from prominent Communist philosophers. In September 1989, Occhetto himself addressed a specific message: the party could continue operating in accordance with the *democratic heritage* of Togliatti and Berlinguer, but it had to abandon any revolutionary aspect of their theoretical and political conceptions once and for all.[15]

We can now draw a few conclusions.

In a rapidly changing world, with the triumph of internationalisation in the West, the reluctant pro-market and democratisation policies of Gorbachev in the East, and mass politics being in retreat everywhere, the

PCI found itself in an awkward predicament: Keynesian policies were no longer effective. In the light of this, the PCI could hardly elaborate a concrete economic policy by strategic references to the public sphere: *this meant that the party could no longer claim the state as a major pivot for the construction of a Socialist economy; in other words, the entire mainstream strategic lines of Togliatti and Berlinguer (the conception of 'structural reform' alongside the gradual and democratic transformation of the capitalist relations of production) were now becoming invalid.* In addition, Gorbachev's political and economic reformism, and his sympathy for free market policies, in a country in which the state has always constituted the only lever of growth, progressively distanced the PCI from the idea of adopting any sort of 'statist' economic strategy.

The crisis of Keynesianism thus becomes a unique crisis for the PCI itself, calling into question the party's strategy, identity and policy. Politically isolated, ideologically confused, electorally in decline and with the trade unions in crisis, the party felt the need to project a new image. The modernisation of the Italian economy and the increase in the rates of growth in the 1980s were not negative evolutions *ad hoc*. The real problem was the governing of this modernity, the implementation of institutional reform and the definition of its contents on the basis of social solidarity and justice. The real question for the PCI was how to dictate socialist rules to neo-liberal-led capitalism once in office. So, although the PCI accepted the progressive character of the modernisation process, it did not merely reflect the neo-liberal development trends underway, but attempted to subordinate them to a new revisionist political project. In this context, the claim for a new civilisation assumes a central position. In a revealing interview in *il Manifesto* in July 1989, the party secretary Occhetto stated:

For a long time the party has criticised the notion that the category of modernity is neutral and has argued that such a notion is totally misleading. Nevertheless, I do believe that we must interpret everything that has happened in these years by having the same courage that Gramsci had when he defined Fascism as 'progressive', on the basis that Fascism was adequately dealing with the modernisation problems presented on a world scale. What today we must criticise is that some directions are leading to modernity without civilisation. We must pose the question of civilisation.[16]

So 'what happened in the 1980s' was, in the last analysis, *progressive*; from this perspective, even Fascism was so and Gramsci did not hesitate to recognise it. Nonetheless, the party did not simply mirror the process under way, but it attempted to govern this process on the basis of its programme, which was informed by the Enlightenment ideas of equality, solidarity and social justice. The PCI started to deepen its analyses in these directions only in November 1987 when the new group of the *quarantenni* substantially took over the party leadership.

The formation of the new ruling group

The more sensitive factions in the party that not only realised the global character of the crisis but also tried to provide concrete analytical formulas in order to overcome it, were those of Ingrao and Occhetto. Both groups shared a common explanation of the causes of the troubles although, at the turn of the decade, they came to provide diametrically opposed alternatives. Since I shall thoroughly examine the theses of Ingrao's faction below, priority must be given to the process of formation of the new ruling group of the *quarantenni* and their conceptions. It is necessary to examine the ideas of Occhetto's majority and the way in which they have hegemonised the party. Thus, we shall be introduced to the meanings implied by formulations such as 'nuovo corso' and 'riformismo forte'.

The serious electoral defeat of June 1987 signalled the beginning of the PCI's transformation and the dominance of the new ruling group of the *quarantenni*. Natta, who appointed Occhetto as deputy party secretary — a post which was not provided for in the statute of the PCI — had previously sent in his resignation but it had been promptly rejected by the party. The nomination of Occhetto as deputy was warmly approved by Ingrao's left and the centrist *berlingueriani* (Aldo Tortorella, Gavino Angius et al.), whereas it encountered the opposition of the *miglioristi* of Napolitano, Lama and Macaluso. Thus, the inner-party alliance between the right and the centre which had emerged victorious from the 1986 Congress, was subverted.[17] With some interruptions and unimportant intra-party mobility, this new balance of forces which emerged around the grouping of Occhetto, would last up until November 1989, when Occhetto announced the change of the party's name and symbols.

At the Central Committee of July 28, 1987, Natta attempted to give a more convincing explanation of the party's dramatic electoral defeat than the one given in the previous CC which took place soon after the election. He endeavoured to further elaborate the strategy of the *alternativa* and highlight possibilities for overcoming the social and political crisis of the country.[18] According to Natta, the most important trends which emerged after the election were the following: **a.** The DC remained the largest party, though its political centrality had been progressively eroded since 1976; **b**. A new balance of forces had been created on the Left; the PSI, PSDI and the Radicals together now totalled 20 per cent of the vote; **c**. A further fragmentation of the political system which embraced the two big parties (the DC and the PCI) — in terms of the representation crisis — was taking place and was being reinforced by the proliferation of minor parties — there were now 10 in the Parliament — which enjoyed less than 4 per cent of the vote; **d**. The exhaustion of extreme versions of the *conventio ad èxcludendum* principle vis-à-vis the PCI.

The contradictions of the ruling coalition, Natta said, concern 'the different views expressed over the process of modernisation', so there are fundamental programmatic differences especially between the DC and the PSI.[19] Therefore, the exhaustion of the *pentapartito* must be seen in conjunction with the new phase of modernity which created political conditions such that the party could talk about a 'new political phase' in the history of the Republic. The PCI secretary went on to argue that, 'the internationalisation of the economy and the challenge of modernisation no longer permit a country like Italy to coexist with backwardness, mass unemployment and such a deterioration of the state'.[20]

In this context, the strategy of the *alternativa*, and despite its conspicuous difficulties following the electoral defeat, acquired another *political meaning*: it would operate more carefully on the basis of the crisis of *the pentapartito*. Consequently, the party's project should be the promotion of a concrete programme able to aggregate and absorb forces dissociating from the ruling coalition. In the words of Natta:

> In Italy and the world, in order to confront the problems of our era, there is the need to work for a broad perspective on the Left which is based not only on its traditional components, but also on new ones which stem from the new contradictions, and also other forces of progress, either lay and/or catholic. It is the convergence of these forces along with a coherent programme for the renewal of the country, upon which the success of the democratic alternative depends.[21]

At the end of his speech, the PCI secretary noted that the party needed to reinforce its mass character and activities and proceeded by openly admitting the serious crisis the party was going through as well as the exhaustion of its 'Communist diversity':

> The concept of our 'diversity' which could be perceived as a sort of sectarian separation towards other political forces, is gradually being exhausted. The secular character of the party was developed in terms of the relationship and solidarity with other political forces of the Left and

> with various societal cultures which are reflected in the party [...]. But it is better to say that we did not succeed in acquiring new values, programmes and political culture for our party, a party which aims at being a modern democratic and reformist force while not dissipating its combativeness, its ties with the masses, its unitary physiognomy.[22]

Natta was certainly very cautious in going beyond certain limits of the party tradition. He defended the welfare state and argued for an increase in wages. He opposed curtailment of public spending and held that the fiscal crisis could be solved via 'the qualified modification of the expenditure apparatus and a modernisation of the omnivorous state machine'. Nevertheless, concrete proposals regarding the constitutional question as a whole were virtually absent.

Natta's motion was contested by Ingrao's left, and the pro-Soviet wing of Cossutta, whereas six *miglioristi* abstained from the vote. Luciana Castellina argued that the PCI secretary failed to make any particular progress in diagnosing the new situation as a whole and pointed out that the party's strategic conceptions were oscillating between Berlinguer's views and the Florence Congress.[23] Ingrao, in the characteristic spirit of his theses, emphasised the incapacity of the centrist ruling group to bring the PCI out of the crisis, and insisted that the party concentrate on two parallel processes opened up by the modernisation of the economy. The first, Ingrao said, was the new form of hegemony brought about by the concentration of big capital; the second, the new antagonistic culture arising out from the critical processes of societal and political fragmentation. According to Ingrao, Natta made no reference to these crucial points, and therefore, he failed to draw the proper conclusion. The extra-reformist Luigi Colajanni, remarked that declaring the crisis of the DC and *pentapartito* to be apparent while admitting the strategic crisis of the *alternativa* after the June electoral collapse, was a profound contradiction that rather led to political confusion and disarray.

Natta and the old centrist group around Tortorella — the *berlingueriani* — failed to provide a balanced project from which tangible results could be expected with regard to the party's renewal and institutional reform. It rather seemed that the alternative to the blocked political system was dependent upon changes in the party's culture and leadership. The great merit of *berlingueriani* was the understanding they showed regarding this reality and that they did not hamper the rise of the *quarantenni* into the leading party positions. On the contrary, they substantially backed them.

The dynamics of the ideas borne by the neo-revisionist ruling group was crystallised by Occhetto in his speech in the party's CC of November 1987.[24] From that date on, the PCI accomplished a major step in its radical renewal by starting to acquire a coherent ideological and political agenda.

Occhetto maintained that neo-liberalism was an *objective* economic policy process which undermined Social Democratic corporatism and statism.[25] The PCI deputy secretary pointed out that the crisis of the ruling coalition reflected its incapacity to respond to capitalist restructuring. This conception began forcefully to correct the party's previous thesis according to which the *pentapartito*'s policies conformed with neo-liberal economics (a position contained in the document of the 17th Congress of Florence). However, he said that the PCI must go even beyond this interpretation. *The proposal of the party did not merely concern a framework to fit the dilemma of a 'more' or 'less' state, but the elaboration of a programmatic alternative reflecting societal, political and institutional functionings.* Contrary to neo-liberals who view market and state as two contrasting entities — Alfredo Reichlin argued in a seminar held in *Botteghe Oscure* in January 1988 — the real problem for the Left was how to reconcile these two social and institutional realities.[26] Therefore, the need was the shaping of a new state and welfarism through a harmonisation process that could be achieved by the democratic control of economic modernisation and a balanced separation between political parties and the administration. It was in this precise sense that a *new phase in Italian politics was opening.* The Left could and should unblock the forty-year long DC-based political system on these grounds. The failure of Craxi's *governability* stemmed from the fact that it did not succeed in implementing those necessary reforms which would have combined institutional renewal, economic growth and social welfare.[27]

In order to interfere within that peculiar and changing institutional context, Occhetto was convinced that the PCI's strategy should distance itself from any notion of Togliatti's 'progressive democracy' and Berlinguer's 'historic compromise', emphasise the centrality of *institutional reforms* and see them as the original prerequisite for the success of the programmatic alternative.[28] After all, both Togliatti and Berlinguer were not freed from a consociational notion of politics. Reichlin also argued that the entire Communist interpretation pattern put forward by Togliatti according to which the working class gains hegemony and completes the bourgeois revolution at the national level, was inadequate today. Therefore, 'the problem is to elaborate a new interpretation of the Italian situation, under the conditions of a process which does not lead to *proletarizzazione* but to *imborghesimento* (diffusion of property or individualistic way of thinking), while new conflicts and sharp contradictions are accumulating [...]. The old *historic bloc* of the Left does not exist anymore' (my emphasis).[29]

In this way, Togliatti's and Berlinguer's political strategies were under attack, and also Gramsci's concept of 'historic bloc'. Capitalist democracy at the national level was no longer the privileged terrain on which Communists could achieve and promote the integration of the masses into the management of the national community in order to apply, once in power, their amply democratic Socialist project. A new linkage between economic and political instances, between political and economic reforms, needed to be envisaged.

This is an appropriate point to draw a parallel between the Labour Party and the PCI concerning the topic in question. At the time the PCI was questioning its own Keynesianism, the Labour Party in Britain, despite the victory of the capitalist restructuring process symbolised by the defeat of the miners' strike in 1984-85, was to preserve the party's constitutional commitment to nationalisation up until 1995 (the famous *clause four* issue). Tony Blair, the new Labour leader, having the overwhelming backing of the party machine, abolished the commitment introduced in 1918.[30] In that qualified context, the *Communist* PCI was far more sensitive to contemporary structural changes and presented more advanced neo-revisionist speculation than British Social Democracy did in the 1980s and even in the early 1990s.

We can now pose the problem, otherwise very similar to the British condition, of the further concretisation/qualification of the *alternativa democratica*, which was proposed by the new ruling group. In point of fact, the whole question was how to prepare the conditions which would enable the achievement of a *democrazia dell'alternativa* (democratic alternation). Therefore, apart from a specific set of reforms which were included in the document on institutional reform presented in March 1988,[31] the abolition of proportional representation appeared an equally crucial point. It would eliminate the fragmentation of the political system and create the stable conditions needed for the new type of democracy. The PCI opted for a French style single member first-past-the-post in two rounds majority system (*doppio turno*) and argued that a *historical discontinuity*, concerning the entire Italian polity, was on the agenda: another form of democracy was required to keep pace with the new global and national realities. Admittedly, the PCI was in crisis, but so was the DC's regime itself: 'If God is dead, if the King is naked, this is equally valid for everybody, not only for the PCI,' Occhetto stated dramatically in a Conference organised by the 'Left Clubs' and the Socialist-Liberal review *Micromega* of Paolo Flores D'Arcais and Giorgio Ruffolo.[32]

Occhetto officially launched the line of 'nuovo corso' just eighteen days before being nominated party secretary (21-6-1988). He did so by way of referring to the category of modernity. He argued:

> I would like to draw an improper parallel with the situation faced by the PSI in 1976. And it is improper because the electoral force of the parties are absolutely different; a bit less than 10 per cent for the Socialists in 1976, much more than 20 per cent for the PCI today. But there is an analogy: we also find ourselves under conditions which force us to delineate a *new course, a new Communist Party* able to design a perspective within an articulated system of the Left [...]. Certainly, we should be moving within modernity knowing, however, that 'modern' is not what is the 'most recent' thing, but the most civilised one.[33]

We can now convincingly advance two points:
i The conceptualisation of 'nuovo corso' along the lines of *modernity* came to emphasise a privileged relationship with the PSI, although other social and political forces, such as lay catholics, were not excluded.
ii What one can call *neo-liberal modernity*, as opposed to the *Keynesian* one, was not seen by the new PCI as a quantitative *continuum* of growth, inasmuch as *modernity* is not identical with *capitalist modernisation:* 'modern' is not what is the 'most recent' thing, but the 'most civilised one'. Both points will be further clarified below.

The discussion between Occhetto and Mussi was positively received by prominent party intellectuals. To Biagio De Giovanni and Mario Tronti the 'language used by Occhetto' was particularly positive, but the former went further by saying that 'talking about a *"nuovo partito comunista"* (new Communist Party) is different from talking about a *"nuovo partito nuovo"* (new new party)', wanting thus to show the necessity of going beyond the Togliattian conception of *partito nuovo*.[34] Giuseppe Vacca pointed out that Occhetto's ideas were very clear because they were not the result of inner-party lobbying and mediation. Nicola Badaloni made a 'soft' criticism by saying that 'more attention should have been paid by Occhetto in fighting modern individualism and egoism'.[35]

At this point, it is worth noting that the PSI kept opposing the PCI. Some months before Occhetto's interview, by taking advantage of the rehabilitation of Nikolai Bukharin by Gorbachev, the Socialist daily *Avanti!* published an unsigned article where a PCI document of 1938 appeared to praise Stalin.[36] The attempt was to equate Togliatti with Stalin, to humiliate the former and, in general, to initiate a concerted attack against the post-war history of the PCI. Officially, the Communists did not give way to these challenges and, at this stage, defended Togliatti who, in the words of Natta, 'was one of the founding fathers of the Republican Constitution'.[37] However, as we have seen, the fundamental strategic notions of Togliatti were being attacked by the new ruling group of the party. In fact, the *nuovo corso* was launched by way of severely contesting the very nature of Togliatti's notion of mass politics and structural reform. Thus, one can recognise a certain 'homologation' of the PCI to the PSI which, besides, was advancing electorally.

On 20 June 1988 Occhetto was again the protagonist in the CC of the PCI. After praising Natta for his 'moral lesson', for he had given the party leadership so humbly to the new generation,[38] Occhetto started his talk by pointing out the party's political isolation and serious crisis. This situation was chiefly due to two basic processes:

> The first is the tendency Western Communist Parties present towards decline, because of their incapacity to define their role in that changing society [...]. The second — and this is a great historical task of the PCI and its ruling group — concerns our ability to originally identify ourselves vis-à-vis today's novelties, to produce ideas and new proposals as a party which is deeply rooted in Italian society.[39]

Undoubtedly, this second point concerns the adaptability and new function the PCI had to acquire in order to face existing challenges. The more the party delayed renewing and adjusting itself to the new economic and political conditions, the more it would jeopardise its mass base and the capacity it had to condition the policy process at the local and national levels. To define precisely 'our' strategic options, Occhetto said, the party should promote a *programmatic convention* — an option already indicated in the theses of the 17th Congress — and prepare another Congress: the common thread of both advances had to be *the definition of a new political course for the PCI as a whole.*

In that CC, Occhetto did not present a complete platform of the PCI's *new course.* Nevertheless, he gave some important indications on the way which this conception should be perceived, clarifying some points made at the above-mentioned interview in *L'Unità* with Fabio Mussi. The PCI had to elaborate such a 'programmatic alternative' that would enable the 'conquest of the centre of the political system by the party and the Left'; this is a 'decisive political question'.[40] In this context, Occhetto proceeded, the strategy of the *alternativa* points to *a different hypothesis in governing the present phase of capitalist development, therefore, it requires the advance of a new relationship between the market and the state.* The crisis of the state, the conflictual nature of the *pentapartito* and the internationalisation of the Italian economy were explicitly interwoven processes. Inasmuch as Communist ideals were undergoing a profound crisis, an overall break with the past, both politico-ideological and organisational (e.g. abolition of 'democratic centralism'), was required to lead the party out of the present crisis.[41]

With three votes against and five abstentions, Occhetto was elected secretary of the PCI on 21 June 1988.[42] Eugenio Scalfari had already pointed out in his daily *La Repubblica*, that 'although Occhetto may not have had any charisma until now, he enjoys a bright political intelligence that distinguishes him from any other rival within his party'.[43]

A month later, in his Report to the CC in 19 July, the new secretary indicated the fundamental lines the party had to follow in order to move successfully towards its 18th Congress. In essence, the Report constituted the first draft for further discussion and does not present any substantial difference with the main themes raised in his Report to the CC four months later (26-11-1988), the date the Congressional theses were drafted. Therefore, we can deal with some crucial party documents of that period as a whole, instead of presenting them in strict chronological order.

Governing the polity crisis: the *new revisionism* of the 18th Congress (March 1989)

Backed by the left of Ingrao and welcomed by the centrist *berlingueriani*, the only opposition being that around the *miglioristi* and Cossutta's pro-Soviet faction, the new leading group acted as a catalyst. To establish its hegemony and qualify its neo-revisionism, Occhetto's majority immediately asked for a new Congress. There was a wide consensus on a number of issues. The institutional impasse of the *pentapartito* further reinforced the thesis that a concrete programmatic alternative solution did exist. The crisis of the Eastern bloc seemed to be irreversible; no one could think in terms of a bi-polar world anymore. None the less, at the moment when the party should have been strong in order to present itself as the only viable alternative, it proved to be equally vulnerable both politically and ideologically. Both capitalist restructuring and the crisis of the Eastern regimes had seriously affected its *mass* character and eroded its Communist ideology. In a revealing formulation during his speech at the 18th Congress, Massimo D'Alema said that: 'what initiated the crisis of really-existing socialism and the welfare state, were not a certain social radicalism or new social movements but, on the contrary, the impetuous development of modern capitalism in the wake of enormous material pressures.'[44]

In such a context, the notion of *nuovo corso* needed to be infused with that of *riformismo forte*, strong reformism. As Occhetto pointed out:

> Strong reformism is a project, a programme [...]. We have already indicated some examples of reform which do not simply cope with the damage caused by conservative policies. I am referring to reforms regarding the position of women; the different view which should be taken vis-à-vis the question of growth; the reduction of the working week and reform of production methods [...]. In short, work, environment and women as the fulcrum of a project which would lead to a qualitative transformation of industrial growth.[45]

And again:

> The entire Italian Left must renew itself [...]. The meaning of strong reformism is that it goes beyond constraints imposed by specific circumstances and it rather commits itself to changing the circumstances, because it is not happy with small changes [...]. The concept of strong reformism implies the real intention of positively guiding the great technological, cultural and economic dynamics expressed by society; asserting a new will for reform and pledging development through justice, democracy and security.[46]

Riformismo forte remained a highly vague concept. It is no accident that it was not further developed and came to be quickly forgotten in the course of 1989. Nevertheless, it played an important *political* role during the period in question, that is, in between Autumn 1988 and Summer 1989.

'New course' and 'strong reformism' came to be seen as two complementary political and ideological moments of the same agenda aiming at the radical renewal of the PCI and the Italian Left as a whole in order to face the consequences of capitalist restructuring, the decay of 'really-existing socialism' and the crisis of the *pentapartito*. Even more importantly, the project was deeply pro-European: any perspective of an alternative to the *pentapartito*'s system of power, Occhetto said in his speech at the party's festival of *L'Unità* in Florence (7-9-1988), must be linked to a European perspective.[47]

The leader of the PCI had in mind the Socialist International. Berlinguer was no longer the mastermind of Eurocommunism, but a 'great *maestro*' of the European Left alongside Olof Palme and Willy Brandt.[48] The last PCI leader who pursued and ended, from a Leftist standpoint, the notion of *compromesso* as the party's principal strategy since the war, Enrico Berlinguer, was now praised for his reformist and evolutionistic views, such as his thesis on the 'universal value of democracy', or his statement that 'democracy is not only a means towards Socialism, but an end state *in itself*.[49] At any rate, the principal thesis elaborated at the 18th Congress according to which 'democracy is not merely *a road* to Socialism but *the road* to Socialism',[50] drew on specific aspects of Berlinguer's notion of socialism. Characteristically, Occhetto would say that party members have always chosen to be Communists alongside the principles of the French Revolution: justice, equality, solidarity and liberty.[51] Elsewhere, the new leader said that 'the PCI is a son of the French revolution of 1789'.[52] I would argue, therefore, that all the themes raised at the 18th Congress of the party and beyond do not regard a mere discontinuity with the past, but apply to the entire question of how to legitimise in full the reformist tradition of the party against the revolutionary one: *how to rehabilitate the former while delegitimising the latter*. The following statement made by Napolitano during his speech at the party's 18th Congress, speaks for itself:

> We cannot speak of a generic or undifferentiated Communist identity. Particular personal elements of our unique Communist Party must be distinguished. Today [...], when we are talking about reformism and challenge other political forces [...], we are not really belated in, or alienated from, this reformism, *but we are finally bringing to light the fundamental part of our historical experience, by giving it a coherent status* (our emphasis).[53]

Occhetto himself was to deal with the question continuity/discontinuity in a different manner. By writing a characteristic article in the party's daily *L'Unità*, he dissipated any doubt:[54] rejecting any *tout court* demonisation of the past, Occhetto praised the reformist ideas of Togliatti and Berlinguer and concluded that the party problems were not the shadows of Stalinism but the understanding of the new socio-economic contradictions. *Our thesis, therefore, is that the PCI of Occhetto achieved a clear-cut break with the past only with regard to the Communist/revolutionary aspect of the party tradition, not with the reformist/revisionist one. In other words, the rupture with the past concerns the 'questione comunista' alone.*[55]

We can now pass on to discuss the major issues raised at the Congress. We have pointed out that a major change established by November 1987 and thereafter was that the *pentapartito*'s system of power was becoming exhausted. This basically meant that the DC-PSI coalition government, as it represented an institutional decay, was unable to deal with the requirements of institutional reform. Thus, the PCI corrected the false thesis presented at the 17th Congress in Florence where it accepted the view that the DC of De Mita and the PSI of Craxi were implementing pro-reformist policies. In an indicative passage of his speech at the 18th Congress, Occhetto argued:

> Whilst the deadline of the single market is approaching — as Delors stressed recently — various resistances increase. For Italy, the European imperative is a reality, but the government forces, with a relevant dose of irresponsibility, are leading the country towards the 1992 appointment in a grave and inadequate condition: the public debt, the fiscal crisis, the degradation of services and the education system, the inefficiency and corruption of the state machine, the deterioration of the South. On these points, we urge the country and the government forces [...]. Posing the basis for an alternative policy [...] is the first task of the Italian Left that really wants to be a European Left.[56]

And in his concluding remarks at the closure of the Congress:

> The DC system of power constitutes a diaphram between demands emerging from society and the political system. It is this very system of power that produces more and more confused and static coalitions which debilitate the state and halt economic progress; it is this system of power that our proposal of alternative wants to transcend.[57]

By fully espousing this thesis, the PCI came to the understanding that the crisis of the *pentapartito's* management of power was irreversible. The chief contradiction of the Italian polity lay between the need for institutional renewal and the conservative resistance of the DC-PSI government axis. In point of fact, anyone who was an expression of 'the old consociational system' was bound to fail. As Occhetto put it: 'Overall, we declare that the pentapartito represents the crisis of the old political system [...]. *In the present situation, it is not groundless to be afraid of a real bankruptcy of the state itself.*' (Emphasis mine.)[58]

Understanding the depth and the meaning of this point is of paramount importance. In point of fact, the PCI came to declare the need for a new political order, based on different democratic principles. *The new ruling group had indeed outlined the contents of a Second Republic, without literally referring to it.* However, vis-à-vis the past, there was an important difference. The methodological horizon of the *autonomy of the polity instance* needs to be amply established and assume a strategic political character. D'Alema stated categorically that 'changing the relations of production first and trying to find out possibilities of guiding the development afterwards, is no longer our guiding thread. This is the new context in which we raise the question of the democratic alternative'.[59]

As we saw earlier, while examining the theses of the party on the fiscal crisis of the state, Fassino opted for the same position. In fact, all the members of the new ruling group espoused the *absolute autonomy of the political*. We thus arrive at the most crucial point of the *nuovo corso*. The crux of the matter for the PCI was to propose such a project which, on the one hand, would advance the intitutional reform required while, on the other, enabling citizens to achieve a real betterment of their social and civil conditions.

The PCI's *nuovo corso* enjoyed the full support of Ingrao. It was fiercely opposed by the pro-Soviet group of Cossutta: 'there is a genetic mutation in the PCI',Cossutta argued; 'some of our leaders', he continued, 'maintain that our party model must be like that of the American Democratic Party'.[60] This anti-capitalist party faction, which presented its own platform in the run-up to the Congress,[61] openly accused the new PCI of being transformed into a liberal party abandoning revolutionary and Marxist traditions forever. We shall comment later on the theses of this faction; for the time being, it is worth mentioning that Cossutta's group, by presenting its own platform, anticipated the future.

Why did Ingrao give his full support to the *nuovo corso* of the *quarantenni*? Did he fail to realise the demise of the *questione comunista* through their neo-revisionist discourse? These are thorny questions because, as we shall see later on, the framework within which Occhetto justified his proposal to change the party's name and symbols does not differ much from that of the *nuovo corso*. On the contrary, after a series of dramatic events that took place between April and November 1989 — the students' revolt in Tienanmen square in Beijing, the change of the name of the Hungarian Communist party and, finally, the fall of the Berlin wall — one would have to expect wholehearted support by Ingrao of the leading group's platform in favour of the complete transformation of the party. Thus, understandably enough, the ex-Communist philosopher Lucio Colletti had difficulty in explaining this bizarre alliance between 'the neo-Berlinguerian centre of the party [the *quarantenni*] and the anti-system Left of Ingrao'.[62]

We shall raise seven particular issues that constituted the core changes established by the Congress and around which the debate was extended from November 1988 onwards. These points are: political ideology, the question of economic democracy, new social subjects, party's alliance policy, the formation of a shadow cabinet, the new party form and the issue concerning the party's name. In this context, we shall attempt to provide a reasonable explanation regarding the support given by Ingrao to the *quarantenni*.

The thesis I shall defend is that Ingrao made a similar mistake to that of Stephen Hellman in his analysis of the strategy of the PCI. The prominent Italianist working in Canada saw in the pro-Communist/libertarian PCI statement 'from each according to his ability, to each according to his needs' included in the Congressional Theses — a famous phrase of Marx in his *Critique of the Gotha Programme* (1875) — the apex of PCI's Communism and commented: 'The course of the 1980s shows that by the 1989 18th Congress, the PCI had probably gone as far as it could as a Communist Party.'[63]

In short, my argument is that Ingrao gave his consensus to the 'new course' not because of the pro-capitalist elements it comprised, but because of the conception of liberation involved in the analyses of Occhetto regarding inner-party democracy, gender and environmental issues, all of which had been central themes for Ingrao's Left since the 1960s. For the purposes of exposition, I shall avoid at this stage examining either the linkage between the European and national contents of the *nuovo corso* or the question of the trade unions, since they will be brought into context when analysing the evolution of the debate over Occhetto's post-Communist proposal for the party's overall transformation.

Political ideology

The importance of the ideological discourse to which, implicitly or explicitly, the conception of the 'new course' referred, does not only involve the adoption of the principles of the French revolution, but also, and perhaps even more significantly, it constitutes a *real revision of the concept of hegemony* as derived from the tradition of Gramsci and Togliatti: this is the key point to an understanding of why the 'new course' started mainly with a fierce criticism of Togliatti. In fact, the concept was prone to two diametrically opposed interpretations.

The first exegesis, which had Norberto Bobbio as its most prestigious supporter, maintained that Gramsci elaborated a revisionist and reformist theoretical thesis, according to which the proletariat, prior to achieving political power, must enjoy the broad consensus of the masses. This, in turn, implied that a Communist Party needs, for example, 80 per cent of the people's vote in order to create the national unity necessary for a Left government.[64] It was on this basis that Bobbio rebuked the PCI for the explicitly reformist assumptions of the *compromesso storico*, as a strategy to achieve the widest popular consensus.

The second interpretation, which was advanced by neo-Marxists such as Perry Anderson, attempts a revolutionary reading of Gramsci's remarks concerning the point at issue. When Gramsci suggested that the working class should have an ideological and political hegemony *before* achieving political power, he simply referred to the hegemony the proletariat must have within the ensemble of dominated classes, not over the capitalist social formation in general. Therefore, the question of national consensus is not posed *before* the conquest of class power. At this stage, the requirement is the hegemony of the proletariat within the boundaries of the dominated classes.[65]

This is not the place to speculate on whether or not the former interpretation implies a Social Democratic/reformist point of view and the second a Communist/revolutionary one. What should be stressed, however, is that both contained in common a stable reference point: the idea of the nation-state as the centre of revolutionary and/or reformist actions. The 'new course' of PCI was unable to fully adopt either of the two interpretations for two main reasons: firstly, the crisis of 'actually-existing socialism' bearing in itself the crisis of Communist revolutionary ideas; secondly, the process of the internationalisation which undermined the ability of the nation-state to act as organiser of hegemony. Taking into account such constraints, Occhetto's 'new course' attempted to establish a conception of hegemony that would have given the party the possibility of going beyond either traditional interpretation. As we saw earlier, one of the first demands put forward was for a functional democracy of *alternanza* and the pre-condition for it was the change of the pure proportional electoral system while insisting on concrete programmatic platforms. In this context, the party began acquiring not merely a Social Democratic identity — although this might imply a mass notion of politics — but a *newly revisionist* one alongside the parties of the Socialist International.

Economic democracy

If hegemony no longer hails from the factory's dominant forces — as Gramsci once claimed — [66] or if the state has serious difficulties in organising financial and political hegemony at the national level, then the problem for the Left becomes the question as to *what form of regulation of the relations of production should be adopted*, a fact which also points to 'the different culture the enterprise should acquire'.[67] In fact, Occhetto appealed to both enterpreneurs and workers on the basis that the latter can participate in the management of company by *stakeholding methods*.[68]

This was seen as a solid foundation upon which a new social contract, replacing the Keynesian-corporatist one, could be built. In an essay written probably by the end of 1989 for the pro-Soviet journal *World Marxist Review*, D'Alema expressed similar thoughts: 'In order to broaden and enhance labour participation in running production with a view to *changing the character of work*, it is necessary to cut back working hours and enable people to engage in voluntary activities, which have an increasing appeal for young men and women...'[69]

These positions stem directly from the programme of the German SPD, approved at its December 1989 Congress.[70] There is one specific criticism which applies to these positions: no PCI document or politician or intellectual of the 'new course' explained *how* stakeholding methods give labourers the possibility of *controlling the means of production as well as the end product which is socially produced*. There is no clarification whatsoever as to how the declared thesis of 'changing the character of work' differs or constitutes an alternative to post-Fordism, flexible productive schemes and voluntary work for unemployed people.[71] The document of the pro-Soviet Cossutta, presented by his faction in the run-up to the Congress, equally failed to give a holistic answer to the aforementioned questions, though rightly warning that 'economic democracy has nothing to do with the holding of enterprise shares on behalf of workers' (the model of 'popular capitalism').[72]

Gender, environment, peace

Governing the new phase of modernity, Occhetto said in his speech at the 18th Congress, means attributing primary importance to the environment, women and security issues.[73] In this context, the fundamental principle was that of 'non-violence between states, individuals, and between human beings and nature'.[74] Environmentalists, the PCI argued, 'launched a real challenge to the Left: will the Left be able to govern today's acute contradictions and guide our complex societies towards a more mature form of civilisation? The ecological restructuring of the economy is one of the most fundamental issues that an alternative Left has to cope with'.[75]

The crisis of heavy industry, the corresponding growth of the service and finance sectors, the increase in dual income families, casualisation and unemployment blur old class and male-dominated categories. In fact, the material basis for the integration of women into the labour market has been laid. An equal representation of sexes in the institutions, however, does not correspond to this real process, a fact which would have helped the overcoming of the antediluvian male culture according to which men are destined for productive labour and women for reproduction (childcare, housework etc.). Nevertheless, these ideological principles still represent the culture of emancipation and liberation of women that had already been established by the movements of 1968-69. Today's societal fragmentation and gender segregation points to a new feminist culture, that of 'sexual difference'.[76] This concept, Claudia Mancina argued, 'does not identify a united historical movement.' Nevertheless, it claims that women express their own new societal condition by way of exclusively referring to themselves.[77]

We shall bring out all the implications that the concept of 'sexual difference' entails while examining the reasons the PCI feminists split and chose different inner-party alignments after Occhetto's ultimate proposal for the transformation of the party in November 1989. What we would like to stress at this stage is the way Ingrao perceived these issues through the discourse of Occhetto and the *quarantenni*. In fact, the leftist leader of the PCI was impressed by the new ruling party generation, as their analyses emphasised the crisis of Keynesianism and the libertarian horizon the new phase of internationalisation was opening up. Ingrao had his own words for translating the 'pro-movementist' discourse of Occhetto and so giving it his consensus:

> Occhetto said that there is no red if it is not green. Yes, I do believe in a convergence, I think the 'green-red' alliance is a fundamental objective [...]. The environmental crisis has a name and a surname. Occhetto has indicated that this crisis is located in the devastating acceleration of a certain industrial model [...] which has been dictated by the general productive paradigm [...]. On the other hand, the culture of the 'sexual difference' is the most radical critique of typical equality and juridical formalism.[78]

Alliance policy

The *quarantenni* made titanic efforts to mobilise the widest possible field of social and political forces for their proclaimed 'new course' project. They addressed a friendly discourse to the Liberal-Socialist *sinistra dei club* of Paolo Flores d'Arcais, they attempted to appeal to the so-called *sinistra sommersa* (the 'submerged Left'), they reinvigorated the relationship with the Independent Left through the formation of a *shadow cabinet* that we shall examine below, and appealed to lay Catholics and other social strata. The DC, the PCI's Congressional theses pointed out, ceased to represent the entire Catholic world. Besides, as we have seen, the party was conscious not only of its own crisis, but also of the crisis of the institutional system in general and the ruling coalition in particular. The analysis further established the thesis already advanced by Fassino in 1986, that capitalist restructuring creates such political conditions that it urges all social and political subjects to align themselves according to the cleavage 'progress/conservatism': 'The differences between Left and Right, conservatism and progress are destined to cut across the present political and cultural alignments and might produce new blocs, new majoritarian and minoritarian alliances.'[79]

Nevertheless, the major political forces, the DC and the PSI, were still there, in office. After so many profound changes, the PCI's 'new course' should have abandoned any sort of erstwhile ambiguity, chosen a stable political ally and concentrated upon building a realistic alliance. Clearing up this difficulty would have given the Italian Communists credibility and political consistency. In order to achieve its strategy of *riformismo forte*, the PCI's *nuovo corso* adopted the contentious line of a privileged alliance with the PSI of Craxi.[80]

Certainly, as we have seen, many in the PCI and the broad Italian Left, for different reasons, either did not share this thesis, or embraced it even more warmly, giving the impression of a subordinate attitude (e.g. the *miglioristi* of Napolitano). However, this is something that goes beyond the purpose of this chapter.[81] We should not fail to mention, however, the position of Massino D'Alema, then editor of the party's daily, *L'Unità*, who, despite being a key supporter of the 'new course', was against Craxi's PSI.[82]

In short, the contradiction of the PCI thesis over the alliance question remained virtually unresolved. The claim of 'reconciliation of the Italian Left in order to build a new political order' was leaving out the DC. Nevertheless, *the transition to another constitutional and political order was claimed to be working together with the PSI, a party of the old regime.*

The shadow cabinet

As we have seen, the idea of setting up a shadow cabinet had been a consistent claim of Occhetto since March 1986. It was one of the themes that the 17th Congress had failed to resolve. We need to pay attention to this issue, because it will only be marginally raised below.

The notion of a 'shadow cabinet' can be traced back to 19th century Britain, when a 'Loyal Opposition' had become a recognised and established part of Britain's unwritten constitution. The rationale was that the British parliamentary system should always be functional by having a democratic alternative in opposition to government.

Admittedly, the idea the PCI put forward drew on the British pattern of majoritarian political rule. At the political-theoretical level, the paradigm was examined by Arend Lijphart, a Dutch political scientist working in the USA and, in Italy, by various political scientists and constitutional lawyers such as Gianfranco Pasquino and Augusto Barbera.[83] Firstly, we shall outline the whole question of 'shadow cabinet' in the theoretical and historical contexts by which it is conditioned. Secondly, we will refer to the reasoning through which the PCI and Occhetto attempted to present it. The aim is to demonstrate that the very structure of the First Republic was alien to the political conditions for which the PCI strived; that is to say, the introduction of innovation by the party did not change the relationship of forces between government (the *pentapartito*) and opposition (the PCI).

Lijphart, having chiefly in mind the British political system, presented some specific elements that majoritarian parliamentary rule consists of:[84] Concentration of executive power in the Cabinet and Cabinet dominance vis-à-vis Parliament; asymmetric bicameralism or near unicameralism, since no substantial power is concentrated in the House of Lords;[85] a two-party system (e.g. the Conservative/Labour opposition in Britain); a one-dimensional party system (the principal axis of conflict consists of disagreements over economic and social policy arrangements, rather than regional, ethnic and religious differences); a majoritarian electoral system (first-past-the-post); a unitary and centralised government, that is, lack of federalist structures; an unwritten constitution and parliamentary sovereignty (e.g. in Britain there is no single written document that specifies the composition and powers of the political instance nor of the rights of citizens. The courts do not have the power of judicial review and the Parliament is the ultimate authority); an exclusively representative democracy, that is, no room for any element of direct democracy exists (e.g. referendum).

In contrast to the Westminster model of majoritarian political rule, Lijphart presented the *consensus-consociative* model which consists of the following distinct elements:[86] Executive power-sharing and formation of grand coalitions; a separation of powers, formal and informal (this makes both the executive and the legislature more independent, and their relationship is much more balanced than the cabinet-parliament relations in Britain, in which the cabinet is clearly dominant); balanced bicameralism (the upper house has to be elected on a different basis from the lower house and, ideally, it must have as much power as the lower house); a multiparty system and proportional representation; a multidimensional party system, that is, instead of one cleavage that dominates political affairs, there are many others such as religious, linguistic, territorial and ethnic; territorial and non-territorial federalism and decentralisation; a written constitution and minority veto.

Pasquino, while accepting the validity of Lijphart's analyses, maintained that the Dutch political scientist makes a '*tout court* examination of opposition',[87] that is, no proper attention was given to the *shadow cabinet*. However, Pasquino himself pays no attention to the fact that the 'shadow cabinet' model pertains to the majoritarian and not to the consensus pattern advanced by Lijphart.[88] In the characteristic spirit of euphoria after the institutional reform proposal of the PCI, some intellectuals and politicians, from either the PCI or the Independent Left, failed to consider the important innovation of the PCI in historical and comparative perspective. In this context, I would argue that the PCI attempted an instrumentalist manipulation of the shadow cabinet pattern and failed, exactly because it did not apply to a consensus democracy — of the kind exemplified by the political structures of the First Republic — but to a majoritarian one.[89] Nevertheless, if the effort failed and the business of the established shadow cabinet slackened off, there were other reasons too. In essence, the dramatic transformation of the party as it took place under the shadow of the collapse of 'really-existing socialism', created a real barrier not only to the success of the shadow cabinet, but also to the general project of the *constituent phase*. In fact, the merit of the PCI lies elsewhere: convinced that the present political system of the First Republic needed genuine institutional reform, the party thought that setting up a 'Westminster-like' institution would have been enough to show the way in which the PCI could achieve its declared intention of separating state administation and party apparatuses. Occhetto referred to this point as a matter of primary importance:

> We affirm, in general, that the functions of the government and the projects of the parties need to be distinguished; and we also think that parties themselves must proceed in the same way. They too must distinguish the function of their political platforms from their task in defining political positions, giving rise to movements, being in close relationship to the tensions raised by society [...].[90]

The main idea that Occhetto and the PCI tried to give to the shadow cabinet was subjected to a twofold conditioning:[91] firstly, the cabinet should represent the transcendance of the consociational phase in Italian politics, thus paving the way for alternative governmental solutions; secondly, the cabinet should establish a different relationship between the institutional system and the political parties, between management and administration. Occhetto went on to outline, rather vaguely, the key political priorities of the party's 'shadow' institution.[92]

The coordinator of the newly-established institution, Giovanni Pellicani, an ex-mayor of Venice, argued that the 'PCI model of a shadow cabinet has very little to do with the British pattern where the whole system operates under the first-past-the-post electoral system'.[93] But this statement is a contradiction in terms: majoritarian electoral systems are the *precondition* for a shadow cabinet to exist and have a substantial role as the opposition that aims to govern. The PCI's effort failed mainly because this precondition did not yet exist.

The party form

The drafting of the Congressional theses has already signalled a fundamental change in the party's methods. Occhetto insisted on a single document which should be drafted by a small commission rather than the *parlamentino* of the CC (small parliament) used for the 1986 theses. With such a reference point, party majorities and minorities might have been formed. The principle of 'democratic centralism' which, in fact, had been in disuse since the 1986 Congress, was now to be *de jure* abolished in the famous article 3 of the new statute approved by the Congress.[94] It allowed party members not only to publicly criticise the official strategy of the party, but also to use party facilities for the dissemination of their ideological and political positions. Admittedly, this sort of *liberalisation* concerning inner-party regulations obviously had the full approval of Ingrao who had been fighting for the democratisation of the rigid Communist apparatus since the early 1960s. In this context, we witnessed the co-interest of the *neo-revisionist* will of the ruling group with the *Communist-libertarian* notion of Ingrao's Left. However, the project of the *quarantenni* aimed to go much further.

The 18th Congress was the 'beginning of the end' of the PCI as a *mass party*. Let us first look at the *organisational aspect* of the reform that was achieved. In the same way as capitalist enterprises were discarding administrative staff so as to shape the new post-Fordist/post-Taylorist flexible production pattern, so the PCI wanted to reduce its apparatus, promote part-time employment for its cadres and transform the overall organisational skeleton of the party. *The PCI's 'new course' was inseparable from a notion of transition from the mass party of Togliatti into a new type of 'cadre' party*: 'Our general point on which the party's clear orientation should be based [...], is that acting as an 'opinion party' is much more organic than acting as a 'mass party' [...]. The Left in Italy needs to acquire both the features of a new mass party and those of an opinion party.'[95]

The verbal reference to a 'new mass party' should not be overemphasised. The general meaning the PCI's Congress attributed to the re-organisation of the party apparatus concerned in fact the launching of a new, flexible and competent form of a 'cadre' party. Along the same lines, the party documents dealt with the abolition of 'democratic centralism' and a number of other intra-party regulations. The final goal was the construction of a *partito leggero* ('light' in the sense of flexible party).

The name

The question of changing the party's name and symbols was discussed even before the date of the 18th Congress.[96] This was not a paradox: since the *communist contents* of the party gave way to *new revisionism*, the same major breakthrough had to be pursued with regard to their *form*, that is, the *name* and the *hammer* and *sickle* symbols. However, the PCI did not wish to be put alongside the names and history of those Communist Parties that stained Communist and Socialist ideals. Therefore, only major changes with wider implications and significance would have forced the party leadership to pursue such a major symbolic change. Characteristically, Occhetto closed his speech at the Congress as follows:

> There are people who think that all this should be translated into changing the party's name. And by doing that, everything would be clear and resolved. We do not put out the cross in front of the devil and do not hang garlic out of the window in order to prevent vampires from coming and sucking our blood. Proposing to change the name of a party is a serious, very serious thing. If a party, in the face of historical facts and transformations of paramount importance [...], decides to give birth to a new political formation, then yes, it would be something serious and no one can be offended [...]. Today, however, we do not face such a critical situation.[97]

The PCI secretary reiterated this thesis while in the USA, in his speech to the Council of Foreign Affairs in May 1989. This time, Occhetto admitted openly that the PCI was acquiring a sort of *liberal* identity and, in the last analysis, Occhetto said referring to the question of the party's name, 'I think that it is quite easy for Americans to understand that *things count more than words*' (our emphasis).[98]

The students' riot in Tienanmen square and the military intervention that followed to suppress it could have been used as reasons for the party's ruling group to propose the change of the historic name. However, the fact that this event coincided with the Euro-election campaign and a certain electoral improvement, prevented the party leadership from pursuing any major radical step. In this conjuncure, the leadership decided only the dissolution of the Communist group in the Euro-parliament, giving birth to a new grouping under the name 'For a United Left'.[99] Nevertheless, Occhetto's assumption, as it was undermined by the facts, could no longer hold. The Eastern regimes were on the verge of collapse.

On July 29, 1989, two pro-PCI intellectuals, Michele Salvati and Salvatore Veca, published an article in the party's weekly *Rinascita* under the characteristic title *Cambiare nome: e se non ora, quando?* (Changing the name: if not now, when?).[100] The authors argued that Communism has been identified with statism and inefficiency, that these regimes were undergoing a profound crisis and disorganisation, that Communist ideals had failed to reconstruct society, while a new pluralistic social order was rising. The PCI had recognised many of the mistakes of the past and made particular efforts to renew itself. The party's 18th Congress was the major step made in this direction. Nevertheless, while the *contents of the policies adopted assumed a Liberal-Socialist dimension, their form, that is, the name of the party, still remained Communist.* Thus, the authors welcomed the 18th Congress only to the extent that it represented a 'tactical passage'.[101] Why did the PCI, even after the Tienanmen events, refuse to change its name and symbols? Because, the authors said, the PCI was afraid of the existence of strong Communist militancy in the party and the shifting of the party's base and electorate towards other Communist forces, such as *Democrazia Proletaria*. However, Salvati and Veca proceeded, it was high time for the PCI to change its name because, after all, tomorrow might be too late. Prophetically, the two intellectuals proposed that the new party be called *Partito Democratico della Sinistra (PDS), Democratic Party of the Left.*[102] Fabio Mussi, of the PCI's politbureau, in the same issue of *Rinascita*, responded but ineffectually.[103] Mussi argued that the PCI should be proud of its name since it has been the chief founder of the Republic. Curiously, he ignored the whole reasoning of the 'new course' which he himself embraced, that is, the existing linkage between the crisis of the DC system of power, the events in the East as well as the dual process of internationalisation/restructuring which had led the PCI to so many strategic revisions.

On 20 August 1989, the PCI leadership received a second important blow, from another distinguished intellectual, this time a member of the party. Biagio de Giovanni, in a famous short article published in *L'Unità*, argued that 'real Communism' was about to conclude its history.[104] Togliatti, the PCI leader who had been fully involved in the business of that obscure period and who had placed at the centre of his political action the principle that the fundamental contradiction is between Communism and Capitalism, should effectively be put aside. Togliatti's *doppiezza* was unquestionable and a serious discussion should follow, de Giovanni said, but the fact that the PCI should abandon its heritage was beyond any doubt: the modern world has dismantled the core of its political theory and practice.

In point of fact, the party leadership was unable to give a definite answer to the question of the name. Occhetto's speech at the festival of *L'Unità* in Genoa on 16 September 1989 made no reference to the name at all. With much rhetoric, Occhetto argued that the problem was not the dissolution but the reconstruction of the PCI, of an autonomous Left aiming at the transformation of Italy and Europe.[105] As regards Togliatti, Occhetto pointed out that serious historical research should start, reminding his audience that the PCI evaluated the personality of its leaders according to the notion of continuity/discontinuity: the party had adopted all the democratic values Togliatti and Berlinguer had fought for, but rejected categorically anything that has to do with antediluvian notions and political practices. The PCI had decided: to throw away the Communist heritage while preserving the revisionist/reformist one. After all, the former was identified with the Stalinist horror, while the latter was identified with the universal values of the French Revolution. The famous 'duplicity' was about to be solved once and for all. Only the question of *name* remained. When the Hungarian Communist party, the old POSU, changed its own in October, the party now found itself being left behind.

The proposal of Achille Occhetto: the European and national meanings of the 'constituent phase'

> Discutemmo a lungo, erano tutti d' accordo sulla necessità di aprire una nuova fase costituente. Ma alla fine mi resi conto il momento decisivo e dissi loro: 'Badate, fate ancora tempo a tornare indietro, perchè dal momento che annunceremo publicamente che ci mettiamo in discussione, non ci sarà più possibilità di ritorno'. Ci furono minuti di silenzio e tensione, poi uno ad uno risposero: 'Sì, andiamo avanti'.
>
> A. Occhetto, *Il Sentimento e la Ragione*, p.66

When the Berlin wall came down in the early morning of 10 November 1989, the secretary of the PCI was in Brussels to meet the then Labour Party leader Neil Kinnock.[106] The day after, he delivered a declaration in which the end of the Cold War was firmly attested and a new appeal for support towards the German Social Democracy of Willy Brandt was made.[107] On 12 November, Occhetto found himself together with a group of Resistance partisans from Bologna celebrating the forty-fifth anniversary of the antifascist struggle, the *Bolognina battle*. When asked if the PCI would change its name in view of the dramatic facts in the East, Occhetto said that 'everything is possible'.[108] In a day, he would write a brief document which was presented in the party's politbureau (*direzione*). Among other things, it stated:

> In my view, it is a matter of posing the question as openly as possible. *It is possible to initiate a real constituent phase, a process which will aim at the formation of a new thing with a new name* [...]. There is a need for a democratic party, for a party of progress, both Socialist and popular, to have Socialism and freedom at the centre of its ideals. It was no accident that I have chosen the veterans' assembly [in Bologna] to raise the question [...]. What is affecting us, affects everybody: no one anymore can define himself as a pure anti-communist alone. The real discussion cannot be that between two contrasting formulas: 'Socialist unity' [Craxi's proposal] and 'neo-Communism' [...]. In essence, we propose to give birth into a new political formation so as to mobilise and express the enormous potentialities of the Left. Our change is subject to this objective: the name shall be the consequence of it, the result.[109]

The 'serious event' which enabled the party to deepen its reform process and proceed with major and even symbolic changes — as Occhetto himself declared during his speech in the 18th Congress — had effectively occurred: it was the fall of the Berlin wall, the symbol of the Cold War era.[110] The party's *name* and *symbols* were finally challenged. For the collective Communist imagination, it was a real blow. The fact as such was to have much more serious implications than the 'pacifist' revision of the 'contents' of the Communist identity established at the 18th Congress.

In that meeting of the politbureau (13/15-11-1989), no one substantially opposed Occhetto. There were many criticisms, such as the 'elitist' way in which the proposal was announced or the lack of possible interlocutors interested in the political process of the 'constituent phase'. In point of fact, only Magri and Castellina were categorically against

Occhetto's Report.[111] As far as Ingrao was concerned, he learnt of Occhetto's *svolta* in the newspapers while in Spain. When he returned (16-11-1989), he pronounced to journalists a few words that were to reverse *de facto* the entire intra-party equilibria established at the Congress: *non sono d'accordo con la relazione di Occhetto* ('I do not agree with Occhetto's Report').[112] In these circumstances, the real inner-party antithesis was finally demystified: Napolitano and *miglioristi* were to ally with Occhetto; Ingrao would be followed by the Eurocommunist wing of the party and a considerable number of *berlingueriani* (Tortorella, Chiarante, Angius et al.). A few days later, when the party's CC had to convene — what came to be called *il Comitato Centrale della svolta* (the Central Committee of the turning point) 20-24 November — in order to decide how the party should proceed on the proposal of Occhetto, the new intra-party alignments had already occurred.

The aim of this chapter is to present, in a historically informed manner, the overall proposal of Occhetto, by focusing particularly on its European dimension. By doing so, we shall become aware that the fundamental meaning of the *fase costituente* was not only 'the reconstitution of the Italian Left' through which 'the reconstitution of the Republic can be achieved'; but also, and perhaps even more importantly, the *svolta* demanded a *simultaneous reconstitution of European power. This was to be achieved via the transformation and the hegemonic presence of the Left at the European level.* To this end, for the PCI, membership of the Socialist International was becoming even more vital.

This claim was not a new one. It had been advanced in the context of the post-1986 Euroleft PCI and the party's awareness of the process of European integration — the Single European Act, various inter-governmental Conferences adumbrating the Maastricht deadline — and culminated in the 18th Congress. In this framework, one of the major hypotheses of this study is reinforced: the fundamental reason for which Occhetto put forward the proposal of the party's dissolution was not because the PCI was dragged down by the critical events in the East, but rather because of the revolutionary process of capitalist restructuring, a process which the PCI began to debate as early as 1979-80 and which intensified after Mitterrand's Keynesian failure (1983) and Berlinguer's death (1984). The collapse of the East was only the reason for more drastic and profound changes: in fact, the end of the Cold War could only invigorate the belief of the ruling group that both the *name* and *communist identities* had become insignificant everywhere. Occhetto and the *quarantenni* were consistent with their ideas formulated as early as 1985-6. Therefore, the overall transformation of the PCI was a continuation of the general political orientations adopted by the party leadership after the death of Berlinguer together with a revisionist interpretation of the 'Italian Road to Socialism'.

The reason why we see these clarifications as particularly important is that a number of discussions on this subject show a certain confusion. As we have already seen, certain writers consider that the transformation of the PCI had been carried through by Occhetto in the form of a total rupture with its Communist past.[113] Others thought that the 18th Congress was the culmination of the PCI's Communist identity,[114] whereas Piero Ignazi has exaggerated the significance of the June 1987 election on the party's transformation.[115] Ignazi goes even so far as to see the dominance of pro-Sovietism in the 17th Congress of the party, giving the impression that the PCI was affected by a sort of antedeluvian Stalinism and not by the fashionable 'Gorbachevism' of the time.[116] Yet, he fails to consider the *duplicity* of the PCI alongside the Social Democratic/Communist cleft, thus clarifying the 'side' which will be 'preserved' in Occhetto's notion of 'breaking with the past'.[117] Finally, I should not fail to mention the deeply misleading notion of Leonard Weinberg who, in his account on the PCI/PDS, argues that the transformation of the party was due to the collapse of the Soviet bloc.[118]

The overall strategic conception of the proposal of the *quarantenni* can be summarised in the following united, but relatively distinct, points:

1 The PCI changed itself in order to change Italy (in that sense, the *fase constituente* concerned primarily the PCI itself);
2 Reconstitution of the Republic via the reconstitution of the Left (here the main goal is to unblock the political system via the PCI's re-unification with the Left-wing forces, primarily the PSI);
3 Institutionalisation of the new social movements and an understanding of governance on the basis of the 'progress-conservatism' cleavage. The contradictions of the present phase of modernity substantiate a new social and political advance especially for environmental and gender issues. Political opinion is divided between those forces recognising the progressive character of the new phase of modernity, and those which resist it. This antithesis cuts across the party system. It follows that the goal of the PCI is to disengage modernist factions of other parties from their conservative and populist matrix;
4 Reconstitution of the European system of governance via the convergence of the European Left and the guidance of capitalist restructuring by it at the European level; to this end, as we shall see, the

PCI put forth a European, rather neo-Keynesian, social contract and raised the role of the Socialist International.

All these points, in one way or another, we repeat, were part and parcel of the 18th Congress as well as of the neo-revisionist discourse of the *quarantenni* before they become the ruling group of the party. In essence, the *fase constituente* was an acceleration of the *nuovo corso*, the culmination of that 'Copernican revolution' launched by Occhetto several years before. In this context, it makes sense to point out that every time Ingrao's opposition castigated the ruling group that the proposal of the *fase costituente* was deprived of any concrete political and ideological contents, it seems not to have understood the entire operation of the *nuovo corso*: in fact, all the four 'neo-revisionist' elements were there and could be found in the Congressional theses and other party documents.[119] Thus, for example, when Giuseppe Vacca, one of the few intellectuals supporting Occhetto's *svolta* — the majority of them sided with Ingrao's opposition — was insisting on the continuity that exists between the 18th Congress and the 'constituent phase', in essence he was at the same time pre-empting the discourse of Ingrao's opposition.[120] Occhetto himself, when he attempted to answer the objections raised by Ingrao at his speech at the 19th Congress held in Bologna in March 1990, in fact did no more than to resort to the conceptions established by the previous year's Congress.[121]

We shall examine the above points consecutively, giving particular attention to the fourth one, since the first three issues are brought into context when analysing the motions of the 19th extraordinary Congress (March 1990).

1 As we saw earlier, when Occhetto officially advanced his proposal in the CC, he tried skilfully to separate the question of the *costituente* from that of changing the name. The aim was to bring the PSI closer and facilitate the process of acceptance of the PCI in the Socialist International: 'first comes the thing and after the name', the PCI secretary said.[122] This meant that the fundamental aspect of the proposal was the definition of the new process opening up, that is, the ways in which new political and social forces would be aggregated and recomposed in the new alignment, how different equilibria would be formed, the new identity created, the party form, new rules, in short, the whole operation of dissolution/reconstruction which was intended to impinge not only upon the PCI and the Left but also the very power system of the First Republic. The question of the name would have to be faced at the end of the day as a sort of 'crowning of all the efforts'. On this basis, Trentin argued:

First comes the *thing*, Occhetto rightly suggested. The *thing*, that is, the redefinition of our identity through our own project, on the grounds of concourse [...] with other subjects and interlocutors [...]. This is what is pushing me to accept the proposal advanced by Occhetto [...]. In my view, the constituent phase is precisely this, and not the declaration of Communism's failure [...] (emphasis by Trentin).[123]

The supposed dissociation of the name from the very context of the *constituent phase*, was to have worked in favour of the ruling group, facilitating the overall transformation of the type of party. After all, posing the question of the name at the start, might have been considered either as a subaltern political attitude vis-à-vis Craxi and his subsequent claim for *unità socialista,* or as a politically unnecessary compromise for the PCI to be accepted in the Socialist International — where the PSI and the PSDI were full members, so any application to join was dependent on their votes.

In short, given the hostile stance of Craxi, the first requirement the PCI set for itself was a 'constituent phase' concerning, basically, the party and those left-wing and democratic forces that had already shown that they favoured the 'new course' (the Leftist Clubs, various personalities etc.). Although highly respectable from an academic point of view, these groupings had a limited political appeal. *In essence, the 'constituent phase' concerned primarily the PCI itself.* Occhetto had no problem whatsoever in admitting it openly in an interview with Eugenio Scalfari in *La Repubblica* in December 1989. When the editor of the daily asked Occhetto with whom the PCI would be allying in the *costituente* since neither the PSI nor the Radicals of Marco Pannella, nor even the Greens showed any interest in joining, the PCI secretary went on to argue:

First of all, we will make it [the constituent] with ourselves. We have decided to transform ourselves, therefore we must decide the modes of our change. Hence, the constituent phase concerns primarily the Italian Communists. Of course, having this as a starting point, we are addressing our message to a large number of interlocutors, many of whom are giving positive signs.[124]

2 Despite its profound crisis, the *pentapartito* was in office. In particular, the party of Craxi and its strategy of 'socialist unity' were gaining support. Communists apart, the PSI was the most significant force on the left of the political stage. If the PCI succeeded in involving part or a large number of Socialist cadres in the constituent process, then the crisis of the corrupt political system would be precipitated and its re-organisation on a new basis would become feasible. *The PCI was indeed conscious of the fact that the pentapartito cabinet had severe difficulties in resolving the political crisis.* Especially after the end of the Cold War, the party was firmly convinced of the sharp and specific character of the crisis of the DC's domination in the political system of the First Republic. The following thesis of Claudio Petruccioli, leading member of the *svolta* and close collaborator of Occhetto, speaks for itself:

> The end of the Cold War will affect our national life in the sense that the problems we already have will be further accentuated. An entire cycle of our national life is drawing to an end. This is one of the central points upon which the 'new course' is based. This necessarily points to a new political class [for Italy], therefore, a new institutional order.[125]

Once this was asserted, the country's new political system was bound up with the new political force emerging from the PCI: *indeed, a dual constituent process involving both the party and the state.*

3 One of the most crucial components of the *costituente* — as in the 'new course' — were the new social movements. The posing of the question of 'ecological restructuring of the economy' as well as that of 'sexual difference', claims which both pertained to a cross-party conception of politics, reinforced the attempt of Occhetto. Thus, the party's transformation was embedded in the actual societal contradictions and crystallised the new process emerging from the restructuring. Contemporary changes demanded that every political force face the dilemma of accommodating itself to the new conditions. Those parties or party factions which refused to do so were objectively allying themselves with conservatism: hence the cross-party character of the new system of political and social alliances emerging. In addition, when the new transforming/transformed progressive party began to rule, it would be neither 'an abstract male'[126] nor an instrumental lever for quantitative growth. The new party would look like the country by mirroring society's sexes and real human needs. Thus, the process of the PCI's 'refoundation' — the term in November 1989 did not have yet the meaning it assumed some weeks later — was seen as a libertarian process which harmonised the liberal-democratic values of equality, fraternity and freedom.

4 All the four components of the 'constituent phase' launched by Occhetto were part and parcel of the 'new course', substantiating the ideas brought in by the *quarantenni* since 1985. One of these ideas, *the European constituent phase*,[127] tended to assume a leading role in the analyses for the transformation of the party, but the events in the East as well as the question of the name obscured this aspect and reduced references to the subject. Thus, in essence, the problematic of 'European constituent phase' ceased to prevail in the party's documents after the Euro-election of June 1989 and got replaced by that of 'constituent phase' at the national level thereafter.

The PCI had declared its commitment to being an 'integral part of the European Left' since 1986. Therefore, whatever the restrictions imposed by the centrist group under Natta were, the modernising discourse of the *quarantenni* could legitimately capitalise on the declaration and advance it further. European developments and the capitalist restructuring of the 1980s were not only the main cause of the crisis of the PCI, but also the principal reason for its renewal and definite transformation. In such a context, the analyses of Occhetto's faction were originally directed well beyond a verbal reference to the Euroleft, by focusing on the very institutional system of the European Union and its potential transformation vis-à-vis the new phase of modernity. From this analytical angle, a united Euroleft had to act as the lever for the construction of a new European polity. In other words, a 'European constituent phase' was necessary: 'Vis-à-vis the process of the reorganisation and concentration of economic and financial powers [...], a new European constituent phase, a new and strong parliament is necessary and urgent, a new and strong European government.'[128]

The demand for an articulation between a strong European executive and a democratic parliament, however utopian it seemed at the time, were to be debated and proposed as a major target of the neo-revisionist strategy of the Euroleft in the years to come.[129] For this to be attained, the PCI's argument went, the hastening of the political and monetary union process was necessary. However, none of these efforts would have any chance of success if conservative and right-wing forces were in power at the national level: *the European and national processes for the unification and reconstitution of the Left were thus seen as inseparable from the reconstitution of Italy and Europe.* As Occhetto himself pointed out in his speech at the 18th Congress, the project aimed at a new, this time, *European* road to socialism.[130] We found a revealing formulation on this topic included in the electoral programme of the party in the run-up to the European election of June 1989:

The question which constitutes the most serious and objective basis upon which the PCI and the Left place their candidature to govern

Italy's Europeanisation, is the indispensable need for the reform of the state and the break-up of that perverse compromise that has been created by the DC and its government allies.[131]

Similarly Pietro Folena argued:

The constituent phase is the lever of that process which aims at the construction of a new national and supranational democracy. The question of government is posed not in line with Togliatti's and Berlinguer's views (progressive association of PCI with the government through the strategy of general unity), but according to a new alternative notion which presupposes a break, a rupture, a refoundation of the relationship between rights and powers, a refoundation of democracy. At the centre of the constituent phase for a new political formation is the question of 'changing' the ruling class.[132]

We are thus coming to grasp the crux of the whole matter: the PCI realised that the process of capitalist modernisation taking place at the national and global levels questions the very existence of the ruling 'historic block' governing Italy since 1948. Although the party itself was actually part of a political structure regulated by the Cold War balance of force, as well as of a certain 'corporatist' mentality contained in its pro-Keynesian attitude, it now came to the understanding that a new political system could be formed only through a new political subject and inspired by a set of new political and ideological values.

Nevertheless, the overriding question to be answered by the PCI was on which *policy grounds* the Left should reconstitute Europe. Without literally saying it, the PCI argued in fact for a *European Keynesianism, for a new European social contract*.[133] As a matter of fact, the party proposed a set of reform policies based on the following points:

a A European *political union* entails a common foreign and even defence policies, as well as full economic and monetary union; therefore, institutions need to be redesigned in order to achieve fiscal harmonisation.

b Because of regional imbalances within the European community area (i.e. Mediterranean countries, the Italian South), re-allocative measures and a reform of the Common Agricultural Policy (CAP) are needed. For example, price disequilibria discourage production and create high income differentials. Peasants should be given qualified services and various incentives for the support and promotion of their products. It is important that the dialogue between the North and the South be based on mutual economic and social interests.

c If 'a European nation is under foundation', as Occhetto stressed in the discussion he had with Eric Hobsbawm,[134] then a European government of the Left must guarantee a general improvement in the social and economic conditions of its citizens. Protection of the weak and immigrants, full employment policies, a thirty five hour working week, creation of special funds for the promotion of programmes regarding infrastructure, research and training and, above all, a strengthening of social rights. In short, a drastic intervention by European authorities to increase the aggregate demand.

d Finally, the PCI argued for a new *European Enlightenment*, a new cultural project of modernity that would offer cultural backing to the cause of unification along the major lines of the Enlightenment: faith in technical progress, human prosperity, justice and creativity. In this respect, the cultural policy imposed should not succumb to 'extraneous' cultures due to their economic supremacy (e.g. Americanism), because they have very few, if any, points of contact with the European tradition and modernity.[135]

Admittedly, this project pointed to a new Keynesianism that now had to work out its agenda at the European level also to 'mitigate the negative effects of market liberalisation that would be particularly devastating in the poorer areas of Europe'.[136] Yet, it aimed at the construction of a *European nation* by using the means of the cultural values of the Enlightenment, their historical *locus* being Europe. On this cognitive grounds, one can address two speculative criticisms.

In the first instance, the party seems to presume a linear conception of capitalist history and development which, based on the supremacy of technical progress, will gradually be advancing to the peripheries under the political pressures exercised by the Left. Thus, the question of *uneven development* becomes of secondary importance and is confronted by proposing corrective measures concerning allocations of resources in the periphery. It is within this context that the most perverse effects of modernisation — caused precisely by *uneven development* either nationally or globally — could have been properly posed. I am referring to the decay of industrial cities, homelessness, alienation, miserable conurbations and appalling tower blocks for immigrants and the poor, the high level of individualism and selfishness, drugs, the uncontrollable dominance of the mass media and the apotheosis of narcissism, the dissolution of the family and the supremacy of singleness, high rates of unemployment and the crisis of welfarism.[137] In short, it seems that the new PCI wanted primarily to address a discourse towards the 'two/thirds' of the society, with the rest coming afterwards.

A second speculation that can be advanced, concerns the question of a *European national identity*. As we have seen, Occhetto attempted to see the European Enlightenment as a homogenised cultural project able to back a European national identity. For all those aware of the study of nationalism and ethnicity, this assimilation is highly debatable. A *European nation* can hardly exist because European modernity, as the PCI itself was aware, is completely different from the American one. European modernity was historically based on an ensemble of sovereign nation-states which achieved their own bourgeois breakthrough by infusing their population and *etnie* with a concrete and coherent *national* ideology, populations which were somewhat 'self-precluded' within entrenched territories whose boundaries were drawn by 'national bourgeoisies', in the case of sovereign industrial states (e.g. Britain, France, Germany), or by their assistance/suzerainty over other nationalities, when and where their indigenous bourgeoisie could not realise, on their own, the 'bourgeois revolution' (e.g. Greece, Italy, Turkey). Thus, Europe's historicity can hardly underpin a united political and cultural dimension, therefore it cannot constitute a nationally homogenised entity: *there can be no European unknown soldier, although there can be a Europe and a world without the military and wars.*

The Central Committee's crucial vote of 24 November 1989

At the end of his introductory speech in the CC in which he presented the main reasoning for the party's transformation (20-11-1989), Occhetto formulated two different 'hypotheses' from which the party had to choose in order to proceed with the declared 'constituent phase'.

The first was the construction of an alignment along which the party would evaluate the contribution of each political and social force willing to join the *fase costituente*. This overt process would have to present its first 'balance sheet' in the Spring and be followed by a re-launch of the *costituente*. The second, which Occhetto called 'more radical', concerned the need for the convocation of an extraordinary Congress in which the proposal of the 'constituent phase' would have been considered for final approval.

That was the crucial point for the success of the *quarantenni*: had the proposal of the 'constituent phase' followed the first road, the transformation of the party would have been faster, the triumph of the strategy more significant and time would have been saved for national policy matters. This did not happen. With a large majority, the CC chose the second path, a fact which can be considered a victory for Ingrao's and Cossutta's opposition, the so-called 'front of Nos', *il fronte del no.*

Occhetto posed the dilemma, though he himself did not have a steady position. On the one hand, he wished the transformation of the party to be made quickly and with the least possible losses; on the other, he felt comfortable with opting for the extraordinary Congress, as he thought that this prolonged process would minimise the possibilities of a split. Thus, Occhetto did not really favour either of the two roads he proposed, though one could pinpoint a certain preference for the second option. For example, in the course of a discusion with Scalfari, Occhetto went even so far as to say that, politically, the chosen path was the most desirable one:

> *Scalfari*: Well, hon. Occhetto, your views about the past are clear. But let us come to the present and future. Could you tell me what will be the itinerary of your constituent?
> *Occhetto*: In March we will have the extraordinary Congress; then there are the local elections of May; soon after the Summer an open programmatic Conference will take place which will discuss the programme and the concrete physiognomy of the new type of party; another Congress will follow which will approve the entire constituent phase (..).
> *Scalfari*: Do not you think that all this is going to be a rather long itinerary? For a year you will still be in the midst of politico-ideological turbulences, exposing yourself to the risks of political conjuncture. Why do you not accelerate the process?
> *Occhetto*: You must be joking if you think this itinerary is a long one! Craxi took two years to turn his party symbols of the hammer and sickle into a rose. And you think a year is too much to give birth into a new political subject? [...]. One year, I think, it is a very short period, believe me.[138]

Occhetto started to realise his mistake in the course of the party's transformation, especially after the administrative election of May 1990. Four years later and after the sweeping changes both in the party and to the Italian Republic, Occhetto admitted that the whole operation was extremely long, a fact which, among others, prevented the PDS from making a better electoral showing in the elections of 1992 and 1994. Even more importantly, the ailing PCI/PDS was virtually unable to advance any major political initiative, thus putting forward its declared candidacy to lead the transition process from the First to the Second Republic.[139] All in all, of the core ruling party fraction, only D'Alema had a clear position: 'an extraordinary Congress will not be useful', he argued.[140]

We will attempt to depict the process of party transformation in parallel with the irreversible crisis of the Italian polity during the period of 1989-1992. The history of the transformation of the PCI is almost inseparable from the transition process towards the Second Italian Republic.

Notes

1   See, G. F. Polara, 'Natta: le vera verifica solo con le dimissioni', *L'Unità*, 29-6-1984, p.1.

2   See in particular, E. Galli della Loggia, 'Natta, non prendertela: al PCI è vietato il sorpasso', *Europeo*, 20-21, 25-5-1985, p.7. The PCI got a 30.2 per cent, the DC polled 35 per cent and the PSI 13.3 per cent.

3   See, L. Bardi, 'The third elections to the European parliament: a vote for Italy or a vote for Europe?', in F. Sabetti-R. Catanzaro (ed.), *Italian Politics; A Review*, v.5 (London: Pinter Publishers, 1991), pp. 138-54.

4   On this subject, see the account made by R. Roscani, 'Quella bilancia tra PCI and PSI', *L'Unità*, 1-6-1988, p.2.

5   W. Veltroni, 'Il successo del nuovo PCI', *Rinascita*, 24, 24-6-1989, pp. 3-4.

6   In the words of B. Trentin, 'the decision of Craxi was a blow not only for the *scala mobile*, but also for the entire Italian contractual system and the principle of the autonomy of collective bargaining itself', B. Trentin, *Il Coraggio dell'Utopia; La Sinistra e il Sindacato dopo il Taylorismo* (Milano: Rizzoli, 1994), p.125. It is worth noting here that the main force which along with the PCI defended the *scala* was the neo-fascist MSI.

7   Among others, see the account of M. Mafai, 'Cgil, il gigante assediato dai Cobas', *La Repubblica*, 7-7-1988, p.6. In 1986, the charismatic reformist leader of the CGIL Luciano Lama was replaced by an ex-worker of Sesto San Giovanni, Antonio Pizzinato. A year later, his leadership was contested by the union's communist majority and November 29, 1988, B. Trentin took over. The worst was yet to come: the left-wing of the union around F. Bertinotti and P. Lucchesi would resist the reformist activism of Trentin and his intention to dissolve the communist faction following the party's changes, taking place under Occhetto's leadership. We shall discuss this latter point further on.

8   Especially on the subject of party militancy and the changing conceptions of party delegates on the question of Communism in the 17th and 18th Congresses, see the very interesting research conducted by the *Cespe* Foundation, 'Il nuovo PCI: due Congressi al confronto; ricerca sui delegati al XVIII Congresso Nazionale', *Politica ed Economia*, 6, June 1989, pp. 1-17.

9   P. Ingrao, 'Le forme della politica...', op. cit., pp. 18-22.

10   Ibid., p.19.

11   M. Notariani, 'Rimettere radici nella rivoluzione tecnologica', *Rinascita*, 2, 19-1-1985, pp. 6-7. Among the participants in the Conference were P. Fassino, G. Angius, V. Giannotti and A. Tortorella. In 1990, in between the two Congresses that marked the

end of the PCI, interesting accounts on the subject were written by R. Armeni, 'Così calano gli iscritti; Quota — 300,000' and L. Benini, 'Nasce la post-sezione?', both in A.Asor Rosa (ed.), *Viaggio nel Cuore del PCI* (attached leaflet of *Rinascita*, 17, 3-6-1990), pp. 11-18 and pp. 19-26 respectively; see also the very interesting essay by N. Magna, 'Dal PCI al PDS: geografia di un declino', *Politica ed Economia*, 12, Dec. 1992, pp. 21-25.

12   G. Napolitano, 'Attualità dell'alternativa', *Rinascita*, 27, 8-7-1983, pp. 1, 39. Along the same lines one should read the article of E. Macaluso, 'Le coerenze dell'alternativa', *Rinascita*, 29, 25-7-1987, pp. 3-6. The importance of Macaluso's long intervention — written from a distance of three years after Berlinguer's death — is that he recognises the ambivalence of the line and Berlinguer's aversion towards the PSI of B. Craxi (a view that was also shared in those years by Macaluso himself). Finally Macaluso called for an alliance with the PSI, because there was no other solution.

13   M. D'Alema, 'Quel che diciamo ai liquidatori della questione comunista', *Rinascita*, 30, 10-8-1985, pp. 4-5.

14   We are referring to G. Pasquino, 'Tre concezioni dell'alternativa', *Rinascita*, 35, 21-9-1985, pp. 28-30. Pasquino, stood for an alliance between the PCI and the DC.

15   See A. Occhetto, 'Il nuovo corso è discontinuità, non è demolizione del passato', *L'Unità*, 14-9-1989, p.2. We shall examine this point in detail below.

16   A. Occhetto, 'Intervista di A. Occhetto', *il Manifesto*, 16-7-1989, now in PCI, *Costruiamo la Democrazia dell'Alternativa* (Roma: ITER, 1989), p.6.

17   On these developments, see among others, M. Lorusso, *L'Era di Achille; Occhetto e la Politica Italiana da Togliatti a Berlusconi* (Firenze: Ponte alle Grazie, 1994), pp. 143-46, P. Ignazi, *Dal PCI...*, op. cit., pp. 60-64, G. Amyot, 'The PCI and Occhetto's new course: the Road to reform', in R. Nanetti, R. Catanzaro (ed.), *Italian Politics; A Review*, v.4 (London: Pinter Publishers, 1990), pp. 146-61.

18   See A. Natta, 'Il programma...', op. cit. The debate of the Central Committee of 25-27 June is thoroughly analysed by D. Sassoon, 'The 1987 elections and the PCI', in R. Leonardi-P. Corbetta (ed.), *Italian Politics; A Review*, v.3 (London: Pinter Publishers, 1989), pp. 138-39.

19   A. Natta, 'Il programma...', ibid., p.13.

20   Ibid., p.14.

21   Ibid.

22   Ibid., p.15.

23   All the speeches we are referring to, in ibid., p.16.

24   A. Occhetto, 'La crisi italiana e le prospettive dell'alternativa' (26-11-1987), *L'Unità*, 27-11-1987, pp. 11-13.

25   A. Occhetto, 'La risposta che si attende il Paese', *Rinascita*, 8, 28-2-1987, pp. 4-6.

26   See M. Villary, 'Le grandi scelte...', op. cit., p.4.

27   Ibid.

28   The party's proposal on the institutional reform would appear as a single document in the party's daily, *L'Unità*, on 16 March 1988, see 'The Communists' document on institutional reform', in *The Italian Communists*, Foreign Bulletin of the PCI, 1, Jan.-March 1988, pp. 3-15.

29   A. Reichlin quoted by M. Villari, 'Le grandi...', op. cit.

30   In the party Conference of April 29, 1995, which took place in the Central Hall of Westminster in London, Blair's proposal received 65.2 per cent, as against 34.8 per cent of the opposition, see our account, V. Fouskas, R. Casale, 'The end of British labourism and the fate of European Social Democracy', *Alpha*, 5, June 1995, pp. 21-25.

31   Among others, the document argued for the abolition of bicameralism, new parliamentary regulation, reorganisation of local government etc., see 'The Communists' document on institutional reform', op. cit.

32   A. Occhetto, 'Per l'egemonia della sinistra', *Rinascita*, 14, 23-4-1988, pp. 5-7. On this occasion, Occhetto suggested a privileged relationship with the PSI, a fact which, as we shall see further on, created a permanent problem between the 'clubists' and the PCI, between Occhetto and D'Arcais in particular. For a summary of the debate, see F. De Vito, 'Sinistra alla sbarra', *L'Espresso*, 16, 24-4-1988, pp. 18-19.

33   Occhetto interviewed by Fabio Mussi, 'Compagni, voliamo o no dare al partito un nuovo corso?', *L'Unità*, 3-6-1988, p.3.

34   See, U. Baduel, 'Comunisti alla prova del "nuovo corso"', *L'Unità*, 5-6-1988, p.2.

35   Ibid.

36   'Quando Bukharin era un «bandito»', *Avanti!*, 7/8-2-1988, p.13.

37   On this point, see the account made by A. P. Salimbeni, 'E su Togliatti al PSI diciamo...', *L'Unità*, 7-3-1988, p.4.

38   A. Natta had sufferred a heart attack while in Gubbio, Umbria, in 30 April 1987, during the electoral campaign in the May 1988 local elections. His resignation letter of 14 June stated, however, that even if no health reasons had necessitated, he would have offered his resignation, A. Natta, 'Letter...', op. cit., p.30, and E. Roggi (interview with A. Natta), 'Così ho vissuto questa prova dura', *L'Unità*, 15-5-1988, p.3. The election confirmed the downward electoral trend of the PCI: its losses were 3.9 per cent vis-à-vis the previous local election and 4.9 per cent vis-à-vis the national result of 1987.

39   A. Occhetto, 'La relazione al CC' (20-6-1988), *L'Unità*, 21-6-1988, p.15.

40   Ibid.

41   Ibid., p.16.

42   The *miglioristi* N. Colajanni, G. Fanti and E. Perna voted against. The absentees were the pro-Soviets A. Cossutta and L. Pestalozza, the vice-mayor of Milan L. Corbani, the historian G. Procacci and A. Boldrini, ex-President of the national association of partisans.

43   E. Scalfari, 'Una pesante eredità...', *La Repubblica*, 14-6-1988, p.4. The article was written on the occasion of Natta's official resignation.

44   M. D'Alema, 'Intervento al 18o Congresso', *L'Unità*, 21-3-1989, p.16.

45   A. Occhetto, 'We must re-define the state, the market and socialism' (interview with F. Ibba, *L'Unità*, 4-9-1988), in *The Italian Communists*, Foreign Bulletin of the PCI, 3, July-Sept. 1988, p.46.

46   A. Occhetto, 'How we are building the new PCI' (speech at the festival of *L'Unità*, 7-9-1988), *The Italian Communists*, ibid., p.62.

47   Ibid., p.71.

48   Ibid., p.75.

49   See also, F. Mussi, 'The ideological objectives of renewal', *World Marxist Review*, vol.32, n.8, Aug. 1989, pp. 43-47.

50   *XVIII Congress*, p.3.

51   See A. Occhetto, 'Nè abiure nè continuismo; un partito nuovo, alternativa per la società' (Report to the CC, 19-7-1988), *L'Unità*, 20-7-1988, p.15.

52   A. Occhetto, 'Siamo figli dell'89' (23-1-1989), now in A. Occhetto, *Un Indimenticabile '89* (Milano: Feltrinelli, 1990), pp. 1 ff.

53   G. Napolitano, 'Intervento sulla relazione di Occhetto', *L'Unità*, 22-3-1989, p.13; see also G. Napolitano, 'Alla ricerca dell'identità perduta?', *Critica Marxista*, 1-2, Jan.-

April 1989, pp. 67-75; In that revealing essay Napolitano argues for the continuity that exists between the PCI's post-war strategy and the present elaboration around the concepts of *nuovo corso* and *riformismo forte*. Obscuring this historical continuity and arguing merely for a break with the past, Napolitano maintained, is totally misleading.

54   A. Occhetto, 'Il nuovo corso è discontinuità...', op. cit., p.2.

55   It seems, for example, that Martin Bull has difficulty in fully understanding the dual historical *continuum* cutting across the strategic character of the party as well as its implications for the important changes introduced by the concept of *nuovo corso*. In his account of the 18th Congress he argued: 'Occhetto even indicated that the name of the party was not something to be held onto at all costs. It could be changed if political developments made it a necessity [...]. None the less, what marked a significant break with the past with respect to the identity of the party was the open declaration that this *was* a break with the past. If the strength of Togliatti's PCI lay in *continuità* the declared strength of Occhetto's PCI lay in *discontinuità*' (emphasis by M.B.), M. Bull, 'The unremarkable death of the Italian Communist Party' in F. Sabetti-R. Catanzaro (ed.) *Italian Politics; A Review*, v.5, op. cit., p.29.

56   A. Occhetto, 'Il nuovo PCI in Italia e in Europa; è il tempo dell'alternativa' (Report to the 18th Congress, 18-3-1989), *L'Unità*, 19-3-1989, p.16. See also, *XVIII Congress*, pp. 7-9.

57   A. Occhetto, 'Conclusioni al 18o Congresso del PCI' (21-3-1989), *L'Unità*, 22-3-1989, p.17.

58   A. Occhetto, 'Il nuovo PCI...', op. cit., pp.16, 17.

59   M. D'Alemma, 'Intervento...', op. cit., p.16.

60   M. Ca., 'Cossutta spara a zero su Occhetto; "nel PCI c'è mutazione genetica"', *Corriere della Sera*, 20-1-1989, p.2.

61   *Un Nuovo Corso per il Socialismo* (il documento di Cossutta), *L'Unità*, 26-11-1988, pp. 11-12. The document was presented in the CC of November 1988 alongside the first draft of the party's Congressional theses. Since it presents substantial similarities with the platform this current presented towards the 19th extraordinary Congress, we shall examine both documents together further on.

62   L. Colletti, 'Il mal di sempre del PCI di Occhetto', *Corriere della Sera*, 1-4-1989, p.2.

63   S. Hellman, 'Italian Communism in the First Republic', in S. Gundle-S. Parker, *The New Italian Republic...*, op. cit., p.83.

64   N. Bobbio, 'La società civile in Gramsci' (first published in *Atti del Convegno Internazionale di Studi Gramsciani*, Cagliari, 23-27 April 1967), now in N. Bobbio, *Saggi su Gramsci* (Milano: Feltrinelli, 1990), pp. 38-65.

65   P. Anderson, 'The antinomies of Gramsci', *New Left Review*, 100, 1977, pp. 5-80.

66   A. Gramsci, 'Americanismo e fordismo', in *Quaderni del Carcere*, op. cit., v.III, p.2146.

67   A. Occhetto, 'La democrazia non può fermarsi al di qua dei cancelli della fabbrica' (from his conclusions at the Congress of Mirafiori workers of FIAT, 11-2-1989), in A. Occhetto *Un Indimenticabile...*, op. cit., p.44.

68   The modernising leadership of Tony Blair in Britain, after abolishing the party's commitment to nationalisation, mapped out the main themes of 1996-7 Labour's election campaign by promising to develop a *stakeholder economy* in which everyone can take part; see T. Blair, *New Britain; My Vision of a New Country* (London: Fourth Estate, 1996), pp. 57-87.

69   M. D'Alema, 'Formulas for progress', *World Marxist Review*, n.1, v.33, Jan. 1990, p.55.

70   The programme was translated into Italian, see *La Socialdemocrazia Tedesca; Il Testo Integrale del nuovo Programma Fondamentale della SPD* (Berlin, Dec. 1989), (Roma: Datanews, 1990), pp. 38 ff.

71   See in particular, 'The PCI's programme for Europe', op. cit., pp. 38, 51, 55.

72   *Un Nuovo Corso per il Socialismo*, op. cit., p.12.

73   A. Occhetto, 'Il nuovo PCI...', op. cit., p.15.

74   *XVIIIth Congress*, p.4.

75   Ibid., p.11. It is worth mentioning here the notion of the 'ecological restructuration of the economy' was derived from the programme of the German SPD.

76   F. Chiaromonte, personal interview (Rome: Camera dei Deputati, 1-8-1995); *XVIII Congress*, p.10; see also the very important document *Carta Itinerante: Dalle Done la Forza delle Donne* (Roma: Nuova Stampa di Mondatori, 1987), pp. 15-32. This document became known as *La Carta delle Donne* and embraced the feminist culture of 'sexual difference' of the French feminist theorist L. Irigaray.

77   C. Mancina, 'Elogio della parzialità comunista', *Politica ed Economia*, 1, Jan. 1989, p.6.

78   P. Ingrao, 'Intervento al 18o Congresso' (20-3-1989), *L'Unità*, 21-3-1989, p.15.

79   *XVIII Congress*, p.8.

80   Among others, A. Reichlin, '1989: è più o meno credibile l'alternativa?', *Rinascita*, 2, 21-1-1989, pp. 3-5, A. Occhetto, 'Per l'egemonia della sinistra', op. cit., p.7, A. Occhetto, 'Chiarezza con i socialisti', *L'Unità*, 11-2-1989, p.2.

81   To give only two examples, S. Garavini had argued for an 'alternative economic policy' instead of a 'ultra-politicised notion of the alternative' ('Intervento al 18o Congresso', *L'Unità*, 20-3-1989, p.12), and L. Magri insisted on the oppositional character the line should assume ('Intervento al 18o Congresso', *L'Unità*, 21-3-1989, p.13).

82   See for example M. D'Alema's articles in the party's daily, 'Noi e i socialisti', *L'Unità*, 3-2-1989, p.2, '...E poi c'è il PCI', *L'Unità*, 19-2-1989, p.2.

83   Our basic references are A. Lijphart, *Democracies: Patterns of Majoritarian and Consensus Government in Twenty-One Countries* (New Haven and London: Yale University Press, 1984), G. Pasquino (ed.), *Opposizione, Governo Ombra, Alternativa* (Bari: Laterza, 1990).

84   A. Lijphart, ibid., pp. 4-9.

85   Ibid., p.7.

86   Ibid., pp. 23-30.

87   G. Pasquino, 'Perchè e come studiare l'opposizione', in G. Pasquino (ed.), *Opposizione...*, op. cit., p.11.

88   The mistake becomes graver when Pasquino, even writting at a distance of three years from the formation of the 'shadow cabinet', fails to pinpoint the real cause of the institution's nonchalant misfunction, see G. Pasquino, 'Programmatic renewal and much more: from the PCI to the PDS', *West European Politics*, n.1, v.16, Jan. 1993, pp. 156-73.

89   Thus, a year after the introduction of the shadow cabinet by the PCI, Ingrao objected to the validity of the whole operation and asked for a serious balance sheet from both, the PCI and the Independent Left; see the debate between Pasquino and Ingrao during the presentation of Pasquino's book on the shadow cabinet, as documented by A. Leiss, *L'Unità*, 21-6-1990, p.5.

90   A. Occhetto, 'Il nuovo PCI...', op. cit., p.18.

91   A. Occhetto, 'Le linee programmatiche del governo ombra per questa legislatura' (speech in the presentation of shadow cabinet, Rome, 19-7-1989), *L'Unità*, 20-7-1989, pp. 14-15.

92   The main issues of Occhetto's neo-revisionist agenda included foreign policy, environmental and gender issues, electoral reform, the question of the South and education. As far as the relationship between state and society was concerned, Occhetto simply stated the need of going 'beyond liberalism and statism', ibid., p.15.

93   G. Pellicani, 'L'opposizione che cambia' (interview with M. Chiara), *Rinascita*, 29, 29-7-1989, pp. 5-6.

94   PCI, *Statuto del Partito Comunista Italiano Approvato al 18o Congresso del PCI* (Roma: Iter, 18/22 March 1989), pp. 11-12.

95   *XVIII Congress*, pp. 15-16.

96   L. Magri, personal interview (Rome, 18-7-1995).

97   A. Occhetto, 'Il nuovo PCI...', op. cit., p.18.

98   A. Occhetto, 'Ecco come lavoriamo per riformare la nostra società', *Rinascita*, 21, 3-6-1989, p.30, also A. Stabile, 'Noi diciamo PCI, voi liberal', *La Repubblica*, 20-5-1989, p.7.

99   That group was composed by the twenty two PCI MEPs, four Spaniards of the *Izquierda Unida*, one Danish MEP from the Popular party and one Greek member of the newly-formed *Coalition of the Left and Progress*. L. Colajanni had been elected President of the group.

100 M. Salvati-S. Veca, 'Cambiare nome: e se non ora, quando?', *Rinascita*, 29, 29-7-1989, pp. 35-39.

101 Ibid., p.35.

102 Ibid., pp. 37, 38.

103 F. Mussi, 'C'è un tempo per ogni cosa', ibid., pp. 36-37.

104 B. de Giovanni, 'C'erano una volta Togliatti a il comunismo reale', *L'Unità*, 20-8-1989, p.1.

105 A. Occhetto, 'Closing speech at the Festa dell'Unità' (16-9-1989), in *The Italian Communists*, Foreign Bulletin of the PCI, 3, July-Sept. 1989, pp. 40-65, esp. p.48; see also, A. Occhetto, 'Discontinuità e comprensione della storia. A proposito di Togliatti' (first published in *L'Unità*, 13-9-1989), in A. Occetto, *Un Indimenticabile...*, op. cit., pp. 116-19.

106 Eight days previously, during the meeting of the Socialist International in Milan, Occhetto had sent a letter to its president Willy Brandt in which the PCI secretary underlined the crisis the Eastern bloc was undergoing and asked to collaborate with the International; see A. Occhetto, 'Al presidente dell'Internazionale Socialista Willy Brandt' (2-11-1989), *P. Fassino Archives*, no file number.

107 See A. Occhetto, *Un Indimenticabile...*, op. cit., pp. 120-123. For a more recent account of the facts by Occhetto himself, see his book published after his resignation as PDS secretary on 13 June 1994, *Il Sentimento e la Ragione* (Milano: Rizzoli, 1994), pp. 63-75.

108 See, W. Dondi, 'Il PCI cambierà nome? tutto è possibile', *L'Unità*, 13-11-1989, p.8.

109 A. Occhetto, 'Cambia il mondo, non possiamo stare fermi' (14-11-1989), in *Un Indimenticabile...*, op. cit., pp. 130-132.

110 Occhetto would remind us again of this part of his speech in the dramatic CC of 20-24 November, see A. Occhetto, 'Una costituente per aprire una nuova prospettiva

della sinistra' (Report to the CC, 20-11-1989), in PCI, *Il Comitato Centrale della Svolta/1* (Roma: L'Unità, 9-1-1990), pp. 15-16 (thereafter: *PCI/1*); see also the speech by Fassino (ibid., pp. 58-60) who also forcefully raised this point again.

111 See in particular, Magri's intervention in *L'Unità*, 15-11-1989, p.6 and *L'Unità* 16-11-1989, pp. 8-10 (the intervention of Castellina on pp. 9-10); also personal interview, op. cit., G. Moltedo-N. Rangeri, *PCI: La Grande Svolta; il Nome, il Simbolo, il Nuovo Partito* (Roma: Associate, 1989), pp. 7-29. Certainly, the long-standing fierce opponent of Occhetto was Cossutta. At the CC of 4 October 1989, he pointed out that 'the PCI, *de facto*, is no longer communist, it remains communist only in name', see *L'Unità*, 5-10-1989, p.16.

112 See, G. Moltedo-N. Rangeri, *PCI: La Grande...*, ibid., p.15. The authors describe perceptively not only the immediate reactions of the party cadres, but also of wider Italian political opinion.

113 This is, for example, the position of M. Bull, 'The unremarkable...', op. cit.

114 S. Hellman, 'The PCI...', op. cit.

115 P. Ignazi, *Dal PCI...*, op. cit. and his 'Il posto della cosa', *il Mulino*, a.XXXIX, 5, Sept.-Oct. 1990, pp. 744-52.

116 P. Ignazi, *Dal PCI...*, p.59.

117 Ibid., pp.15, 21, passim.

118 See, L. Weinberg, *The Transformation of Italian Communism* (New Brunswick: Transaction Publishers, 1995).

119 We exclude the opposition of A. Cossutta and G. M. Cazzaniga in this case, because it had been suggested for a long time that the PCI had lost its Communist identity, being communist only in name. The same, but on the opposite side of course, was the position of Napolitano: 'Already, a long time ago, the PCI had become a different thing from the name it bears' (20-24/11/1989), in *PCI/1*, p.129.

120 See, among his various speeches and interviews, G. Vacca, *Dal PCI al PDS* (Bari: Delphos, 1991), pp.77-78, passim.

121 See, A. Occhetto, 'Un nuovo inizio: la fase costituente di una nuova formazione politica' (Occhetto's Report to the 19th Congress), *L'Unità*, 9-3-1990, p.24.

122 A. Occhetto, 'Una Costituente...', in *PCI/1*, p.23 and A. Occhetto, 'Le conclusioni', PCI, *Il Comitato Centrale della Svolta/2* (Roma: L'Unità, 16-1-1990), pp. 165-66 (thereafter: *PCI/2*).

123 B. Trentin, *PCI/1* (20-24/11/1989), pp. 123-24.

124 A. Occhetto, 'Ho fatto quel che dovevo' (*La Repubblica*, 17-12-1989), now in *Un Indimenticabile*, op. cit., p.162.

125 C. Petruccioli, in *PCI/1* (20-24/11/1989), p.216.

126 See the speech of A. Cavalero in the CC of PCI, in *PCI/1* (20-24/11/1989),pp.73-74.

127 The concept was also elaborated by the 'Left of clubs', see Paolo Flores D'Arcais, 'Lettera aperta al Congresso del PCI', *Micromega*, 1, 1989, pp. 25-27.

128 A. Occhetto, 'Come costruire la democrazia Europea', *Rinascita*, 43, 26-11-1988, p.7. See also Occhetto's speech to the conference of the German SPD in Bonn (26-1-1989), 'Come disegnare l'Europa delle riforme', *Rinascita*, 5, 11-2-1989, pp. 3-5.

129 For an implicit agenda, D. Sassoon, *Social Democracy at the Heart of Europe* (London: IPPR, 1996).

130 A. Occhetto, 'Il nuovo PCI...', op. cit., p.16. The same statement can also be found in the Congressional theses, see *XVIII Congress*, p.3.

131 'The PCI's programme for Europe', in *The Italian Communists*, Foreign Bulletin of the PCI, 2, April-June 1989, p.35.

132 P. Folena, 'Un nuovo sogetto di cambiamento', *Critica Marxista*, 1, Jan.-Feb. 1990, p.118.

133 Our basic arguments are drawn from the PCI's programme for the European election of 1989.

134 A. Occhetto, 'Il PCI al punto di svolta nella storia della sinistra', in *Un Indimenticabile...*, op. cit., p.187.

135 See, 'The PCI's programme...', op. cit., pp.80-83.

136 *XVIII Congress*, p.4.

137 With reference to American society in the 1970s, Christopher Lasch has perceptively developed all these points in his *The Culture of Narcissism; American Life in an Age of Diminishing Expectations* (New York: Norton, 1978).

138 A. Occhetto, 'Ho fatto quel che dovevo', interview with E. Scalfari in *La Repubblica* (17-12-1989), now in *Un Indimenticabile...*, op. cit., pp. 161-62.

139 A. Occhetto, *Il Sentimento e la Ragione* (Milano: Rizzoli, 1994), pp. 106-07, passim. The party's daily, *L'Unità*, went even further. In a vignette it presented Occhetto leaving a message on his answer machine saying: 'the opposition is absent; please leave a message of thirty minutes maximum after the long tone' (quoted by M. Braun, *L'Italia...*, op. cit., p.97). Due to its internal troubles, the PCI was unable to interfere in the critical developments taking place in the ruling coalition, therefore to direct these developments providing a visible outlet amidst the institutional crisis. We shall return to this point below.

140 See D'Alema's speech in the CC of 20-24 November, in *Documenti/1*, p.133.

5   Governing the Party Crisis (1): The Retreat of *New Revisionism* in the 19th Congress (March 1990)

The conjuncture

In the preceding chapters we have become increasingly aware of the fundamental elements which characterised the Italian crisis of the 1980s. We have explained the strategic ambiguities of the PCI as well as its ideological and organisational decline. We have seen that both the Italian and the PCI's crises were linked with the process of capitalist restructuring and the demise of 'actually-existing socialism'. From this perspective, we have asserted that the principal difference between the PCI and the ruling coalition was that while the former showed particular sensitivity to international and national developments, the latter failed to grasp their very meaning. Thus, when the PCI launched its transformation, both the DC and the PSI saw in the above interlinked developments a verification of their own political choices.[1] History showed that they got it wrong all along.

As we saw earlier, a large part of the 1980s was shaped around the conflicts of De Mita and Craxi. Among other things, this pair attempted to consolidate a hegemonic presence in politics and society by using a modernising, though highly rhetorical, discourse. By the late 1980s, this device was exhausted. In 1989, the DC-PSI power axis turned further to the right. The *Craxi-Andreotti-Forlani* axis (CAF) loomed large on the political stage, won over any resistance by De Mita's reformist faction and, most importantly of all, ensured that De Mita's appeal for institutional and electoral reform was shelved. De Mita, at least, made references to these issues. The CAF axis cancelled them altogether. The new hegemonic grouping began to shape its agenda at the 18th Congress of the DC (Rome, 18-22 February 1989).

De Mita faced accusations by Andreotti and Forlani that his declared political regeneration of the party was a dead letter and that he had quite arbitrarily violated the 'unwritten DC rule that a party secretary could not, at the same time, be prime minister'.[2] After all, the hypothesis of a functional democracy based on a DC-PCI alternation in government was no longer valid since the PCI received a serious blow in the 1987 election. In fact, the party which did particularly well was the PSI, whose successful electoral results were, from time to time, called by Craxi *l'onda lunga* (the long wave), meaning the slow, but steady, process leading to the overtaking of the PCI. De Mita lost out as party secretary at the February Congress (1989) and in his place delegates elected Forlani. One month after the closing of the Congress, the DC national council elected De Mita as its President. A few months later, he gave up the Premiership to Andreotti. On 20 February 1990, De Mita also resigned as DC President, accusing the party of being too subordinate to the PSI.

The PSI's forty-seventh Congress held in Milan in May 1989, relaunched the party strategy along two major lines: firstly, it affirmed the line of 'socialist unity' and viciously attacked the 'new course' of Occhetto; secondly, it welcomed the new power set-up in the DC with Craxi in particular victoriously ending his long vendetta with De Mita.

The line of 'socialist unity' simply reformulated the old intention of the PSI of overtaking the PCI and becoming the hegemonic force of the Left.[3] However, given that the PCI's *nuovo corso* considered the PSI to be a privileged interlocutor as well as the latter's favourable electoral results, the conception of 'socialist unity' could claim a certain success. *In fact, during the period in question and given the predicament of the PCI, Craxi's line put the PCI on the defensive.* However, Craxi's attacks on the 'new course' did not stop here. The PSI repeated the proposal of a Presidential democracy, though not clarifying the concrete form of Presidentialism it wished to have.[4] Finally, on the international front, the PSI had a great advantage: without the votes of the PSI and PSDI, the PCI could not become a full member of the Socialist International.[5]

At the PSI Congress Craxi demanded the resignation of De Mita and proposed the formation of a new cabinet. Mario Caciagli has reconstructed a remarkable episode of the Socialist Congress in the following way:

> In the course of an encounter with Forlani, which took place in a 'camper', the two party secretaries allegedly drew up a general agreement which, under the aegis of Andreotti, was not only to make the latter prime minister, but also to draw a map of power-sharing for the entire political system. The appointments to public bodies, the alliances with several large industrial groups and the control of major media outlets apparently constituted the terms of agreement among the three politicians.[6]

The 'new cross-party' alliance was set up. Its agenda and governing methods were not different from the previous cabinets: expansionary policies along corporatist lines, corrupt use of public finance, incompetence in dealing with the fiscal crisis and so forth. Filippo Sabetti and Raimondo Catanzaro argued:

The critical difference between the De Mita and Andreotti governments is that the former represented the apex and the beginning of a decline of efforts to create stable and long-lasting coalitions. Whereas the De Mita government seemed to be open to the prospects of institutional reform, the Andreotti government seemed to have put aside the theme of institutional reform altogether, even though its very creation brought into question, in a dramatic way, the powers and the prestige of the President of the Republic.[7]

It would be easy enough to give several quotations along the same lines, but the matter is already perfectly clear: *the 'CAF' political pact was a step backward compared with the era of De Mita; it consolidated corporatist practices at the moment when national and international constraints were pointing in the opposite direction.*[8] This pure anti-reformism caused tough political resistance particularly within the DC itself. It was no accident that two of the most important political movements that played a major role in the breakdown of the First Republic, the referendum movement of Mario Segni and the anti-Mafia movement of Leoluca Orlando in Palermo, both came from inside the DC and began to seriously challenge their party at that time.

Nine days before the formation of the sixth Andreotti cabinet on 23 July 1989, the distinguished DC cadre, Segni, announced that if the Parliament was to turn down his proposal for electoral reform, then he would be forced to call for a referendum. By the end of the year, Segni, his DC supporters (around seventy deputies) and the Radicals of Marco Pannella started taking up the challenge. The PCI supported the effort. In the words of Occhetto:

> I had no hesitation at all in approving the referendum initiative because we need to step out of this suffocating climate which characterises the present political phase. It is a new fact that tends to decompose parties and their inner-factions [...]. In general, we are interested in every electoral reform that gives citizens the possibility of choosing, on a programmatic basis, alternative coalitions and governments.[9]

As we saw earlier, the electoral reform was discussed by the *Commissione Bozzi* from November 1983 to January 1985. However, no progress was made 'because of a series of cross-cutting vetoes and the Communist opposition that allowed the Socialists to disguise their hostility and aversion to any form of decisive action'.[10] Nevertheless, speculation and mobility around the subject did not cease and in February 1990, a committee for the promotion of a referendum for the reform of the electoral law was set up. Headed by Segni, the movement was composed of Radicals, Liberals, Republicans, DC supporters, Communists and the Independent Left, ACLI, FUCI and the National Women Voters' Association. Nor did Gianfranco Pasquino fail to see that the referendum movement of Segni was one of the first 'cutting across all political groups'.[11]

The crisis of the DC continued. On 8 April 1989, the left-wing DC mayor of Palermo, Leoluca Orlando, resigned, accusing the DC-PSI government of 'contiguity' with the mafia. Soon afterwards, he formed a *giunta* consisting of PCI, DC, PSDI, Greens, Independent Left and other members from Catholic organisations. When Orlando triumphed once again in the election for the local council in 1990, he had to encounter the open hostility of the DC.[12] It is worth noting that neither of these two movements seriously thought of abandoning the DC for the time being (Orlando left the party in November 1990 and Segni as late as October 1992): both acted as reform pressure groups within the party.

In Palermo there was the 'reign' of Orlando and in Rome the star of Segni started to rise, while in the North the Leagues were gaining ground. The Leagues entered Italian politics in the North as early as the early 1980s, each claiming the autonomy of their region from the clientelistic and unproductive system of the South as well as the corrupt parties of Rome. With the first League appearing in Veneto — the *Lega Veneta* which at the 1983 election gained 4.2 per cent of the vote — the effort, nevertheless, developed seriously in Lombardy, one of the richest Italian regions. In 1987, the *Lega Lombarda* of Umberto Bossi got 3 per cent of the vote in Lombardy while in the 1989 Euro-election, gains were about 500,000 votes and 8.1 per cent. After this success, Bossi unified various other Leagues and autonomous formations under the name *Lega Nord*, Northern League (4-12-1989). Being now a wider alliance including not only the Northern regions but also some groups in the Centre, the Northern League was no longer propagating the autonomy of single regions but a tri-partite division of the country, that is, Republics of the North, the Centre and the South.

Having said this, I wish to suggest that, in light of sharpening social and political contradictions towards the end of the decade, some of the principal forces which destabilised the First Republic, namely, the Lega Nord and the referendum movement of Segni, showed a particularly strong desire for reform almost at the time as the PCI was completing its 'new course' and launching its total transformation. In this context, *I would argue that the dissolution of the party goes pari passu with the dissolution process of the Republic, though it is clear that the two processes enjoyed a distinct autonomy.*

Late in the Autumn and after the closure of the PCI's *Comitato Centrale della svolta* in November, the Chancellor of West Germany, Helmut Kohl, presented in the Bundestag a platform in which the steps towards the re-unification of Germany were indicated. America's President George Bush agreed on the grounds that Germany should be fully integrated into Europe. Gorbachev, on his visit to Italy and the Vatican on 29 and 30 November, made some ambiguous statements, saying that the 'Cold War is ending not because there are victors and vanquished, but precisely because there are neither'.[13] Obviously, however, the post-war period was ending at the expense of 'actually-existing socialism'.[14] When the last ten days of the 'unforgettable 1989' saw a unique disorder in Romania and the execution of Nicolae and Elena Ceausescu, the end of Eastern regimes seemed to be not only an indisputable reality, but also a justification for the party's constituent process initiated by the PCI.

Before I pass on to analyse the Congress as such, the student movement known as *pantera* (panther) should be mentioned. The movement played an important role in shaping the socio-political determinants of the conjuncture and, insofar as it was the only radical event taking place amidst the general malaise of the Left, favoured the opposition of Ingrao.

From January 1990 when the first occupations of *Atenei* (Universities) began in Palermo, students contested the very meaning of the law 168 promoted by the Socialist Minister of Education, Antonio Ruberti, which claimed:[15] i) collaboration between private and public sectors in order to modernise University infrastructure, research etc.; ii) in the administrative council of *Atenei*, private enterpreneurs would have one fifth of the total composition and ordinary professors would have half of the posts with students having only a consultative say; iii) Universities would give diplomas, Bachelor and PhD degrees; University diplomas could be organised in association with the private sector.

The students argued that the Ruberti law implied the privatisation of the *Atenei*, downgraded Arts and Humanities while upgrading science, computing, and engineering. In addition, it widened the gap between Southern and Northern Universities and made the students' role in the decision-making bodies parochial. Apart from those opposing the *svolta*, the movement's theses were also welcomed by Orlando who considered students and the University of Palermo as 'the last healthy zone in the entire city'.[16] The leadership of PCI and Aureliana Alberici — Minister of

Education in the PCI shadow cabinet and wife of Occhetto — proposed a counter-reform centred on the modernisation/Europeanisation of the Universities, asked for further investment policies and denounced the Ruberti law as 'centralised masquerade that reproduces the existing order of things'.[17] Thus, while both the PCI leadership and students opposed the law, they did so from radically different points of view. The students thought that the *Atenei* were about to fall into the private sector, whereas the PCI saw no reform whatsoever but a repetition of the same statist rhetoric.[18]

To recapitulate: in 1989 the Craxi-Andreotti-Forlani grouping succeeded in defeating the lay left-wing faction of De Mita who, at least on paper, had raised the question of institutional and electoral reforms from the early 1980s. This situation was to drive the country many steps backwards, and ignored the emergency status of the political system as well as the consequences of the end of the Cold War. The PCI, on the other hand, through its 'new course' and the qualified proposal of the 'constituent phase' was fully conscious of the crisis of the *pentapartito* and warned about the decomposing tendencies the new ruling bloc contained within itself. The 19th Congress of the party, which had to decide the future of the PCI, took place under these extremely peculiar circumstances. Nevertheless, the PCI's ruling group proved unable to manage the government of 'both transitions': *from the First to the Second Republic and from the PCI to the PDS*. Its own transformation being an extremely difficult, long and self-alienating procedure, the PCI/PDS would fail to provide a sound political alternative, thus conceding the governance of the crisis to forces which, most of the time, did not sympathise with and/or were alien to its *costituente*.

The ruling group and the gendered discourse of the transformation

According to the platform signed by the *quarantenni* and the *miglioristi* of Napolitano — an alliance established at the CC of November 1989 — the *grande svolta* was not dictated by the collapse of 'really-existing socialism'. It was argued that Italian Communism

> ...is not misguided by the crisis of the East. Its political and ideological autonomy, its deep roots in the Italian society and great history, its criticism of the statist, authoritarian and bureaucratic models of Socialism, are very old and recognised facts: these make the party one and the same with the history of Italian democracy and liberty. In fact, the events in the East confirm the validity of our theses.[19]

Nevertheless, the account goes, 'we had a wrong perception believing that certain reforms of these social and political models would have been possible. This notion has inhibited us from categorically stating that these societies needed a profound political revolution'.[20]

This sort of self-affirmation and, at the same time, self-criticism vis-à-vis the Eastern regimes, helped the ruling group to present the whole party within the 'continuity/discontinuity' framework, in the sense that while the party, on the one hand, had been criticising the Stalinist regimes, on the other, its criticism was somewhat entrapped by the notion that democratic reforms in the East alone were enough to establish an ideal society. Thus, even from this perspective, the PCI was justified and, at the same time, unjustified.

As the world was moving away from the juxtaposition between the two military and socio-economic blocs, the struggle for progress could no longer be reduced to either of them.[21] Capitalism, the ruling group's argument went, is now becoming more vulnerable since the challenges to it have been multiplied. Indeed, 'post-Yalta capitalism' must be able to govern that interdependent world, respond to new libertarian claims, reconcile the complexity and diversity of modern society, redistribute the relationship of forces among sexes; all in all, the collapse of the East does not promise a paradise for the West. That is why Socialism is not only necessary, but must also be seen as a *world*, that is, *global process*.

The real danger for the party, the neo-revisionist argument proceeded, was that the collapse of Communism might lead to the collapse of Socialist ideals in general. To avoid such an evolution, a new set of values and goals, which would replace the Communist ones, was absolutely necessary. In fact, with the internationalisation of capital on the European and world scale, new potentialities of cooperation among left-wing forces were opening up. The need in the present phase of modernity was to be governed by the European Left in Europe and by the reconstituted Left in Italy. To this end, the Socialist International served not only the prospects for a new hegemonic projection at the European level, but also the convergence between the PCI and the PSI. So vital was the PCI's entry into the International, that the party's diplomacy was forced to conceal some aspects of its activities in order to appease the internal opposition towards the crucial Congressional appointment. In a letter to the President of the International Willy Brandt in 6 February 1990, Occhetto maintained:

Dear President [...],
As you know, at the beginning of March the PCI has an extraordinary Congress to decide on the proposal I put forward on November 14 in the party Directorate: a proposal aimed at transforming the PCI into a

wider political formation of the Left, which could make a fundamental contribution to the construction of an alternative government in Italy. We are aware that such an alternative implies a rapprochement of the left-wing forces and therefore an agreement with the Italian Socialist Party. We hope that this agreement may be facilitated by the proposal I made [...]. *The proposal that I put forward has been dictated by our own autonomous considerations and evaluations. We have never referred to conditions posed or suggestions made by the Socialist International* (our emphasis).[22]

Quite the opposite, in fact. We are conspicuously witnessing here that (a) the proposal forwarded by the leader of PCI had very much taken into account the policy framework and the informal suggestions made by the International and the SPD in particular; (b) the fundamental pre-requisite for the entry of the PCI to the Socialist International was its relationship with the PSI. Nevertheless, the political situation in the country was far more complex and such 'furtive' diplomacy had to be presented in a different fashion. Since the real objective was the *unblocking of the Italian political system*,

the constituent phase we wish to advance, is a unitary process which, on new bases, intends to aggregate an ample reformist area. It is a process that is developing before, during and after the constitution of the new political formation. It aims, moreover, at promoting a profound transformation of the entire political system.[23]

As Macaluso argued: 'We must look at our problems in a strict relation to the travail of our Italian democracy. This is the only measure with which the validity of our proposal can be measured [...]. The primary condition is to unblock the Italian political system [...].'[24]

This original claim of transforming the PCI *and* the Republic through an open constituent process enabled the neo-revisionists to identify some analytical points of paramount importance and even, I would say, be prophetic. Rejecting the proposal of Craxi who called for a 'socialist unity' but insisting upon a privileged rapport with the PSI during the constituent phase, the PCI further advanced some analyses made at the 18th Congress. Assisted by developments in the Central and Eastern Europe, the *quarantenni* were far more assertive in the view that the new world equilibria demanded from all the political forces a re-examination of their role and specific function in the political and institutional system of the Republic. The DC could no longer use the alibi of anti-Communism alone to keep itself in power — the ruling group argued — and if it did not want to be the mere expression of the current institutional decay, it had to become familiar with the challenges posed by the new national and international order and adopt the notion of the *political alternative*.[25]

Quite surprisingly, both the ruling group's platform and the introductory address of Occhetto to the Congress attempted to infuse a radical dimension into the very notion of the *costituente*. They overlapped, at some crucial points, with the theses of Ingrao's and Tortorella's opposition. We read, for example, that 'governing the world' meant also 'going beyond the logic and horizons of capitalism',[26] while arguing for a *costituente di massa* (mass constituent) and rejecting the idea of an 'opinion party' all along which, as we have seen, was introduced a year earlier at the 18th Congress.[27] As far as the new social movements were concerned, Occhetto proceeded with verbal puns to mollify Ingrao's demands, saying that the party would concede a certain political autonomy to them. On these grounds, the ruling group speculated upon his old thesis of a new 'grouping on a programmatic basis'.[28] Moreover, being aware of the appeal that the PCI's symbols and political rites exercised upon party members, the *quarantenni* made use of the old symbolism to counter-balance the general climate.[29] Overall, this is what we can call the 'retreat of new revisionism' vis-à-vis Ingrao's neo-Communism.

This pro-radical attitude did have some negative repercussions with regard to Occhetto's major allies, the *miglioristi* of Napolitano and the 'Left of Clubs', the latter being the only significant forces external to the PCI interested in joining the *costituente*. Let us outline here the most influential theses put forward by this last group, in order to decipher the tensions raised more easily.

The group was gathered around the theoretical review *Micromega* (founded in 1986). For a certain period it was a reference point for a potentially broader social grouping, the so-called *sinistra sommersa* (submerged Left) to which Occhetto appealed.[30] Key figures of the group shared some ideological principles close to a libertarian and revisionist idea of Socialism. A considerable number of intellectuals were under the influence of the Socialist-liberal tradition (e.g. Norberto Bobbio), and some revisionist versions of the Second International; others had espoused post-modernist theories, this being the case, for example, of the influential philosopher Gianni Vattimo. Politically, they were a rather pluralist *corpus* with various socialist and liberal nuances, but united on the general grounds of friendly attitudes towards the PCI. The group was fully conscious of the fact that the proposal of Occhetto represented a radical break not only with regard to the PCI's revolutionary tradition, but also with the corporatist system of the First Republic.[31] Paolo Flores D'Arcais in particular, was in favour of a radical reconstitution of the PCI and the Republic on the basis of 'smashing' the party's bureaucratic machine. Thus, he asked for a drastic reduction of party professional cadres and deputies.[32] In the characteristic spirit of *libertarian Socialism*, D'Arcais argued that the new party must be a *party of the citizens*, a fact which would enable the extirpation of inefficiency, corporatism, corruption and clientelism. Thus, he disagreed with the idea of considering the PSI of Craxi a component of the 'constituent phase' and even maintained that the new party should not consider its entry in the Socialist International as a legitimising factor of its democratic physiognomy.[33] Nevertheless, a number of other influential figures around the Socialist, Giorgio Ruffolo, who also had strong links with the pro-Socialist area of PCI (Napolitano-Macaluso), opted in favour of a PCI-PSI axis.[34]

The whole picture became rather complicated: on the one hand, D'Arcais and a large part of the 'Left of Clubs' implicitly agreed with Ingrao on the question of the PSI but, on the other, no satisfactory grounds for discussion with the *miglioristi*, the force with which the group shared similar ideological values, were found. Occchetto tried to mediate and fix a 'working disagreement' by articulating the different views. In doing so, though, he failed to present a new synthesis, giving rather the impression of an instrumentalist composition. In his reply to D'Arcais he wrote that 'the PCI is certainly opposed to Craxi's "socialist unity" strategy because it represents an ideological unity regarding the past' but, at the same time, he remarked that 'the new party will not be an anti-Socialist force',[35] meaning anti-PSI force. In this context, one can argue that Occchetto's main contradiction was that he argued for the refoundation of the Republic via the reform of the existing forces within it.

We can conclude that Occchetto's attempt to incorporate elements from Ingrao's platform whilst cautiously favouring a pact with Socialists, was dictated by two overriding needs: party unity, on the one hand, and the aim of achieving the widest possible participation of forces in the *constituente*, on the other. It follows that many of concessions made were only tactical in order to defuse the tensions. Up to a certain point, I therefore agreed with the criticism of Umberto Curi, a pro-*svolta* intellectual and member of the party's CC, who blamed the leadership that 'succumbed to that sort of consociational and mediation practices which are followed by the governing coalition itself'.[36] However, one needs to go further. The real problem for the leader of PCI was not how to avoid mediation in order to keep 'consociationalism' away. To a certain extent, this was rather unavoidable. In point of fact, the crux of the matter was how to produce, *through mediation*, a new, superior political synthesis going *beyond* the divergencies of the partners involved.

Despite the fact that the *quarantenni* appealed to Socialists, Greens, lay Catholics and the Radicals of Pannella, no significant external force was willing to join the *costituente*. Thus, any time Ingrao's opposition raised the questions 'with whom' and 'how' the *costituente* would really lead to a new political formation, Occhetto, in fact, would have to fall back on 'some powerful ideas which have already been established at the 18th Congress'.[37] Other pro-*svolta* intellectuals, like Michele Salvati, worried about the purpose of calling the whole operation *fase costituente*, inasmuch as it had only to deal with internal divisions of the PCI, that 'old and big organisation'.[38] So as we can see, the ruling group gave no real answer to the questions raised. In this respect, I conclude that the criticism of Occhetto advanced by various voices within the Italian Left and the pro-Ingrao opposition was, in the main, correct. Conditioned by the real absence of interlocutors, the *quarantenni* had to proceed with the *costituente* on the grounds of its own potential and by way of raising the gender question: *women should become a fundamental constituent component of the whole process, thus the transformation of the party assumed a gendered dimension.*

Although politically divided — an important section of women would choose the platform of Ingrao and Tortorella, signing the document 'Our liberty is only in our hands'[39] — this pressure group inside the PCI, played a vital political role for the party, particularly during the period in question. I shall deal here with some major claims of the PCI feminists and I will attempt to assess them in the political context of the party divisions. By doing so, the main point of divergence between the two factions will be raised and some significant issues concerning the new social movements as such will be touched on.

The *Carta delle Donne* of 1987, was the first document of Communist women which attempted to overcome the traditional feminist discourse of the 1960s and 1970s based on the notion of 'emancipation' and, instead, advanced the concept of 'sexual difference', a term employed by the French school of Luce Irigaray and post-structuralist theorists.[40] The starting point of these analyses was no longer a 'real capitalism' which the gender, after the working class, should oppose in order to liberate itself, but the sexualisation of society *ad hoc*, as it encompassed the contradiction — and therefore the hegemonic terrain — male/female. In the opposition between men and women, the latter have the sexual prerogative of determining the genealogy of the gender: 'women reproduce life',[41] the *Carta* argued. This theoretical premise gave the advantage to the argument that the societal can no longer be constructed on the predominance of a masculine archetype but, quite the opposite, it should be based on female centrality.[42] Although this argument seemed to be quite matriarchal, the *Carta* moderated its discourse by putting forward claims such as equity and equality: 'In our country, working women form 28 per cent of the workforce; female students form 52 per cent of our Schools and Universities; many of them are businesswomen and managing directors; *however, the women elected in the Parliament are only 7 per cent of the total, the same proportion as in 1946*' (emphasis in the original).[43]

Thus, there was underway a *feminisation of the societal but not a corresponding feminisation of the political instances* (party and state). In this context, the system of 'quotas' which would enable women to achieve an equal representation of sexes in the party apparatuses, should be introduced;[44] the abolition of the 'sexual division of labour' was endorsed, while an attempt to reshape society, working time and everyday life according to the new feminist conception, was proposed.[45] In short, the cardinal issues for the feminist discourse were three: equal representation of the female sex in political bodies, self-reference to their own sex (*dalle donne la forza delle donne*, the force of women stems from women themselves), reorganisation of the state and society on the basis of the female's centrality.[46]

While no serious disagreement was raised among the PCI women in drafting the *Carta*, severe interpretation problems appeared when the party split over the proposal of Occhetto. Criticisms of the mainstream pro-Occhetto feminists were made by Franca Chiaromonte, Maria Luisa Boccia, Letizia Paolozzi, Gloria Buffo and Marisa Nicchi. Their chief argument was that Communist women, by accepting promotion by men through the 'quota' system, in essence gave over their autonomy and the movement as a whole was in danger of being manipulated by the party bureaucracy. Hence, feminism would lose its autonomy and the claim of 'sexual difference' be absorbed in the dominant discourses of male and class powers. Consequently, women would not be a real constituent part of the new political force, but a politically institutionalised appendage of masculinity.[47] After all, Gloria Buffo argued, women were called by men to be 'founding partners' of the new political formation, simply because of the crisis spreading through the PCI.[48] This tendency endorsed the platform of Ingrao, which firmly insisted on the autonomy of the new social movements from the party apparatuses. By advancing a discourse of autonomy and body self-determination, Ingrao in fact won over the most radical part of the women's movement.

In replying to these criticisms, Claudia Mancina, Livia Turco, Anna Maria Crispino and Francesca Izzo quite rightly argued that their decision to sign the platform of Occhetto was in accordance with the political choices that all the PCI women endorsed at the 18th Congress and the *Carta*.[49] In addition, the opportunity offered to women to take part *equally* in the foundation of the new party, was unique: after all, symbols, rhythms, social timing, mechanisms and the relationship of force between the sexes could not change via an 'external' reflexion of demands, for they must struggle for their autonomous presence and radicalism 'from within'. All in all, while no divergencies were manifested in drafting the *Carta*, the PCI women were split on whether or not the institutionalisation of their movement was beneficial for the promotion of their cause.

We can now pass on to examine the platform headed by Ingrao, Natta and Tortorella, the main ideological and political faction which opposed the ruling group.

Cesare Luporini, Pietro Ingrao and gli orizzonti del comunismo

As we saw earlier, the principal requirements of the *svolta* advanced by the neo-revisionists, dealt with four points: i) The PCI change itself — inclusive of its name change — to change Italy; ii) reconstitution of the Republic and unblocking of the political system via the reconstitution of the Left; iii) institutionalisation of the new social movements and emphasis on cross-party contradictions; iv) reconstitution of the European system of governance through the Socialist International and advance of European integration. The platform of Ingrao opposed these points all along, one by one. Let us give an introductory table, summarising the principal points of divergence between the motions.

Table 11   The strength of the motions at the 19th Congress of PCI (1990)

(percentage received by each motion and main topics of disagreement)

RULING GROUP/*MIGLIORISTI* 67%	INGRAO-TORTORELLA 30%	COSSUTTA-CAZZANIGA 3%
Constituent phase/ re-name the party	Communist horizon of history	Against PCI's dissolution
Euroleft/Socialist International	Unimportant/beyond the two blocks/SPW	Toward socialist European polity
Institutionalisation of NSM	Autonomy of NSM	Union centrality
Privileged interlocutor: PSI	Illusion	Illusion
Bi-polar alternation in government	alternativa	alternativa
Programme's centrality	Masses' centrality	Working class centrality
Separation between public and private spheres	Capitalising on existing economic and political contradictions	Politico-economic power as a neo-liberal mono-lithic bloc

Key: SPW= Southern Peripheries of the World inclusive of Italy's South; NSM = New social movements. The allocation of votes regards the congressional vote where 1088 out of 1092 delegates voted. The vote in lower level regional congresses reflects almost identical levels. Source: PCI, P. Fassino archives, no file number; also, R. Armeni, 'PCI: prossimo venturo', *Rinascita*, 5, 11-3-1990, pp.4-8

1 According to Ingrao, and the platform *Per un vero rinnovamento del PCI e della Sinistra* (For an authentic renewal of the PCI and the Left), the internationalisation of capital, the crisis of 'really-existing socialism' and the 'post-Yalta' era objectively open a historical itinerary *towards Communism* to the party, not the thin end of the wedge *towards Social Democracy*. Communism is not a mere ideal but an *immanent tendency of capitalist society*. The Communist physiognomy of the party draws its meaning from this very fact and constitutes a substantial and not a formal matter for its political course. Led by the analyses of the Communist philosopher, Cesare Luporini, Ingrao vindicated an authentic Communist renewal and the party's heritage.

On 19 November 1989, Luporini published an article in the Communist daily *il Manifesto* where he attempted to theorise the concept of *Communism* as a category inherent to capitalist development and history.[50] Communism was to be seen as a *possibility to be achieved in the course of history*, inasmuch as it is innate to it by way of constituting its permanent *shadow*.[51] If 'historical materialism' has any sense, Luporini argued, this is precisely its *Communist real horizon*.[52] Yet Gorbachev's democratic experiment showed that this possibility was now broadened. This in turn implies that if Gorbachev lost the democratisation battle, the consequences for Italy and Europe would be enormous and the defeat far more serious.[53] In essence, the problems posed by the 'post-Yalta' era have a totally different nature. Gorbachev's proposals help Communists to understand that priority should be given to the transcendence of the two blocs and the issue of disarmament, while the question of the Southern peripheries of the world press for immediate solution. This was the real basis on which Gorbachev's efforts at injecting democracy into socialism must be conceived. The East was in turmoil and the whole process is rather libertarian and positive. Nevertheless, the crisis of the USSR was really dramatic and the transition would not be smooth and free of risk: 'The dissolution of the one camp can be the premise towards a world of cooperation and interdependence, but it can also very well give way to the dominance of the other camp.'[54] Therefore, the 'Eurocommunist' — though the term as such had never been used in the debate [55] — claim of going beyond the two blocs, was valid as never before.

Having said all this, the question of the *name* was not merely a formal *thing*. Communism was written in the objectivities of the societal axes, was a sort of *verità effettuale della cosa* — to use a Machiavellian wording — so it did exist beyond the single will of the party's leadership. Therefore, it was not an abstract ideal which can be faked by temporary events, such as the developments in the East. After all, Ingrao characteristically argued, *the Stalinist regimes have never been Communist regimes*;[56] there is not only 'one Communism', but 'many Communisms' and, in the final instance, Italian Communism has always, in one way or another, differed from Stalinism. These were some of the principal reasons for which 'the PCI can and must be transformed without neglecting itself'.[57] 'It is true', Tortorella argued in the Congress, 'that the name of Communism has been dishonoured by others; so they must change their name'.[58] So, in the first instance, the name must be defended for three main reasons: i) embedded in the capitalist mode of production and reproduction, Communism is not an abstract ideal; ii) it represented the cultural stronghold of Italian Communism; iii) by changing it now, while Eastern Communism was in deep disarray, it would give the impression that Italian Communism too had had no autonomy vis-à-vis Stalinism.[59] All in all, the Ingrao-Tortorella platform accused the ruling group of *empiricism* and *political opportunism*.

2 The vagaries of Occhetto's group did continue, since it employed a *classless* conception of politics,[60] set aside the historical role of the PCI in the foundation and democratic expansion of the Republic and, most importantly of all, misconceived the party's function in the political system. In a characteristic passage, Ingrao's motion stated powerfully:

> Many comrades argue that the dissolution of the party into a new political formation was the necessary pre-condition for the 'unblocking of the Italian political system' so to break the hegemony of the DC. This assertion means that the Italian political system is blocked due to the existence of the PCI itself.[61]

Presenting the issue in such a blunt fashion, the *fronte del no* wanted to make clear not only the defensive nature of Occhetto's proposal and the deadlock in which the party was directed, but also to stress the crucial disagreement regarding the issues of *alternativa* and *alternanza*.

The dissociation of the *political* from the *societal* and *economic* instances implied a politically misleading notion according to which the political change was seen simply as an institutional one. This, in turn, led to a, rather insignificant, conception of the political, obscured the impact of large private interests on politics and discouraged a rational radicalism from the bottom up. So instead of simplifying the political spectrum by lending more power to it, a supposed political bi-polarism would further intensify the links with private capital and its hegemonic presence in the political sphere. The *alternativa*, however, has nothing to do with the *alternanza*. The former points to a social/class notion of politics whereby political dominance is linked with the exploitative nature of the relations of production: opposing this bourgeois unity constitutes the constant democratic strategy of the Left. The latter refers to the *autonomy of the political power as such*, so no matter *who* holds it. Hence the categorical position of Ingrao: 'You cannot go into office without previously conducting a concrete struggle against the government, which in fact enables you to open, and thus capitalise on, some crucial contradictions present within the Conservative governing bloc.'[62]

Why was Ingrao *now* opposed to that 'Anglo-Saxon' notion of politics in Italy, since he was the first leading Communist politician to opt for institutional and electoral reforms? After all, similar — if not identical — theses drafted by the ruling group were endorsed by Ingrao at the 18th party Congress just a year earlier.

Apart from the qualified explanation given earlier concerning Ingrao's consent to the line advocated by the *quarantenni* between November 1987 and 1989, the fresh question posed involved a conjunctural dimension. I suggest that, under the specific circumstances — the probable debâcle of the USSR, the serious crisis of the *pentapartito* and institutions, the challenge of the party's historical name and symbols — it was impossible for Ingrao, Tortorella, Magri, Natta and all those who had conceived politics along the *mass paradigm*, to see a pure institutional reform *prior* to an overall change of class determinants. They dismissed the idea that the PCI had any drawbacks and saw no link between institutional reform and the party's transformation. In point of fact, Ingrao thought that the proposal advanced by Occhetto and others put the PCI on the defensive at the moment when it needed to advance a concerted attack against the *pentapartito*. In the last analysis, a functional 'bourgeois democracy' borne out of such a reform is a matter to be dealt with under different international and national circumstances. Thus, the political notion of *alternanza* proposed by the ruling group had catastrophic effects, disorientated the party, caused disorder: instead of presenting a strong Communist Party and mass initiatives throughout the country against the corrupt and 'Conservative governing bloc', the PCI too retreated.

Firmly against any hypothesis of making an alliance with the PSI and rejecting the idea that the 'Left of Clubs' represented a significant socio-political force, the *fronte del no* concluded that, even from a limited political standpoint, Occhetto's proposal was inadequate to find a way out of the crisis: precisely, it did not indicate an alliance policy, failed to design a new party identity and lacked any sound ideological principles; thus, for the time being, 'the proposal advanced by the ruling group, did not indicate a strategy for the future, while having already caused serious damage in the present'.[63]

3   The third point, namely, the cross-party conception of politics and the role of new social movements, was of particular importance. Strictly linked with the previous issue of the *alternativa* and the new *party form* under construction, the platform of Ingrao objected to the institutionalisation of the new social movements and claimed their autonomy as a *conditio sine qua non* for Communism.[64] Political structures, Ingrao's argument went, are tendentially closed, introverted, characterised by traditional classist structures which, as such, are prone 'to making politics on the basis of co-optation by imposing orders and propaganda from above'.[65] The vital space of new social movements was civil society itself which, via its inherent inequalities and injustices, constituted the chief motivation for their radicalism. To Ingrao, the *pantera* students' movement was indicative of the validity of such a position. Students did not demand the nationalisation of Universities: motivated by what was really happening *in* the Universities, they aimed at being recognised as 'autonomous subjects', and demanded the Universities be 'civil not public'.[66] In all, the new type of party should reflect the 'polycentric', differentiated and anti-hierarchic condition of Communism,

in such a framework that was external to capitalist institutions *ad hoc.* To preserve the *Communist horizon of history* and distance humanity from *barbarism*, the new political formation must be subjected to these imperatives. In point of fact, Ingrao never abandoned the conception of the 'socialisation of politics' via social radicalism, the very notion running through the pages of his masterpiece *Masse e Potere*, written in 1977. On the other hand, there was the need for the rehabilitation of the party's image and autonomy, damaged by the way Occhetto's group dealt with the crisis in the East. Ingrao asked for a sound identity and more independence of the party.[67]

4   This is the appropriate point to deal with objections regarding the issue of the Socialist International. Facing the challenge, the opposition was rather cautious, avoided harsh criticisms of the Euroleft and preferred references to the notion of 'new internationalism', established at the 17th Congress in Florence: disarmament, regional allocation of resources in favour of the South, environmental protection, struggle against concentration of power in the big monopolies and the media. However globalising are the dimensions that capitalist development assumes, they could never overcome the division between North and South, developed and underdeveloped peripheries. *Uneven development* was central to the structuring of economies, both nationally and globally. Certainly, Ingrao did not leave out an issue which was dear to him: once more, the leader of the opposition pointed out that *alienation* and *individualism* that were bound up with the production and reproduction of advanced capitalism depoliticise the subaltern classes. That is why the *real renewal* of the party should begin by way of *re-politicising* the masses, finding new links between their needs and their demands.[68] In this context, the platform of the opposition — under the influence of Tortorella and Angius — was very close to the Eurocommunism of the late Berlinguer. The following statement of Ingrao was particularly strong:

> If we fail to organise a popular action along these issues, then 'world administration' becomes rather a bitter phrase. Why not? We can try to build a new internationalism even by using the means of strike action [...]. A real struggle toward the overcoming of the two blocs which, in turn, is a battle against the 'military-industrial' complex [...], must begin. Otherwise, that great word 'non violence' will remain an ethical aspiration [...], but it will not reform politics. It is a highly demanding word and needs cohesion: *it cannot be pronounced without blaming the French Socialists who still defend their own atomic arsenals. I do not believe in a discussion with the Socialist International, and on the*

Socialist International, that does not enjoy such a cohesion [*our emphasis*].[69]

Ever since he began his research on the crisis of the nation-state and the internationalisation of capital (the early 1980s), Ingrao had been particularly aware of the evolutions in European Social Democracy. Interested in deciphering the way in which Social Democracy copes with the crisis of Keynesianism, he never really attacked the very notion of its reformist policies. Instead, Ingrao preferred, occasionally, to expose the main theses of the PCI in terms of the Eurocommunist notion, though not referring to it literally. The aforementioned statement, however, raised the problem from a different angle: at the moment when the PCI applied to join the International, both defects and merits would have to be openly announced. In that qualified context, the real issue for the party was not whether or not it would succeed in getting full membership. This was a parochial question. Rather, the fundamental tasks of the movement in the 'post-Yalta' world were disarmament, transcendence of the two blocs, pro-Southern policies and sustainable development. If the International agreed on these points, then there was no problem for the PCI in joining it. If it did not, then it would be better to stay out.

To recapitulate: Ingrao's platform opposed the four principal arguments of the ruling group all along. It dismissed any idea of supporting the 'constituent phase' with the PSI, and opted for a genuine alternative/anti-capitalist solution while the issue of the International was considered of secondary importance. The motion, focusing on the Marxist conception of *uneven development*, paid particular attention to the North/South divide, both globally and nationally (the Italian South). Motivated by the analyses of the Marxist philosopher Luporini, Ingrao maintained that the new *forma partito* must reflect the 'Communist horizon' of history: pledging the autonomy of new social movements and pointing to an anti-hierarchical organisational pattern against the division ruler/ruled. Thus, the name of the party went far beyond a question of semantics. In essence, the name *comunista* indicated the historical tendency which was embedded in the capitalist reality by way of constituting its permanent and innate possibility for achievement. Italian Communists have genuinely struggled since 1924 to bring this about: 'If the originality of the PCI was going to be cancelled', Ingrao said in a dramatic formulation in January 1990, 'then the history of Italy since 1925 is incomprehensible'.[70] We shall explore all the dimensions of Ingrao's faction in a broader context, while examining the contradictory pair of *new revisionism/communist refoundation*, which was the real combination of antitheses finally giving birth to the *Democratic Party of the Left* (PDS), on the one hand, and the *Party of Communist Refoundation* (PRC), on the other.

The orthodoxy of Armando Cossutta and the Socialist European Polity

The limited appeal the platform of Armando Cossutta-Gian Mario Cazzaniga had in the party — only 37 out of 1,088 delegates voted for Cossutta's platform — had little to do with its real contents, or the political positions this faction assumed soon after Occhetto took over the party leadership. After all, it was the only party group which remained consistent with its Marxist orthodox theses, for it presented a unique political continuity and cohesion while dealing with inner-party political and ideological debates or specific circumstances. For example, by skilfully using key theses of Marxist orthodoxy, Cossutta 'succeeded' where Ingrao 'failed': in point of fact, the document Cossutta presented in the run-up to the 18th Congress had clarified some crucial revisionist aspects of the positions put forward by the *quarantenni* and suggested that the identity of the PCI had definitely ceased to be a Communist one. In the words of Cossutta's document presented in November 1988 for the 18th Congress, 'strong reformism' is always reformism and as such 'is an inadequate political strategy; capitalism can absorb it'.[71] In my view, this methodology has a fallacious rationale: *the very essence of every political dogmatism, inclusive of the liberal one, is that they take ideological principles for reality, thus dismissing any possibility of conquering sufficient historical knowledge of both.*

Nevertheless, this has not always been the case. As we shall see — and despite defects which will be raised — the Cossutta-Cazzaniga trend attempts to outline a concrete and realistic programmatic proposal, while also offering, *in some respects*,[72] an original speculation over the issue of European integration. So the category of 'political dogmatism' is only partly applicable to Cossutta and his political followers. But if this is true, then what was the main reason behind the failure of the faction? Was it due to a certain isolation from the main *corpus* of the opposition of Ingrao, or should we go beyond this reasoning? I would suggest that the political débâcle of the 'Third platform' was due to the political history of the group as a whole, namely, the pro-Soviet position it took when Berlinguer was fighting to disengage the PCI from Brezhnevism and the Soviet Union in the 1970s and 1980s as well as its openly expressed opposition to the line of *compromesso storico*.[73] In short, with the USSR collapsing, this party faction had in fact very little chance of any success.

According to Cossutta's motion, the crisis of the PCI throughout the 1980s had no links with the social, economic and political changes of the period. Rather, it reflects the failed strategy of *compromesso* during the years of 1976-79, which subordinated the PCI to the DC and showed the limits of its political autonomy.[74] The capitalist restructuring of the decade was seen as an advance of the capitalist relations of production led by the *pentapartito*. The essence of the ruling group's ideas, according to the Cossutta-Cazzaniga account, was that they simply wanted to lead the process of restructuring by using the ultra-politicised notion of 'democratic alternative', whereby the opposition has an equal chance of becoming government and vice versa, while leaving intact the very exploitative nature of the capitalist mode of production. The November 1988 document argued:

> The party must choose. There are nowadays those who opt for a solution *à là Mitterrand*, that is an organic transformation of the PCI into a non Communist force [...]. All these people see the PCI as a force which is capable of putting itself forward as a candidate for the government of capitalist modernisation [...] on the basis of a reformist programme able to conquer the 'centre' of the political stage [...]. Both the internal contradictions and the points of divergence in the *pentapartito*'s cabinets are the expression of the Italian variant of neo-liberal policy.[75]

Seen in such a *reductionist* framework, the *pentapartito* was presented as a mere instrument manipulated at the will of the bourgeoisie, thus lacking any sort of institutional autonomy which was necessary to organise its own interests.[76] In point of fact, Cossutta's faction equated the political theses of the *quarantenni* with the actual policies applied by the *pentapartito*. A unique tautology was thus raised, in which it was difficult to understand why the bourgeoisie should opt for the liberal PCI and not once again — or forever — for the *pentapartito*, since both were experts in supply-side economics. In point of fact, the pro-Cossutta notion fell roughly into line with that of the party's 17th Congress, where the PCI, still caught up in ambiguity, focused on the claim that the *pentapartito* applied fully-fledged neo-liberal policies.

The PCI, since Togliatti, has *due anime* (two souls): the reformist/Social Democratic and the Communist. After all, that was the gist of the inner-party conflict in the 1960s after the death of Togliatti. The motion of the faction stated explicitly that it subscribed to that 'anti-imperialist and pro-workerist culture of Togliatti' that recognised political pluralism and endorses class unity with the PSI.[77] In this respect, the centrality of anti-imperialist struggles and the workers' movement was indisputable. What had to be done was the *Communist refoundation* of the party alongside the reform of the bureaucratised trade union. Cazzaniga, who was also director of the pro-Cossutta bi-monthly *Marxismo Oggi*, urged a reform/refoundation of the party and considered out of context Occhetto's proposal for a Conference in the Autumn: it was too late, he said.[78]

The motion of Cossutta-Cazzaniga, like that of Ingrao, backed Gorbachev's reforms. However, the arguments forwarded by the faction did not deal very much with the crisis of the USSR and the Eastern bloc. In fact, in the official documents of the group, the thesis often declared with regard to these regimes was deeply mistaken: 'The new Soviet revolution', the motion argued, 'returns to the Leninist legacy of self-government, Soviet and the NEP [New Economic Policy], all of which were abandoned by Stalinism and the Brezhnev era.'[79]

Admittedly, we can distinguish here two set of misconceptions.

The first concerns the ability of the faction to decipher the real developments in the East, which in fact were heading towards capitalism, not a deepening of Socialism. The second has to do with the policy of V.I. Lenin after 1921: in point of fact, Lenin's New Economic Policy, his famous 'tax in kind', his slogan 'let us learn how to trade and do business', the full application of Taylorist methods in labour relations — whereas before the revolution of October he was a fierce opponent of Taylorism — were only a *pro-capitalist economic policy and highly authoritarian in its own inner logic to advance the development of social productive forces in backward Russia.*[80] Cossutta's theses, various documents of this party faction dealing with that particular issue, failed to understand this crucial historical fact with regard to Bolshevism: hence the inept conclusion drawn.

The end of the Cold War was seen as a result of the demise of American hegemony due to the advances of West Germany, Japan and Europe. Thus, the USSR of Gorbachev was assessed positively since it promoted and propagated disarmament, peace and democracy.[81] Globalisation and interdependence are the new world economic, social and political realities with which the world and European Communist movement has to deal. This said, the PCI, with its principles and distinct Communist culture, should have acted as a catalyst in order to advance both a *Socialist Democracy for Europe* and a *Socialist Democracy for Italy*. The great merit of the Cossutta-Cazzaniga motion was that it offered *concrete* proposals in both cases. Let us outline the main ideas of this dual project.[82]

The trade unions must assume a non-bureaucratic form and, for this to be achieved, the transcendence of the centralised tri-partite deals (state-union-enterpreneurs) in contractual bargaining is required. Not far from the proposal of the ruling group — with the cardinal exception of the *electoral reform* — the institutional reform sketched by the motion comprised, among other demands, the abolition of bi-cameralism, full autonomy of the judiciary, reinforcement of the national character of the National Health System and anti-trust legislation. Women were seen as a distinct social subject whose proposed institutionalisation damaged their autonomy, while the critical environmental situation pointed once again to the need for state planning and the transcendence of capitalism. The question of disarmament remained central — the motion talked about a 'de-militarised development'[83] — and the loss of the party's identity as 'collective intellectual' needed to be rehabilitated: 'The party is no longer that collective intellectual inspired by Gramsci and Togliatti; it is rather subordinate to capitalist modernity, legitimates the existing order and succumbs to ideologies disseminated by the information monopolies of Agnelli, Berlusconi and De Benedetti.'[84]

As far as the Southern question was concerned, a rather bleak picture was drawn: the capitalist restructuring in the 1980s worsened its endemic problem, inasmuch as scant attention was given to it either by private entrepreneurs or the Italian authorities.

Nonetheless, the aforementioned reasoning was not to search for solutions in the restricting bounds of the Italian nation-state alone. If it is true that capitalism is becoming globalised, problems and solutions are becoming equally globalised. For instance, the fiscal crisis of the state, the motion argued, should be solved not via technocratic avenues at the national level by damaging citizen's income. Welfare legislation and the reinforcement of European welfarism were an urgent need. In this respect, a *European coordination* via the construction of a European bank and common monetary policy were raised. The reinforcement of the European Parliament was necessary also as an instrument to counterbalance Germany's hegemony in Europe.[85] Having said all this, the key question became the ideological and political premises by which the European Left would deal with the process of European integration. The claim for the entry of the PCI into the Socialist International was completely out-of-date. As original developments were taking place on the world scale, the founding of a *new International* was required. The Socialist International was no longer adequate to express the new developments. After all, this organisation hosted parties that were explicitly 'reactionary' (e.g. the PSI).

In conclusion, I would argue that the political discourse of the Cossutta-Cazzaniga motion was affected by *reductionism*, as it is linked to the structural predominance of capitalist relations of production to which no degree of autonomy of the institutional materiality — on the basis of which ruling political classes constitute their hegemony — was recognised. Had not this been the case, the Cossutta-Cazzaniga faction would have understood that the *pentapartito* was not eager to implement neo-liberal policies. Moreover, the opportunity the PCI enjoyed to organise its own interests once in office would have been recognised. On the other hand, however, the faction attempted a courageous exit to 'the world of the concrete': in fact, as far as its proposals over Europe and institutional reform were concerned, it made far more concrete proposals than the platform of Ingrao-Tortorella. Many of the themes proposed were in fact accepted by the ruling group. The sole principal disagreement with it was certainly the insistence of Cossutta on the proportional electoral system.

Reflections on cross-inner-party alliances

The neo-revisionists feared a split. Nor was such an evolution improbable, inasmuch as Cossutta's group had been seriously advocating it since the 18th Congress.[86] Nevertheless, a careful study of the whole situation shows that, for a whole series of reasons, an extended split comprising the Ingrao-Tortorella faction, was highly unlikely.

Admittedly, with the *pentapartito* in crisis, Ingrao would never have offered it the chance to recover by splitting the PCI. His political culture, otherwise strongly identified with the post-war history of the party, was one of party unity, not division.[87] On the other hand, he knew that none of the motions involved in the debate — inclusive of his own — was without serious problems. Yet, Ingrao was conscious of the fact that, despite the clear-cut party consensus enjoyed by the core group around Occhetto, an extreme party emergency could only be handled collectively. Occhetto's problem was not only the ultra-reformism of *miglioristi* (Napolitano, Chiaromonte, Macaluso, Lama), but also various objections put forward by prominent party cadres who finally supported his proposal in the decisive Congress in March.

Since I have dealt with the positions of the *miglioristi* and their major points of divergence from the core ruling group of Occhetto, I will illustrate here some important personal initiatives concerning, I would say, a sort of 'cross-factional alliances', since cadres from both principal motions examined so far shared some fundamental political and ideological conceptions. The document presented by Antonio Bassolino in the run-up to the 20th party Congress due in January-February 1991, was hemmed in by this 'cross-cutting nature'.

Alberto Asor Rosa, leading theorist of *nuovo corso* and editor of the new series of *Rinascita*,[88] argued that the majority *Ingraiani/Occhettiani* — to which he belonged — formed during the 18th Congress, was not a myth and that many comrades shared this position. Since then, there is no doubt that new questions were posed by these developments. But instead of facing them by capitalising on the real conquests of that Congress, Asor Rosa continued, the current alignments towards the new one reflect either mere *idealism* or pure *pragmatism*. Opting for Ingrao's motion, which was rather a utopian document, did not necessarily mean sharing all its positions. However, better utopia than Occhetto's pragmatism. Asor Rosa called his thesis a 'counter-motion' and hoped that the Congress of Bologna would give the party the possibility of recomposing its internal equilibria, the current ones being false and mystificatory: 'From the documents presented', the PCI intellectual argued, 'very little is understood.'[89] Mario Tronti, of the *fronte del no*, too, reached similar conclusions as he was engaged in investigating the new type of party adequate for the Italian Left. As far as the ruling group was concerned, I confine myself here to observing the doubts put forward explicitly by party and trade union leaders like Bassolino and Trentin.[90] Bassolino went so far as to challenge the neo-revisionist cohesion of the *quarantenni* as follows: 'In essence, we like the crisis. The more serious — and even catastrophic — it is, the more challenging the perspective for a radical change becomes.'[91]

However, if we take into account any single view expressed especially by party politicians (e.g. D'Alema, Veltroni) or intellectuals (e.g. Vacca, Badaloni et al.), the whole question of cross-intra-party speculation becomes extremely complicated while, from an analytical point of view, it jeopardises the validity of the research by giving the impression of underestimating the main cleavages raised.

Table 12 Divisions and factions in the PCI

19th Congress; cadres and intellectuals expressing intentions at going beyond the
pro-Occhetto/anti-Occhetto cleavage

Pro-Occhetto/*fronte del sì*		Anti-Occhetto/*fronte del no*
B. Trentin		M. Tronti
A. Bassolino		A. Asor Rosa
L. Turco	(Pro-Occhetto)	A. Minucci
	M. D'Alema*/W. Veltroni**	

* M. D'Alema had reservations about the alliance strategy and tactical objections to the
way Occhetto was handling the whole operation of the *svolta*;
** W. Veltroni had demonstrated pro-liberal/democratic positions, see also, R. Armeni,
'PCI: prossimo...', op. cit.

The analysis leads us to several reflections. First of all, given the degree of
fragmentation at the time, no party group or faction could handle the
political consequences of a real organisational split. The party was already
dramatically divided on a number of key issues, while serious divisions
existed even within the same alignments or groupings. In the second
place, the 'picture' was read by Ingrao not only in terms of halting the
party fragmentation, but also in the belief that a future 'reshuffling' of
these fluid components might work in his favour. Thirdly, every time
Ingrao raised — always implicitly — the issue of the split, he did so in
order to shift, as much as possible, the positions of the ruling group
toward the left. And he succeeded in this. In essence, Ingrao had never
thought a split likely *immediately* after the Congress or in the short-run.
*This was the main reason why he aligned himself with Cossutta in the run-
up to the next party Congress in Rimini, although the latter was always
threatening a split.*[92] After all, his platform had been defeated
democratically while the *pentapartito*, despite its profound crisis, was still
there, in office. Therefore, the split would have been unrealistic, politically
unacceptable and party militants would not have understood it. Indeed, a
careful study of Ingrao's and Tortorella's speeches during the campaign of
the *fronte del no* in the run-up to the Bologna Congress, shows that they
had no intention whatsoever of splitting. For example, in his first public
pre-Congressional debate in Milan in the *Sala della Provincia* on 11
January 1990, the leader of the Communist opposition, facing the
crowded hall, announced: 'What I can see here, is that the party is moving
on. This is what we wanted: defeat the frustration and ask Occhetto's
supporters to recognise, at least, the merit of this very fact.'[93]

Occhetto had tears in his eyes on hearing the aged communist leader at the end of his speech at the Bologna Congress saying:

> I have read in some newspapers about the threat of a split. Those making similar suggestions deceive themselves. I do not intend to leave the party! [*altro che andarsene*!] We invite men and women of this country, now, to become members *of this party*: because we are here to show that this party must live and renew itself.[94]

Assessing these trends from a specific angle that goes beyond the party's 'duplicity', we are witnessing that the PCI was also subjected to a different kind of *duality*. On the one hand, it gave the impression of solid alignments gathered around prestigious leaders and sound ideological references. On the other, serious cross-party mobility was taking place challenging the existing relationship of forces. Given that Ingrao had no intention of splitting, I suggest that the ruling group should have acted with more determination on the basis of the theses it formulated, rather than mediating among the intra-party 'unstable equilibria of compromises' simply to compose the diversity for the sake of party unity, a practice which had so often led to instrumental politico-ideological syntheses.

Notes

1   See, for example, B. Craxi, 'Diffido di questo PCI: non è l'ombelico del mondo', *Corriere della Sera*, 9-3-1989, p.2, F. Geremica, 'Gli auguri di De Mita, l'anatema dei socialisti', *La Repubblica*, 11-10-1990, p.5.

2   M. Caciagli, 'The 18th DC Congress: from De Mita to Forlani and the victory of «neodoroteism»', in F. Sabetti, R. Catanzaro (ed.), *Italian Politics; A Review*, v.5, op. cit., p.16.

3   On more than one occasion Occhetto would maintain that 'the line of socialist unity is an idea of the past' while the PCI's operation 'is addressing a proposal for the future' see, among others, his interview with P. Mieli in Turin's daily *La Stampa*, 'Sbloccare il sistema è una necessità democratica', 14-1-1990, now in *Un Indimenticabile...*, op. cit., p.177.

4   See G. Pasquino, 'The De Mita government crisis and the powers of the president of the Republic: which form of government?', *Italian Politics; A Review*, v.5, op. cit., pp. 49, 53. The most conspicuous allies of Craxi who supported his proposal were the neo-fascist MSI and the then President of the Republic, Francesco Cossiga.

5   The agony of the PCI over this question can clearly be seen when going through the correspondence of Occhetto and Napolitano with leading figures of European Social Democracy. Characteristically, on March 7, 1989, the PCI secretary wrote to the SPD president Hans-Jochen Vogel: 'I wish to let you know about the tensions which suddenly came into being between the PSI and the PCI. We regret the fact that the PSI secretaryship has disseminated the idea that I have "speculated" on the positions of the

SPD. Nothing similar happened [...]. I have never said that in the course of my talks in Bonn there were expressed on behalf of the SPD or Willy Brandt a favourable position vis-à-vis the PCI's entry into the Socialist International'. Occhetto sent the same letter to M. Guy Spitaels, then President of the union of European Socialist parties; see PCI, *P. Fassino archives* (7-3-1989), no file number.

6   M. Caciagli, 'The 18th DC Congress...', op. cit., p.19. M. Braun in his *L'Italia...* (op. cit., p.100) will state: 'At the top management of IRI Franco Nobili was appointed, from Andreotti's current; the general direction of RAI was given to Gianni Pasquarelli, a follower of Forlani [...]. Craxi put at the top management of ENI the socialist Gabriele Cagliari. The third industrial corporation, EFIM [...], had a philo-Craxi president and pro-Andreotti vice-president'.

7   F. Sabetti, R. Catanzaro, 'The 1989 events in perspective: the end of an era or the past as the future?', in F. Sabetti-R. Catanzaro, *Italian Politics*, v.5, op. cit., p.3.

8   The PCI was fully aware of these negative developments as well as their impact on the political system; see, among others, the articles of Claudio Petruccioli written on the eve of the DC's Congress, 'Qualche domanda al Congresso DC', *L'Unità*, 17-2-1989, p.2, and E. Macaluso, 'Ciriaco al finale di partita', *L'Unità*, 14-4-1989, p.2, written a month before the official resignation of the De Mita government.

9   A. Occhetto, 'Sbloccare il sistema...', op. cit., pp. 176-177, and also the view of the PCI constitutionalist A. Barbera, 'Riforme elettorali, si può anche mediare sulle differenze', *L'Unità*, 1-10-1990, p.2.

10   G. Pasquino, 'The electoral reform referendums', in R. Leonardi, F. Anderlini (ed.), *Italian Politics: A Review* (London: Pinter Publishers, 1992), v.6, p.9.

11   Ibid., p.11.

12   See, L. Di Mauro, 'Palermo che resiste', *Rinascita*, 4, 4-3-1990, pp. 4-7.

13   Quoted in J. B. Urban, 'Gorbachev's visit to Italy and the Vatican', in F. Sabetti, R. Catanzaro (ed.), *Italian Politics; A Review*, v.5, op. cit., p.131.

14   On 28 January 1990, Gorbachev was forced to recognise the dynamics of the whole situation and agreed on Germany's unification. On 26 February 1990, another dissapointing event took place: the front of Sandinistas of Daniel Ortega in Nicaragua lost the election against the anti-Communist alignment of Violeta Chamorro.

15   See L. Benini's articles: 'Il novanta in movimento', *Rinascita* (new series), 1, 11-2-1990, pp. 6-12 and 'Occupati e preoccupati', *Rinascita*, 2, 18-2-1990, pp. 20-23; for a more general speculation outlining the pros and cons of students' demands see S. Bruno, 'L'iceberg che sta sotto la riforma Ruberti', *L'Unità*, 15-2-1990, p.2.

16   L. Benini, 'Il novanta...', ibid., p.7.

17   L. Benini, 'Occupati...', op. cit., p.23.

18   The students' criticism of the PCI touched this very point, see the correspondence between Occhetto and students in *L'Unità*, 3-3-1990, p.4.

19   PCI, *Documenti per il Congresso Straordinario del PCI; le Mozioni*, 3 (Roma: L'Unità, 23-1-1990), p.3-4, thereafter: *PCI/3: Mozione 1*, A. Occhetto, 'Un nuovo inizio...' (Report to the 19th Congress, 7-3-1990), op. cit., p.25.

20   *PCI/3: Mozione 1*, op. cit., p.12.

21   *PCI/3: Mozione 1*, p.8. On this subject, see also P. Bufalini, G. Chiaromonte, 'Per un partito riformista, socialista e democratico', *Critica Marxista*, 1, Jan.-Feb. 1990, pp. 39-45.

22   A. Occhetto to W. Brandt (Rome 6-2-1990), *P. Fassino archives*, no file number.

23   *PCI/3: Mozione 1*, p.14.

24   E. Macaluso, 'Intervento al 19o Congresso', *L'Unità*, 11-3-1990, p.26.

25   See, A. Occhetto, 'Un nuovo inizio...' (Report to the 19th Congress, 7-3-1990), op. cit., p.26.

26   *PCI/3: Mozione 1*, p.4.

27   In fact, Occhetto himself would admit, by the end of his speech, that some fundamental elements from the platforms opposing his own had been incorporated into his analyses since the CC of November 1987; see, A. Occhetto, 'Un nuovo inizio...', op. cit., p.26.

28   *PCI/3: Mozione 1*, pp. 25 ff.

29   On this subject, D. I. Kertzer, 'The 19th Congress of the PCI: the role of symbolism in the communist crisis', in R. Leonardi — F. Anderlini, *Italian Politics; A Review*, v.6 (London: Pinter Publishers, 1992), pp. 69-83. Kertzer theorises further his views in his *Politics and Symbols; The Italian Communist Party and the Fall of Communism* (New Haven and London: Yale University Press, 1996).

30   Occhetto's speeches apart, see on this topic in particular G. F. Serra (ed.), *Una Magnifica Avventura...*, op. cit., pp. 17-24.

31   'The *pars destruens* of Occhetto's proposal points to the institutional reform *par excellence*, points to the end of the First Republic', L. Caracciolo would maintain in his essay 'La sinistra che non è', *Micromega*, 1, 1990, p.35.

32   See P. Flores D'Arcais's letter to A. Occhetto, 'Un partito del cittadino' (5-1-1990), *Micromega*, 1, 1990, pp. 13-14.

33   D'Arcais, moreover, would denounce the Craxi-Berlusconi pact and call the leader of PSI 'populist-reactionary'. 'Craxism', D'Arcais wrote, 'represents a new Right for Italy', see ibid., pp. 15-16.

34   See, among others, G. Ruffolo, 'Le tre vie dell'alternativa', ibid., pp. 25-31.

35   A. Occhetto, 'Una scelta obbligata' (12-1-1990), *Micromega*, 1, 1990, pp. 19, 22.

36   U. Curi, 'La genesi del Partito democratico della sinistra', in U. Curi-P.F.D'Arcais, *L'Albero e la Foresta; il Partito Democratico della Sinistra nel Sistema Politico Italiano* (Milano: Franco Angeli, 1991), p.26; also his *Lo Scudo di Achille* (Milano: Franco Angeli, 1990).

37   In particular, A. Occhetto, 'Un nuovo inizio...' (7-3-1990), op. cit., p.24.

38   M. Salvati, 'La sinistra ridisegnata: note per una Convenzione', *Politica ed Economia*, 3, March 1990, pp. 9-13. Salvati outlines the agenda of the new party which should be discussed in the programmatic Convention on the new type of party due the following Autumn.

39   To a certain extent, the division of women on the proposal of Occhetto challenged the authority of the joint document *La Carta delle Donne* [see *Dalle Donne la Forza delle Donne* (Trento: Mondatori, 1987), henceforth: *Carta*] in which the contents of 'sexual difference' was supposed to be constitutionalised within a Communist, not another, political horizon. On this subject, see the debate between L. Turco and R. Rossanda in *il Manifesto* (19-12-1989 and 10-1-1990).

40   The books of Irigaray were translated in Italy in the mid-1970s by Luisa Muraro, leader of the *Libreria delle Donne* (Womens' Bookshop) in Milan.

41   *Carta*, p.27.

42   On this topic also, L. Turco, 'Il mondo comune delle donne', *L'Unità*, 8-3-1990, p.2.

43   *Carta*, p.15.

44   'The communist women intend to incise onto politics the *sexual contradiction*', ibid., p.15. Turco and Mancina fought for a 30 per cent quota in the leading organs of the PCI and in the CC elected from the 18th Congress achieved an increase in the

number of women from 40 to 93; for a satisfactory 'Who's who' of the PCI feminists, see S. Brusadelli, F. Caccarelli, 'Chiedo aiuto compagne', *Panorama*, 1237/38, 7-1-1990, pp. 54-59.

45 *Carta*, pp. 32-34.

46 See also, 'Lettera alle donne comuniste', in *PCI/3: Le Mozioni*, pp. 80-84. Among the most prominent women who intervened in the debate were Miriam Mafai and Rossana Rossanda. Both criticised the concept of *sexual difference* as 'separatist' (Mafai) and 'lacking in social problematic' (Rossanda); see M. Mafai, 'Le vedove di Lenin e la deriva feminista', *Micromega*, 4, 1990, pp. 7-15, R. Rossanda, 'La creatura del patriarca', *il Manifesto*, 2-2-1990, p.10.

47 See, G. Buffo, 'Identità politica e differenza sessuale', *Critica Marxista*, 1, Jan.-Feb. 1990, pp. 47-54.

48 Ibid., p.49.

49 See, *inter alia*, L. Turco, 'Il mondo comune...', op. cit. and her 'La mia coerenza', *il Manifesto*, 10-1-1990, p.6 and *Idee e Proposte per la Costituente* (16-6-1990), Sezione Propaganda del PCI (Roma: Iter, 1990), F. Izzo, 'Le donne da «questione sociale» a «soggetto fondante»', *Critica Marxista*, 1, Jan.-Feb. 1990, pp. 157-62.

50 C. Luporini, 'L'utopia della liberazione ha un futuro?', op. cit.

51 D. Sassoon operates in a similar theoretical framework (D. Sassoon, *One Hundred Years of Socialism*, op.cit.); the difference being that Sassoon, in contrast to Luporini, maintains that *Socialism, not Communism, is the real shadow of capitalism*.

52 Since then, many attempts have been made to apply the term to the current political debate; see, for example, G. Ferrara, 'Per la rifondazione dell'identità comunista', *Critica Marxista*, 1, Jan.-Feb. 1990, pp. 107-15.

53 See P. Ingrao, 'I comunisti e l'Est', *il Manifesto*, 4-2-1990, p.10. Nonetheless, Ingrao formulated similar theses much earlier, see for example his interview with C. Valentini, 'Gorbachev ti voglio bene', *L'Espresso*, 8, 26-2-1989, pp. 36-41.

54 *PCI 3/Mozione* 2, p.40. On this point, the principal mover of the *fronte del no* in his Introductory speech in the Congress, Aldo Tortorella, also insisted, see 'Mozione 2: L'Intervento di A. Tortorella', *L'Unità*, 9-3-1990, p.15.

55 Instead, however, Ingrao's current used the term 'new internationalism'. We shall deal with this issue further on.

56 P. Ingrao, 'Non toccate il nome' (interview with G. Corbi), *La Repubblica*, 7/8-1-1990, p.5. The same thesis by Ingrao in his speech at the CC of the *svolta* in 20-24 November 1989, in *Documenti/1*, p.50, or in his answer to C. Testa in *Micromega*, 'Con Marx oltre Marx', *Micromega*, 5, 1990, p.73.

57 *PCI 3/Mozione* 2, p.38.

58 A. Tortorella, 'Mozione 2: Intervento...', op. cit.

59 Within that characteristic spirit, Rossanda reacted to Occhetto's proposal from the beginning of the *grande svolta*, see R. Rossanda, 'Dove è finita l'autonomia dei comunisti Italiani?', *Il Manifesto*, 17-11-1989, now in G. Moltedo-R. Rangeri, *PCI: La Grande...*, op. cit., pp. 139-40.

60 'A doctrine which ignores the nexus between economy and politics, state and society, will not solve anything but, I fear, the contrary: it will rather aggravate the crisis of the Italian Left', A. Tortorella, 'Mozione 2: l'intervento...', op. cit., p.15.

61 *PCI 3/Mozione* 2, p.47 and also, S. Garavini, 'Cambiar pelle al PCI per rifondare la politica? Sarebbe troppo semplice', *L'Unità*, 6-1-1990, p.2. It should be noted that that was the position of many PSI cadres too.

62 P. Ingrao, 'Non toccate...', op. cit.

63   *PCI 3/Mozione* 2, p.37. At this point, however, I should not fail to mention efforts made by a few pro-*svolta* PCI intellectuals on the topic of the party's cultural identity. I would distinguish the contribution of G. Vacca who, in two series of articles in *L'Unità*, attempted to present an innovative notion of hegemony, deepening the Gramscian and Togliattian conceptions, see G. Vacca, 'Ciò che la cultura italiana deve al Marxismo', *L'Unità*, 29-4-1990, p.2, 'Nè dittatura nè egemonia della "cultura di sinistra"', *L'Unità*, 30-4-1990, p.2 and his books relevant to the subject.

64   *PCI 3/Mozione* 2, pp. 53-56.

65   Ibid., p.55.

66   See also the interesting discussion between Ingrao and Rossanda in *il Manifesto*, 21-2-1990, pp. 6-7.

67   Ingrao was paying particular attention to this point especially while campaigning for the Congress. We distinguish here the following statement of Ingrao made at the event organised in Rome on 15 January 1990 in the Metropolitan cinema: 'there is no party renewal whatsoever, if a lack of capacity in deepening the autonomy and the identity of the party, is manifested.' See R. Cagliardi, 'Ingrao: nuovo è comunista', *il Manifesto*, 16-1-1990, p.7.

68   *PCI 3/Mozione* 3, p.45.

69   P. Ingrao, speech in the CC of the *svolta*, 20-24 Nov. 1989, in *PCI-1*, p.52.

70   P. Ingrao, 'Non toccate...', op. cit., p.5.

71   *Un Nuovo Corso per il Socialismo* (26-11-1988), op. cit., p.11.

72   For example, the faction of Ingrao-Tortorella-Magri was so focused on ideological and political matters, that no concrete attention was given to European integration and globalisation processes.

73   Characteristically, when after the electoral retreat of the party in the extended local election of May 1990 (see below) Cossutta asked Occhetto to resign, D'Alema answered the challenge as follows: 'I have great respect for every comrade, inclusive of Cossutta, but when I think of the way he conducted such a harsh polemic against Berlinguer (on the question of Soviet Union etc.), then certainly he should be silent for another 15 years', M. D'Alema, *La Repubblica*, 9-5-1990, p.11.

74   See Cossutta's speech in the Congress, 'L'Intervento di Cossutta' (8-3-1990), *L'Unità*, 9-3-1990, p.16.

75   *Un Nuovo Corso per il Socialismo*, op. cit., p.12. Costanzo Preve, an orthodox Marxist intellectual, in his criticism of the 'new course' of Occhetto, will go so far as to call it *una sintesi culturale neo-borghese, aristocratica ed elitaria* (a neo-bourgeois cultural synthesis, aristocratic and elitist). However, the Marxist philosopher will recognise that 'our neo-Communist and neo-Marxist platform [of Cossutta] does not yet exist', see C. Preve, 'Una Bad Godesberg Italiana: Note per una discussione seria sul nuovo corso del PCI di Occhetto', *Marxismo Oggi*, 3-4, May-July 1989, pp. 1-7.

76   See also formulation of the Cossutta-Cazzaniga motion in the run up to the 19th Congress, *PCI 3/Mozione* 3, p.68.

77   Ibid., pp. 65-68.

78   M. Cazzaniga, 'Mozione 3: Le Conclusioni al 19o Congresso' (9-3-1990), *L'Unità*, 10-3-1990, p.22.

79   *PCI 3/Mozione* 3, pp. 64-65.

80   For a full development of these points, V. Fouskas, *Populism and Modernisation; the Exhaustion of the Third Hellenic Republic, 1974-1994* (Athens: Ideokinissi, 1995), pp. 20-99.

81   What is dubious, however, is the extent to which this sort of 'pro-Gorbachevism' indicated a real belief of the faction or, because of Gorbachev's popularity at the time, a disguised political opportunism.

82   *PCI 3/Mozione 3*, pp. 71-79.

83   Ibid., p.75.

84   Ibid., pp. 76-77.

85   Ibid., p.78.

86   See in particular, A. Cossutta, 'Vogliamo l'unità del PCI? Allora consentiamo liste distinte di Candidati', *L'Unità*, 13-4-1989, p.2.

87   Rossana Rossanda, in referring to the case of the expulsion of the Manifesto group from the party in 1969, answered the question as to why Ingrao had not left the party and joined the group, as follows: 'For those knowing Ingrao, this is not a mystery. His judgement was that our struggle was an acceleration of the events making the intra-party battle more difficult instead of helping the cause of internal democracy', R. Rossanda, 'Comunismo Manifesto' (interview with P. Meli), in *Storia* (supl. in n.2035 of *Epoca*), 8-10-1989, p.31.

88   *Rinascita* suspended publication on March 3, 1991, after 47 years (the first issue appeared in Naples in 1944).

89   See A. Asor Rosa, 'È un'operazione a perdere', *L'Unità*, 11-1-1990, p.2; from his various contributions to the party weekly *Rinascita*, we distinguish 'Per essere antagonisti', *Rinascita*, 7, 25-3-1990, pp. 4-5. For a reply to Asor Rosa, see G. Vacca, 'L'argomento Asor Rosa', *L'Unità*, 1-2-1990, now in his *Dal PCI al PDS*, op. cit., pp. 162-64.

90   See A. Bassolino, 'PCI, oltre i sì e i no' (interview with G. Moltedo), *il Manifesto*, 20-1-1990, p.8, B. Trentin, 'Al di là del Sì e del No' (interview with R. Cagliardi), *il Manifesto*, 31-1-1990, p.10. For a more general speculation on this topic, V. Fouskas, 'Il nome della cosa: Eurocommunism, the Euroleft and the crisis of PCI' (in Greek), *Economicos Tachidromos*, v.20, n.188, 17-5-1990, pp. 68-70.

91   A. Bassolino, 'Intervento al 19o Congresso' (9-3-1990), *L'Unità*, 10-3-1990, p.19. This statement, would not only challenge the *miglioristi* allies of Occhetto and the leading group: in fact, it would be too leftist to be adopted in such an open fashion even by the platform of Ingrao's opposition.

92   P. Ingrao, personal interview, op. cit.

93   S. Menichini, 'Ingrao sveglia Milano', *il Manifesto*, 12-1-1990, p.7.

94   P. Ingrao, 'Mozione 2: le conclusioni...', op. cit., p.22.

6   Governing the Party Crisis (2): Internal Realignments and Ambiguous Identities

The conjuncture

'The facts', Edward Carr argued in a notorious passage in his *What is History?*, 'speak only when the historian calls on them: it is he who decides to which facts to give the floor, and in what order or context [...]. The historian is necessarily selective'.[1]

As we are amidst the most fascinating events of the period, it is worthwhile underlining this speculative proposition which, after all, has been used throughout the study. In the previous section, for example, while dealing with conjunctural events before examining the 19th Congress, we have necessarily distinguished some of the most fundamental movements and events which were to contribute to the destabilisation of the First Republic. In this section, I will focus on some specific conjunctural determinants affecting both the transformation of the party and the political system. These determinants are: i) the administrative election of May 1990, the first electoral test for the PCI's *fase constituente* and a general test for the national election of 1992; ii) the crisis of the CGIL due to the proposal put forth by the general secretary, Bruno Trentin, for the dissolution of the union's factions (20-9-1990), and thereby, of the Communist one too; iii) the crisis in the Persian Gulf in which the anti-war and pacifist mentality of Communists was gauged; iv) the *Gladio* affair which was the first post-Cold War test contesting the political boundaries of the ruling coalition; v) the role of judges in the crisis, which decisively added yet another important destabilising factor, perhaps the most crucial one, contributing to the disintegration of the regime. I shall deal with these conjunctural determinants separately, though it will become clear that at least some of them are strictly connected.

i   As early as November 1989, Giancarlo Pajetta — *il ragazzo rosso*, as he used to be called by his veteran comrades — warned the ruling group in the following manner: 'Before putting your hands together celebrating victory, you should wait for the electoral results.'[2] Pajetta's gaze was drawn to the administrative election of 6-7 May 1990: should the party results be good, the *svolta* would be verified and its premises reinforced; if they were bad, everything would have become much more difficult, not only for Occhetto but also for the party as a whole. The election was called in order to renew 15 regional, 87 provincial and 6,274 communal councils. They were devastating for the PCI, as the table below shows.

Table 13 1990 regional election results, compared to the 1985 regional elections

Parties	1990	1985
DC	33.4	-1.6
PCI	24.0	-6.2
PSI	15.3	+2.0
MSI	3.9	-2.6
PRI	3.6	-0.4
PLI	2.0	-0.2
PSDI	2.8	-0.8
DP*	1.0	-0.5
Leagues**	5.4	+4.8
Greens***	5.0	+3.3
Others	3.7	+1.2

*DP = Democrazia Proletaria; **Total sum of votes received by various regional Leagues; ***Greens: the figure refers to the totality of Green lists. Source: *Corriere della Sera*, 9-5-1990, p.1

During the electoral campaign, Occhetto's appeal to the electorate was based on the major themes of the *svolta*: the whole world was dramatically changing, Italian governments could no longer be formed on the principle of 'Communism/anti-Communism', therefore the PCI must also change in order to change the country and prevent a new government centred on DC: 'The vote for the PCI means that Italians say no to a new Christian Democrat political cycle; they say yes to unblock the political situation, facilitating the unity of the Left towards a new reformist political force.'[3] Occhetto's reasoning and appeal met with no response. The PCI dropped to 24 per cent of the vote and the administrators of the *svolta* became more susceptible to criticism, especially from the left.

Soon after the election, Cossutta asked the ruling group to resign. Sergio Garavini, Aldo Tortorella, Gavino Angius and others insisted on the salvation and renewal of the PCI, relinquishing any idea of changing the name. The reasons of the defeat, they argued, could be traced back to November 1989, when Occhetto launched the *svolta*.[4] In the CC held between 15 and 17 May, Mario Santostasi further argued that 'the *svolta* itself has precipitated a tricky politicisation, without social subjects; that the whole thrust of the operation was deeply conservative by drawing resources from the system which it supposedly had to replace'.[5]

Occhetto dealt with the arguments of the opposition by asserting that the kernel of the *svolta* had already been approved at the 18th Congress of the party and that both the Central Committee of November 1989 and the 19th Congress had initiated the *fase costituente*.[6] Consequently, Occhetto continued, the argument according to which the party's electoral losses were due to its subordinate political strategy, did not stand up. Quite the opposite: it hampered a serious reflection over the deepest causes of the defeat which, in turn, should also be seen as a defeat, though a less conspicuous one, for the ruling bloc itself. As Occhetto put it: 'the vote does not give a satisfactory consensus to the ruling bloc, while castigating the Left.'[7] What were the key social and political trends revealed by the vote?

According to the PCI secretary, the vote should be analysed along two major roads. The first concerned a crisis of political representation, a fact which could be seen from the electoral success of the Leagues, forces that were external to the corrupt system of power, as well as from the high number of abstentions, the blank and invalid votes. The second had to do with a sort of 'merging' between the Southern civil society and the *pentapartito*'s system of power on the basis of clientelism. 'We are witnessing the phenomenon of southernisation of the five-party coalition and its essential components, both of the DC and the PSI', Occhetto argued.[8] In this context, the party's defeat was due to (a) the general crisis of the national system of power and (b) the delay of the party itself in undertaking and accomplishing its renewal. The rise of the Leagues in the robust civil society of the North on the one hand, and the clientelistic basis of politics in the fragile and weak civil society of the South on the other, reinforced the validity of the party's institutional reform proposal.[9] Consequently, had the PCI not been developing its radical transformation, the electoral result would have been even more devastating. The party therefore needed to precipitate its constituent phase, acquiring a concrete identity so as to cease being *nè carne nè pesce* (neither meat nor fish).[10]

There are two major interlinked conclusions that can be drawn from Occhetto's survey: the first is that the PCI was fully conscious that the political system of the First Republic had seriously started to fragment. Having said that — and this is the second conclusion — the *fase costituente* needed to be hastened and the transformation of the party accomplished as soon as possible.[11] Accordingly, any view based on the motto 'the longer the *fase costituente* lasts, the better it is for the party' — a variant of which, as we saw, was expressed by Occhetto himself — had to be abandoned. In point of fact, the sooner the transformation was completed, the better the chances for the new party would be to achieve its programmatic alternative and lead the transition process. Nevertheless, the party's soul-searching continued and the only serious initiative in which it has been involved was the referendum movement of Mario Segni.

ii As we have seen, Segni's initiative constituted the first type of a 'cross-party alliance' which, potentially, threatened the DC's monopoly of power. The original idea was that three referenda should be held. The first was to determine whether Italians wished to reduce the preferential votes in each constituency in parliamentary elections for the Lower House. The second was to abolish the ceiling of 65 per cent for direct election to the Senate, replacing it with a simple majority system for 237 seats while allocating the other 77 seats by proportional representation. The third was aimed at the extension of the majoritarian rule which assigns 80 per cent of the seats to the winning lists in towns with a population of less than 5,000. On 2 February 1991, the Constitutional Court declared that the second and third referenda were inadmissable. Therefore, Italians had to vote only for or against the first one. On 9 June 1991, despite Craxi's ironical invitation to voters to 'go to the seaside', 62.5 per cents of Italians refused to go and voted overwhelmingly in favour of the reform.[12]

Having said this, it is worth noting that the ruling group of the party, in its attempt to back the referendum initiative, found itself in conflict with both *miglioristi* and *ingraiani*. The former group only paid lip service to the cause of electoral reform and the campaign in the run up to the 9 June referendum, because it did not want to displease its privileged allies, the PSI. The latter saw no organic link between electoral reform, the democratic extension of civil rights and social struggles. As for the CGIL, while it called on people to vote in favour of the electoral reform, it was indeed more concerned with its internal problems. In short, one should not fail to note that this sort of sluggishness coincided with the unwillingness of the ruling bloc to reform the political system.[13]

iii As early as February 1990 in the party's weekly *Rinascita*, Riccardo Terzi speculated on the dissolution of the CGIL's Communist faction. If the PCI dissolved itself into a new political formation, he argued, then so should the Communist component of the trade union.[14] This fact added another difficulty to the crisis of the union in the 1980s and made its reform ever more pressing.

The CGIL was traditionally associated with both the PCI and the PSI and with their respective organisational factions as well as a cumbersome bureaucratic machine. It now needed to initiate its own complete transformation so as to adjust itself to the new industrial (e.g. post-Fordism) and social (e.g. immigrants' work) trends. In addition, it had to cope with the institutional crisis and the fiscal question which affected the redistributing capacity of the state — hence, its welfare dimension — the effects of a common European labour market as well as the ever-persisting problem of the modernisation of the South.[15] It was obliged to elaborate a new comprehensive proposal which overcame traditional factionalism.[16] In short, the CGIL's set of problems resembled those which challenged the very existence of the PCI. The main difference was that the whole gamut of the crisis now had to be adapted to the specific 'nature' and needs of the union. In this perspective, Trentin attempted to explain that the real point at issue was not the Communist or the Socialist identity of trade-unionists *per se*, but the profound changes in labour relations *ad hoc* caused by the capitalist restructuring that had taken place throughout the 1980s. These changes dictated a *new form* of trade unionism. A union of 'rights and solidarity' was required:

> The trade union of rights is founded on the premise which unites the whole world of labour: we are not referring to income-based social strata or old professional identities alone, but also to the dependent, subordinated, heterodirected labour, whether manual or not. In the trade union of rights the factor which unites intellectual and manual labourers is their own being as executive, dependent labourers.[17]

Though the issue of the dissolution of the union's Communist faction was already raised in the wake of Occhetto's proposal, it was accepted much later in the 12th Congress of the CGIL which was held at Rimini from 23 to 27 October 1991. Rimini, it should be remembered, was not only the cemetery of the old PCI, but also the death-rock of the Communist faction of the CGIL and the beginning of a new era for the biggest Italian union.

'Whatever its eventual effect on parties', Carol Mershon maintained in her account of the CGIL's 12th Congress, the decision to dissolve the Communist faction 'was surely affected by changes in the Italian Communist Party'.[18] This can be seen not only by the way personalities positioned themselves vis-à-vis Occhetto's proposal (e.g. Trentin was in favour of Occhetto, while Fausto Bertinotti adopted Ingrao's motion), but also through the concrete theses expressed in the documents presented in the run up to the 12th Congress. The Congressional theses of the majority around Trentin echoed the views of the party's ruling group: the reform of the state was a pre-requisite for a fairer distribution of resources, the humanisation of work and a profound reform of the union was necessary for it to become a decisive co-determinating partner in the policy-making of enterprises.[19] On the other hand, the motion *Essere Sindacato* advanced by Bertinotti, Buffardi and Gremaschi saw the trade union as an intransigent actor of the class struggle, fighting against alienation and exploitation of labour-power, calling for a 'different model of development'; in other words, the themes of Ingrao's left.[20] Tension between the Communist minority and the Secretariat were also raised over the Gulf War issue. While soon after the attack of the allied forces in Iraq (16-1-1991) the CGIL Secretariat with other trade union federations asked for diplomatic initiatives to mitigate the effects of the crisis and end the war, Bertinotti's faction advocated an intransigent anti-war position and called for a strike. In this perspective, one can also add a further factor, namely, the intentions on the part of the CGIL's ruling group to agree on the abolition of the *scala mobile*. In fact, on 31 July 1992, the leaders of the three biggest trade union confederations — the CGIL, the CISL which was traditionally tied to the DC and the UIL which was linked to the PSDI, PRI and PSI — signed an agreement with the *Confindustria* (the employers' federation) which effectively abolished the *scala*. The real antithesis raised was between the culture of 'co-determination' implying the participation of the trade union in choices taken within the bounds of firms, and the 'conflictual' character of the union centred along the notion of class struggle. Since we shall discuss the wider framework of this conflict later, let us move on to another conjunctural determinant.

i v On 3 August 1990, the Iraqi leader **Saddam** Hussein, in an attempt to present himself as leader of united Arab world awakening old 'irredentist' claims, invaded Kuwait. The Andreotti government decided on the participation of Italian warships in NATO's mission to the Persian Gulf. Both Italian Houses of Parliament approved the mission. The PCI abstained on the vote and asked for the opening of a new phase in international relations, while calling on the United Nations to assume full responsibility.[21] Ingrao and the *fronte del no* made a gesture not seen in the post-war parliamentary history of the party: instead of abstaining, they opted for openly expressing their opposition to the government. This was the reasoning of Ingrao:

> I do not share De Michelis' thesis that the American intervention in the Gulf is preventive. I do not agree with that speech of praise [elogio]. I do not feel secure at all about the role of the USA as gendarme of the world, at a moment when the Warsaw Pact and the Red Threat no longer exist [...]. I am sensible too, and I understand the

responsibility of my act. I did not do it easily; but in certain moments one cannot, one cannot really remain silent.[22]

On the other hand, Napolitano and the *miglioristi* accused Occhetto's faction of succumbing to Ingrao's left and argued that such a stance would isolate the PCI from mainstream politics. In fact, the *miglioristi* put pressure on the ruling group to support a pacific mission in the Gulf via the initiative of the United Nations.[23]

That the 20th Congress of the PCI — which was to take place a few months later during the Gulf War — saw Ingrao and Napolitano as the chief actors was no accident. Their arguments symbolised, in the best of ways, the two different roads along which the new identity of the PDS could be shaped: competence, pragmatism, responsibility and respect in the decisions of international official bodies for Napolitano; radicalism, the right of the peoples to self-determination, anti-capitalism and anti-Americanism for Ingrao and the neo-Communist Left. This is also another particular angle from which one can look at the party's *historical duplicity*, which was about to come to an end.

v   Ironically, at the moment the Americans were witnessing anti-war and hostile behaviour by the PCI, they were also beginning to withdraw their support from the DC-PSI government axis. On 9 October 1990, that is, one day before Occhetto presented the new party name and symbols at a press Conference, a bricklayer in Montenevoso Street in Milan, the ex-hide-out of the Red Brigades, discovered a documentary dossier belonging to the ex-DC stateman and protagonist of the *compromesso storico*, Aldo Moro. The document included serious implications against Andreotti and Cossiga, Premier and President of the Republic respectively. It also implied, in a codified form, the existence of a 'stay-behind' para-military and clandestine structure, what later came to be known as *Gladio*. The purpose of *Gladio* was to prevent, by any means, the participation of the PCI in government power. In particular, Moro's document alluded to the whole 'strategy of tension' in the 1970s which began with the bomb blast in *Piazza Fontana* in Milan in 1969, as having taken place under the auspices of Andreotti, Cossiga and highly regarded politicians of the DC. In fact, Moro argued that he had been the victim of a strategy orchestrated by the Americans, Andreotti and DC officials working 'behind the scenes'.[24]

Andreotti openly admitted the existence of such a structure even before the appearance of the Moro document.[25] He dated it back to the 1950s, though he tried to fend off accusations regarding his personal involvement, adding that such structures existed everywhere; therefore it was legitimate, necessary and opportune in the very system of power created by the Cold War. Cossiga, who was minister of Interior during Moro's kidnapping by the Red Brigades, went some steps further and, in taking the whole affair personally, made a harsh attack on the institutions, the *partitocrazia* and, in particular, the PCI and judges. By making extraordinary use of his Constitutional powers, Cossiga threatened both to dissolve parliament and offer his resignation.[26] At the same time, he demanded the limitation of the powers assigned to judges. Additionally, by opting to support a Presidential system, Cossiga expressed theses very similar to Craxi's and the MSI's. This all added another problem for the newly formed alliance of Craxi-Andreotti-Forlani and in fact prompted its disintegration.[27]

As Stephen Gundle and Simon Parker have argued, the crux of the whole matter was that American diplomacy no longer had any intention of backing a DC-PSI axis of power at any cost. In addition, both the DC and the PSI, by 'assuming that the "triumph of capitalism" was an endorsement of the rather peculiar form it had assumed in the context of post-war Italy',[28] fell short of understanding the impending revolutionary changes stemming from the end of the international relations system established at Yalta.

The PCI immediately grasped the meaning of the events and reacted forcefully. On 17 November 1990 the PCI organised a very successful anti-*Gladio* rally in Rome and the ruling group did not cease to demand both the dissolution of *Gladio* and the resignation of the ruling political class.[29] 'Everything in Italy', Occhetto explained in an interview, 'was done in order to stop the Left's coming to power. Any kind of Left, even the DC left on certain occasions: against Nenni in the 1960s, against Moro, against the students in 1968, against us. Why? because everything had only one goal: making the power of those who already held it eternal.' And the PCI secretary went on to argue:

> A year ago we launched our transformation. Its very meaning was to take account of the fact that the whole world is changing. I talked about a new start. All the parties should have the capacity to understand these changes [...]. It must be clear that we propose the radical change of the whole system of power.[30]

As mentioned above, Occhetto presented the *dichiarazione di intenti* (declaration of intent) and the party's new name and symbols on the day after the Moro document was discovered. The PCI's process of dissolution/reconstitution was at its height when the disintegration of the political and institutional system was beginning: *we are witnessing in fact two parallel forms of transition which, on the one had, saw the PCI in a position of 'catching-up with the events' while, on the other, the ruling coalition was lagging far behind them.*

vi We can now look at the role of the judiciary in the crisis. In their attempt at exercising in full the independent role assigned to them by the Constitution,[31] the magistrates were constantly at odds with the governing parties and the PSI in particular during the 1980s. On 20 July 1990, that is before the revelation of the Moro document, Felice Casson, a judge from Venice, asked Andreotti for access to the documents of SISMI in order to investigate the Paetano bomb blast in 1974.[32] Andreotti was positive and gave his permission. However, when the eruption of the *Gladio* affair resulted in a judicial investigation and Casson asked Cossiga himself to testify, the President refused to do so. Casson was forced to resign, with Cossiga taking further steps in frenziedly accusing of corruption the judiciary, political personalities and parties.[33] It is worth noting in closing that the Socialist Claudio Martelli — then Minister of Justice — in an attempt to control the activities of the CSM, made an alliance with Cossiga with both demanding a limitation of the judiciary's excessive powers.[34] In short, the *Gladio* affair and the serious frictions between the judiciary and the ruling political class in 1990-91, paved the way for what was yet to come: the extensive scandals of *Tangentopoli* (Kickback City), which saw the judges as crucial actors in the struggle against the corrupt ruling class, a prolonged affair which finally brought about the downfall of the First Republic.

We possess now an entire critical overview of the framework within which the transformation of the PCI took place. Moreover, we are also aware of the fact that in the wake of the PCI's crisis and dissolution, the whole DC-PSI regime began to tremble. In point of fact, all the principal symptoms of the crisis, which were present in a latent form throughout the 1980s, as well as the emergence of the forces which led to the final destabilisation of the First Republic, had appeared between 1989 and 1991: the *Lega Nord* of Bossi, the referendum movement of Segni, the distinct role of the judges in the *Gladio* affair. The PCI's diagnosis was correct, for it promptly saw the symptoms of the crisis as they were visible in the electoral result of the May 1990 administrative election and talked about a 'crisis of political representation', meaning that the ruling forces no longer represented the unity of the popular will, that is, the *real country*.

In the run-up to the 20th Congress — with some important 'reshufflings' — three platforms were also presented: a. the ruling group with the *miglioristi*; b. Ingrao and Tortorella allied with Cossutta in a joint motion of the *fronte del no*; this turned out to be a highly fragile pact, since Cossutta's supporters left Rimini soon after the foundation of the PDS; c. Bassolino, in an attempt to straddle the two positions, split from the *quarantenni* and, while accepting the name change and symbols, proposed a qualified 'labour-style' motion; this attempt too proved precarious; a week after the Rimini Congress and to the surprise of many of his followers, Bassolino turned back to re-join the neo-revisionist ruling group. Undoubtedly, the most surprising characteristic of the Congress was that no imaginative ideological and/or political problematics emerged, since in fact all of them had been presented in the run-up to and during the 19th Congress in Bologna and party factions confined themselves to arguing about the Gulf War.[35]

I shall first examine the neo-revisionist positions, seeking to pinpoint the issues around which significant progress was made since the Bologna Congress. In this context, I will pay attention to the party's programmatic Conference held in late October 1990, whose main aim was to establish the conception of a new *type of party* as well as to propose a *federalist* notion of the state, around which the political renewal of the PDS was to be constructed.[36] Thereafter, I will deal with the theses of Bassolino-Tronti-Asor Rosa, which are bound up with the question of the *party identity* and *programmatic physiognomy*, inasmuch as Bassolino himself was to have been appointed by the party as coordinator of the working groups in the run-up to the October programmatic Conference. By calling for a *partito antagonista e riformatore* ('antagonistic and reforming party'), Bassolino's move was intended to be the real innovation of the Rimini Congress although, as we shall see, it fell short of expectations. In this respect, I will present the joint theses of Ingrao's and Cossutta's currents, which appeared under the name of *Rifondazione Comunista* and which were metamorphosed into the future Communist Party of Italy. The *miglioristi* refused to present their own platform by arguing that such a move would weaken the ruling group in confronting Ingrao's left. In short, I will attempt to discuss the arguments shaping the identity of the PCI/PDS, and then offer general speculation on the juxtaposition of *new revisionism-communist refoundation*, which is intrinsic to the tensions existing within the Italian Left up until the present.

The PDS, the second Italian republic and the question of federalism

The 20th Congress of the PCI, which was the 1st Congress of the PDS, was held in Rimini between 29 January and 2 February 1991. While the previous Congress in Bologna had taken place simply to authorise the principle of the new party, that is, the process of the constituent phase, the present one was a founding Congress: it had to establish the new party, the PDS, ratify its new symbolism and constituting principles, elect its new leaders and seek to accommodate itself in the given political relationship of forces in Italy and Europe. In view of the fragmentation of the political system and the internal political *status* of the party, the difficulties for the ruling group were far from imaginary.

The *dichiarazione di intenti* ('declaration of intent') presented by Occhetto on 10 October 1990 together with the party's new name and symbols, was the first official document of the new party. It had been announced a few weeks before in Modena during his speech at the festival of the party's daily, *L'Unità*.[37] Occhetto explained that the *dichiarazione* was neither a systematisation of ideological principles nor a concrete medium-term programmatic platform. Rather, it aimed at 'constituting the basis of a proposal which will be further enriched during the preparation and the unfolding of the 20th Congress'.[38]

The document further specified some points with regard to the crisis of the Eastern regimes asserting their collapse with more confidence; it argued that a *governo mondiale* (world administration) in the post-Yalta era was possible, implying that this role would be taken over by the United Nations;[39] it also explained with particular clarity the crisis of the ruling bloc and the role of a 'new reformist party' which, in Italy, 'has never existed'.[40] The present *social, ideological* and *political* crisis, Occhetto argued, was bound up with the process of European unification and the collapse of 'actually-existing socialism'. If the new party wished to decipher properly the organic crisis of the *pentapartito* and lead the process of modernisation — Occhetto talked about 'a different government of the modernisation process' — then it had to read developments in an *organic* manner. All the three dimensions of the crisis cannot be seen separately from each other. Occhetto's 'organic reading' of the crisis had a *peculiar leftist connotation*. Let us decipher this peculiarity.

Occhetto argued that the present phase of modernity and technological advances in particular, are not to be identified with human progress. Modernity included *in se* a distorted notion of development and progress, because it had been achieved under capitalism, therefore under the supremacy of *profit*.[41] In this context, the Left had to 're-think the entire notion of progress' and assume as its major objective 'a coherent projection for the transformation of society'. In his words, '...modern economic development which brought the primacy of exchange-value over use-value and the reduction of every good into a commodity, has shown its limits today. This forces us to think of a new relationship between the two terms'.[42]

He went so far as to consider purposeless any political notion whose rationale is based on a mere programmatic logic:

> A different government of modernity cannot be achieved through programmes, behavioural and political locations which accept the existing mechanisms. In fact, it requires a real mutation of power equilibria and programmes which promote profound changes. Without a profound mutation in the relationship of force, without the knowledge of the necessity of such a concrete and coherent alternative project, the defeat and the humiliation of the Left is the logical outcome.[43]

There is no need to explain further here that this discourse is affected by Ingrao's critique of *capitalist* modernity. The point at issue, however, is to understand why Occhetto decided to accompany the important historical moment of the birth of PDS with such a leftist argumentation.

When Occhetto presented the *dichiarazione* of the PDS, his right-wing allies gathered around Napolitano-Macaluso were increasingly isolated, inasmuch as the USA was moving toward an armed conflict challenging the anti-war sentiments of the PCI. Meanwhile, Bassolino's group, though not yet having put forward a platform, had taken the first steps by demanding a class identity for the new party. Fears of splits and inner-party manoeuvring apart, two further important reasons which pushed Occhetto into a left-wing position can be pinpointed. First of all, the international conjuncture in which the transformation of the party was taking place gave the impression that the PCI had changed itself because there was a dramatic shift in public opinion against Communism after the collapse of the Eastern regimes. Thus, the party had succumbed to the masses' 'false consciousness', employing opportunistic *tout court* decisions. Secondly, by claiming that 'the PCI change itself to change Italy', a possible interpetation was that it was impossible to change Italy hitherto because of the very existence of a Communist anti-capitalist party. As we have seen, both these arguments were developed by Ingrao's opposition, which accused the ruling group of *omologazione* (homologation), meaning the party's surrendering to (a) a false notion of Communism and (b) the capitalist process of modernity. Having said this and taking into account the intra-party unstable equilibria of compromises, *our thesis is that Occhetto attempted to give a left-wing identity to the PDS to fend off accusations from the party's left and tip the relationship of forces.* In this context, the judgement passed on the *dichiarazione* by Tortorella, Angius and others, according to which 'the dichiarazione is founded on democratic liberalism',[44] was made in rather a hurry, hence it was completely untenable. It was no accident that almost all the members of the party minority later recognised that the ruling group had shifted toward the positions of the minority, especially over the Gulf War issue.[45] Therefore, I argue that a certain retreat of *new revisionism* in the face of the positions of *Communist refoundation* represented by the left of Ingrao marked the whole period between the two Congresses.

At the end of his speech, Occhetto referred to organisational questions: he proposed the *de jure* abolition of 'democratic centralism', argued for a party based on the principle of *differenza* (difference), though not opting for a 'discussion club' party: 'the party must be united on the field of representation, political action and direction.'[46] Finally, he presented the new name and symbols of the party: *Democratic Party of the Left*, the same name as that proposed by Salvati and Vecca several months previously, with its symbols — designed by Bruno Magna — being an oak tree (the symbol of the French revolution) with a reduced version of the old PCI logo at the base. Occhetto added that 'none of these roots must ever be cut off',[47] thus replying indirectly to speculation that the PCI logo would be dropped in the future.

The eruption of war in the Persian Gulf influenced all aspects of the Congressional debate and overshadowed critical issues, such as the question of the party's entry to the Socialist International. Faced with the American initiative and determination to solve the crisis by violent means, not only did the lack of importance of the International become clear, but the weakness of Europe as a political force having a say in the whole operation became even more evident. As Tortorella rightly put it: 'The party faction to which I belong, has not made the question of the entry of the party to the Socialist International a question of principle. Nevertheless, the insignificance of this organisation in these critical circumstances is more than obvious.'[48]

Only the left-wing of Ingrao and the *miglioristi* of Napolitano-Macaluso had expressed clear-cut views on the Gulf War. While, for Napolitano a mere denunciation of the war was not enough if the PDS wished to acquire a 'culture of government',[49] for Ingrao only a pacifist culture promoted by the new party through mass movements would enable the European Left to play a leading role in the post-Yalta era.[50] Occhetto held a 'centrist' position and looked sympathetically to the verbal pacifism of the American Democratic party.[51] His speech, though now more concrete and detailed, was along the lines of the *dichiarazione*. Despite the fact that he compromised with Ingrao's fraction on a number of issues, on the questions of the reform of the state and the need for a new *forma-*

partito, both Occhetto and the leading group remained firm. Yet, they improved their analyses, while the *fronte del no* often gave the impression of not having understood that the debate had moved ahead into another phase; that the point at issue was no longer the defence of the name and symbols but, as D'Alema put it, 'what sort of party needs to be constructed and along with what set of principles'.[52] In addition, the ruling group employed more than assertive tones in arguing that the DC-PSI axis was unable to rule the country, that the 'real enemy is the DC system of power', hence a profound change of the Republic was required. In the words of Occhetto in his introductory speech in Rimini:

> We need to take into account and act on the grounds of the crisis of the DC as a party-state, its organic impossibility of interpreting, today more than ever, the exigencies of the development of the country [...]. *The taking the field* [scendere in campo] *of a new political force* [meaning the PDS] *that has at the centre of its programme the reform of the political system and the democratic refoundation of the state, is almost a national emergency* (emphasis added).[53]

Thus, amidst all the intra-party manoeuvres and the question of the Gulf War, the PCI/PDS had to deal with issues such as the new party's programme and identity (political, organisational, ideological), themes that were seen as inseparable from the broader questions of the new *forma-partito* and the *federal reform of the state*. As we have mentioned above, Bassolino was the coordinator of the working groups preparing the *programmatic platform*, while Fassino and Barbera were responsible for the issues of the *forma-partito* and *forma-stato* respectively. The programmatic Conference of the party scheduled in late November and announced, as we have seen, since the very inception of the *svolta*, was to be the culmination of these interlinked issues. An analysis of them is of particular significance for many reasons.

First, comes the mistaken notion that the new party's programmatic platform is the result of the very recent revolutionary changes taking place in the party. This was, for example, the thesis of Gianfranco Pasquino who thought that the PDS' programme was only a 'brand-new formulation which came in response to some of the Bologna Congress decisions'.[54] Secondly, by failing to pinpoint the subtle division of labour between Bassolino and Fassino in the run up to the Conference, even sharp analysts such as Stephen Hellman saw the Conference as an unimportant event inasmuch as 'its rapporteur was Bassolino who used the occasion to spell out what became the third motion to the 20th Congress'.[55] This is merely an exaggeration, simply because the principal innovation on organisational and other matters related to the new *forma partito* came from Fassino, not Bassolino. In point of fact, Hellman's thesis is valid to the extent it refers to the general programme drawn up by Bassolino, which in fact was identical with his own motion, and not to the working groups and the Conference as a whole. The last point I would like to draw attention to is that, to the best of my knowledge, no study of the transformation of the PCI pays proper attention to the serious programmatic effort of the PCI/PDS on the *federal reform of both the state and the party*.[56] Thus, the degree of awareness of the PCI/PDS of the crisis of the First Republic, is generally underestimated. The issue of federalism, which turned out to be of paramaount importance for the coming years due to the political success of the *Lega Nord*, was one of the three core problematics of the Conference, the other two being the electoral/institutional reform and the new *forma-partito*. The coordinator of the working group on the regional/federalist reform of the state was the party constitutional expert Augusto Barbera.[57] We shall now turn to examine these points in detail.

Both Barbera and Fassino presented identical views on the crisis of the nation-state, which somewhat further qualified Occhetto's conclusions drawn after the May 1990 administrative election. Barbera, who talked clearly about a *federalist refoundation of the state*,[58] argued that, under the present circumstances, a set of three major reforms were required: i) individualisation of the spheres in which the state should intervene; these include, for example, foreign and defence policies, market regulation and social protection, civil rights and relationship with the Church etc.; on the other hand, local and federal governments should enjoy, for example, legislative autonomy;[59] ii) transformation of the parliamentary system; this implied abolition of bicameralism, reduction of deputies for the House and the founding of a federal parliament; iii) the 'taxation question' as a specific issue to be looked at, simply because of the importance given it by the Leagues. Being strictly linked with the dramatic situation of public finance, the Leagues argued that the fiscal crisis should not be staved off on the basis of increasing the contributions of the robust civil society of the North. Barbera recognised that the problem posed by the Leagues was real and argued that only *l'autonomia impositiva* (autonomous tax regulation by the regions) could provide a viable solution. All three points met with the approval of Occhetto in his concluding remarks.[60]

Fassino's task was rather more difficult, for he had to present not only a full reasoning along organisational and political lines, but also to provide a radical departure and a detailed account of organisational and constitutional party matters, which were to be the governing institutions of the party (e.g. the party's new statute). Fassino convincingly summed up the two crucial factors which determined the very changes of the party identity in the 1980s: firstly, the crisis of the nation state and Keynesianism questioned the capacity of the party system — and first of all of the opposition, that is, the PCI — to respond to and satisfy increasingly differentiated societal demands; secondly, the crisis of 'actually-existing socialism' added yet another difficulty in the formulation of a successful Communist political strategy. He then proceeded with a sharp remark, which basically constituted the only convincing answer to the opposition of Ingrao on the *Communist question*:

> Certainly, if it is true that Communism as an ideal of equality belongs — and will continue to belong — to the history of human thought [...], it is likewise true that Communism as a concrete political experience and historical form of state organisation of power, has failed.[61]

The way the problem of *Communism* was posed by Fassino significantly improved the neo-revisionist argumentation as a whole and, furthermore, contributed to the clarification of the notion of *new revisionism* vis-à-vis that of *Communist refoundation* which derived from the analyses of Ingrao. In point of fact, Fassino implied that the ideal of *Communism as a libertarian perspective* did not differ from that of *libertarian Socialism*, which was adopted by the ruling group. However, while the former experienced a failed historical reification, the latter was inherent in the actual phase of socio-economic development. It was precisely on this basis that the party could formulate its own political and ideological renewal. We shall draw out all the implications of this position while examining the juxtaposition, specific to the Italian political system, between *new revisionism* and *Communist refoundation*. For the time being, it is important to discuss Fassino's agenda on the new *forma-partito*, that is the PDS.

Fassino had no difficulty in admitting that 'the future political formation stems from the PCI itself, so it is the result of its cultural, historical, political and organisational experience'.[62] This remark was also a clear-cut confirmation, for it posed the question as it stood, beyond the circumstantial rhetoric of Occhetto, who envisaged constituent partners at the moment when they did not exist. Political and ideological changes in the party, Fassino proceeded, *must necessarily be accompanied* by organisational ones, because it was the very form of the party apparatus which condensed and reified the programmatic, ideological and political instances. With regard to its past, the new party form presented elements both of *continuity* and *discontinuity*.

The elements of continuity were:[63]

a   The party remained a *collective intellectual* (Gramsci) to promote intellectual and moral mobilisation throughout the country as well as the autonomous development of citizenship.

b   It should continue to be a *mass party*, in terms of its capacity to organise the masses in an increasingly complex society.

c   The party ought to be a *non-ideological* organism in which membership was based on whether its concrete programme was acceptable, independently of philosophical, religious or other biases.

d   The party had to become an *organisation for change*, which was not limited to collecting demands, but also promoted and directed them by virtue of increasing the autonomy of citizens.

The new elements to be introduced were:[64]

a   The *coscienza del limite della politica* ('the notion of limit of politics'), which referred to the very fact that any 'polity' or 'political instance' could not represent the social whole, that is, the 'totality' of the societal. This, in turn, implied that the new party must accept the notion of *difference* (e.g. 'sexual difference') and appeal to commonly accepted values via the method of 'political negotiation'.

b   abolition of *democratic centralism*, since 'ideological cohesion, validity and programmatic options were no longer centred on a given ruling group, which had to act, by definition, as the only possessor of tools for applying the party's policies'. Once the principle of discipline imposed from above was over, the only guarantor of party unity was the 'democratic and collective experience as well as the principle of responsibility and majority'.[65] In such a context, the new party was only an *opinion party* adopting new communicative codes and attitudes, for example, networking activities at the national and international levels, what Fassino called *struttura a rete*. Thus, what remained to be defined were new regulatory rules pledging the collective and individual rights of the party members, for it was the founding element of the PDS to be a 'party of citizenship and civil rights'.

c   A *flexible organisational model*, which enabled the new party to present itself successfully in light of the new contradictions. Accordingly, a new decentralised party machine had to be built on the grounds that a *federal party form* was required.[66]

In line with Barbera's analyses concerning the *federal form of the state*, Fassino thus proposed the notion of a *federal form for the PDS* which, without neglecting its nation-wide character, aimed at developing a federalist organisational structure alongside the concrete demands which emerged from regional communities. As examples, Fassino referred to the Socialist and Communist parties of Catalonia (Spain) and the German

Christian Democrats CDU-CSU.[67] Fassino, however, rejected the type of the federal party claimed by some fractions of *Rifondazione Comunista's* platform (Cossutta and Garavini), according to which each party faction in the new party would have the right to be organised on the grounds of its own logic, alongside a proper organisational structure, politico-ideological agenda etc. This, however, would have meant, as Stephen Hellman rightly put it, 'a permanent all-out factional warfare'.[68] On the contrary, 'recognition of difference', Fassino said, meant adoption of a 'regulatory framework and an associative form of action'.[69]

The PCI/PDS rapporteur went on to outline the concrete organisational forms of the new party. After being further qualified, they were enshrined almost entirely in the new statute of the PDS approved by the Congress.[70] In this respect, the major innovation proposed by Fassino concerned his distinction between *policy makers* and *political cadres*, both of whom are employed on a full-time basis, but the former are not necessarily linked with any party political authority. Thus, Fassino introduced the notion of *technocrat/assessor* into the PDS to improve the competitive performance/know-how of the party in an open political market. Fassino also gave substance to his proposal of party flexibility by suggesting a generous introduction of part-time staffing of the PDS. The aim of this new structure which Fassino called *struttura di supporto*,[71] was to advance the functioning of the party apparatus alongside the expertise and specialisms required.

There are two important sets of remarks that can be made about this survey. The first has to do with the way the PCI/PDS advanced its reform: being fully conscious of the worsening of the Italian crisis, it proposed a federal reform of itself in the wake of a federal reform of the state. Coupled with the institutional reform and the European perspectives of the PDS, both questions substantiate the thesis that the party had not only foreseen the crisis of the First Republic, but had also outlined concrete solutions which were not far from the real reforms required in the critical years yet to come.

The second point concerns our criticism of Hellman and Pasquino. If it is true that Bassolino's theses did not coincide with those of the ruling group — therefore his commitment to leading the PDS's programmatic renewal could only fall into line with his own motion which he was about to launch — it is equally true that the new party's programmatic renewal came also from other sources. The most relevant were the analyses of Barbera and Fassino, who both attempted to present a concrete proposal to reform the party and the state along federal lines, something which

Pasquino in particular, in his attempt to outline the PDS's programme, failed to point out.

Limits and merits of Antonio Bassolino's motion

As we have seen, Bassolino was a lukewarm supporter of the ruling group up to and after the 19th Congress. One would have expected that his entry into the 'war of motions' would have damaged the cohesion of Occhetto's faction. This fact would have further added to the critique made by the right-wing *miglioristi*, thus contributing to the opening up of alternative hegemonic discourses in the party. As the 20th Congress approached, it became clear that such thoughts were groundless. In point of fact, Bassolino's attempt to drive a wedge between the Centre-right alliance and *Rifondazione Comunista*, harmed the latter. There were several reasons for this.

Firstly, Bassolino had always been close to Ingrao's position, though in the 1980s he began to distance himself from the Eurocommunist leader. The immediate result of this was that many medium-ranking cadres and rank-and-file who supported Bassolino's motion were recruited by Ingrao's fraction. Yet, his most important collaborators, such as Mario Tronti (also working on the notion of *forma-partito*), Asor Rosa and Adalberto Minucci, came from the former group of Ingrao. This fact was coupled with the discontent of Asor Rosa and Tronti on the grounds of: 'how is it possible for Italian Communism to ally itself with the Stalinists of Cossutta?' This created visible breaches in the newly-formed platform of *Rifondazione Comunista*. Asor Rosa, in particular, would delve deeper and speak out, saying that Ingrao's attitude after the Bologna Congress did nothing but confirm some generally accepted notions of Communism. He also distinguished two contrasting attitudes in Ingrao: on the one hand, there was his *prejudiced will* which regarded his perennial belief in staying *in* the party while appealing against splits and, on the other, his *fierce critique* of whichever ruling group controlled the party.[72] In addition, the political mobility around Bassolino (noticed even before the Bologna Congress) which paved the ground for a more solid alignment afterwards, accounted for the general weakening of Ingrao's motion.

While both the strengthening of the *quarantenni* and *Rifondazione's* weakening are understandable, what is difficult to explain is the poor performance of Bassolino's motion, which in practical political terms meant that alternative hegemonic discourses vis-à-vis both Occhetto's and Ingrao's groupings were hard to produce. Though it can be argued that Bassolino's failure stemmed from the fact that the alignments were already consolidated, thus making a radical hegemonic 'reshuffling' of the inner-party relationship of forces impossible, I would rather maintain that the real reasons for his failure lay in the political and ideological conceptions of the grouping *ad hoc*.

Table 14 The strength of the platforms at the 20th Congress (1991)

Percentage received by each platform		
Occhetto+*miglioristi*	Bassolino+A.Rosa+Tronti	Ingrao+Tortorella+Cossutta
[PDS]	[PDS]	*Rifondazione Comunista**
67.69	5.4	26.85

**Rifondazione Comunista* comprised the area of 'democratic communists' (Ingrao+Tortorella) which, contrary to *cossuttiani* (ex motion 3), was against the split. The proportion refers to the percentage of members who attended and voted in lower level party Congresses; The party delegates to the Congress were 1259 and 300 were the *outsiders* ('Leftist Clubs', Independent Left et al.) without voting rights. Source: L. Benini, 'Il partito numero per numero', *Rinascita*, 4, 3-2-1991, pp.62-64

The thesis I shall defend relates to some analyses already put forward by Umberto Curi, who has implied that Bassolino's motion was only an expressive reality of both major intra-party groupings, so that it could be absorbed either by Ingrao's left when proclaiming the *oppositional character* of the PDS, or by Occhetto's faction when arguing for the *reformist physiognomy* of the PDS.[73] The *migliorista* philosopher and member of the PCI's Central Committee, Curi, went so far as to see in Bassolino's theses a sort of 'Togliattian duplicity'.[74] My attempt here is to illustrate further the account of Curi, by outlining the positions of Bassolino's group in the historical and theoretical context of the three platforms presented in the run up to the Rimini Congress. I will take this picture as the necessary yardstick to evaluate other criticisms addressed to Bassolino. At the same time, I will attempt to pinpoint some inaccuracies in Curi's account.

So far, we saw that throughout the 'new course' and the 'constituent phase' of the party, the ruling group was constantly challenged by the *miglioristi* on a number of issues: they demanded an opening toward the Socialists, pressed for a more pragmatic agenda and demanded a more responsible attitude over the Gulf War issue. To these, the new name and symbols of the party came to add yet another controversy, inasmuch as the *miglioristi* were dissatisfied both with the appearance of the old PCI logo in the new symbol and the absence of the word 'socialism' or 'socialist unity' from it, wordings which were dear to Craxi.[75] All these frictions notwithstanding, the *miglioristi* decided not to present their own platform in order to boost the ruling party majority vis-à-vis the challenges of Ingrao, Bassolino and Cossutta. Yet, the *quarantenni* had strengthened their positions: working uninterruptedly on the thorny questions raised by the debate, Occhetto's fraction corroborated the cause of the party transformation. The motion presented marked a further attempt at establishing, in a politically coherent way, the major principles of the *svolta*: the need to create a new party in the changing (and critical) Italian political scene; that this new force should be as open to external societal and political forces as possible; that *alongside the federal form of the new party a federal refoundation of the Republic was required*; yet, after the collapse of Eastern Communism, the ideological principles upon which the new Left based itself were those of the Enlightenment and the French revolution as well as the libertarian nucleus of Marxism, for which 'a different power can only be founded on a real liberation and humanisation of labour';[76] it is on these precise grounds that the democratic reform of the *economy* (economic and industrial democracy) and *polity* (institutional and federal reform) will be based. Therefore,

> the struggle for the transformation of power relations consists of an integral democratisation process of politics and civil society, assuming parties, movements, trade unions, associations and organisations of volunteers as autonomous political actors of that democratic reform. Such a political perspective should be based on a mass initiative calling for simple objectives that can mobilise the people.[77]

Until the formation of *Rifondazione's* motion, the *fronte del no* passed through many tumultuous stages of convening, agreeing and disagreeing. Having lost the battle over the opening up of the *costituente* and the formation of another *cosa* — 'thing', meaning party — the *fronte* now concentrated on two main issues: i) how to avoid the split threatened by Cossutta and other radical Communists as well as finding ways of mitigating the effects of the so-called *scissione silenziosa* ('silent split'); ii) how to build a convincing ideological and political platform by summing up the theses of the faction and shaping its identity. To these, one could add a third point, which was in fact present in the shaping of the *fronte* from the very beginning and which had to do with the definition of the role and the position of the group in the new political formation, the ways it could influence the party's policy making so as to counter-balance the *miglioristi* etc.

Ingrao and Tortorella faced the first question by addressing a unitary call to Cossutta and Cazzaniga. Aspects of the second issue concerned the *reform of Italian Communism ad hoc*, that is, its *refoundation* vis-à-vis the process of capitalist modernity and the collapse of 'actually-existing socialism'. We shall deal with these aspects in the next chapter. For the time being, we shall confine ourselves to unravelling the main points put forward in the joint platform of Ingrao-Cossutta as well as the rivalries developed within the fraction.

Admittedly, the shaping of the *Rifondazione* group which, in turn, led to the formation of the Party of Communist Refoundation, was a long process whose roots can be found in the early documents of Ingrao's and Cossutta's fractions and, later, in their proposals in the run-up to the Rimini Congress. The motion as such was the crystallisation of views drawn up basically in the course of two conventions of the group held in Rome (Arriccia, 9/10-6-1990) and Trento (Arco, 28/30-9-1990). The Arriccia gathering was important not so much for its politico-ideological formulations as for the fact of inaugurating a new reality within the party, the area of *democratic Communists*.[78] Yet, Ingrao himself began to soften his frontal attack on the ruling group. For example, he made a significant change of position on the question of the party's entry into the Socialist International, arguing that 'never mind so much the name with which the new party will get into the International as its "mind" *per se*, its reasoning, its culture'.[79] In Arco, although the debate seemed to be better prepared and organised,[80] it was nevertheless stifled by the very fact that not all the leaders of the *fronte* were in accord with Ingrao's position that the area of *democratic Communism* must *anyway* remain in the post-Rimini party of Occhetto. Cossutta and some of Ingrao's followers (Niki Ventola, Sergio Garavini, Rino Serri) argued that the *fronte* could not commit itself to pronouncing such a thesis in advance, inasmuch as nobody knew what sort of party would emerge after Rimini. Ingrao remained somewhat alone, a sort of *monaco metropolitano*, as Renato Armeni described him.[81] The debate went on even after Occhetto's *Dichiarazione* and the need for a joint platform became stronger especially after pressures exercised by Magri and Castellina that in the case of absence of a joint motion, they themselves would not support any.[82] By November 1990, the joint document was drafted.

Ingrao's thesis, which can be summarised comprehensively in his phrase *dobbiamo costruire nel gorgo*,[83] meaning that Communists *must* stay in the new party which, in the last analysis, would be the *locus* of the majority of the Left, was ultimately enshrined — though in a different form — in the joint motion.[84] The thesis proved spurious, for it was already repudiated *de facto* in Rimini with the walk-out of *Cossuttiani* and a handful of other radical Communists from the Congress. Most of the speculative interest, however, lies in the analyses developed by the motion with regard to the question of *forma-partito* and a certain concretisation of the criticism against the process of capitalist modernity. The motion argued that the idea of Communist refoundation was seen on the part of 'democratic Communists' as a process linked to a concrete critique of capitalist modernity, which constantly produced unjustices, inequalities and an extension of exploitation. Communism, therefore, was alien to the collapsing regimes of the East and drew its *criticità* from the mass movements and the working class: the latter, being particularly harmed by the restructuring process (precarious labour market, flexible regulation of working time, part-time contracts or no contracts at all etc.), established the claim for its liberation as a primary condition for any programme of societal and political transformation.[85] Taking this into account, the new *foma partito* must develop the grounds of a theoretical and practical refoundation so as to re-launch its mass and amply democratic physiognomy.[86] Neither the course followed by the party since November 1989, nor Fassino's proposal fulfilled this condition. Instead, a new emphasis on leaders and the 'media-based' profile of professional politicians was outlined, while the party representation of societal levels proved to be fragmented and corporatist. Consequently, 'all this would not bring in a true innovation of the organisational form, but a party where no *locus* of collective experience could possibly be found; certainly, this leads right up to asking citizens for passive support and delegating procedures to the party'.[87]

The motion, however, attempts to develop some ideas which were already present in Fassino's agenda: it made reference to a *party form* alongside networking activities (the model of *struttura a rete* which the motion explicitly referred to), while also adopting the idea of a *federal* party structure. Equally, it was not negative either to the institutional and electoral reform — though the latter 'has been lately overemphasised'[88] — or to the federal reform of the state. Thus, we witnessed a specific overlapping of positions between the ruling group and *Rifondazione*, a fact which left Bassolino with even less room for manoeuvre to have an autonomous political presence.

This is certainly the appropriate point to begin an examination of Bassolino's attempt. His group was built around the hypothesis that the proposal of the *quarantenni* in its very essence was only institutional engineering disengaged from the social and class conflicts. As early as March 1990, Bassolino alluded to his intention: 'I think that in the constituent phase, the party must immediately open up and assume the specific character of a social and political Left, otherwise it will be destined to end up in a conservative management of power.'[89]

As inner-party mobility around this assumption increased, the new grouping began to qualify its positions.[90] Bassolino enjoyed the advantage of being the coordinator of the working group drafting the party's new programme. Accordingly, he had the opportunity not only of attempting to incorporate his own analyses into the programme,[91] but also of employing a wide range of conceptions and analytical tools which could attract various leaders from both party fractions and thus achieve a new hegemonic synthesis. The former attempt proved impossible, since Bassolino had to present his own ideas *coram populo* to the PCI/PDS. The latter was only partly successful, for it failed to advance a hegemonic alternative, though it gave rise to a new political grouping in the run-up to the Rimini Congress. This is what we must analyse now.

Bassolino held that the PCI had in fact had a 'fundamental programme' since the second world war, though it was never written.[92] Its strategic axis was built around the so-called 'Italian Road to Socialism' and framed within the constitutional bounds. The *partito nuovo*, the centrality of alliance strategy, the idea of 'progressive democracy', the projects of 'structural reform' and 'democratic planning of the economy', were only some of the crucial aspects of that 'fundamental programme' of the PCI, whose principal aim was the modernisation of the country under the leadership of the labour movement. Therefore, Bassolino proceeded, 'either as labour movement or PCI, both culturally and politically, we are still the most modern political force of the country'.[93] Did this perhaps mean that no changes should be made? Quite the opposite.

The new world order emerging after 1989 and the shaping of societies along neo-liberal ideas, required fundamental changes and proposals be made by the party. The end of the juxtaposition between the East and the West and the dissolution in practice of the Warsaw Pact pointed to a transcendence of NATO.[94] To this end, both Europe and the European Left were of particular help. The Italian Left, Bassolino's documents argued, should commit itself to work for a *joint programme of European Socialism*, assessing the experience of the third phase of capitalism which, in turn, corresponds to the third phase of the development of the labour movement.[95] The new Left must have, first of all, an 'anti-war culture'; it should be deeply European and learn 'not to be deflected by the process of americanisation of politics';[96] it should liberate the Italian polity — particularly the South — from the perverse powers of the Mafia;[97] the programme of the new party must reflect 'a concrete definition of the nexus Democracy-Socialism';[98] it must comprise its *opposition* to capitalism and the existing order of things but, equally, it should always apply a concrete set of democratic reforms within the bounds of capitalism. For instance, the transition to post-Fordism can lead to a different articulation of working time in favour of labour and economic/industrial democracy. Bassolino accepted the claim of 'sexual difference' and the 'ecological reconversion of economy', while admitting the limits of the political institutions in encompassing the increasingly differentiated societal demands. Interestingly enough, however, the issue of 'federalism' did not receive much attention, though documents of the grouping mention the concept of 'autonomous refoundation of the state'. As a matter of fact, Mario Tronti, the theorist of the group dealing with these questions, conceived the dialectics between *forma partito* and *forma stato* on merely speculative grounds.

In this context, as I pointed out earlier, I would agree with the intuition of Umberto Curi that Bassolino's motion, by claiming both principles of Italian Communism, indeed failed to express either. In point of fact, *where Bassolino tried to match an oppositional/anti-capitalist identity for the new party, he was already within Ingrao's discourse; conversely, where he attempted to put forward concrete reformist demands, he was in the entrenched conceptual framework of the ruling group.* Bassolino understood this contradiction quite clearly and soon after Rimini returned to support Occhetto. Beyond that, however, commentators of the Italian Left, including Curi, failed to grasp a particularly significant issue that Bassolino's motion raised: I refer to the vigorous insistence of the group on the centrality both of *labour* and the *capital-labour* contradiction.[99]

The reason for considering the question of *labour* as particularly important in the analyses of Bassolino, stems from the fact that, *in a very specific sense*, it is presented in a piecemeal manner in both Ingrao's and Occhetto's agreggations. In fact, these party factions confer an extremely privileged space to the question of 'differences' (e.g. 'sexual difference') giving the impression that their discourses are but a dissipated reflection of neo-liberal differentiations. To take only one example, when pro-Ingrao or pro-Occhetto feminists argued for the construction of an autonomous *female identity* which, in turn, was cut across by class, religious, racial and other contradictions/identities, they in fact undermined the benefits of a *universalist appeal* and tended to dissipate the dynamics of their discourse into a pure and instrumental alliance of minorities.[100] Bassolino, however, attributed to the notion of 'labour' a universal centrality and seemed to overcome the handicap presented in the other motions: *in point of fact, only if the question of labour is grasped in all of its forms, divisions and dimensions can it potentially become a solid unified actor in the fragmented neo-liberal societal and pave the way for a new social solidarity.*[101] Let us follow the way the question was put by Bassolino in successive phases:

> To raise the question of workers and dependent labour as a general — and not sectorial — fundamental question, requires a long-term commitment to the cause, in which not only relevant social categories, but also the ruling group of the party are called to participate.[102]

And again:

> I think of a party which — though not exclusively — represents the working class and the huge world of labour, the latter conceived through its various articulations and in light of modern transformations. I do not think of course that a modern classist point of view alone is enough in interpreting the complex contradictions of our era. Nevertheless, an alternative strategy must search for possible common boundaries, common aims between these new contradictions and the insuperable fundamental contradiction between capital and labour.[103]

I could go on giving quotations along the same lines, but the point has already emerged clearly. Bassolino conceived the category of labour as the analytical starting point wherein many differentiations are articulated *ipso facto*, while it seems that both the analyses of the ruling group and those of Ingrao follow the opposite path: first recognition of 'differences' and then search for 'unity'. Thus, Occchetto's universalist appeal alongside the ideological values of the Enlightenment (peace, solidarity, liberty, equality) risks the loss of their leftist connotation and dissipates itself in the antagonisms of the societal taking place under the aegis of neo-liberal hegemonic discourses (e.g. the media, market forces).

Few analyses recognised this merit of Bassolino's faction. Salvati, Salvatori and Tamburrano blamed Bassolino for speculative, abstruse and improper use of political language. Michele Salvati in particular, diagnosed that all this was only the *quarantenni*'s fault, inasmuch as Bassolino's appointment as programme coordinator served the inner-party balance of forces for the cause of party unity. Therefore, Salvati concluded, 'Bassolino's argument does not address the masses but the party cadres'.[104] Giampiero Borghini of the ruling group, who took part in the working groups directed by Bassolino, took pains to explain to Salvati that Bassolino's appointment as programme coordinator had nothing to do with intra-party lobbying and that the real problem was whether or not

Bassolino's theses were a proper base for discussion. Borghini himself criticised Bassolino on the grounds that the proposals lacked any concrete analysis of the post-Cold War situation and the failure of Communism. He also went so far as to see no contribution to what we have here considered as the most significant thesis of Bassolino's faction: 'What is really absent from the [Bassolino] document is precisely this: there is no assessment of the productive structure of the country [...]. There is no such an analysis indicating ways in which the South can be developed.'[105]

There was indeed a certain misunderstanding on the part of the ruling group over the most striking position of Bassolino. In point of fact, Bassolino's group as a whole did pay attention to the question of the South and the structural productive potential of the country.[106]

To recapitulate: seen in the historical and ideological context of the other two motions, Bassolino's attempt to straddle the two positions emerged as his political limit, for he failed to go beyond them and create a new hegemonic aggregation. This was due chiefly to his *dualism* intrinsic to the position 'oppositional and reforming party', a position which was already expressed in Ingrao's and Occhetto's motions. However, the merit of Bassolino's motion lay in the emphasis given to the question of labour as a unifying factor of the societal, an issue which was poorly expressed in the other platforms.

Notes

1   E. H. Carr, *What is History?* (London: Pelican Books, 1967), pp. 11-12.
2   G. Pajetta, quoted by G. Moltedo-N. Rangeri (ed.), *PCI: La Grande Svolta...*, op. cit., p.28. Pajetta opposed the proposal advanced by the leading group, though firmly being in favour of party unity until his death (14-9-1990), see for example G. Pajetta (interview with S. Messina), 'Ma di partito ce n'è uno solo', *La Repubblica*, 26/27-8-1990, p.10.
3   A. Occhetto, 'Un voto per sbloccare la democrazia' (speech in Bologna, 9-4-1990), *L'Unità*, 10-4-1990, p.14.
4   See PCI, 'I verbali del dibattito in Direzione', *L'Unità*, 11-5-1990, p.4.
5   M. Santostasi 'Intervento al CC', *L'Unità*, 18-5-1990, p.15.
6   A. Occhetto, 'Relazione al CC', *L'Unità*, 16-5-1990, p.10-11 and his 'Conclusioni al CC', *L'Unità*, 18-5-1990, p.16.
7   A. Occhetto, 'Relazione al CC', ibid., p.10.
8   Ibid., p.10.
9   The PCI's institutional concern caused by the vote was characteristically expressed by Nilde Iotti, then President of the Chamber of Deputies, see N. Iotti, 'Una tavola rotonda dei partiti e poi un referendum popolare', *La Stampa*, 13-5-1990, p.3.
10   On this particular phrasing of Occhetto, see the comments of Flores D'Arcais, 'Nè carne nè pesce', *La Repubblica*, 15-5-1990, p.12.

11 See also, A. Occhetto, 'Questa Repubblica è in crisi grave' (interview with F. Rondolino), *L'Unità*, 26-5-1990, p.5.
12 See P. McCarthy, 'The referendum of 9 June', in S. Hellman-G. Pasquino (eds), *Italian Politics: A Review*, v.7 (London: Pinter Publishers, 1992), pp. 11-28.
13 Some further developments and positions taken up in the run-up to the 9 June referendum should be pointed out here. De Mita, despite his pro-reformist stances throughout the 1980s, did not support Segni. The President of the Republic, Cossiga, had also supported Craxi and undermined any attempt at reform. As we shall see below, Cossiga's stance in particular was linked with fears with regard to the *Gladio* investigation. Finally, in the Leagues, G. Miglio was in favour of the reform, as was the Confindustria, see P. McCarthy, ibid., pp. 20-23; for a general speculation about the role of 1991 and 1993 referenda in the transformation of the political system, see M. Donovan, 'The referendum and the transformation of the party system', *Modern Italy*, v.1, n.1, Autumn 1995, pp. 53-69.
14 R. Terzi, 'Si scioglierà l'ala comunista della CGIL?', *Rinascita*, 2, 18-2-1990, p.61.
15 For a general account concerning the crisis of trade unionism in Italy caused by the capitalist restructuring of the 1980s, see S. Negrelli, 'Rappresentanza, rappresentatività e conflitto: il sindacato nell'Italia post-industriale', *Prospettiva Sindacale*, 82/2, II Semestre 1992, pp. 26-36.
16 B. Trentin, personal interview, op. cit.
17 B. Trentin, 'La mia CGIL' (interview with R. D'Agostini), *Nuova Rassegna Sindacale*, 12, 8-4-1991, p.10.
18 C. A. Mershon, 'The crisis of the CGIL: open division in the 12th national Congress', in S. Hellman-G. Pasquino (ed.), *Italian Politics: A Review*, v.7, op. cit., p.91.
19 See 'CGIL: Tesi Congressuali', in *CGIL: Sindacato dei Diritti, Etica della Solidarietà. I Documenti del XII Congresso della CGIL* (Roma: Ediesse, 1992), pp. 77-243.
20 See the motion 'Essere sindacato', ibid., pp. 245-94.
21 See, PCI, *Sulla Grave Crisi del Golfo Persico* (Roma: Fratelli Spada, 1990).
22 Ingrao's speech in the Lower House, quoted by P. Banca, 'Ingrao: non posso tacere il mio dissenso', *L'Unità*, 24-8-1990, p.5.
23 G. Napolitano, 'Ci sono ancora vie per evitare la guerra' (interview with M. Sappino), *L'Unità*, 30-11-1990, p.2.
24 The entire document was published by the PCI's daily *L'Unità* in a special insertion, see A. Moro, *Le 400 pagine di Moro riemerse dal covo brigatista*, *L'Unità*, 23-10-1990.
25 See F. Ferraresi, 'A secret structure codenamed Gladio', in S. Hellman-G. Pasquino (ed.), *Italian Politics: A Review* (London: Pinter Publishers, 1992), v.7, pp. 29-48.
26 See F. De Vito — G. Quaranta, 'Seconda Republica', *L'Espresso*, 48, 2-12-1990, pp. 8-10, M. Braun, *L'Italia...*, op. cit., pp. 106-109, S. Mannuzzu, 'Il retrobottega della Repubblica', *Rinascita*, 40, 18-11-1990, pp. 10-12.
27 See E. Balboni, 'The President of the Republic, judges, and Superior Council of the Judiciary: chronicle of a bitter constitutional struggle', in S. Hellman-G. Pasquino (ed.), *Italian Politics: a Review*, v.7, op. cit., p.51, and the account by N. Tranfaglia, 'Cossiga, Craxi, Andreotti e i giorni di Gladio', *L'Unità*, 16-7-1991, p.2.
28 S. Gundle-S. Parker, 'Introduction: the new Italian Republic', in S. Gundle-S. Parker (eds), *The New...*, op. cit., p.7.

29   See B. Tucci, 'La verità sulle stragi', *Corriere della Sera*, 18-11-1990, p.9.

30   A. Occhetto, 'Ecco chi era il grande vecchio' (interview with P. Sansonetti), *L'Unità*, 31-10-1990, p.2; also, A. Occhetto, 'Tutta la verità' (interview with S. Roscani), *Rinascita*, 41, 25-11-1990, pp. 4-6. In that second interview, Occhetto insisted on an alliance with the PSI in order to refound the Republic.

31   As Paul Ginsborg noted: 'the post-war settlement was crucial, for it decreed the establishment of the Consiglio Superiore della Magistratura (CSM) and established the potential for independent action by prosecuting magistrates [...]. Judges and magistrates were beholden only to the Law', P. Ginsborg, 'Explaining Italy's crisis', in S. Gundle-S. Parker, *The New...*, op. cit., p.26.

32   SISMI and SID were names for the secret services of the Italian military during different periods; the original designation was SIFAR, see F. Ferraresi, 'A secret structure...', op. cit., pp. 30-31, 43, passim.

33   See E. Baloni, 'The President...', op. cit., pp. 53 ff.

34   For the 'Giardana case', from the name of Pasquale Giardana who was nominated against the will of Martelli, effectively causing the open alliance between Cossiga and Martelli, see E. Baloni, 'The President...', ibid., p.60.

35   The fact was noticed by D'Alema: 'I continue to think that the best things were produced by the party during the first period. [...] It was somewhat inevitable vis-à-vis such a radical discontinuity which was invested within our being as political force...', M. D'Alema, 'Arrichire le culture della sinistra' op. cit., p.7. Certainly, this is far from assuming that 'the 20th Congress of PCI was but a faded photocopy of the 19th', P. Ignazi, *Dal PCI...*, op. cit., pp. 127, 173.

36   The reports of the major working groups of the party can be found in *Critica Marxista*, 5-6, Sept.-Dec. 1990.

37   See A. Occhetto, 'Il discorso a Modena', *L'Unità*, 23-9-1990, pp. 15-16.

38   A. Occhetto, 'Dichiarazione di Intenti', in his *Il Sentimento...*, op. cit., p.206.

39   In fact, Occhetto avoided stating explicitly so in the *dichiarazione* and refers only to *governo mondiale* in general. A clear statement by Occhetto of the United Nations as world administrator and regulator of the Gulf crisis can be found in his speech in Modena, see A. Occhetto, 'Il discorso...', op. cit., p.15 and also in his Report to the Congress where he drew up a balance-sheet on the successive positions taken by the party on the question of the Gulf war and presented a qualified explanation of his views, see A. Occhetto, 'Relazione al 20o Congresso', *L'Unità*, 1-2-1991, p.15.

40   A. Occhetto, 'Dichiarazione...', op. cit., p.221.

41   Ibid., p.212.

42   Ibid., p.218.

43   Ibid., p.223.

44   See, *inter alia*, A. Tortorella, 'Un Congresso unitario? Ancora spero' (interview with M. Sappino), *L'Unità-Lettera sulla Cosa* (special insert), 19-10-1990, p.11-13. Cossutta went even further: he saw no class enemy in Occhetto's discourse and denounced the content of *dichiarazione* as a 'strategic vacuum', see A. Cossutta, 'Il dibattito alla direzione del PCI', *L'Unità*, 12-10-1990, p.7.

45   See in particular the speeches of Tortorella (the mover of the *fronte del no*), G. Angius and P. Ingrao in the Congress, *L'Unità*, 2-2-1991, p.15, *L'Unità*, 3-2-1991, pp.16-17.

46   A. Occhetto, 'Dichiarazione...', op. cit., p.230.

47   Ibid., p.233.

48   A. Tortorella, 'Intervento al 20o Congresso', *L'Unità*, 2-2-1991, p.15.

49   See G. Napolitano, 'Intervento al 20o Congresso', *L'Unità*, 3-2-1991, pp. 16-17.
50   See P. Ingrao, 'Intervento al 20o Congresso', *L'Unità*, ibid., p.17. For a detailed account on the Congressional re-alignments while voting on the Gulf as well as the shrewd tactic of D'Alema, see S. Hellman, 'The difficult birth...', op. cit., pp. 75-77.
51   See A. Occhetto, 'Relazione al 20o Congresso', op. cit., and also his conclusions 'Conclusioni al 20o Congresso', *L'Unità*, 4-2-1991, pp. 15-16.
52   M. D'Alema, 'Arricchire le culture...', op. cit., p.7.
53   A. Occhetto, 'Relazione al 20o Congresso', op. cit., p.17.
54   G. Pasquino, 'Programmatic renewal...', op. cit., p.157.
55   S. Hellman, 'The difficult birth...', op. cit., p.73.
56   We have referred to these contributions in objecting to other aspects of their analyses relevant to specific sections of our study, see *inter alia*, P. Ignazi, *Dal PCI...*, op. cit., M. Lorusso, *L'Era di Achille*, op. cit., U. Curi, *Lo Scudo di Achille*, op. cit. As early as July 1990, however, Vacca pinpointed the significance of federalist dimensions in Fassino's agenda, see G. Vacca, 'L'organizzazione del nuovo partito', originally published in *Tribuna del Sud*, 7-7-1990, now in his, *Dal PCI al PDS*, op. cit., pp. 198-200.
57   See A. Barbera, 'Per un moderno stato regionale', *Critica Marxista*, 5-6, op. cit., pp. 237-58.
58   Ibid., pp.241, 246 ff. It should be noted that Barbera uses the terms 'federalism' and 'regionalism' as identical and attempts to concretise his proposals alongside the Spanish (Catalonia) and German models.
59   Barbera clarifies that article 117 of the Constitution can be modified so as to give legislative powers to the regions that are either not specified by the Constitution or do not form part of the duties assigned to supranational organisations. The central state will continue to regulate welfare, economy, defence and other policies. Thus, Barbera argued, a certain 'Reaganisation of the federal notion', where the central state discharges its welfare dimension to the regions, will be avoided.
60   A. Occhetto, 'Intervento conclusivo', ibid., pp. 207-23.
61   P. Fassino, 'Un contributo alla "fase costituente" per una nuova forma-partito', in PCI, *Idee e Proposte per la Costituente* (Roma: Fratelli Spada, 1990), p.7. The same formulation by Fassino in his more qualified and detailed intervention to the programmatic Conference, 'Per una nuova forma-partito', *Critica Marxista*, op. cit., pp. 137-38; also his 'Una forma partito nuova per una sinistra nuova', *L'Unità*, 1-7-1990, p.2.
62   P. Fassino, 'Per una nuova...', op. cit., p.135.
63   Ibid., pp. 139-40.
64   Ibid., pp. 140-41.
65   Ibid., pp. 140-41.
66   Ibid., p.141.
67   See ibid., p.155, passim. Nevertheless, it should be noted that no equivalent of Catalonia or Bavaria existed in Italy.
68   See S. Hellman, 'The difficult birth...', op. cit., p.75. Cossutta would speak out on this point — which, after all, was discussed in various gatherings of the current from May 1990 to January 1991 — in his speech to the Congress, see A. Cossutta, 'Intervento al 20o Congresso', *L'Unità*, 3-2-1991, p.16.
69   P. Fassino, 'Per una nuova...', op. cit., p.159; see also his interview with F. Rondolino, 'Scriviamo insieme la carta comune del PDS', *L'Unità*, 8-1-1991, p.10.
70   See Partito Democratico della Sinistra, *Lo Statuto* (Roma: Fratelli Spada, 1991).

71   P. Fassino, 'Per una nuova...', op. cit., p.159.
72   See A. Asor Rosa, 'Monaci e monachesimi', *Rinascita*, 35, 14-10-1990, p.14.
73   U. Curi-P.F.D'Arcais, *L'Albero...*, op. cit., pp. 36-46.
74   Ibid., p.42.
75   See in particular the explicit agenda of Macaluso-Napolitano, 'Coerenza riformista: Ecco la "cosa" che vogliamo', *L'Unità*, 14-7-1990, p.2. Also, in January 1991, the reformist faction (Macaluso, Barbera, Chiaromonte, Napolitano, Ranieri, Veca et al.) published the volume *Noi Riformisti*, edited by G. Polillo and P. Valenza (Rome: Cuen).
76   *PCI-20o Congresso: Mozioni, Documenti, Regolamento*, 'Mozione presentata da A. Occhetto per il Partito Democratico della Sinistra' (Roma: Fratelli Spada, 1990), p.4.
77   Ibid., p.7.
78   The term was envisaged before Ariccia by the *berlingueriani* of Tortorella and Angius, see, *inter alia*, F. Rondolino, 'Il «no» indice un'assemblea nazionale a Roma', *L'Unità*, 13-5-1990, p.5; also, Assemblea del No, 'Il documento di Ariccia', *L'Unità*, 16-6-1990, p.4, A. Tortorella, 'Alla ricerca di un nuovo centro' (interview with N. Vendola), *Rinascita*, 20, 24-6-1990, pp. 20-21.
79   See F. De Vito, 'Ingrao meravigliao', *L'Espresso*, 25, 24-6-1990, p.18.
80   See Rifondazione Comunista, *Materiali di Dibattito per la Rifondazione Comunista. In Nome delle Cose* (Roma: Tipolitografia Iter, 1990).
81   R. Armeni, 'L'arco del No', *Rinascita*, 35, 14-10-1990, pp. 20-24; see also G. Vacca, 'Le frecce di Arco', in his *Dal PCI al PDS*, op. cit., pp. 228-30, who blames ex-members of PDUP and *cossuttiani* 'for not following Ingrao's thesis'.
82   L. Magri, personal interview, op. cit.
83   See, *inter alia*, G. Battistini, 'Lo shock Ingrao', *La Repubblica*, 2-10-1990, p.13.
84   *PCI-20th Congress: Mozioni, Documenti, Regolamento*, 'Rifondazione Comunista', op. cit., p.14.
85   Ibid., p.11.
86   Ibid., p.13. Many of the theses enshrined in the motion with regard to the *forma partito*, were formulated by Magri in his Report at Arco.
87   Ibid., p.13.
88   Ibid., p.12.
89   A. Bassolino, 'Quella legge sui diritti è giusta' (interview with A. Leiss), *L'Unità*, 13-3-1990, p.5.
90   It can be said that Bassolino's fraction was somewhat helped by the conjuncture. From May until September, strikes and demonstrations by Northern metal workers were very frequent; then, a law against arbitrary lay-offs in small and medium size enterprises was enacted. Both events enjoyed active support by the PCI and its left-wing tendencies in particular.
91   In a party seminar of his working group in June, Bassolino made his intention clear: 'It seems right to me to work not for a programme for the party majority alone, but for the entire party as well as for all the forces which are interested in our project', A. Bassolino, 'I programmi dei partiti della sinistra Europea e la nostra elaborazione programmatica' (18-6-1990), in *Idee e Proposte per la Costituente*, op. cit., pp. 25-26.
92   We are referring to his Introductory speech in the Programmatic Conference of October, A. Bassolino, 'Relazione introduttiva', *Critica Marxista*, 5-6, op. cit., p.9.
93   Ibid.
94   Ibid., p.12.

95   Ibid., p.13, and also, *PCI-20o Congresso...*, 'Per un moderno partito antagonista e riformatore', op. cit., p.19, PCI, *Idee e Proposte per il Programma. Testo Elaborato dall'Ufficio del Programma Diretto da A. Bassolino* (Roma: Fratelli Spada, 1990), A. Bassolino, 'Idee per il programma di un nuovo partito della sinistra', *L'Unità*, 31-5-1990, p.2. For a general speculation on the concept of 'third wave of capitalism' — the previous two phases being the 'liberal' and the 'Keynesian' ones — with special reference to the Left, see A. Schiavone, *La Sinistra del Terzo Capitalismo* (Bari: Laterza, 1989).

96   A. Bassolino, 'Relazione introdutiva', op. cit., p.14.

97   For a concrete pro-Bassolino agenda on the Southern question, see M. Magno-P. Soriero-I. Sales, 'Una costituente nel Mezzogiorno: Riformista, cioè antagonista', *L'Unità*, 11-8-1990, p.2.

98   'Per un moderno partito antagonista e riformatore', op. cit., p.19.

99   No doubt, the shaping of such a view was only a qualified result both of Tronti's 'workerist' culture whose roots are traced back in pre-1968 leftism and Bassolino's pro-Ingraoist formation. Tronti — together with Raniero Panzieri and Antonio Negri — was one of the most distinguished writers and founders of the *Quaderni Rossi*, a leftist critique of the official Left (PCI and PSI).

100   As Eric Hobsbawm so perceptively put it: 'Today both the Right and the Left are saddled with identity politics. Unfortunately, the danger of disintegrating into a pure alliance of minorities is unusually great on the Left because the decline of the great universalist slogans of the Enlightenment, which were essentially slogans of the Left, leaves it without any obvious way of formulating a common interest across sectional boundaries', 'Identity politics and the Left', *New Left Review*, 217, May-June 1996, p.45. Fausto Bertinotti, leader of the Party of Communist Refoundation since 24 January 1994, grasped the point. In an attempt to present the degree of emergency of the Left, Bertinotti said: 'Why, after the disappearance of the socialist regimes, is the Church the only grand international force left? Because it faces the question of internationalisation on the terrain of universal values', F. Bertinotti, *Tutti i Colori del Rosso* (Milano: Sperling and Kupfer, 1995), pp. 97-98.

101   Ernesto Laclau and Chantal Mouffe, in their first 'post-modern' statement, failed to consider this point in theoretical perspective. The failure of the authors to pose at the heart of their problematic the question of *labour* and *value-theory* as central unifying and unified parameters of the social whole, led them to define the social 'as a non-sutured space' and society 'as a non-valid object of discourse', see, E. Laclau-Ch. Mouffe, *Hegemony and Socialist Strategy...*, op. cit., pp. 111, 126.

102   PCI, *Conferenza Nazionale del PCI sulla FIAT*, 'Relazione Introduttiva di A. Bassolino' (22-23 June 1990) (Roma: Fratelli Spada, 1990), p.14.

103   A. Bassolino, 'Riproporrò le mie idee' (interview with A. Leiss), *L'Unità*, 14-10-1990, p.5.

104   M. Salvati, 'Non basta la mediazione per fare un programma', *L'Unità*, 15-8-1990, p.2.

105   G. Borghini, 'L'antagonismo al sistema è minoritario, non alternativo', *L'Unità*, 22-8-1990, p.2.

106   See, for example, the account by Gianni Militello, 'Nuove idee per vincere la sfida della democrazia economica', *L'Unità*, 11-9-1990, p.2.

7   New Revisionism *vs* Communist Refoundation: Once again on the *Questione Salariale*

Tu parli di un comunismo astratto e irrealizzato [...]. Ma il socialismo democratico si è realizzato? E dove? O queste parole significano un' altra cosa, e allora diciamolo. Le parole sono pietre. Socialismo non è capitalismo.

P. Ingrao, *Le Cose Impossibili*, op.cit., p.210.

As we saw earlier, the secretary of the PCI was keen to base his *svolta* on the contribution of 'outsiders' (e.g. Independent Left, 'submerged Left' et al.). Thus, though he succeeded in getting the consensus of the new party in electing the prominent jurist, Stefano Rodotà, to the position of President and so replacing Tortorella, the Rimini Congress reserved a surprise for him: Occhetto failed to be elected secretary of the PDS, for he had received 10 votes less than those required by the statute.[1] Though there were some technical difficulties — members of the National Council of the party that elected the secretary had rushed home — Occhetto himself alluded to the fact that 'technical factors cannot explain everything, therefore I am forced to withdraw my candidature from the secretaryship of the new party'.[2] The issue was resolved a few days later, when Occhetto was overwhelmingly elected by the National Council of the PDS.

His election notwithstanding, Occhetto was much contested: he was at odds not only with Napolitano and Ingrao, but also with the ex-leader of the PCI, Natta, to whom he owed his promotion to the party's leadership.[3] In addition, signs of friction within the ruling group itself began to appear.[4] Indeed, going beyond personal recriminations and ambitions concerning the leadership of the PDS, these frictions took place on the grounds of 'different points of view'. As Occhetto admitted, there were in fact 'two readings of the *svolta*': the *locus* of the PDS in the Italian political system in transition and the degree of its action towards the de-structuring of the old system.[5] However, the *demarcation line* in the Italian Left was not self-evident: it did not lie among the different politico-ideological views expressed periodically by prominent figures of the Communist or non-Communist Italian Left. Our thesis is that the major ideological and historical contradiction within the Italian Left, and perhaps not only the Italian Left, was — and still is — that between *new revisionism* and *Communist refoundation*. The purpose of this chapter is to explore this contradiction, analyse its theoretical and historical connotations and open a new area for debate. Once the necessary historical and descriptive horizons for such a speculative exposition are in place, I will address the problem through four major instances: the historical, the ideological, the political and the economic. In the latter case, I shall refer almost exclusively to the *questione salariale* (the 'question of wages'), thus keeping pace with our previous analyses relevant to the issue.

History

The history we have traced of Italian Communism and its transformation features some very interesting dimensions. The battle of *ingraoismo* in the PCI since the early 1960s was not a historical contingency, nor was it a specific variant intrinsic to Italian Communism, whose supposed uniqueness was written in the history of Italian Marxism, from Antonio Labriola to Antonio Gramsci.[6] True, Gramsci's thought and (ambivalent) theoretical legacy were a founding bond for the PCI. Nevertheless, the leader who marked the party's concrete political steps and established it as a force *par excellence* of the First Italian Republic and the Left, was Palmiro Togliatti. His 'duplicity' did not concern domestic/international policy alone, where the former met pro-reformist and democratic demands and the latter pro-stalinist and revolutionary ones; it had also, and even more importantly, to do with the *Communist identity of the PCI itself vis-à-vis its actual political conception.* The 'Italian Road to Socialism' brought *in se* this very contradiction: on the one hand, the PCI began to play a substantial national role by presenting itself not as a striking force aiming to take advantage of capitalist crises and thus capture power in a revolutionary situation (the Russian case of *dual power* and its theorisation by Lenin); it rather wanted to act *within* capitalism, achieve a welfare situation for the masses and gain their consensus, thus attaining Socialism by parliamentary means. On the other hand, the PCI never abandoned its anti-capitalist principles and identity, the *Modern Prince* of the First Republic considered itself a mass party, with the principle of 'democratic centralism' always in force, while also acting as a major mobilising force for Socialist and Catholic strata. Yet the PCI had a conception of continuously expanding democracy and civil liberties and used the state — which should be transformed — as the principal lever for a Socialist economic strategy pointing the way to Communism: hence the name, *Communist Party.* This 'duplicity' took some very specific forms in the post-war history of the party.

    Ingraoismo was a *revisionist* effort to advance Communist ideas *within* a Communist Party. Although containing some original features, it nevertheless was only a qualification of specific theoretical and historical conjunctures. For example, in the plurality of Marxisms recognised and embraced by Ingrao, he had a privileged rapport with 'austro-Marxism', while never ceasing to declare, both theoretically and practically, his profound anti-Stalinism.[7] On the other hand, *ingraoismo* was deeply *revisionist*, for it saw the changes in Italian capitalism and sought to capitalise on the dynamics of student, feminist and ecological movements that capitalist advances had generated.

If *ingraoismo* was the leftist side in the system of 'duplicity', Amendola's and Napolitano's reformist positions were its right-wing. *Amendolaismo* was a further concretisation of the party's reformism, a highly pragmatic Social Democratic view. Its blatant reformism can be seen in the position taken on the question of inflation in the 1970s, or — by Napolitano — over the Gulf War issue in 1990-91, or its insistence in considering the PSI as a privileged ally. The latter claim unnecessarily went so far as to be repeated even when the PSI was sinking into the *tangentopoli* scandals of 1992-93. However, it is obvious even here that this sort of *riformismo* was no more than the Italian variant in the wide-range framework of European Social Democracy, either traditional or contemporary. A few words on the ruling centre of the party is appropriate here. As happens in every political party, the 'centre' provided the regulatory framework: Togliatti, Longo and Berlinguer guaranteed both continuity of Communist identity and reformist competence. By keeping 'duplicity' alive under the conditions dictated by the Cold War, the PCI also flourished. To recall Ian Mikardo and Harold Wilson: 'In order for a bird to fly, you need a left-wing and a right-wing.' This applied perfectly to the PCI.

All this was no longer the case in the 1980s, let alone in the post-1989 situation. The party was in a vertical decline all along: globalisation and European integration were undermining the very essence of its strategy, that is, *the use of the state to achieve Socialism* (the Italian Road to Socialism). We saw that Gorbachev's reformism overshadowed the Berlinguerian line of Eurocommunism. The collapse of 'actually-existing socialism' questioned the very existence of the name 'Communist'. The situation was 'revolutionary', though not in the Leninist sense, and whatever the conditions, clear-cut positions were required. The PCI had only to take sides: with which side of its own *doppiezza* should it ally? The road chosen was the most 'natural' one. The PCI opted for the path which, as practical necessity and political orientation, had always prevailed in the party's post-war tradition: the reformist/Social Democratic road. In this context, I would argue that the 'duplicity introduced in the debate'[8] during the transformation of the party between *Communist refoundation* and *new revisionism* drew from this historical root. The motion of Cossutta-Cazzaniga, presented in the run-up to the Bologna Congress, put the question succinctly: the PCI, the motion argued, has *due anime* ('two souls'); these are the product of its own post-war history.[9]

Ideology

What are the ideological premises of 'new revisionism' and 'communist refoundation' in the contemporary Italian context? In answering the question, we must first shed light on the general differences between *reformism*, on the one hand, and *revisionism*, on the other. As Ernesto Laclau and Donald Sassoon have argued, the notion of *revisionism* presents three features unique to Edward Bernstein's thought and not to be found in any orthodox versions of Marxism (e.g. Karl Kautsky) or of 'austro-Marxism' (e.g. Otto Bauer). Lenin's revisionism is of quite a different type.[10] Revisionism's first distinctiveness recognises the link between the *political strategy* of the party of the working class, on the one hand, and the *very changes capitalism undergoes* in its various developmental phases, on the other. In this context, the first pillar of revisionism is that once capitalism undergoes changes, the labour party must re-adjust its strategy according to the new requirements and constraints imposed. Its second tenet is the *autonomy of the political instance*. While reformism and orthodox Marxism or Bolshevism argue that capitalism, in the last analysis, can be overcome by first starting changes in the infrastructure, revisionism holds that this was to be achieved through autonomous political intervention. Yet, reformism and its political practices imply 'political quietism and the corporatist confinement of the working class', while revisionism tends to isolate itself from these determinants.[11] Last but not least, revisionism's third tenet is in line with Bernstein's famous motto: 'the goal is nothing, the movement is everything.'

Having clarified this, we can understand why the ideological *locus* of the *quarantenni* was a *revisionist* one: it argued for 'institutional reform' and political changes in the 'superstructure', assuming the autonomy of both the economic and political instances. This revisionism, however, was *historically new*, for it came into being under the conditional framework of dramatic changes in the capitalist mode of production: hence the need to revise the party's political strategy and to give it a new impetus. Undoubtedly, the whole picture became profoundly dramatic because, to the capitalist changes underway, came to be added the collapse of Eastern regimes. Nevertheless, the speculative question does not stop here because *the faction of Communist refoundation claimed a revisionist notion too, for it understood the revolutionary meaning of capitalist restructuring and held that a Communist revisionism is not only possible, but also necessary.* In a decisive passage of the motion *'Rifondazione Comunista',* presented by Ingrao and Cossutta in the run-up to Rimini, we can read:

> What the workers suffer everyday in their workplace is a form of dominance which operates at the international level. *The need for a political revision on the Left stems precisely from here.* Among its programmatic priorities must be the notion of a new cycle of struggle aiming at a sharp reduction of the working time and a minimum standard of protection for every worker in every country (my emphasis).[12]

So where does the real demarcation line between *new revisionism* and *Communist refoundation* lie?[13] My thesis is that *Communist refoundation* conceived the transformation of capitalism as changes occurring in the *capitalist* relations of production; thus it drew its identity by opposing these relations, which are reactionary/exploitative. In contrast, *new revisionism* assumed the development of social productive forces as its analytical starting point and, in particular, its 'technical/technological' aspects. We saw, for example, the emphasis which Occhetto and the ruling group gave to the technological advances achieved through the internationalisation/ globalisation of economies, the way Occhetto himself raised the issue of the party's renewal, drawing on the notion of the German SPD and Peter Glotz etc. On the other hand, it is evident that Ingrao's 'Communist point of view', establishes a 'Communist revisionism' through an opposition to capitalist restructuring, claiming a *critica aggiornata contro le nuove forme di sfruttamento e di dominio* (a critique adjusted to the new forms of exploitation and dominance). In point of fact, we are almost within the field of the most contradictory aspect of Marxist theory itself: should the political subject of the Left prioritise the exploitative character of the capitalist relations of production, and the damage it causes to nature, so as to advance a political conception of social/political/ideological opposition, or should it be adjusting itself to the evolution of capitalism and to the constraints imposed *per se* by this very development?[14] This said, there is no need to point out that neo-Communist revisionism is opposed to the notion of the 'autonomy of the political'. Instead, it adopts that of 'relative autonomy', which was the option of Gramsci and neo-Marxist theoreticians in the 1970s (Nicos Poulantzas, Etienne Balibar, Christian Palloix, Elmar Altvater et al.).

Having covered the ideological/theoretical ground, we can now turn to an examination of the *political* aspects of the antithesis. We shall chiefly focus on the issue of *alternativa* versus *alternanza*, whereby the former implies a Communist notion and the latter, a revisionist one.

Politics

As we saw earlier, the question of altering the political class of the First Republic was seen by both factions within the critical framework of the internationalisation of economies along neo-liberal lines which, in turn, weakened the interventionist role of the nation-state and led to the crisis of mass politics. Both fractions agreed on this evolution of capitalism, *because they were revisionist*. From a political point of view, the real *structural hiatus* separating them was the strategy to be followed. *New revisionism* saw that the political refoundation of the Republic — so, in practice, the *Second* Italian Republic — could be achieved through the political notion of *alternation* along the British (Westminster) pattern, whereas *Communist refoundation* held that this was to be attained through an intensification of social and political oppositions against the dominant power block and the big monopolies, thus implying an *alternative* political stategy going beyond the boundaries of capitalist democracy. In this context, however, *Communist refoundation* seems unable to disentangle itself from Ingrao's notion of the 'socialisation of politics' (see his *Masse e Potere*, 1977) which presupposed a *mass, and even corporatist, conception of the polity*. Thus, the real contradiction of *Communist refoundation* was that, whereas the crisis of mass politics was grasped, the means of overcoming it were based on the very premise of mass politics which, first and foremost, referred to mass participation in political instances. This is why Ingrao, while being among the first to announce the need for institutional and electoral reform, never really embraced the claims of Segni's referendum movement and the PDS, let alone the abolition of proportional representation. To Ingrao and the neo-Communists, only an electoral system based on proportional representation — or a *form* of it — can ensure mass participation and involvement of wider popular strata in politics.

Economy

The aforementioned question of alternation/alternative involved the notion of *hegemony* as it stretched between the antithesis *capital-labour* and the *welfare aspects* of the Keynesian state. Although it is impossible here to examine the issue in all its complexity, I will proceed with an important aspect which has emerged from this the study: the question of 'social compromise' alongside that of *wages*, which took place during the most critical historical periods of the First Republic by involving *compromising strategies at the level of political governance* led chiefly by the DC and PCI. We are referring to the period of reconstruction and the 'compromises' of Togliatti over wages and political co-administration with the DC; also to the years of 'historic compromise' of Berlinguer, the question of *austerità* and the notion of a 'medium-term programme', launched by the reformist wing of the PCI (Amendola-Napolitano). In this context, the issue we intend to raise is the way in which *a third period of compromise was formed*, in the wake of the capitalist restructuring of the 1980s. Theoretical jargon apart, it is clear that the issue enjoyed a straighforward relationship with the notion of *hegemony*, meaning the terrain of dominant articulation of powers between the political, ideological and economic instances.

As we saw in earlier chapters, Togliatti's political compromise and the PCI's participation in the governments of 'national unity' (1944-1947) during the chaotic post-war years, were accompanied by his appeal to the working class that, if the country's reconstruction was to be successfully achieved, workers should be less concerned with how to increase their wages. Instead, they had to be conscious of how to increase production and welfare capitalism. Similarly, Berlinguer's strategy of *compromesso*, as it was carried out through the unique recession of the mid-1970s and the sharp problem of inflation, raised the question of *austerity* for the working class to bring inflation down. This implied that part of the unions' achievements following the conquests of the 'Hot Autumn' (1969), such as *high wages*, had to be restricted. *The argument I will outline, is that the socio-economic restructuring of the 1980s, and the fall of the First Republic's ruling political class, created a third historical form of social and political compromise, hence a new basis of disagreement between new revisionism and Communist refoundation over the question of wages.* In this context, the difference with the past lies in the fact that no *organisational link* between the two factions exists.

As we have seen, beginning with FIAT in 1980, Italian capitalism dealt a severe blow to the trade union movement and the PCI, especially when the latter failed to defend the *scala mobile* in the referendum of 1985. The reduction of the *scala* was only the start of what was yet to come. In fact, the disarticulation of the Fordist paradigm and the fragmentation of the ruling political class of the First Republic — including the crisis and transformation of the PCI — reduced both the rates of unionisation and the bargaining power of the unions.[15] Furthermore, as the tripartite corporatist 'social contract' — trade union/government/ enterpreneurs — was in crisis, it gave way to new negotiations and compromises among the partners. Among the first targets of the new ruling authorities was the control of wage increases via the halting of the principal mechanism promoting them in company with inflationary trends: that is, the *scala mobile*. Thus, in an attempt to bring down inflation and mitigate the fiscal crisis to meet European requirements, the *scala* was completely abolished by Carlo Azeglio Ciampi's cabinet at the end of 1993, a policy initiated by the previous government of the Socialist, Giuliano Amato, in 1992.

All this happened while the First Republic was on the verge of collapse. The *tangentopoli* (kickback city) investigation for corruption scandals by the judges had already begun in Milan.[16] The April 1992 election was a further indication of the irreversible crisis of the ruling bloc, confirming the analyses of the *quarantenni* in the wake of the 1990 administrative elections. On Monday 7 April 1992, the headline of *L'Unità* acknowledged the end of the DC regime.[17] The electoral results spoke for themselves: spectacular gains for Bossi's Northern League, while the 'limited collapse' of the PSI and the DC was to be accelerated by the *tangentopoli* scandal as it went on through 1992-93. The PDS achieved a very modest 16.1 per cent, while the newly-founded *Party of Communist Refoundation*, then led by Sergio Garavini, scored 5.6 per cent.[18]

Table 15   Electoral results of 5-6 April 1992 national election

	Parliament		
Parties	Votes	Percentage	Seats
DC	11,627,657	29.7	206
PDS	6,315,815	16.1	107
Communist Refoundation	2,202,574	5.6	35
PSI	5,336,358	13.6	92
MSI	2,103,692	5.4	34
PRI	1,721,658	4.4	27
PLI	1,119,492	2.8	17
PSDI	1,063,048	2.7	16
League	3,394,917	8.7	55
Pannella	485,339	1.2	7
Greens	1,092,783	2.8	16
Rete/L. Orlando	728,661	1.9	12
Others	2,016,983	5.1	6

Source: *La Repubblica*, 8-4-1992, p.7

In the negotiations occurring in the tumultuous post-1992 conjuncture, *new revisionism* compromised over the abolition of the *scala*, though it did not succumb to Confindustria's request to reduce everything to contractual level of *capital* (enterpreneurs) — *labour* (the union).[19] By contrast, *Communist Refoundation* emerged as a fierce opponent of the compromise, defended the existence of the *scala* and argued for its re-establishment.[20] I would argue that the *neo-revisionists* attempted to work out a *new compromise* between all the national players and take into account the new framework of national and international constraints, whereas *neo-Communists* tended to operate through an external/ oppositional relationship to them, inasmuch as they were *capitalist constraints*, that is, constraints imposed by the bourgeoisie. In this context, the neo-Communist strategy might turn to the *defensive*, that is, the logic of *vested interests*. Yet, *mutatis mutandis*, neo-revisionism considered its policy in parallel with the mainstream strategic lines of the post-war PCI, while *Communist Refoundation* was in a conflictual/class relationship to them. Ultimately, *new revisionism* wanted to consolidate its presence by seeking a new *social* and *political compromise* in a more and more globalised world.

Having said this, the risk for *Refoundation* is to stay out of the principal bodies where crucial decisions are taken, thus being unable to influence the developments with its own specific policies and rationale. The new leading group of *Rifondazione* around Bertinotti, seems to be conscious for this. In point of fact, *Rifondazione* attempts to develop a conflictual relationship with the PDS and the government of Romano Prodi by opposing them 'from within' the bounds of political power, though not assuming, for the time being, any ministerial responsibility.

The risk for *new revisionism* is precisely that it may be absorbed by capitalism and the requirements of its highly specialised institutional bodies. History shows that this is an only too familiar story, which might imply a *structuralist approach to history*, according to which, as the historical trajectory of the Left is merely a return to the initial 'conflictual centres' shaped by the Second and Third Internationals, no real distance can ever be covered.

Notes

1   Of all the votes cast, 264 of 415 were favourable; 102 were opposed to Occhetto and 43 were blank or null; see F. Rondolino, 'A sorpresa il PDS senza segretario', *L'Unità*, 5-2-1991, p.3.

2   See G. F. Polara, 'Come uscirne? Con una candidatura unitaria', ibid.

3   Occhetto would acknowledge his debt to Natta in his *Il Sentimento e la Ragione*, op. cit., p.105.

4   In an interview with M. Franco in *Panorama*, D'Alema announced that 'he himself was loyal but not faithful to Occhetto'. He even went so far as to say that 'he was not born as an member of Occhetto's team since, after all, it was he who proposed Occhetto's entry to the party's politbureau to Berlinguer', M. D'Alema, 'Craxi? Calma', *Panorama*, n.1297, 24-2-1991, pp. 50-52.

5   A. Occhetto, *Il Sentimento...*, op. cit., pp. 153-54.

6   For an excellent account of the intellectual history of Western Marxism, P. Anderson, *Considerations on Western Marxism* (London: Verso, 1979).

7   It is worth noting here that Nicos Poulantzas' last theoretical statement which marked his passage to left-wing Eurocommunism, draws on the problematics of Ingrao; see on this topic the analyses of B. Jessop, *Nicos Poulantzas: Marxist Theory and Political Strategy* (London: Macmillan, 1985), pp. 23 ff., 293-297, 321.

8   See G. Vacca, 'La proposta e la leadership', in his, *Dal PCI...*, op. cit., p.161.

9   *PCI 3/Mozione 3*, op. cit., pp. 65-68.

10   D. Sassoon, *One Hundred Years of Socialism...*, op. cit., E. Laclau-Ch. Mouffe, *Hegemony and Socialist Strategy*, op. cit., pp. 8-46.

11   E. Laclau-Ch. Mouffe, ibid., p.30.

12   *PCI-20o Congresso*, op. cit., p.11; for a concrete elaboration of *communist revisionism/refoundation* in Italy, see the following unpublished essays of P. Ingrao, 'Relazione introduttiva', PDS-Area Comunisti Democratici, Rome, 23-3-1991, 'Relazione in Assemblea dell'area dei comunisti democratici del PDS', Roma, 23-2-1992; also, P. Barcellona, 'Per una sinistra che vada oltre l'orizzonte socialdemocratico', *L'Unità*, 12-7-1990, p.2.

13   The problem could also be posed in a non-historical and therefore purely speculative, context: what is the principal difference between *communism*, on the one hand, and *revisionism*, on the other? Because of the specific purposes of the study, I will confine myself to exploring the case only within its Italian context.

14   I have examined some of the implications of this contradiction in my 'Political society/civil society and base/superstructure' (in Greek), *Scientific Thought*, 48, Jul.-Aug. 1990, pp. 11-25 and *Populism and Modernisation*, op. cit.

15   Unionisation fell from 51 per cent to 39 per cent in 1989; see, M. Carrieri, 'Industrial relations and the labour movement', in S. Gundle-S. Parker (ed.), *The New Italian Republic...*, op. cit., pp. 294-307.

16   *Tangentopoli* began in 17 February 1992, when Mario Chiesa, the socialist-appointed President of the municipal of Milan (the Old People's Home), was arrested. It involved the principal ruling figures of the Republic (Craxi, Forlani, Andreotti) and accelerated the crisis of the old power system; see, *inter alia*, D. Sassoon, '*Tangentopoli* or the democratization of corruption: considerations on the end of Italy's First Republic', *Journal of Modern Italian Studies*, v.1, n.1, Fall 1995, pp. 124-43.

17   M. Sappino, 'Finito il regime democristiano', *L'Unità*, 7-4-1992, p.1.

18   For a short, though comprehensive, narrative on the formation of the Party of Communist Refoundation, see L. Libertini, 'Quei nostri dieci mesi', *Liberazione*, 21-12-1991, pp. 17-19.

19   The national level of negotiation established was compulsory, while the decentralised was optional, see Carrieri M., 'Industrial relations...', op. cit., pp. 302-303.

20   For an overall account, see F. Bertinotti, *Tutti i Colori del Rosso*, op. cit.

8   A Tentative Conclusion

A

The year the Maastricht Treaty was signed, the Italian Left split and the Republic was on the verge of collapse. The 1992 national election marked the beginning of the end of the old ruling political class. Involved in a series of financial scandals and various embezzlements, neither the Christian Democrats of Giulio Andreotti and Arnaldo Forlani, nor the Socialists of Bettino Craxi managed to survive. Minor parties such as the Republicans and the Social Democrats followed suit. In essence, all the parties which had dominated the government of the country for fifty years disappeared (see table 16). *Tangentopoli's* judges and the *mani pulite* (clean hands) operation swept away the ruling elites and what was left from the old system represented a fragmented body of Catholic factions and *partitini* (small parties).

Table 16   March 1994 national election and June 1994 Euro-election

Parties	March 1994 national election*	June 1994 Euro-election
Forza Italia (Berlusconi)	21.0	32.4
Alleanza Nazionale (ex-neo-fascists)	13.4	12.3
Lega Nord (Umberto Bossi)	8.3	6.7
Pannella Lists	3.5	2.0
PDS	20.3	18.1
Rifondazione	6.0	5.9
Greens	2.7	3.4
Rete (L. Orlando)	1.9	1.0
Socialists/Democratic Alliance	3.4	1.8
Republicans (PRI)	—	0.7
Social Democrats (PSDI)	0.5	0.5
Popular Party (PPI–ex DC)	11.0	9.0
Segni's Pact (Referendum Party)	4.7	4.0

* The election was held under a new electoral system, where 75 per cent of the seats were allocated according to the *first-past-the-post* mechanism, whilst the remaining 25 per cent were distributed in proportion to the votes gained nationally by the parties.
Source: *Corriere della Sera*, 29-3-1994, pp.1-5, *La Repubblica*, 13-6-1994, pp.1-3

The collapse of the political class was prompted by the separatist Northern League of Umberto Bossi, which claimed the independence of the North against the corrupt bureaucracy of Rome, and by the referendum movement of Mario Segni for the abolition of the proportional electoral system.

As we saw earlier, PCI neo-revisionists and, later, the PDS advocated fiscal restriction, institutional and electoral reform as the key to the 'unlocking' of the political system and a renewed democracy of alternation; they also outlined a federal programmatic platform for the party and the country which, potentially, could pre-empt the strategy of Bossi. The transformation of the party assumed for itself the slogan 'the PCI changes itself because it wants to change Italy'. Nevertheless, the PDS failed to play a hegemonic role during the transition period (1992-94) and the victory in the 1994 election — both European and national — was captured by the newly-formed party of the media tycoon, Silvio Berlusconi. The reasons for this failure are a matter of ongoing debate. In this place, I will confine myself to list the most important reasons for this failure with reference only to the mistakes of the PDS itself.

i   That the PCI/PDS was paralysed by the internal debate over the question of transformation is the least controversial point. This produced a lack of political initiative as all party matters were translated in terms of the cleavage between *Ingraoiani* and *Occhettiani*. The PDS had no united strategy on the Gulf War issue nor on which political ally to choose for the declared aim of refounding the Republic. The party moved into the era of *tangentopoli* in a totally confused state. Instead of capitalising on *tangentopoli*, it felt wounded by it: it was revealed that *tangenti rossi* (Soviet financial help to the PCI) had continued even after Berlinguer's *strappo* with the USSR in 1981, while the involvement of some PDS cadres in *tangentopoli* further weakened the party's political initiative.[1] Thus, the PDS failed to play a leading role in some very important movements, such as Orlando's anti-Mafia effort in Palermo and Sicily, and the referendum movement of Segni, merely giving them rather unenthusiastic or belated support. Therefore, there was a failure of political initiative and leadership.

ii   The PDS insisted *too strongly* on the reform of the DC and PSI: once these parties changed themselves, they could then take part in the refoundation of the Republic. It proved a chimera simply because these parties were unreformable. At least after *Gladio*, the PDS ought to have seen this fact and distanced itself from both the DC and the PSI. In this respect, one should not fail to mention the privileged attitude of the PDS towards the PSI of Craxi, even when the latter was sinking in corruption scandals.[2] This is exclusively attributable to pressures exercised by the ultra-reformist wing of the PDS around Napolitano-Macaluso as well as the tolerance of the ruling group with the sole, steady exception of D'Alema.

iii Between 1992 and 1994, Giuliano Amato and Carlo Azeglio Ciampi respectively became successive Prime Ministers. A tactical mistake recognised by Occhetto himself, but which his political biographer fails to see,[3] was the decision of the PDS to participate in Ciampi's cabinet on 28 April 1993. Only when parliament refused to vote for Craxi's committal to investigation for embezzlement did the PDS realise that the Ciampi government was merely a government of the old regime and its three ministers resigned. It is at this conjuncture that Ingrao and Bertinotti left the PDS, with the former announcing he 'can no longer share a common language of political communication with the ruling group of the party'.[4] Soon after the completion of the 'first period of life' of the PDS,[5] the Party of Communist Refoundation began its reorganisation on the premises that neo-revisionism assumes a technocratic vision of politics, hence becoming absorbed by the institutions of neo-liberal economic development.

iv In the light of this, the PDS proved unable to substantially extend its alliance policy towards the centre of the political stage during the 1991-94 period. The crucial difference between Occhetto and D'Alema was in fact that the former had failed to lead the party towards the centre of the political scene, whereas the latter urged this strategic imperative quite effectively. Contrary to Occhetto's political indecision, D'Alema saw no objection to a political leadership of the 'dispersed' lay and Catholic forces at the expense of the PDS. These are the 'two different readings of the *svolta*' to which, as we saw earlier, Occhetto avoided clear reference.[6] During the debate in the politbureau of the party over the succession of Occhetto after the two successive defeats in the national and European elections of 1994, D'Alema categorically stated:

> Our political proposal was not to the level required by the Italian crisis itself. The real agenda needed to be a broad democratic coalition in which the Left, with its own identity and strategy, could have made a programmatic and ideological compromise with other components of the Italian society, lay and catholic forces [...]. This was not done.[7]

v The leadership crisis affecting both left-wing parties, the PDS in particular. Sergio Garavini stepped down as *Rifondazione*'s leader in January 1994 and Bertinotti, after thirty consecutive years serving the trade union movement, took over the party leadership. In July 1994, after the defeat in the European election, the politbureau of the PDS elected Massimo D'Alema as party secretary, with Occhetto subsequently engaging in recriminations.

Had the Left and the PDS in particular avoided making these mistakes, the political avenues taken since 1992 might have been different. From this perspective, the disintegration of the ruling political class of the First Republic is the least interesting. More important is the fact that the PDS missed the opportunity of capitalising on the crisis and laying the foundations of a new socialist polity for Italy and Europe.

B

The victory of the *Ulivo* (Olive Tree coalition) in the election of 21 April 1996 marks a notable watershed for Italy: for the first time since the war, a Left-dominated government will rule the country.

Table 17   The April 1996 national election

Lower House — Proportional

Parties	%	Votes	Seats
Ulivo			
PDS	21.1	7,897,044	26
PPI/Prodi	6.8	2,555,082	4
Dini	4.3	1,627,191	8
Rifondazione	8.6	3,215,960	20
Polo			
Alleanza Nazionale	15.7	5,875,391	28
Forza Italia	20.6	7,715,342	37
Pannella-Sgarbi	1.9	701,033	—
CCD/CDU	5.8	2,190,019	12
Northern League	10.1	3,777,786	20

Lower House — Majoritarian

Coalition	Seats
Centre-Left	246
Progressists	15
Polo delle Libertà	169
Northern League	39
Others	6

Source: *La Repubblica*, 23-4-1996, p.4

The PDS forms the backbone of the cabinet led by Romano Prodi — a Catholic professor of economics at the University of Bologna and former President of IRI — while *Rifondazione*, for the time being, offers critical backing to the government.[8] The political priority of both PDS and Prodi is Italy's inclusion in the launch of the monetary union in 1999.[9]

The success of the Northern League and its extreme federalism shows the importance of the federalist question that the Italian Left has raised since 1989-90. *Alleanza Nazionale*, drawing heavily on conservative and even fascist matrixes of the past, represents the best of Italian Euroscepticism, the worst being the neo-liberal hotch-potch of Silvio Berlusconi and Giuliano Ferrara.

This is the appropriate point to summarise the arguments advanced by this study. I will also attempt to survey some crucial points of disagreement with other arguments in works discussed throughout.

1 The First Italian Republic was a *Republic of compromises* underpinned, in one way or another, both by its major constitutive political forces (DC, PSI, PCI) and the State which could generate growth by institutionalising the political management of aggregate demand (the Keynesian state). In this respect, the history of the PCI is inseparable from the history of the First Republic. This means that Italian Communists shared both the merit of struggling for the expansion of political democracy and civil liberties *and* the flaw of being part of the democracy built around the DC's corrupt system of power. In this context, and after the collapse of 'actually-existing socialism' and the acceleration of European integration under the aegis of neo-liberalism, the dissolution of the PCI could only 'act' as a harbinger for the dissolution of the First Republic. This was noted by Eugenio Scalfari who, soon after Occhetto announced the *grande svolta*, categorically argued: 'If the PCI as such disappears and transforms itself into another political subject, then the entire political system of Italy will be transformed, just as if some similar process were to happen to the Christian Democratic party.'[10]

To the best of my knowledge, no accounts of the transformation of the PCI develop a similar context. Rather, they marginalise the European dimension in the analyses of the PCI and, instead, see events in the East as the major factor contributing to the *grande svolta*. Furthermore, it also had perverse effects on studies that have tried to explain the transition to the Second Italian Republic. By focusing on the ahistorical category of 'consociationalism' advanced by Arend Lijphart, they concluded that the corporatist and corrupt political form of management intrinsic to the power system of the First Republic could not meet the needs of neo-liberal economic restructuring, therefore its polity was bound to collapse and pave the way for a functional administration of neo-liberal orientation. As we have seen, this is, among others, the thesis of Gianfranco Pasquino and, in a more general South European comparative framework, that of Giulio Sapelli.[11] *We are experiencing here a form of reductionism, where the political system mirrors the ordinances of neo-liberal economics, the latter seen as the essentialist evolutionary substratum intrinsic to the new phase of capitalist development.*

2   The triple (political, organisational, ideological) crisis of the PCI in the 1980s was the result of a complicated process concerning major changes in the international and European system of power. The process involved the weakening of the nation-state, the shaping of economic policy along Keynesian lines, the crisis of unionism vis-à-vis new forms of industrial relations (flexible specialisation, part-time contracts etc.), and a crisis in the ideologies of 'mass struggle' and 'collectivism' in the wake of the prevailing culture of individualism and 'self-fulfilment'. All this, in turn, entailed a crisis of representation, distanced civil society from mass politics and raised the question of 'citizenship' and 'regulation by legislation' as a left-wing alternative. The PCI discussed these issues throughout the 1980s, and completed its passage to *new revisionism* well before Occhetto announced the constituent phase for the party's dissolution. In this context, the transformation of the party identity must be seen as a long process of inner-party debate which had already begun under the leadership of Berlinguer and the introduction of *alternativa democratica*, but was completed under the leadership of the *quarantenni* and Occhetto at the 18th Congress of the party in March 1989. Up to that point, the neo-revisionists capitalised on the reformist-democratic tradition of the party at the expense of the anti-capitalist one. In fact, we can formulate the following somewhat paradoxical proposition: *without the duplicity of the PCI, its transformation would have been impossible.* Furthermore, the *quarantenni* could base their arguments on the exhaustion of Eurocommunism and Gorbachev's activism which, in fact, undermined the party's democratic image and initiative in Europe. When the PCI declared itself an 'integral part of the European Left' at its 1986 Congress in Florence, it had already taken the path of no return: that of renewing itself by keeping pace with the renewal of European Social Democracy (the German SPD was seen as the privileged interlocutor). The crisis of 'actually-existing socialism' and the fall of the Berlin Wall accelerated the constituent process of the party transformation, accelerated the change of name and symbols, while corroborating the belief that the power system of the First Republic, after the end of the Cold War, would no longer hold.

3 The picture we have presented is of a process of splits and fragmentations through which the disaggregation of the PCI took place. However, this did not leave a void. *New revisionism* (PDS) and *Communist refoundation* (PRC) emerged as two new political paradigms of the Italian Left, recomposing the system of tensions and hegemonic articulations of the old PCI. We thus came to see the principal contradiction in the Italian Left as a *corpus* of two distinct political entities which, *although both are revisionist*, did not share the same political priorities. New revisionism emphasises the institutional and ideological leadership over the process of capitalist restructuring, while Communist refoundation stresses the antagonistic relationship to the capitalist relations of production, which in the current political jargon is often called *capitalismo opulente*. In this context, any strategic revision or identity change, on the part of *new revisionism* or *Communist refoundation*, which does not affect these very contents will continue to be partial by virtue of changes in the historical process of capitalist development *per se*. Otherwise, the distinction will lose its significance. Having said this, the real problem was perhaps not whether the Italian Left had overcome the separating principles between the Second and the Third Internationals respectively, but whether or not such a transcendence was — and is — possible *under* capitalism.

4 Since 1943, the PCI backed major social and political compromises: it formed and supported governments of *national solidarity* (1944-1946 and 1976-1979), backed the formation of the Centre-Left in the 1960s and did not hesitate to propose austerity measures for the benefit of the country's capitalist recovery. The principal tension was created around the question of wages, the *questione salariale*. As a predominantly revisionist and reformist force, the PCI presented moderate views on the question and, in critical periods, often at the expense of the working class. Nevertheless, the PCI in the 1980s and the PDS in the 1990s was obliged to proceed with a major revisionist break: they had to give up the defence of the *scala mobile*, an index which counterbalances the dynamic relationship between wages, inflation and purchasing power. The crisis of Keynesian economics also undermined the social balance of forces between capital and labour. Thus, as we have seen, a new social and political compromise is being formed on the premises of a post-Keynesian consensus.

I have attempted to trace the history of the PCI and its transformation in conjunction with the history and the crisis of the First Italian Republic. As I pointed out in the preface to the study, the entire methodological framework of my attempt in fact can be traced back to Gramsci who, in criticising the political party theory of Roberto Michels, remarked: 'To write the history of a political party means to write the history of a country from a monographic point of view.' I can now state with confidence that this is far more than a simple methodological assumption. In point of fact, it includes the whole notion of *hegemony over a given national formation*: once the 'monographic reading' is completed, the whole notion of how to build the hegemony is much more easily conceived. This is the case of the modern Italian Left today, seen as a *mèlange* of Italian and European Socialist traditions, operating in an increasingly integrated political system.

Notes

1   All these points have been admitted by Occhetto himself, see his *Il Sentimento...*, op. cit.
2   For further comments, see my 'Is there a *Modern Prince* for the Second Italian Republic?', paper presented in the Conference *Contesting the Boundaries of Italian Politics*, held at Carleton University, Canada, 21-23 March 1996, pp. 16-18.
3   A. Occhetto, *Il Sentimento...*, op. cit., p.116 and M. Lorusso, *L'Era di Achille*, op. cit., pp. 311-16.
4   P. Ingrao, personal interview, op. cit., also, R. Roscani, 'Il comunista eretico', op. cit.
5   On this topic, P. Ciofi, *Passaggio a Sinistra. Il PDS tra Occhetto e D'Alema* (Messina: Rubbettino, 1995).
6   A. Occhetto, *Il Sentimento...*, op. cit., pp. 153-54.
7   M. D'Alema (30-6-1994), in his *Un Paese Normale; La Sinistra e il Futuro dell'Italia* (Milano: Arnoldo Mondatori, 1995), pp. 82-83.
8   For a brief speculation on this topic, on the occasion of the victory of the Centre-Left in the election of 21 of April, see T. Abse, 'The Left's advance in Italy', *New Left Review*, 217, May-June 1996, pp. 123-30, V. Fouskas, 'Sotto i rami dell'*Ulivo*', *Il Punto*, n.66, June 1996, pp. 8-9.
9   For an account of the European strategy of the PDS and *Rifondazione*, see my 'The Italian Left and the Enlargement of the European Union', *Contemporary Politics*, v.3, n.2, June 1997, pp. 119-37.
10   E. Scalfari, 'Il vecchio PCI e la coperta di Linus', *La Repubblica*, 19-11-1989, now in G. Moltedo, N. Rangeri (ed.), *PCI: La Grande...*, op. cit., p.69.
11   G. Pasquino, 'Introduction: the case of a regime crisis', op. cit., G. Sapelli, *Southern Europe since 1945...*, op. cit., and my review of Sapelli 'Review of G. Sapelli *Southern Europe since 1945*', op. cit.

Bibliography

Abse T., 'Judging the PCI', *New Left Review*, 153, Sept., Oct. 1985.

Abse T., 'The Left's advance in Italy', *New Left Review*, 217, May-June 1996.

Accornero A., 'Nella "terza Italia" maggiore coesione', *Rinascita*, 25, 23-6-1978.

Agnelli G., 'European industry and Southern Italy', *Questions for Debate*, 27-28, Naples, 6-6-1980.

Amendola G., 'I comunisti e il movimento studentesco. Necessità della lotta su due fronti', *Rinascita*, 23, 7-6-1968.

Amendola G., 'I contrasti fra Secchia e Togliatti (1944-1954)', *Rinascita*, 17, 4-5-1979.

Amendola G., 'Ipotesi sulla riunificazione', *Rinascita*, 45, 7-11-1964.

Amendola G., 'Lotta di classe e sviluppo economico dopo la liberazione', in Istituto Gramsci (ed.), *Tendenze del Capitalismo Italiano* (Roma: Riuniti, 1962).

Amendola G., 'The Italian Road to Socialism', *New Left Review*, 106, Nov., Dec. 1977.

Amendola G., *Il Rinnovamento del PCI* (Roma: Riuniti, 1978).

Amyot G., *The Italian Communist Party; the Crisis of the Popular Front Strategy* (London: Croom Helm, 1981).

Anderson P., 'The antinomies of A. Gramsci', *New Left Review*, 100, 1977.

Anderson P., *Considerations on Western Marxism* (London: Verso, 1979).

Angius G., 'Intervento al 20o Congresso', *L'Unità*, 2-2-1991.

Armeni R., 'L'arco del No', *Rinascita*, 35, 14-10-1990.

Armeni R., 'PCI: prossimo venturo', *Rinascita*, 5, 11-3-1990.

Asor Rosa A., 'Monaci e monachesimi', *Rinascita*, 35, 14-10-1990.

Asor Rosa A., 'Per essere antagonisti', *Rinascita*, 7, 25-3-1990.

Asor Rosa A. (ed.), *Viaggio nel Cuore del PCI* [attached leaflet of *Rinascita*], 17, 3-6-1990.

Asor Rosa A., 'Un'operazione a perdere', *L'Unità*, 11-1-1990.

Assemblea del No, 'Il documento di Ariccia', *L'Unità*, 16-6-1990.

Baduel U., 'Comunisti alla prova del "nuovo corso"', *L'Unità*, 5-6-1988.

Bagnasco A., *Tre Italie; La Problematica Territoriale nello Sviluppo Italiano* (Bologna: il Mulino, 1977).

Baldassari M., Briotti G.M., 'The government budget and the Italian economy during the 1970s and 1980s: causes of the debt, strategy for recovery, and prospects for restructuring', in Baldassari M.(ed.), *The Italian Economy: Heaven or Hell*? (London: St. Martin's Press and SIPI, 1994).

Banca P., 'Ingrao: non posso tacere il mio dissenso', *L'Unità*, 24-8-1990.

Barbera A., 'Per un moderno stato regionale', *Critica Marxista*, 5-6, Sept., Dec. 1990.

Barcellona P., 'Oltre la crisi del Welfare, più autonomia sociale', *Rinascita*, 12, 20-3-1981.

Barcellona P., 'Per una sinistra che vada oltre l'orizzonte socialdemocratico', *L'Unità*, 12-7-1990.

Barcellona P., *Il Ritorno del Legame Sociale* (Torino: Bollati Boringhieri, 1990).

Bassolino A., 'Idee per il programma di un nuovo partito della sinistra', *L'Unità*, 31-5-1990.

Bassolino A., 'Intervento al 19o Congresso', *L'Unità*, 10-3-1990.

Bassolino A., 'Oltre i sì e i no', *il Manifesto*, 20-1-1990.

Bassolino A., 'Quella legge sui diritti è giusta', *L'Unità*, 13-3-1990.

Bassolino A., 'Relazione introduttiva', *Critica Marxista*, 5-6, Sept., Dec. 1990.

Bassolino A., 'Riproporrò le mie idee', *L'Unità*, 14-10-1990.

Battini M.(ed.), *Dialogo su Berlinguer* (Firenze: Giunti, 1994).

Battistini G., 'Lo shock Ingrao', *La Repubblica*, 2-10-1990.

Benini L., 'Il novanta in movimento', *Rinascita*, 1, 11-2-1990.

Benini L., 'Occupati e preoccupati', *Rinascita*, 2, 18-2-1990.

Benini L., 'Il partito numero per numero', *Rinascita*, 4, 3-2-1991.

Berlinguer E., 'Il partito di cambiamento', *Rinascita*, 25, 19-6-1981.

Berlinguer E., 'Imperialismo e coesistenza alla luce dei fatti Cileni', *Rinascita*, 38, 28-9-1973.

Berlinguer E., 'Riflessione sull'Italia dopo i fatti del Cile', *Rinascita*, 39, 5-10-1973.

Berlinguer E., 'Riflessioni sull'Italia dopo i fatti del Cile', *Rinascita*, 40, 12-10-1973.

Berlinguer E., 'Prospettiva di trasformazione e specificità comunista in Italia', *Critica Marxista*, 2, March-April 1981.

Berlinguer E., *Attualità e Futuro* (Roma: L'Unità, 1989).

Berlinguer E., *Austerità, Occasione per Trasformare l'Italia* (Roma: Riuniti, 1977).

Berlinguer E., *La Questione Comunista*, v.1-2 (Roma: Riuniti, 1975).

Berlinguer E., *Relazione al XVI Congress Nazionale del PCI* (Milano: Bozze di Spampa, 2-3-1983).

Bertinotti F., *Tutti i Colori del Rosso* (Milano: Sperling and Kupfer, 1955).

Bianchi P., 'The IRI in Italy: strategic role and political constraints', *West European Politics*, v.10, n.2, April 1987.

Bianchi P., Della Salla V., 'Privatisation in Italy: aims and constraints', *West European Politics*, v.11, n.4, Oct. 1988.

Blair T., *New Britain; My Vision of a New Country* (London: Fourth Estate, 1996).

Bobbio N., *Saggi su Gramsci* (Milano: Feltrinelli, 1990).

Boccia Maria L., 'Part-time tra passato e futuro', *Rinascita*, 15, 16-4-1982.

Boffa M., 'La difficile prova di Mitterrand', *Rinascita*, 13, 1-4-1983.

Bolaffi A., 'Il teorema Glotz incroccia il dilemma PCI', *Politica ed Economia*, 12, Dec. 1985.

Borghini G., 'L'antagonismo al sistema è minoritario, non alternativo', *L'Unità*, 22-8-1990.

Braun M., *L'Italia da Andreotti a Berlusconi; Rivolgimenti e Prospetive Politiche in un Paese a Rischio* (Milano: Feltrinelli, 1995).

Brusadelli S., Caccarelli F., 'Chiedo aiuto compagne', *Panorama*, 1237/38, 7-1-1990.

Bufalini P., Chiaromonte G., 'Per un partito riformista, socialista e democratico', *Critica Marxista*, 1, Jan., Feb. 1990.

Buffo G., 'Identità politica e differenza sessuale', *Critica Marxista*, 1, Jan., Feb. 1990.

Cagliardi R., 'Nuovo è comunista', *il Manifesto*, 16-1-1990.

Caracciolo L., 'La sinistra che non c'è', *Micromega*, 1, 1990.

Carr E. H., *What is History?* (London: Pelican Books, 1967).

Cassese S., 'Italy: Privatisations announced, semi-privatisations and pseudo-privatisations', in Wright V.(ed.), *Privatisation in Western Europe: Pressures, Problems and Paradoxes* (London: Pinter Publishers, 1994).

Catanzaro R., Sabetti F. (eds), *Italian Politics; A Review*, v.5 (London: Pinter Publishers, 1991).

Cazzaniga M., 'Mozione 3: Le Conclusioni al 19o Congresso', *L'Unità*, 10-3-1990.

CENSIS, *Italy Today: Social Pictures and Trends* (Rome: F. Angeli, 1990).

CGIL, *I Documenti del XII Congresso della CGIL* (Rome: Ediesse, 1992).

Chiarante G., 'Compromesso, solidarità, alternativa', *Rinascita*, 25, 23-6-1984.

Chiarante G., 'Le ricette di De Mita, le alternative di Ruffolo', *Rinascita*, 4, 27-1-1984.

Chiarante G., *Da Togliatti a D'Alema* (Bari: Laterza, 1996).

Chiaromonte G., 'La via Italiana che noi proponiamo', *Rinascita*, 23, 22-6-1985.

Chiaromonte G., 'La sua analisi del Centro-Sinistra', *Rinascita*, 47, 7-11-1964.

Ciofi P., *Passaggio a Sinistra; il PDS tra Occhetto e D'Alema* (Messina: Rubbettino, 1995).

Clough B. S., *The Economic History of Italy* (New York: Columbia University Press, 1964).

Colletti L., 'Il mal di sempre del PCI di Occhetto', *Corriere della Sera*, 1-4-1989.

Cooper J., 'Soviet resources options: civil and military priorities', in Hasegawa T., Pravda A.(eds), *Perestroika: Soviet Domestic and Foreign Policies* (London: Sage, 1990).

Cossutta A., 'Il dibattito alla direzione del PCI', *L'Unità*, 12-10-1990.

Cossutta A., 'Intervento al 19o Congresso', *L'Unità*, 9-3-1990.

Cossutta A., 'Intervento al CC', *L'Unità*, 5-10-1989.

Cossutta A., 'Intevento al 20o Congresso', *L'Unità*, 3-2-1991.
Cossutta A., 'Per il superamento del capitalismo', *Critica Marxista*, 1, Jan., Feb. 1986.
Cossutta A., 'Vogliamo l'unità del PCI? Allora consentiamo liste distinte di candidati', *L'Unità*, 13-4-1989.
Craxi B., 'Diffido di questo PCI: non è l'ombelico del mondo', *Corriere della Sera*, 9-3-1989.
Curi U., *Lo Scudo di Achille* (Milano: F. Angeli, 1990).
Curi U., D'Arcais P.F., *L'Albero e la Foresta; il Partito Democratico della Sinistra nel Sistema Politico Italiano* (Milano: Franco Angeli, 1991).
D'Alema M., 'Intervento al 18o Congresso', *L'Unità*, 21-3-1989.
D'Alema M., 'Arrichire le culture di sinistra', *L'Unità-Letera sulla Cosa*, 19-10-1990.
D'Alema M., '...E poi c'è il PCI', *L'Unità*, 19-2-1989.
D'Alema M., 'Craxi? Calma', *Panorama*, n.1297, 24-2-1991.
D'Alema M., 'Noi e i socialisti', *L'Unità*, 3-2-1989.
D'Alema M., 'Formulas for progress', *World Marxist Review*, v.33, n.1, Jan. 1990.
D'Alema M., *Un Paese Normale; La Sinistra e il Futuro dell'Italia* (Milano: Arnoldo Mondatori, 1995).
D'Arcais P. F., 'Nè carne nè pesce', *La Repubblica*, 15-5-1990.
D'Arcais P. F., 'Lettera aperta al Congresso del PCI', *Micromega*, 1, 1989.
D'Arcais P. F., 'Lettera a Occhetto', *Micromega*, 1, 1990.
Dalamasso S., *Il Caso 'Manifesto' e il PCI degli Anni '60* (Torino: Cric Editore, 1989).
De Giovanni B., 'C'erano una volta Togliatti e il comunismo reale', *L'Unità*, 20-8-1989.
De Mita C., *Politica e Istituzioni nell'Italia Repubblicana* (Milano: Bompiani, 1988).
De Vito F., Quaranta G., 'Seconda Repubblica', *L'Espresso*, 48, 2-12-1990.
Degras J., *The Communist International. Documents (1929-1943)*, v.3 (London: O.U.P., 1965).
Dondi W., 'Il PCI cambierà nome? Tutto è possibile', *L'Unità*, 13-11-1989.
Donolo C., 'Social change and transformation of the state in Italy', in Scase R. (ed.), *The State in Western Europe* (London: Croom Helm, 1980).
Donovan M., 'The referendum and the transformation of the party system', *Modern Italy*, v.1, n.1, Autumn 1995.
Ehmke H., 'SPD-PCI, le ragioni di un confronto', *Rinascita*, 5, 9-2-1985.
Fabbrini S., 'The end of consensual politics in Italy', paper presented in the Conference *Contesting the Boundaries of Italian Politics*, Carleton University, Ottawa, 22-23 March 1996.
Fassino P., 'La sinistra e la questione delle modernità', *Critica Marxista*, 1, Jan., Feb. 1986.
Fassino P., 'Per una nuova forma-partito', *Critica Marxista*, 5-6, Sept., Dec. 1990.

Fassino P., 'Scriviamo insieme la carta comune del PDS', *L'Unità*, 8-1-1991.

Fassino P., 'Una forma partito nuova per una sinistra nuova', *L'Unità*, 1-7-1990.

Fattorini E., 'Una sfida possibile al moderno', *Rinascita*, 3, 25-2-1990.

Ferrara G., 'Per la rifondazione del identità comunista', *Critica Marxista*, 1, Jan., Feb. 1990.

Foa V., *Sindacati e Lotte Operaie, 1943-1973* (Torino: Loescher, 1975).

Folara G. F., 'Come uscirne? Con una candidatura unitaria', *L'Unità*, 5-2-1991.

Folena P., 'Un nuovo sogetto di cambiamento', *Critica Marxista*, 1, Jan., Feb. 1990.

Fouskas V., 'The Italian Left and the enlargement of the European Union', *Contemporary Politics*, v.3, n.2, June 1997.

Fouskas V., 'Il nome della cosa: Eurocommunism, the Euroleft and the crisis of PCI', *Economicos Tachidromos*, v.20, n.188, 17-5-1990.

Fouskas V., 'Is there a *Modern Prince* for the second Italian republic?', paper presented in the Conference *Contesting the Boundaries of Italian Politics*, Department of Political Science, Carleton University, Ottawa, 22-23 March 1996.

Fouskas V., 'Political society/civil society and base/superstructure', *Scientific Thought*, 48, Jul., Aug. 1990.

Fouskas V., 'Sotto i rami dell'Ulivo', *Il Punto*, 66, June 1996.

Fouskas V., *Populism and Modernisation; the Exhaustion of the Third Hellenic Republic* (Athens: Ideokinissi, 1995).

Fouskas V., 'Review of G. Sapelli, *Southern Europe since 1945*', *Modern Italy*, v.1, n.2, Autumn 1996.

Fouskas V., 'New americanism and post-fordism', *Utopia*, 18, Nov., Dec. 1995.

Fouskas V., 'The end of British labourism and the "clause 4" issue', *Alpha*, 5, June 1995.

Galli della Loggia E., 'Natta, non prendertela: al PCI è vietato il sorpasso', *Europeo*, 20-21, 25-5-1985.

Galli G., *Storia del Partito Comunista Italiano* (Milano: il Formichiere, 1976).

Garavini S., 'Intervento al 18o Congresso', *L'Unità*, 20-3-1989.

Garavini S., 'Cambiar pelle al PCI per rifondare la politica? Sarebbe troppo semplice', *L'Unità*, 6-1-1990.

Gentili M. A., Panebianco A., 'The PCI and International relations, 1945-1975: the politics of accommodation', in Serfaty S., Gray L.(eds), *The Italian Communist Party; Yesterday, Today and Tomorrow* (London: Aldwych Press, 1980).

Geremica F., 'Gli auguri di De Mita, l'anatema dei socialisti', *La Repubblica*, 11-10-1990.

Germani G., 'Lo sviluppo dei ceti medi', in Ragone G.(ed.), *Mutamanto e Classi Sociali in Italia* (Napoli: Liguori Editori, 1981).

Germani G., *Autoritarismo, Fascismo e Classi Sociali* (Bologna: Il Mulino, 1975).

Giavazzi F., Spaventa L., 'Italy: the real effects of inflation and disinflation', in Baldassari M. (ed.), *The Italian Economy: Heaven or Hell?* (London: St. Martin's Press and SIPI).

Ginsborg P., *A History of Contemporary Italy; Society and Politics 1943-1988* (London: Penguin Books, 1990).

Glotz P., *Manifesto per Una Nuova Sinistra Europea* (Milano: Feltrinelli, 1986).

Gorbachev M., *Le Idee di Berlinguer ci Servono Ancora* (Roma: Sisifo, 1994).

Gorbetta P., Leonardi R., Nanetti R. (eds), *Italian Politics: A Review*, v.2 (London: Pinter Publishers, 1987).

Gramsci A., *Quaderni del Carcere* (Torino, Einaudi, 1977), v.I-IV.

Gramsci A., *Sul Fascismo* (Roma: Riuniti, 1974).

Graziani A. (ed.), *L'Economia Italiana: 1945-1970* (Bologna: il Mulino, 1972).

Graziano L., 'Partito di regime e clientelismo di massa', *Rinascita*, 33, 8-8-1975.

Graziano L., 'Patron-client relationships in Southern Italy', *European Journal of Political Research*, v.1, n.4, 1973.

Gundle S., 'The Italian Communist Party: Gorbachev and the end of "really existing socialism"', in Bell (ed.), *Western European Communists and the Collapse of Communism* (Oxford: Berg, 1993).

Gundle S., Parker S., *The New Italian Republic; from the Fall of the Berlin Wall to Berlusconi* (London: Routledge, 1996).

Hanson P., 'Gorbachev's economic policies after four years', in Hasegawa T., Pravda A. (eds), *Perestroika: Soviet Domestic and Foreign Policies* (London: Sage 1990).

Hellman S., Pasquino G. (eds), *Italian Politics: A Review*, v.7 (London: Pinter Publishers, 1992).

Hine D., *Governing Italy; The Politics of Bargained Pluralism* (Oxford: Clarendon Press, 1993).

Hoare Q. (ed.), *A. Gramsci: Selections from Political Writings (1910-1920)* (London: Lawrence and Wishart, 1977).

Hoare Q. (ed.), *A. Gramsci: Selections from Political Writings (1921-1926)* (London: Lawrence and Wishart, 1978).

Hoare Q., Smith N.G. (ed.), *A. Gramsci: Selections from the Prison Notebooks* (London: Lawrence and Wishart, 1973).

Hobsbawm E., 'Identity politics and the Left', *New Left Review*, 217, May-June 1996.

Ignazi P., 'Il posto della cosa', *il Mulino*, a.XXXIX, 5, Sept., Oct. 1990.

Ignazi P., *Dal PCI al PDS* (Bologna: il Mulino, 1992).

Indrio U., *Dieci Anni: La Lotta Politica in Italia dal 1978 al 1988* (Roma: Edizione Lavoro).

Ingrao P., 'Alternativa di Stato', *L'Espresso*, 7, 23-2-1986.

Ingrao P., 'Con Marx oltre Marx', *Micromega*, 5, 1990.

Ingrao P., 'Gorbachev ti voglio bene', *L'Espresso*, 8, 26-2-1989.

Ingrao P., 'I comunisti e l'Est', *il Manifesto*, 4-2-1990.

Ingrao P., 'Il sistema di potere del capitalismo di stato', *Rinascita*, 47, 30-11-1973.

Ingrao P., 'Intervento al XI Congresso del PCI', in *XI Congresso del PCI. Atti e Risoluzioni* (Roma: Riuniti, 1966).

Ingrao P., 'Intervento al 18o Congresso', *L'Unità*, 21-3-1989.

Ingrao P., 'Intervento al 20o Congresso', *L'Unità*, 3-2-1991.

Ingrao P., 'La sinistra oltre i limiti dello stato-nazione', *Rinascita*, 17, 29-4-1983.

Ingrao P., 'La grande politica dell'epoca atomica', *Rinascita*, 39, 19-10-1985.

Ingrao P., 'Le forme della politica e il rapporto tra masse e democrazia', *Rinascita*, 23-1-1981.

Ingrao P., 'Mozione 2: Le conclusioni al 19o Congresso', *L'Unità*, 10-3-1990.

Ingrao P., 'Non toccate il nome', *La Repubblica*, 7/8-1-1990.

Ingrao P., 'Novità dalle Regioni', *Rinascita*, 19, 11-5-1973.

Ingrao P., 'Relazione in Assemblea dell'area dei comunisti democratici del PDS', Roma, 23-2-1992.

Ingrao P., 'Relazione Introduttiva', PDS-Area Comunisti Democratici, Rome 23-3-1991.

Ingrao P., 'Sistema di potere e tipo di sviluppo economico-sociale', *Rinascita*, 21, 25-5-1973.

Ingrao P., 'In Polonia e altrove c'era altro da fare', *Rinascita*, 50, 18-12-1981.

Ingrao P., 'The European Left and the problems of a new internationalism', *Socialism in the World*, 53, 1986.

Ingrao P., *Crisi e Terza Via* (Roma: Riuniti, 1978).

Ingrao P. et al., 'La politica del PCI per una nuova direzione del paese', *Rinascita*, 4, 24-1-1975.

Ingrao P., *Le Cose Impossibili* (Roma: Riuniti, 1990).

Ingrao P., *Masse e Potere* (Roma: Riuniti, 1977).

Ingrao P., Rossanda R., 'Alla vigilia del Congresso', *il Manifesto*, 21-2-1990.

Ingrao P., Rossanda R., *Appuntamenti di Fine Secolo* (Roma: Manifesto Libri, 1995).

Iotti N., 'Una tavola rotonda dei partiti e poi un referendum popolare', *La Stampa*, 13-5-1990.

Istituto Gramsci/Sezione di Firenze, *Togliatti e il Centro-Sinistra, 1958-1964*, v.1-2 (Firenze: Cooperativa Editrice Universitaria, 1975).

Izzo F., 'Le donne da "questione sociale" a "sogetto fondante"', *Critica Marxista*, 1, Jan., Feb. 1990.

Jessop B., *N. Poulantzas: Marxist Theory and Political Strategy* (London: Macmillan, 1985).

Kertzer I.D., *Politics and Symbols; The Italian Communist Party and the Fall of Communism* (New Haven and London: Yale University Press, 1996).

Kissinger H., 'Communist parties in W. Europe: Challenge to the West', in A. Ranney-G. Sartori (eds), *Eurocommunism: The Italian Case* (Washington: American Enterprise Institute for Public Policy Research, 1978).

Kostoris F.P.S., *Italy: the Sheltered Economy* (Oxford: Clarendon Press, 1993).

Laclau E., Mouffe C., *Hegemony and Socialist Strategy; Towards a Radical Democratic Politics* (London: Verso 1985).

Lange P., Vannicelli M. (eds), *The Communist Parties of Italy, France and Spain: Post-war Change and Continuity* (London: George Allen, 1981).

Lasch C., *The Culture of Narcissism; American Life in an Age of Diminishing Expectations* (New York: Norton, 1978).

Leonardi R., Anderlini F. (eds), *Italian Politics; A Review*, v.6 (London: Pinter Publishers, 1992).

Leonardi R., Corbetta P. (eds), *Italian Politics; A Review*, v.3 (London: Pinter Publishers, 1989).

Libertini L., 'Quei nostri dieci mesi', *Liberazione*, 21-12-1991.

Lijphart A., *Democracies: Patterns of Majoritarian and Consensus Government in Twenty-One Countries* (New Haven and London: Yale University Press, 1984).

Longo L., 'Il movimento studentesco nella lotta anti-capitalista', *Rinascita*, 18, 3-5-1968.

Lopes A., 'Scelte di portafoglio, tassi di interesse e debito pubblico in Italia. Una verifica empirica per gli anni '80', in Giannola A., Marani U. (eds), *Tassi di Interesse e Debito Pubblico* (Napoli: Edizioni Scientifiche Italiane, 1990).

Lorusso M., *L'Era di Achille; Occhetto e la Politica Italiana da Togliatti a Berlusconi* (Firenze: Ponte alle Grazie, 1994).

Macaluso E., 'Ciriaco al finale di partita', *L'Unità*, 14-4-1989.

Macaluso E., 'Intervento al 19o Congresso', *L'Unità*, 11-3-1990.

Macaluso E., 'Le domande sulla P2 alle quali Forlani poteva rispondere', *Rinascita*, 21, 22-5-1981.

Macaluso E., 'Le coerenze dell'alternativa', *Rinascita*, 29, 25-7-1987.

Macaluso E., Napolitano G., 'Coerenza riformista: Ecco la "cosa" che vogliamo', *L'Unità*, 14-7-1990.

Mafai M., 'Le vedove di Lenin e la deriva feminista', *Micromega*, 4, 1990.

Mafai M., *Dimenticare Berlinguer; La Sinistra Italiana e la Tradizione Comunista* (Roma: Donzelli, 1996).

Magna N., 'Dal PCI al PDS: geografia di un declino', *Politica ed Economia*, 12, Dec. 1992.

Magno M., Soriero P., Sales I., 'Una Costituente nel Mezzogiorno: Riformista, cioè antagonista', *L'Unità*, 11-8-1990.

Magri L., 'Alternanza o alternativa: omologazione o nuova identità comunista?', *Critica Marxista*, 1, Jan., Feb. 1986.

Magri L., 'Intervento al CC', *L'Unità*, 16-11-1989.

Magri L., 'Real socialism and possible socialism: The problems of the East European societies and the European Left', in *Power and Opposition in Post-Revolutionary Societies* (London: Links, 1979).

Magri L., 'Intervento al CC', *L'Unità*, 15-11-1989.

Magri L., 'Intervento al 18o Congresso', *L'Unità*, 21-3-1989.

Magri L., 'La spesa sociale è un falso imputato', *Rinascita*, 35, 21-9-1985.

Magri L., 'Non è solo un ritorno, siamo cambiati tutti', *L'Unità*, 20-10-1984.

Mancina C., 'Elogio della parzialità comunista', *Politica ed Economia*, 1, Jan. 1989.

Mancina C., 'Intervento al 19o Congresso', *L'Unità*, 9-3-1990.

Mannuzzu S., 'Il retrobottega della Repubblica', *Rinascita*, 40, 18-11-1990.

Marx K., *Capital*, v.1 (London: Penguin Books, 1976).

Marx K., *Capital* v.3 (London: Lawrence and Wishart, 1959).

Marx K., *Grundrisse* (Middlesex: Penguin Books, 1973).

Marx K., *Selected Writings* (Oxford: O.U.P., 1970).

Masi A.C., 'Economic performance, government policies, and public opinion in Italy', in Gottlieb A., Yuchtman Yaar E., Strumpel B. (eds), *Socio-Economic Change and Individual Adaptation: Comparing East and West* (Connecticut: JAI Press, 1994).

Mattfeldt H., 'Eurokeynesimo: una base per un programma economico alternativo', *Politica ed Economia*, 5, May 1985.

McCarthy P., 'The Italian Communists divide — and do not conquer', in Pasquino G., McCarthy P. (eds), *The End of Post-War Politics in Italy; the Landmark 1992 Elections* (Oxford: Westview Press, 1993).

Menichini S., 'Ingrao sveglia Milano', *il Manifesto*, 12-1-1990.

Militello G., 'Nuove idee per vincere la sfida della democrazia economica', *L'Unità*, 11-9-1990.

Minucci A., 'La logica dei blocchi', *Rinascita*, 51, 25-12-1981.

Moltedo G., Rangeri N. (eds), *PCI: La Grande Svolta; il Nome, il Simbolo, il Nuovo Partito* (Roma: Associate, 1989).

Moro A., *Le 400 Pagine di Moro Riemerse dal Covo Brigatista* [special insert], *L'Unità*, 23-10-1990.

Mouzelis N., *Post-Marxist Alternatives; The Construction of Social Orders* (London: Macmillan, 1990).

Murray R., 'The internationalisation of capital and the nation-state', *New Left Review*, 67, May-June 1971.

Mussi F., 'C'è un tempo per ogni cosa', *Rinascita*, 29, 29-7-1989.

Mussi F., 'The ideological objectives of renewal', *World Marxist Review*, v.32, n.8, Aug. 1989.

Nanetti R., Catanzaro R. (eds), *Italian Politics; A Review*, v.4 (London: Pinter Publishers, 1990).

Napolitano G., 'Alla ricerca dell'identità perduta?', *Critica Marxista*, 1-2, Jan., April 1989.

Napolitano G., 'Attualità dell'alternativa', *Rinascita*, 27, 8-7-1983.

Napolitano G., 'Ci sono ancora vie per evitare la guerra', *L'Unità*, 30-11-1990.

Napolitano G., 'Governare da sinistra un arduo periodo di transizione', *Critica Marxista*, 1, Jan., Feb. 1983.

Napolitano G., 'Intervento al 20o Congresso', *L'Unità*, 3-2-1991.

Napolitano G., 'Intervento al 18o Congresso', *L'Unità*, 22-3-1989.

Napolitano G., 'Le nuove dimensioni della via Italiana', *Rinascita*, 25, 23-6-1984.

Napolitano G., 'Le condizioni del dialogo tra eurocomunismo e socialismo europeo', *Rinascita*, 19, 8-5-1981.

Napolitano G., 'Polonia, una vicenda cruciale', *Rinascita*, 50, 18-12-1981.

Napolitano G., 'Proposte per un confronto su un programma a medio termine', *Rinascita*, 38, 26-9-1975.

Napolitano G., 'Senza timidezze per nuove prospettive di progreso e di unità', *Rinascita*, 5, 9-2-1985.

Napolitano G., 'Un polo europeo per le forze di progresso', *Rinascita*, 42, 27-10-1984.

Napolitano G., Hobsbawm E., *The Italian Road to Socialism* (London: Journeyman, 1977).

Natta A., 'Così ho vissuto questa prova dura', *L'Unità*, 15-5-1988.

Natta A., 'Disarmament, Europe, the Left', in *The Italian Communists* (Foreign Bulletin of the PCI), 4, Oct., Dec. 1987.

Natta A., 'Letter to the CC of the PCI', in *The Italian Communists* (Foreign Bulletin of the PCI), 2, April-June 1988.

Natta A., 'Il programma e la lotta del PCI per aprire una nuova fase politica', *L'Unità*, 29-7-1987.

Negrelli S., 'Rappresentanza, rappresentatività e conflitto: il sindacato nell'Italia post-industriale', *Prospettive Sindacale*, 82/2, II Semestre 1992.

Negrelli S., Santi E., 'Industrial relations in Italy', in Baglioni G., Crouch C. (eds), *European Industrial Relations. The Challenge of Flexibility* (London: Sage Publications, 1992).

Occhetto A., 'Al Presidente dell'Internazionale Socialista Willy Brandt', *P. Fassino Archives*, 2-11-1989, no file number.

Occhetto A., 'Chiarezza con i socialisti', *L'Unità*, 11-2-1989.

Occhetto A., 'Closing speech at the Festa dell'Unità', in *The Italian Communists* (Foreign Bulletin of the PCI), 3, July-Sept. 1989.

Occhetto A., 'Come costruire la democrazia Europea', *Rinascita*, 43, 26-11-1988.

Occhetto A., 'Come disegnare l'Europa delle riforme', *Rinascita*, 5, 11-2-1989.

Occhetto A., 'Compromesso storico e alternativa democratica', *Critica Marxista*, 2-3, May-June 1985.

Occhetto A., 'Conclusioni al 20o Congresso', *L'Unità*, 4-2-1991.

Occhetto A., 'Conclusioni al 18o Congresso', *L'Unità*, 22-3-1989.

Occhetto A., 'Ecco come lavoriamo per riformare la nostra società', *Rinascita*, 21, 3-6-1989.

Occhetto A., 'Ecco chi era il grande vecchio', *L'Unità*, 31-10-1990.

Occhetto A., 'How we are building the new PCI', in *The Italian Communists* (Foreign Bulletin of the PCI), 3, July-Sept. 1988.

Occhetto A., 'Il partito di programma', *Rinascita*, 8, 1-3-1986.

Occhetto A., 'Relazione al 18o Congresso', *L'Unità*, 19-3-1989.

Occhetto A., 'Ingrao o Napolitano? Io selgo Occhetto', *L'Unità*, 10-2-1991.

Occhetto A., 'La crisi Italiana e le prospettive dell'alternativa', *L'Unità*, 27-11-1987.

Occhetto A., 'La sinistra dopo Palermo', *Rinascita*, 18, 1-5-1981.

Occhetto A., 'La risposta che ci attende il Paese', *Rinascita*, 8, 28-2-1987.

Occhetto A., 'Le linee programmatiche del governo ombra per questa legislatura', *L'Unità*, 20-7-1989.

Occhetto A., 'Le Conclusioni al CC', *L'Unità*, 18-5-1990.

Occhetto A., 'Letter to M. Guy Spitaels', 7-3-1989, *P. Fassino Archives*, no file number.

Occhetto A., 'Letter to Hans-Jochen Vogel', 7-3-1989, *P. Fassino archives*, no file number.

Occhetto A., 'Lettera ai Studenti', *L'Unità*, 3-3-1990.

Occhetto A., 'Nè abiure nè continuismo; un partito nuovo, alternativa per la società', *L'Unità*, 20-7-1988.

Occhetto A., 'Non un cartello di potere ma un programma riformatore', *Rinascita*, 4, 2-2-1985.

Occhetto A., 'PCI: sulla Lauro occorre un' indagine parlamentare', *L'Unità*, 2-11-1985.

Occhetto A., 'Per l'egemonia della sinistra', *Rinascita*, 14, 23-4-1988.

Occhetto A., 'Questa Repubblica è in crisi grave', *L'Unità*, 26-5-1990.

Occhetto A., 'Relazione al CC', *L'Unità*, 16-5-1990.

Occhetto A., 'Relazione al 20o Congresso', *L'Unità*, 1-2-1991.

Occhetto A., 'Relazione al CC,', *L'Unità*, 21-6-1988.

Occhetto A., 'Tutta la verità', *Rinascita*, 41, 25-11-1990.

Occhetto A., 'Un nuovo modo di pensare e fare politica', *Rinascita*, 41, 24-10-1987.

Occhetto A., 'Relazione al 19o Congresso', *L'Unità*, 9-3-1990.

Occhetto A., 'Un voto per sbloccare la democrazia', *L'Unità*, 10-4-1990.

Occhetto A., 'Una contrastata partenza', *Rinascita*, 27, 3-7-1981.

Occhetto A., 'Il nuovo corso è discontinuità, non è demolizione del passato', *L'Unità*, 14-9-1989.
Occhetto A., 'Una scelta obbligata', *Micromega*, 1, 1990.
Occhetto A., 'We must re-define the state, the market and socialism', in *The Italian Communists* (Foreign Bulletin of the PCI), 3, July-Sept. 1988.
Occhetto A., *Il Sentimento e la Ragione* (Milano: Rizzoli, 1994).
Occhetto A., *Un Indimenticabile '89* (Milano: Feltrinelli, 1990).
Occhetto A., Mussi F., 'Compagni, voliamo o no dare al partito un nuovo corso?', *L'Unità*, 3-6-1988.
OECD Economic Surveys, *Italy 1984-5* (Paris: OECD, 1985).
OECD Economic Surveys, *Italy 1992-3* (Paris: OECD, 1992).
Paci M., 'Il mercato e la sfida della cittadinanza sociale', *Politica ed Economia*, 11, Nov. 1986.
Paci M., 'Quali principi per il Welfare', *Politica ed Economia*, 4, April 1985.
Paggi L., D'Angelillo, M., *I Comunisti Italiani e il Riformismo; Un Confronto con le Socialdemocrazie Europee* (Torino: Einaudi, 1986).
Paggi L., 'Comunismo e riformismo', *Rinascita*, 32, 24-8-1979.
Pajetta G., 'Alle origini del partito nuovo', *Rinascita*, 35, 7-9-1973.
Pajetta G., 'Ma di partito ce n'è uno solo', *La Repubblica*, 26/27-8-1990.
Palombelli B., 'Occhetto: un post-Marxismo per l'alternativa', *Corriere della Sera*, 22-1-1989.
Parlato V., *Spazio e Ruolo del Riformismo* (Bologna: il Mulino, 1974).
Pasquino G., 'Introduction: a case of a regime crisis', in Pasquino G., McCarthy P. (eds), *The End of Post-War Politics in Italy; the Landmark 1992 Elections* (Oxford: Westview Press, 1993).
Pasquino G., 'Programmatic renewal and much more: from the PCI to the PDS', *West European Politics*, v.16, n.1, January 1993.
Pasquino G., 'Tre concenzioni dell'alternativa', *Rinascita*, 35, 21-9-1985.
Pasquino G. (ed.), *Opposizione, Governo Ombra, Alternativa* (Bari: Laterza, 1990).
PCI, 'I verbali del dibattito in Direzione', *L'Unità*, 11-5-1990.
PCI, 'Materiali e proposte per un programma di politica economico-sociale e di governo di economia', *Rinascita*, 50, 18-12-1981.
PCI, *Costruiamo la Democrazia dell'Alternativa* (Roma: ITER, 1989).
PCI, 'Riflessione sui dramatici fatti di Polonia: aprire una nuova fase della lotta per il socialismo' (resolution of the CC, 29-12-1981), in *Rinascita*, 1, 8-1-1982.
PCI, 'The Communists' document on Institutional reform', in *The Italian Communists* (Foreign Bulletin of the PCI), 1, Jan., March 1988.
PCI, 'The PCI's programme for Europe', in *The Italian Communists* (Foreign Bulletin of the PCI), 2, April-June 1989.
PCI, *Conferenza Nazionale del PCI sulla FIAT* (Roma: Fratelli Spada, 1990).

PCI, *Documenti per il 17o Congresso; Progetto di Tesi, Programma, Emendamento; Statuto, Criteri e Proposte*, attached in *Rinascita*, 5, 8-2-1986.

PCI, *Documenti per il Congresso Straordinario del PCI; Il Comitato Centrale della Svolta/1* (Roma: L'Unità, 1990).

PCI, *Documenti per il Congresso Straordinario del PCI; Il Comitato Centrale della Svolta/2* (Roma: L'Unità, 1990).

PCI, *Documenti per il Congresso Straordinario del PCI; Le Mozioni, il Regolamento, La Lettera delle Donne, La Carta della FGCI/3* (Roma: L'Unità, 1990).

PCI, *Idee e Proposte per la Costituente* (Roma: Fratelli Spada, 1990).

PCI, *Idee e Proposte per il Programma. Testo Elaborato dall'Ufficio del Programma Diretto da Bassolino* (Roma: Fratelli Spada, 1990).

PCI, *La Politica Economica Italiana, 1945-1974; Orientamenti e Proposte dei Comunisti* (n.d.), Roma.

PCI, *Proposta di un Programma a Medio Termine* (Roma: Riuniti, 1977).

PCI/Sezione Propaganda, *Idee e Proposte per la Costituente* (Roma: Iter, 1990).

PCI, *Statuto del Partito Comunista Italiano Approvato al 18o Congresso del PCI* (Roma: Iter, 1989).

PCI, *Sulla Grave Crisi del Golfo Persico* (Roma: Fratelli Spada, 1990).

PCI, *Tesi, Programma, Statuto: I Documenti Approvati dal XVII Congresso del PCI* (Roma: L'Unità, 1987).

PCI, *XV Congresso del PCI; Atti, Risoluzioni, Documenti* (Roma: Riuniti, 1979).

PCI, *XVI Congresso del PCI; Atti, Risoluzioni, Documenti* (Roma: Riuniti, 1983).

PCI, *XVIII Congresso del PCI* (supplement in *L'Unità*), 272, 4-12-1988.

PCI-20o Congresso, *Mozioni, Documenti, Regolamento* (Roma: Fratelli Spada, 1990).

PCI-Documento Cossutta, 'Un nuovo corso per il Socialismo', *L'Unità*, 26-11-1988.

PCI-Donne, *Carta Itinerante: Dalle Donne la Forza delle Donne* (Roma: Nuova Stampa di Mondatori, 1987).

PDS, *Lo Statuto* (Roma: Fratelli Spada, 1991).

Pecchioli U., 'Armi, Petrolio e P2', *Rinascita*, 23, 5-6-1981.

Pellicani G., 'L'opposizione che cambia', *Rinascita*, 29, 29-7-1989.

Perelli L., 'Part-time purchè non diventi un ghetto', *Rinascita*, 19, 21-5-1982.

Petruccioli C., 'Qualche domanda al Congresso DC', *L'Unità*, 17-2-1989.

Polara F.G., 'Come uscirne? Con una candidatura unitaria', *L'Unità*, 5-2-1991.

Poulantzas N., *Classes in Contemporary Capitalism* (London: Verso, 1978).

Poulantzas N., *Fascism and Dictatorship; the Third International and the Problem of Fascism* (London: NLB, 1979).

248   *Italy, Europe, the Left*

Poulantzas N., *State, Power, Socialism* (London: NLB, 1978).
Pravda A., 'Introduction: linkages between Soviet domestic and foreign policy under Gorbachev', in Hasegawa T., Pravda A. (eds), *Perestroika: Soviet Domestic and Foreign Policies* (London: Sage, 1990).
Preve C., 'Una Bad Godesberg Italiana: Note per una discussione seria sul nuovo corso del PCI di Occhetto', *Marxismo Oggi*, 3-4, May-July 1989.
Reichlin A., '1989: è più o meno credibile l'alternativa?', *Rinascita*, 2, 21-1-1989.
Reichlin A., 'L'economia si fa progetto', *Politica ed Economia*, 11, Nov. 1986.
Reichlin A., 'La sinistra del post-Reaganismo', *L'Unità*, 12-9-1990.
Reichlin A., 'Note per un programma', *Politica ed Economia*, 11, Nov. 1987.
Reichlin A., 'Se l'Italia discende di un gradino', *Rinascita*, 3, 25-1-1986.
Reichlin A. (ed.), *La Riforma del Welfare; Materiali per un Programma di Politica Economica*, attached to *Rinascita*, 47, 14-12-1985.
Rey M. G., 'Italy', in Boltho A. (ed.), *The European Economy: Growth and Crisis* (Oxford: O.U.P., 1991).
Rifondazione Comunista, *Materiali di Dibattito per la Rifondazione Comunista. In Nome delle Cose* (Roma: Tipografia Iter, 1990).
Rodotà S., 'Potere e democrazia nel futuro elettronico', *Rinascita*, 15, 16-4-1982.
Rondolino F., 'A sorpresa il PDS senza segretario', *L'Unità*, 5-2-1991.
Rondolino F., 'Il 'no' indice un' assemblea nazionale a Roma', *L'Unità*, 13-5-1990.
Roscani R., 'Il comunista eretico', *L'Unità*, 16-5-1993.
Rossanda R., 'Comunismo Manifesto', in *Storia*, supplement in *Epoca*, 2035, 8-10-1989.
Rossanda R., 'La creatura del patriarca', *il Manifesto*, 2-2-1990.
Rubbi A., 'Let us discuss the USSR, socialism and our choices', in *The Italian Communists* (Foreign Bulletin of the PCI), 1, Jan., March 1988.
Rubbi A., *Incontri con Gorbachev* (Roma: Riuniti, 1990).
Ruffolo G., 'Le tre vie dell'alternativa', *Micromega*, 1, 1990.
Salimbeni P.A., 'E su Togliatti al PSI diciamo...', *L'Unità*, 7-3-1988.
Salvati M., 'Muddling through: economy and politics in Italy, 1969-1979', in Lange P., Tarrow S. (eds), *Italy in Transition. Conflict and Consensus* (London: Frank Cass, 1980).
Salvati M., 'Non basta la mediazione per fare un programma', *L'Unità*, 15-8-1990.
Salvati M. 'The travail of Italian communism', *New Left Review*, 202, Nov., Dec. 1993.
Salvati M., *Economia e Politica in Italia dal Dopoguerra a Oggi* (Milano: Garzanti, 1984).
Salvati M., 'La sinistra ridisegnata: note per una convenzione', *Politica ed Economia*, 3, March 1990.

Salvati M., Veca S., 'Cambiare nome: e se non ora, quando?', *Rinascita*, 29, 29-7-1989.

Salvati M., 'May 1968 and the Hot Autumn of 1969: the responses of two ruling classes', in Berger S.B. (ed.), *Organising Interests in Western Europe* (Cambridge: C.U.P., 1981).

Santostassi M., 'Intervento al CC', *L'Unità*, 18-5-1990.

Sapelli G., *Southern Europe since 1945; Tradition and Modernity in Portugal, Spain, Italy, Greece and Turkey* (London: Longman, 1995).

Sappino M., 'Finito il regime democristiano', *L'Unità*, 7-4-1992.

Sassoon D., '*Tangentopoli* or the democratization of corruption: considerations on the end of Italy's first Republic', *Journal of Modern Italian Studies*, n.1, v.1, Fall 1995.

Sassoon D., 'The Italian Communist Party's European Strategy', *The Political Quarterly*, v.47, n.3, 1976.

Sassoon D., *Contemporary Italy; Politics, Economy and Society since 1945* (London: Longman, 1986).

Sassoon D., 'La sinistra in Italia e in Europa; elezioni e governi 1945-1988', *Italia Contemporanea*, 175, June 1989.

Sassoon D., *The Strategy of the Italian Communist Party; from the Resistance to the Historic Compromise* (London: Frances Pinter, 1981).

Sassoon D., *The Italian Communists Speak for Themselves* (Nottingham: Spokesman Books, 1978).

Sassoon D. (ed.), *P. Togliatti: On Gramsci and other Writings* (London: Lawrence and Wishart, 1979).

Sassoon D., *One Hundred Years of Socialism* (London: I.B. Tauris, 1996).

Sassoon D., *Social Democracy at the Heart of Europe* (London: IPPR, 1996).

Sassoon D. (ed.), *Looking Left: European Socialism after the Cold War* (London: I. B. Tauris, 1997).

Scalfari E., 'Una pesante eredità...', *La Repubblica*, 14-6-1988.

Scalfari E., 'Il vecchio PCI e la coperta di Linus', *La Repubblica*, 19-11-1989.

Schiavone A., *La Sinistra del Terzo Capitalismo* (Bari: Laterza, 1989).

Schumacher F. E., *Small is Beautiful* (London: Abacus, 1973).

Secchia P., 'Introduzione', in Secchia P., *I Comunisti Italiani e l'Insurrezione, 1943-1945* (Roma: Edizioni di Cultura Sociale, 1954).

Serra Francesco G. (ed.), *Una Magnifica Avventura: Dalla Sinistra Sommersa alla Sinistra dei Club* (Roma: Associate, 1990).

Socialdemocrazia Tedesca, *Il Testo Integrale del Nuovo Programma Fondamentale della SPD [Dec. 1989]* (Roma: Datanews, 1990).

Somaini E., 'Crisi della sinistra e ripresa neo-conservatrice in Europa; dinamiche distributive e mediazioni politiche', *Critica Marxista*, 5, Sept., Oct. 1979.

SPD, *La Socialdemocrazia Tedesca; il Testo Integrale del Nuovo Programma Fondamentale della SPD* (Berlin, Dec. 1989) (Roma: Datanews, 1990).

Spriano P., *Gramsci in Carcere e il Partito* (Roma: Riuniti, 1977).

Stabile A., 'Noi diciamo PCI, voi liberal', *La Repubblica*, 20-5-1989.

Tamburrano G., *Storia e Cronaca del Centro-Sinistra* (Milano: Feltrinelli, 1971).

Tarrow S., 'Historic compromise or bourgeois majority? Eurocommunism in Italy 1976-9', in Machin H. (ed.), *National Communism in Western Europe; A Third Way for Socialism?* (London and New York: Methuen, 1983).

Terzi R., 'Si scioglierà l'ala comunista della CGIL?', *Rinascita*, 2, 18-2-1990.

Togliatti P., 'Federalismo Europeo?', *Rinascita*, 11, Nov. 1948.

Togliatti P., 'Postilla a Garaudy', in *Il PCI e la svolta di Salerno*, *Rinascita*, 14, 12-4-1986.

Togliatti P., 'Un partito di governo e di massa', *Rinascita*, 32, 24-8-1973.

Togliatti P., *Lectures on Fascism* (New York: International Publishers, 1976).

Togliati P. [ed. Istituto Gramsci], *Togliatti e il Centro-Sinistra, 1958-1964*, v.I, Ib (Firenze: Cooperativa Editrice Universitaria, 1975).

Tortorella A., 'Intervento al 20o Congresso', *L'Unità*, 2-2-1991.

Tortorella A., 'Mozione 2: Intervento al 19o Congresso', *L'Unità*, 9-3-1990.

Tortorella A., 'Un Congresso Unitario? Ancora spero', *L'Unità: Lettera sulla Cosa*, 19-10-1990.

Tortorella A., *Berlinguer Aveva Ragione; Note sull'Alternativa e la Riforma della Politica* (Roma: Critica Marxista, 1994).

Tranfaglia N., 'Cossiga, Craxi, Andreotti e i giorni di Gladio', *L'Unità*, 16-7-1991.

Tranfaglia N., 'Ma la storia dice il contrario', *La Repubblica*, 23/24-9-1990.

Trentin B., *Il Coraggio dell'Utopia; La Sinistra e il Sindacato dopo il Taylorismo* (Milano: Rizzoli, 1995).

Trentin B., 'Al di là del sì e del No', *il Manifesto*, 31-1-1990.

Trentin B., 'La mia CGIL', *Nuova Rassegna Sindacale*, 12, 8-4-1991.

Turco L., 'Il mondo comune delle donne', *L'Unità*, 8-3-1990.

Turco L., 'La mia coerenza', *il Manifesto*, 10-1-1990.

Vacca G., 'Ciò che la cultura Italiana deve al Marxismo', *L'Unità*, 29-4-1990.

Vacca G., 'Nè dittatura nè egemonia delle "culture di sinistra"', *L'Unità*, 30-4-1990.

Vacca G., 'Per non dire crisi si discute di governabilità', *Rinascita*, 6, 6-2-1981.

Vacca G., *Dal PCI al PDS* (Bari: Delphos, 1991).

Vacca G., *Gorbachev e la Sinistra Europea* (Roma: Riuniti, 1989).

Vacca G., *Gramsci e Togliatti* (Roma: Riuniti, 1991).

Vacca G., *Saggio su Togliatti e la Tradizione Comunista* (Bari: De Donato, 1974).

Valenza P. (ed.), *Il Compromesso Storico* (Roma: Newton Compton Editori, 1975).

Valenzi M., 'La difficile victoria di Togliatti', *Rinascita*, 13, 29-3-1944.

Van Der Wee H., *Prosperity and Upheaval. The World Economy, 1945-1980* (London: Viking, 1986).

Vattimo G., 'Post-moderno, tecnologia, ontologia', *Micromega*, 4, 1990.

Villary M., 'Le grandi scelte per portare la sinistra al governo', *L'Unità*, 12-1-1988.

Weinberg L., *The Transformation of Italian Communism* (New Brunswick: Transaction Publishers, 1995).

Zamagni V., *The Economic History of Italy; Recovery after Decline, 1860-1990* (Oxford: Clarendon Press, 1993).

[Ca. M.], 'Cossutta spara a zero su Occhetto; 'nel PCI c'è mutazione genetica', *Corriere della Sera*, 20-1-1989.

[Unsigned] 'Quando Bukharin era un "bandito"', *Avanti!*, 7/8-2-1988.

Interviews*

Claudia Mancina, Cultural policy and MP (PDS), Rome, 12-4-1995.

Giorgio Napolitano, ex-President of the Parliament and MP (PDS), Rome, 12-4-1995.

Bruno Trentin, ex-general secretary of CGIL (PDS), Rome, 30-6-1995.

Alfonso Gianni, Political adviser of Bertinotti and MP (PRC), Rome, 11-7-1995.

Pietro Ingrao, ex-PCI MP and ex-President of the Parliament, Rome, 14-7-1995.

Lucio Magri, MP (PRC), Rome, 18-7-1995.

Aldo Tortorella, MP (PDS), Rome, 17-7-1995.

Armando Giallombardo, jurist and member of 'gruppo sicurezza sociale PCI', London, 15-11-1993.

Riccardo Azzolini, Economist (Cespe), Rome, 25-7-1995.

Fulvia Bandoli, Environmental policy (PDS) and MP, Rome, 26-7-1995.

Piero Fassino, International Relations (PDS) and MP, Rome, 31-7-1995.

Franca Chiaromonte, Gender issues (PDS) and MP, Rome, 1-8-1995.

Questionnaires Answered*

Walter Veltroni, Director of *L'Unità* and MP (PDS), date issued 26-5-1995.

Luigi Tagliaferri, ex-MP of PCI, Piacenza, date issued 13-7-1995.

* Interviewees have been assigned their official status as at the time of interview or of their response to questionnaires.

Index